MW00769960

HOLLYWOOD CONFIDENTIAL

Books by Dan E. Moldea

The Hoffa Wars:
Teamsters, Rebels, Politicians, and the Mob
1978

The Hunting of Cain:
A True Story of Money, Greed, and Fratricide
1983

Dark Victory:
Ronald Reagan, MCA, and the Mob
1986

Interference:
How Organized Crime Influences Professional Football
1989

The Killing of Robert F. Kennedy:
An Investigation of Motive, Means, and Opportunity
1995

Evidence Dismissed:
The Inside Story of the Police Investigation of O. J. Simpson
(With Tom Lange and Philip Vannatter)
1997

A Washington Tragedy:
How the Death of Vincent Foster Ignited a Political Firestorm
1998

Confessions of a Guerrilla Writer:
Adventures in the Jungles of Crime, Politics, and Journalism
2013

Hollywood Confidential:
A True Story of Wiretapping, Friendship, and Betrayal
2017

Hollywood Confidential

A True Story of Wiretapping, Friendship, and Betrayal

Dan E. Moldea

MOLDEA.COM

Portions of this book have appeared on Dan Moldea's website,
www.moldea.com, where updates about this work will appear.

Library of Congress Cataloging-in-Publication Data
Moldea, Dan E., 1950-
Hollywood Confidential / by Dan E. Moldea
1. Moldea, Dan E.—Crime. 2. Hollywood. 3. Journalism.

ISBN-10: 0692383409

ISBN-13: 9780692383407

Library of Congress Control Number: 2015902300
Moldea.com, Washington, DC

First Edition

To Roger C. Simmons

and in memory of C.P. Chima, Pat Clawson, Darah Farris, Traudis Kennedy, Alex Kura, Jon Kwitny, Larry Momchilov, Nancy Nolte, Barbara Raskin, John Sikorski, and Natalie Simmons . . . as well as to Nicolas Craciun, Grayson Parker Davis, Maureen Farris, Nyere Miller, Jasmine-Simone Morgan, Alex Sopko, and Casey and Rachel Wexler whose lives are just beginning. . . .

"No good deed goes unpunished"

—credited to Billy Wilder,
Clare Boothe Luce
and Oscar Wilde,
among others

CONTENTS

CHARACTERS

Anita Busch sphere of influence

Anita Busch: Entertainment reporter, investigated by Anthony Pellicano
"The Car Guy": Alleged mob associate listed in Nevada's "black book;" Anita's former lover
John Connolly: New York cop-turned-stockbroker-turned-investigative reporter
Bernie Ebbins: "Like a grandfather" to Anita
Mickey Freiberg: Literary agent, close friend of Anita's
Matthew Geragos: Former attorney for Anita
Ian Herzog: Current attorney for Anita
Brian S. Kabateck: Former attorney for Anita
Evan Marshall: Current attorney for Anita
Dan Moldea: Author, investigative journalist; "like a brother" to Dave Robb
Marvin Rudnick: Former attorney for Anita; friend of Moldea and Robb
David Robb: Hollywood journalist; Anita's best friend; "like a brother" to Moldea
Lou Tedesco: Close friend, former housemate of Anita's
Bernie Weinraub: Reporter, *New York Times*; Anita's partner on the Ovitz series in 2002

Law-enforcement community

Tom Ballard: Special agent, FBI's Los Angeles Field Office
Elihu Berle: Judge, Superior Court of California County of Los Angeles
Frederic L. Block: Judge, U.S. District Court, New York; presided over the Nasso case
Dale S. Fischer: Judge, U.S. District Court, Los Angeles; presided over Pellicano conspiracy trial

Mike Howard: Organized Crime Intelligence Division, LAPD
Kevin Lally: Assistant U.S. Attorney, Los Angeles
Corrie Lyle: Special agent, FBI
Roslynn Mauskopf: U.S. Attorney, Brooklyn
Stan Ornellas: FBI special agent, Los Angeles; lead investigator on the Pellicano case
Victor V. Pohorelsky: U.S. Magistrate Judge, New York
Stephen Reinhardt: Circuit judge, U.S. Court of Appeals for the Ninth Circuit
Dan Saunders: Assistant U.S. Attorney, Los Angeles; lead prosecutor in the Pellicano case
Dickran Tevrizian: Judge, U.S. District Court, Los Angeles

Los Angeles Times sphere of influence

John Carroll: Editor of the *Los Angeles Times*
Karlene Goller: Deputy general counsel for the *Los Angeles Times*
Paul Lieberman: Investigative journalist; Anita's partner on the Nasso-Seagal investigation
John Montorio: Deputy managing editor for the *Los Angeles Times*
Jim Newton: Investigative journalist, Metro editor, Karlene Goller's husband
Chuck Philips: Investigative journalist
Reporters and investigative journalists: Rachel Abramowitz, James Bates, Andrew Blankstein, Michael Cieply, Claudia Eller, Scott Glover, Patrick Goldstein, Carla Hall, Victoria Kim, Caitlin Liu, Greg Krikorian, Matt Lait, Paul Pringle, David Rozenzweig, Richard Verrier, Henry Weinstein, and Richard Winton.

Journalists

Cindy Adams: Gossip columnist, *New York Post*
Ken Auletta: Media critic and columnist, *New Yorker*
Kate Aurthur: Reporter, *Daily Beast* and *Newsweek*
Rick Barrs: Editor of the now-defunct *New Times L.A.*, an alternative weekly
Bill Bastone: Editor, *TheSmokingGun.com*; published the Patterson-Proctor transcript
Matthew Belloni: Journalist, *Hollywood Reporter*
Alex Ben Block: Senior editor, *Hollywood Reporter*
Howard Blum: John Connolly's partner for his first article on Pellicano in *Vanity Fair*
John Brodie: Senior writer, *GQ*
Bryan Burrough: Connolly's partner for his second story on Pellicano in *Vanity Fair*
Christopher Byron: Investigative journalist, *New York*
Danny Casolaro: Independent journalist, committed suicide in 1991

George Christy: Columnist, *Hollywood Reporter*

Cynthia Cotts: Media columnist, *Village Voice*

Diane Dimond: Television journalist

Robert Dowling: Publisher, *Hollywood Reporter*

Nikki Finke: Columnist and investigative journalist, *L.A. Weekly* and *Deadline Hollywood*

Charles Fleming: Author, editor, adjunct professor, University of Southern California

Mike Fleming, Jr.: Co-Editor-in-Chief, *Deadline Hollywood*

Roger Friedman: Correspondent, Fox News

Eriq Gardner: Journalist, *Hollywood Reporter*

William Glaberson: Investigative journalist, *New York Times*

Lloyd Grove: Reporter, *New York Daily News*

David Halbfinger: Investigative journalist, *New York Times*

Laura Holson: Investigative journalist, *New York Times*

Richard Johnson: Columnist, "Page Six," *New York Post*

Debbe Jonak: Reporter, *Daily Herald* (of suburban Chicago)

Gina Keating: Correspondent, Reuters

Allan Lengel: Investigative journalist; editor, *Tickle the Wire*

Steven Mikulan: Reporter, *LA Weekly*; now an editor with *Capital & Main*

Christine Pelisek: Reporter, *Daily Beast* and *Newsweek*

David Poland: Editor, *Movie City News*

Greg Risling: Reporter, Associated Press

George Rush: Columnist, "Rush & Molloy," *New York Daily News*

Janet Shprintz: Reporter, *Variety*

Jeff Stein: "SpyTalk" columnist, *Congressional Quarterly*; now with *Newsweek*

Frank Swertlow: Correspondent, *TheWrap*

Laura Sydell: Correspondent, National Public Radio

Sharon Waxman: Former staff reporter, *Washington Post*, now at *The Wrap*

Allison Hope Weiner: Journalist who covers the entertainment industry and the media

Jeffrey Wells: Columnist, *Reel.com*

Del Quentin Wilber: Reporter, *Washington Post*

Peter Wilkinson: Reporter, *GQ*

Ned Zeman: Contributing editor, *Vanity Fair*

Steven Seagal sphere of influence

John Carman: San Diego private investigator; former agent, Secret Service

Robert DeBrino: Former New York City police officer

Phil Goldfine: President of production at Steven Seagal's Steamroller Productions
Kelly LeBrock: Actress, Seagal's ex-wife
Robert Booth Nichols: Reputed arms dealer, appeared in *Under Siege*
Martin Pollner: Former lawyer for Seagal
Danny Provenzano: Alleged Mafia associate, film producer
Steven Seagal: Action-adventure actor, former partner of Jules Nasso
Marty Singer: Former lawyer for Seagal

Jules Nasso sphere of influence

Andrew Catalan: Private investigator who investigated Dan Patterson
Robert J. Hantman: Lawyer for Jules Nasso
John Leekley: Screenwriter, friend of Jules Nasso
Barry Levin: Lawyer for Vincent Nasso
Jack Litman: Attorney for Jules Nasso
William McMullan: Jules Nasso's private investigator
Julius "Jules" Nasso: Film producer, former partner of Steven Seagal
Vincent Nasso: Jules Nasso's younger brother and co-defendant
Thomas Vinton: Former FBI special agent and private investigator for Jules Nasso

Michael Ovitz sphere of influence

Michael Eisner: Chairman and CEO, The Walt Disney Company
Eric George: Lead defense attorney for Ovitz in *Busch v. Ovitz* civil case
Jonathan Gottfried: Defense attorney for Ovitz in *Busch v. Ovitz* civil case
Bryan Lourd: Followed Michael Ovitz as the head of Creative Artists Agency
Ron Meyer: Co-founder of Creative Artists Agency; president, Universal Studios
Michael Ovitz: Co-founder of CAA; former president of Disney; founder of AMG
Abigail Page: Defense attorney for Ovitz in *Busch v. Ovitz* civil case
Cathy Schulman: Served as president of Ovitz's Artists Production Group

Anthony Pellicano sphere of influence

Mark Arneson: Former LAPD detective who did work for Pellicano; co-defendant
Paul Barresi: Los Angeles private investigator, former porn actor
Sandra Will Carradine: Actress; Pellicano girlfriend; ex-wife of Keith Carradine
Steven F. Gruel: Pellicano's principal criminal attorney, former federal prosecutor

Kevin Kachikian: Creator of Telesleuth, Pellicano co-defendant

Lynda Larsen: Pellicano's private investigator

Anthony Pellicano: "Sleuth to the Stars," target of multiple federal and state investigations

Kat Pellicano: Pellicano's former wife and the mother of four of his nine children

Alexander Proctor: Pellicano covert operative, reputed drug dealer

Donald Re: Former attorney for Pellicano

Craig Stevens: Beverly Hills police officer who allegedly did work for Pellicano

Rayford Turner: Employee of Pacific Bell, Pellicano co-defendant

Denise Ward: Pellicano associate; former LAPD officer

Friends and colleagues of Dan Moldea

Jim Agnew: Crime researcher, also a friend of Anthony Pellicano

Jim Bamford: Best-selling author, also a friend of Linda Fiorentino

Susan Eisner: Attorney, associate of Roger Simmons, Moldea's attorney

Jodi Foss: Attorney, associate of Roger Simmons, Moldea's attorney

Deborah Grosvenor: Literary agent based in Washington, D.C.

William Jahoda: Soldier and bookmaker, Chicago Outfit, Wit-Sec Program

Tom Lange: Lead detective O.J. Simpson case; Moldea co-authored his book (with Philip Vannatter)

Laurence Leamer: Best-selling author and biographer

Larry Flynt: Exposed right-wing hypocrisy during President Bill Clinton's impeachment drama

Nancy Nolte: Moldea's long-time writing coach

Mark Olshaker: Best-selling author and crime reporter

Deborah Jeane Palfrey: The D.C. Madam

Gus Russo: Best-selling author and mob reporter, partner of Moldea on the Nasso book project

Roger Simmons: Moldea's attorney and close friend

Richard Stavin: Former prosecutor, U.S. Strike Force Against Organized Crime

Frank Weimann: New York literary agent who occasionally worked with Mickey Freiberg

Supporting cast

Jay Acton: New York literary agent who occasionally worked with Mickey Freiberg

Keith Carradine: Actor, Oscar-winning singer/songwriter
Terry Christensen: Attorney, represented Kirk Kerkorian; Pellicano co-defendant
Anthony "Sonny" Ciccone: Ex-union leader; reputed member of Gambino crime family
Kissandra Cohen: A former associate in the law firm of Ed Masry who sued her boss
Tom Cruise: Actor and filmmaker
Gavin de Becker: Private investigator, based in Los Angeles
Bertram "Bert" Fields: Los Angeles entertainment attorney
Linda Fiorentino: Actress
Luke Ford: Hollywood web blogger and celebrity profiler
John "Sonny" Franzese: Capo, Joseph Colombo crime family
Peter Gotti: Former acting boss, Carlo Gambino crime family
Brad Grey: President of Paramount Pictures; former business manager
Chad Hummel: Attorney for LAPD detective Mark Arneson
Michael Jackson: "The King of Pop"
Carmen La Via: Literary agent for Moldea and Russo on their Nasso project
Rod Lurie: Film critic who became a screenwriter and film director
Ed Masry: Criminal and tort attorney
John McTiernan: Movie director, *Die Hard*, among other films
John Nazarian: Los Angeles-based private investigator
Daniel and Abner Nicherie: Brothers and business partners; Pellicano co-defendants
Denise Oswald: Editor, Faber & Faber
Dan Patterson: The key informant who tape recorded Alexander Proctor's confession
Robert Joseph Pfeifer: Former president of Hollywood Records, Pellicano co-defendant
Angelo Prisco: Capo, Vito Genovese crime family
Chris Rock: Comedian, actor, writer, producer, and director
Mark Rossini: Former FBI agent
Arnold Schwarzenegger: Actor, former governor of California
Terry Semel: Former chairman of Warner Brothers and Yahoo!
Garry Shandling: Comedian, actor, and writer
Erich Speckin: Handwriting expert, Speckin Forensic Laboratories
Sylvester Stallone: Actor, screenwriter, and director
Elizabeth Taylor: Actress
Lew Wasserman: Former chairman, president, and CEO of MCA, Inc.
Howard Weitzman: Attorney who "discovered" Pellicano and introduced him to Hollywood
Bo Zenga: Film producer

Characters for whom Anita Busch created code names

"Baby": Steven Seagal

"Babysitter": Jules Nasso

"Bird": Anthony Pellicano

"Dinosaur": An elderly Mafia figure with whom Anita was acquainted via "The Car Guy"

"ED" or "Ed": Anita's exclusive code name for Michael Ovitz, aka "Evil Doer," "Evil Dude."

"Janus": A Hollywood investment manager

"Lambchop": A mobbed-up Los Angeles businessman

"Mister Chuckles": One of Anita's sources on her Nasso-Seagal stories

"The Mystery Man": Dan Patterson

"Nighthawk": A Los Angeles businessman

"The Poet": A reputed member of the Chicago Outfit

"Songbird": One of Anita's sources in the entertainment industry

Character for whom the author used a code name

"***Mister X": Moldea used this as a code name for Michael Ovitz in a 2005 book proposal. The three asterisks (***) were Moldea's edit-needed signal to Anita Busch to decide how she wanted Ovitz identified.

PREFACE

This is a true story about friendship and betrayal, as well as loyalty and greed—along with an offbeat new dimension to what is known about one of Hollywood's most-publicized scandals: the federal investigation of Anthony Pellicano and his illegal wirctapping activities.

As with all of my previous works, everything in this book has been extensively fact-checked with the documentation on file. Whenever necessary, I used the databases of the *New York Times*, the *Washington Post*, and the *Los Angeles Times*—along with the Hollywood trades and other authoritative sources in the entertainment industry—as the final arbiters when discrepancies arose over the spellings of proper names.

In short, I have always worked hard to get my facts straight. However, I do make mistakes, and I am more than willing to atone for them. When informed, I will immediately list provable errors on an errata sheet on my website, *www.moldea.com*, and I promise to make any and all necessary corrections in future editions of this book as quickly as possible.

Further, I have attempted to be as scrupulous as possible to credit those reporters who broke major news stories about the events discussed in this book. Their important works are referenced either in the main text or in the endnotes.

Significantly, I earlier cited many of these journalists' articles, along with other public sources of information, in my unpublished book written with reporter Anita Busch and titled, *Woman at Risk*. She unilaterally took that project off the table in 2005—because, as she wrote to me, it gave too much "free information" to the defense in her civil litigation against Pellicano and others. During her sworn testimony in the midst of Pellicano's criminal trial in 2008, she underscored this decision by telling the court, "There will never be a book."

Because I had spent two years working completely on spec with Busch on her project, I refused to accept her decision. But in lieu of filing a lawsuit against her, I opted to write my own book, based upon my own experiences with the Pellicano case, which included my association with Busch.

Notably, I have cited many of the same media stories and public documents in both books. Those articles and official papers provide a permanent timeline of the key events in this complicated case. Of course, I cannot change that written record, so these quoted words in both books are exactly the same.

———

I would like to thank my personal attorney and "big brother," Roger C. Simmons of Frederick, Maryland, and his associate, Susan Eisner, along with one of my oldest and most trusted friends, George L. Farris of Akron, Ohio, who has been the Moldea-family attorney for over thirty years.

Also, I want to express appreciation to my lecture-booking agents, Jodi Solomon and Bill Fargo of Jodi Solomon Speakers in Boston, along with my friends and colleagues, author Gus Russo and legal researcher Julie Payne. In addition, I want to extend my deepest gratitude to investigative journalist and long-time friend Kristina Rebelo for her outstanding editorial assistance and heartfelt encouragement, as well as to my friend, Tim Hays, a New York literary agent whose editorial suggestions helped polish the finished manuscript. Further, I send my great respect to Nancy Nolte of Boulder, Colorado, my writing coach since 1970 to whom I have dedicated two of my previous books.

To complete this work, I received a generous grant from The Charlotte von Stein Charitable Trust for which I am very grateful.

Finally, thank you to my good friend, Robert, as well as to his wife, and, most of all, thank you dear Mimi.

Dan E. Moldea
Washington, D.C.
November 11, 2017

PROLOGUE

"A blessing and a curse"

We were the best of friends who became the worst of enemies.

This story chronicles the most horrible nightmare in my long career as an author and investigative journalist, a career that has also included several attempts on my life and an unsuccessful libel lawsuit against the *New York Times*. That litigation went on longer than World War II, giving some in the media plenty of time to portray me as the Darth Vader of the First Amendment. While living through it, I could not imagine a more painful experience.

Notably, I was winning that case when a federal appellate court—in an unprecedented moment in American jurisprudence—took away my apparent victory.

But this latest episode of my life has been worse, much worse.

In Cameron Crowe's wonderful 1996 movie, *Jerry McGuire*, a top sports agent loses his most-treasured client, the much sought-after first-round draft pick, on the night *before* the NFL draft.

In this book, a crime reporter loses the exclusive inside story about the most explosive scandal in the history of Hollywood on the eve of the widely anticipated federal indictments that will light the fuse. But then, while scrambling to salvage the time and work he has invested in the project, he discovers a better, more effective way to tell his version of events.

I am that journalist, a specialist on organized-crime investigations and the author of eight previous non-fiction books, who was writing about the highly publicized illegal wiretapping activities of Hollywood's reputed "Sleuth to the Stars," Los Angeles private detective Anthony Pellicano.

I spent much of that time working with Anita Busch, the person who was the genesis of the Pellicano investigation and at the epicenter of the wiretapping case. A now-infamous threat against her on June 20, 2002, led to all of the remarkable disclosures that followed, as well as many of the events I chronicle in this book.

I had been introduced to Anita in 1994 while I was in California, wrapping up the research for my fifth book, *The Killing of Robert F. Kennedy*. I met her on or about the same day as my third and final prison interview with the assassin, Sirhan Sirhan, at the home of tall and lean David Robb of Los Angeles, a cranky and tough but extremely talented and honest investigative journalist. At that time, Dave and Anita, who often shot pool together, worked for rival publications: Dave, then 45, was the top labor and legal reporter for the *Hollywood Reporter*. Anita wrote breaking stories about the entertainment industry for *Variety*.

Because of Dave's admiration for the professional abilities of Anita—an intelligent and attractive woman with blonde hair and brown eyes who stood just shy of five-feet-seven—I immediately liked and respected her, too. She was born on May 31, 1961, and raised in Granite City, Illinois. After graduating from Eastern Illinois University with a degree in speech communications, she wrote for Crain Communications in Chicago before moving to Los Angeles to work for the Hollywood trades.

A few years after I met Anita, Dave received much of the credit when she was named the top editor of the *Hollywood Reporter* in 1999 by its publisher Robert Dowling. Dave had lobbied heavily on her behalf for the position.

Shortly after her appointment, Bernard Weinraub, the chief Hollywood reporter for the *New York Times*, published a story about Anita's new job, saying:

> [Since] *The Hollywood Reporter* handed over the top editor's job to Anita M. Busch, a strong-willed and aggressive former top reporter at *Variety*, the competition has intensified as Ms. Busch has challenged her former employer in the hard-fought battle for readers and advertisers in the insular world of Hollywood. In the process, the 37-year old editor, who as a reporter was as feared by executives

PART ONE:
Denial

1. *"Forget it, Dan. It's Chinatown."*

I didn't see the minefield ahead.

On April 12, 2002, Anita Busch sent an email, asking me for a favor. She wanted me to collect three articles that Bernard Weinraub of the *New York Times* had written about one-time Hollywood super-agent Michael Ovitz, two from 1996 and the third from 1999. She provided no explanation, and I didn't need any. I just did what she asked.

Later that day, I sent Anita two of the three articles that she had requested, along with six other stories in which Weinraub had discussed Ovitz.

At the time of her email to me, Anita was freelancing for the *New York Times*. She and Weinraub were in the midst of what would become a seven-part series which began on March 22 about Ovitz and his latest business venture, the Artists Management Group, a broadly based management company for those involved in film and television productions.

The two reporters alleged that Ovitz had engaged in financial mismanagement, based on a recent audit of the company's records. The final part of their series appeared in the newspaper on May 7.[6]

The day before that final installation, Anita and Weinraub published a story about Ovitz, "A Faded Hollywood Power Broker Relinquishes His Talent Business," which seemingly added insult to injury:

> Even by the turbulent and often cruel standards of Hollywood,
> Mr. Ovitz's downfall has been startling. As a founder of the Creative
> Artists Agency, he emerged as a strong-willed and intimidating figure
> who sought to inspire fear, and succeeded. But Mr. Ovitz, who is 55,
> has seen his career fall into a downward spiral since 1997 when he
> was fired as president of the Walt Disney Company.
>
> Today, Mr. Ovitz reached one of the lowest points in his career.
> He agreed for a company called The Firm to acquire the major units
> of his current company, the Artists Management Group. . . .
>
> For Mr. Ovitz, the deal is a serious financial and personal blow.

In lieu of continuing to freelance for the *New York Times* and other publications upon the completion of her work on Ovitz, Anita accepted a job on or about May 21, working under contract for the *Los Angeles Times*.

On June 3, her first day with the newspaper, Hollywood legend Lew Wasserman, the retired chairman of MCA, died. As part of her research, she called me to discuss my third book, *Dark Victory: Ronald Reagan, MCA, and the Mob*, in which Wasserman was a major character.

In that 1986 work, I concentrated on MCA, a powerful Hollywood corporation, and its fifty-year relationship with President Reagan who was in the midst of his second term in office. During the next two years, I watched the Reagan Justice Department, specifically the U.S. Attorney's Office in Los Angeles, kill a federal investigation of MCA, as well as another broader probe of the Mafia's penetration of the motion-picture industry.

With life imitating art, these cases were embodiments of the dramatic conclusion of the 1974 film, *Chinatown*, in which wealthy powerbrokers used their influence with the law-enforcement community to evade responsibility for their roles in major crimes. In fact, one federal prosecutor placed a fine point on this analogy when—after hearing of my frustrations with reporting on the aborted MCA case—he told me, "Forget it, Dan. It's *Chinatown*."

The newspaper's obituary of Wasserman the following day referred to my work.[7]

On June 4, federal prosecutors indicted Julius "Jules" Nasso, along with sixteen reputed members of New York's Carlo Gambino crime family as part of a major 68-count conspiracy case.[8] Nasso had been the business partner of motion-picture star Steven Seagal, whose popular action-adventure films included *Above the Law*, *Out for Justice*, and *Under Siege*.

In effect, Anita, who usually covered show business, was now investigating the Mafia.

Her partner for this investigation was Paul Lieberman, a respected veteran investigative reporter who worked in the New York bureau of the *Los Angeles Times*.

The first Busch-Lieberman story appeared on June 5, stating:

> Nasso, 49, of Staten Island, was charged with two counts, conspiracy to commit extortion and attempted extortion of a figure in the motion picture industry. Although prosecutors did not identify the extortion target in the indictment, Nasso's lawyer said after court that Seagal is the film figure.
>
> "It's definitely Steven Seagal," said Nasso's lead attorney, Barry Levin. "Steven Seagal has been seen talking to the grand jury."
>
> Nasso had a 15-year business relationship with Seagal until a bitter falling-out. In March, Nasso filed a $60-million lawsuit against the actor, alleging the star of such films as *Under Siege* had backed out of a contract to perform in four movies. The two have not spoken in more than a year."[9]

In her follow-up article the next day, Anita, without the participation of Lieberman, wrote: "The alleged extortion attempt was caught on FBI wiretaps. The wiretaps recorded a conversation between Nasso and Gambino associate Anthony 'Sonny' Ciccone in which Ciccone allegedly chastised Nasso for trying to share some of the extorted money with others without 'prior approval.'"[10]

Anita and Lieberman co-authored a third story on June 12, adding: "The Mafia captain who rules the Staten Island waterfront threatened to kill an entertainment figure, identified previously as actor Steven Seagal, as part of a multimillion-dollar extortion scene. . . .

"Anthony 'Sonny' Ciccone 'demanded millions of dollars from this individual and threatened his life,' Assistant U.S. Atty. Andrew Genser said at a court hearing for the accused Gambino family docks boss."[11]

However, Anita did not appear to trust her partner. In her personal notes, she wrote:

> I am sharing information with the reporter I'm working with,
> Paul Lieberman. But something doesn't smell right. Lieberman is
> too close to these guys, I believe. He's going out drinking with them.
> I tell an editor at the paper this. I told him I don't feel comfortable
> telling [Lieberman] things because I believe he's too close to Nasso
> and his friends. . . .
>   I decide not to tell Lieberman anything else. Period.

In the midst of her research on Seagal and Nasso, Anita called, asking me about mystery man Robert Booth Nichols, a shadowy associate of Seagal's, who had appeared in the movie *Under Siege*, and was supposedly connected to mobsters and spooks.

Nichols first came to my attention shortly after the tragic death of freelance journalist Danny Casolaro, who was found dead in the bathtub of his room at a motel in Martinsburg, West Virginia, on August 10, 1991. Police discovered his wrists slashed and a shoe string tied around his neck. They also found a half-full bottle of wine and a broken glass near the tub.

After a note from the reporter was found in the room, the local coroner quickly declared Casolaro's death a suicide. However, his body was embalmed before any notification to his family. This hasty action did nothing but incite legitimate questions about what had really happened to him. During that probe, Nichols's name surfaced as someone Casolaro had planned to meet.

Even though I believed that Casolaro had committed suicide in the midst of widespread speculation that he was murdered, I was intrigued by his relationship with Nichols, who was both a source and a target for Casolaro's wide-ranging probe of organized crime, drug trafficking, and money laundering. He wanted to place all of this information in a book that no publisher seemed to want.

Overcommitted and underfinanced, as well as way over his head with this investigation, Casolaro had started to call his bottomless-pit investigation, "The Octopus."[12]

I told Anita what I knew about Nichols and suggested that she call Richard Stavin of Los Angeles, a trusted friend of mine and a former federal prosecutor who had investigated him.

While working at home in Washington, D.C. during the afternoon of Thursday, June 20, 2002, I received a telephone call from Dave Robb in Los Angeles. Also on the line was Anita. As always, I was happy to hear from either of them and certainly both at the same time.

When Dave and Anita, almost in unison, asked me to guess what had just happened, I shouted with considerable glee that they had finally run off to Las Vegas and gotten married.

Scoffing at that suggestion and now deadly serious, Dave informed me that Anita had been threatened that morning. Someone had placed an upside-down tin-foil baking tray on the windshield of her 1996 silver Audi convertible. Inside the pan were a dead fish and a rose. Also, taped to the windshield, which appeared to contain a bullet hole, was a hand-lettered sign that simply said, "STOP."

After discovering the montage on her car, Anita called Dave, as well as the Los Angeles Police Department. Soon after, the local cops arrived at the scene, along with detectives from the LAPD's Organized Crime Intelligence Division and special agents with the Federal Bureau of Investigation. They were interested in the subject of Anita's most recent investigation for the newspaper.

Hearing then that she suspected Seagal and/or Nasso, along with their alleged Mafia associates, of being behind the threat against her, I suggested that she contact John Connolly, a former New York City police detective-turned-investigative reporter with whom I had been a friend for several years. Connolly had published stories about Seagal. Dave Robb, whom I had earlier introduced to Connolly, added that the New York reporter's life had been threatened during his work on Seagal.

In a 1993 article for *Spy* magazine, Connolly had written:

> Seagal stands apart from his action-hero brothers. With Seagal, the gap between myth and reality makes the shortcomings of Arnie, Chuck and Sly look like kid stuff. After a six-month-long investigation, *Spy* has concluded that Seagal is not simply a fraud, a liar, a coward and a bully but also a onetime bigamist who on at least two occasions said he wanted to contract out a murder, who had

to settle a nasty sexual-harassment claim and who, not surprisingly,
hires and does business with people having ties to organized crime.[13]

Along with contacting Connolly, I advised Anita to start a
timeline of any and all potentially relevant events leading up to
the threat and to continue updating it as the law-enforcement
investigation proceeded.

I told her to remain calm, adding that the Mafia did not kill
honest reporters. Specifically, I mentioned to her that the murder
of reporter Don Bolles of the *Arizona Republic* in June 1976 was an
anomaly, and had never been actually proven to have been a Mafia
hit.

With regard to my own personal security problems, especially
during the research for my first book, *The Hoffa Wars*, which
detailed the rise and fall of Teamsters boss Jimmy Hoffa, I had never
been targeted by the Mafia. If I had been, I would already be dead.

At first, I did not take the threat against Anita very seriously. A
victim of a mere act of vandalism, she was physically unscathed,
completely uninjured. Though it seemed to be a real threat, no one
had raised a hand to her. I assumed that she would continue her fine
reporting about the entertainment industry, and that she would laugh
about this incident someday.

———

On July 11, three weeks after the threat against Anita, the *New
York Daily News* published the first story about it, saying:

> Reporting can be a risky business. . . . After digging into
> the [Seagal-Nasso] story for a couple of weeks, Busch recently
> discovered that someone had come to her L.A. home and smashed
> her car's windshield, leaving a note that said, 'Stop,' sources tell us.
>   She also found a metal box on the car. Bomb-squad cops found
> a dead fish in it.
>   While police investigate the incident . . . , Busch has resigned
> from the story and is in hiding, say sources.[14]

I was particularly surprised to read that Anita had actually left the Seagal-Nasso story in the wake of what I still viewed as an act clearly designed to do nothing more than to frighten her.

The following day, July 12, an online publication that featured news about Hollywood repeated the reported threat against Anita, stating that she "hasn't been to work for close to three weeks." The writer of this short piece added: "I would be less than candid if I didn't disclose that certain voices within the small community of industry reporters and observers are reacting to this story with arched eyebrows. Let's let it go at that . . . for now."[15]

The writer appeared to be implying that some journalists did not believe that Anita had actually been threatened.

Dave Robb confirmed to me during a telephone conversation that Anita had left the Seagal-Nasso story. He did not give me any details, and I didn't ask for any.

With regard to the skepticism of her peers in the Hollywood-reporting community, I was concerned that Anita might have lost the respect of some of her colleagues if they viewed her as a coward because she had abandoned the Seagal-Nasso story and gone into hiding. That aside, even though I did not know Anita very well, I felt confident that she was incapable of concocting the threat scenario. Essentially, I believed her story because Dave completely trusted her. And that was good enough for me.

What I did not realize then was that on the day after the June 20 threat, an alleged con artist under federal indictment for fraud, Dan Patterson, had called Anita repeatedly at her office. When she finally received his messages and called him back, he warned that her life was in danger and that someone was planning to place a bomb in her car. Identifying himself by name, he said that he did not want to see her get hurt.

Patterson later told *The Smoking Gun*: "If someone is gonna hurt a young woman, I'm not gonna sit by and let that happen. I knew it was gonna cause me a problem when I did it. . . . You got to look at yourself in the mirror."[16]

Patterson had no idea of what had happened the previous day.

Considering that federal agents were taking this threat seriously, it was understandable that Anita, who never billed herself as a crime reporter, had left the story and decided to disappear while the investigation proceeded.

Paul Lieberman of the *Los Angeles Times*, Anita's former partner who was not threatened, stayed with the story and published his first solo-bylined article on July 12 about the relationship between Seagal and Nasso in which he wrote:

> During a partnership that lasted more than a decade, Seagal starred in films that grossed hundreds of millions of dollars, and Nasso helped produce them. They were close, almost like brothers. Seagal bought the house next to Nasso's mansion on Staten Island and they often dressed alike, all in black, just in different sizes. Nasso was a foot shorter than the imposing actor.
>
> Nasso also was the easy one to deal with. Like many performers, Seagal could be self-centered and moody—"a stubborn, maniacal idiot," as he once described himself. But it was hard to find anyone who didn't like Nasso. "I would go in," he said, "and clean up the mess."
>
> Yet it was worth it, he insisted. Every minute with Seagal.
>
> "I went on the magic carpet ride with him," Nasso explained.
>
> He says that even as the magic carpet ride threatens to land him in prison.[17]

Five days after his story about Seagal and Nasso, Lieberman published another, saying:

> New York-based Mafia figures pursued their attempted extortion of a "petrified" Steven Seagal in Canada, on the West Coast and in a restaurant here, according to newly filed court papers.
>
> In one episode resembling a scene from *The Godfather*, Seagal's former producing partner, Julius "Jules" Nasso, startled the action star by switching the location of a meeting "at the last moment" and taking him to the Brooklyn restaurant, where mob captain Anthony "Sonny" Ciccone demanded money from the actor. . . .
>
> Two weeks later, an FBI bug recorded the mob crew joking about the incident. . . . Julius Nasso's brother, Vincent, is quoted as quipping, "It was like right out of the movies."[18]

2. *"It freaks me out that they are still out there"*

Two months after the threat to Anita, Dave Robb, while doing research for a book he was writing about the Pentagon's influence on the motion-picture industry, flew to Washington, D.C. and stayed with me during his two-week visit. Anita's predicament was the big topic of conversation—although Dave still seemed to hold back on some of the details. Respecting that Dave was Anita's best friend and that she had told him some things in confidence, I took no offense.

What I did not know was that shortly after her return home in early August, two men in a dark-colored Mercedes with no license plate had supposedly made an "attempt to run over" Anita on August 16. Then, after missing her, the driver of the car pulled up next to Anita while the passenger in the car "leaned out of the window and made menacing gestures" at her.

When I later heard about this bizarre incident, I could not figure out why the alleged assailants, who had allegedly just attempted to kill Anita, would then stop, back up, and allow her to get a good look at them.

Two days after Dave arrived in Washington, Ned Zeman, a reporter for *Vanity Fair*, who was finishing his own article about Seagal and Nasso, also received an apparent death threat.[19] A little after 10:00 P.M. while driving north on Laurel Canyon Boulevard, the driver of a car tailing Zeman flashed his headlights. In response, Zeman moved to the side of the road. Pulling next to Zeman, the driver of the other car, another dark-colored Mercedes, turned on a flashlight and pointed it at Zeman while the passenger pointed a handgun at the reporter. As Zeman got down on the floor of his car, he heard a metallic click, indicating that the passenger had fired an empty chamber. Before the driver took off, the passenger yelled, "Bang. . . . Stop it!"

Even before that incident, Zeman, while checking his mailbox, had supposedly found a toy soldier with its head cut off.

In light of what had supposedly happened to Zeman, Anita's concerns seemed quite legitimate. But there were still people who did not believe her.

On August 29, Jim Romenesko of the *MediaNews* website highlighted an article about Anita, published by *New Times Los Angeles*.[20] The article was written by the free weekly's editor, Rick Barrs, who wrote a regular column called "The Finger." Titled "Busch League," Barrs wrote:

> What The Finger's wondering is, do Gambino greaseballs read West Coast papers, and even if they do, why would they give a rancid cannoli about Anita Busch? . . .
>
> Commented one former *Times* staffer familiar with the alleged threat: "Most people at the *Times* think it's bullshit. . . . One current *Times* reporter whispered, "Talking about the Busch situation has kind of turned into a sport around here. She's a person who has a certain reputation in town, and the fact that this is going on has only added to her lore." . . . .
>
> One of The Finger's *Times* sources said, "Look, I'm just suggesting that it could be some kind of elaborate prank."[21]

Dave was furious, and so was I, recognizing the blatant unfairness of Barrs's reporting. In fact, Anita had been threatened at least once and possibly twice. And now she was being forced to take all of this grief?

On September 1, I received an email from an acquaintance, John Carman, a former Secret Service agent, who attached an article from that day's *New York Times* about the U.S. Attorney's indictments in Brooklyn of the Gambinos and Jules Nasso.[22] The ex-agent, now a California-based private investigator who had a business relationship with Steven Seagal, wrote, in part, "I know Steven personally and I am a little concerned. Is he in trouble with the mob?"

Dave, with whom I shared this communication, instructed me to call Anita, which I did. Anita told me that there were rumors that "a private investigator" might have been involved in the threat against her.

Three days later, the *New York Times* published the first mainstream news article about the recent threats against both Anita and Ned Zeman.[23] However, as Dave explained to me, while *Vanity*

Fair stood behind its reporter, the *Los Angeles Times* appeared to be distancing itself from Anita.

The following day, September 5, the Associated Press reported:

> [Sergeant John] Pasquariello said despite the similarities between the threats, detectives have yet to link them, so for now the two investigations are separate. He said police advised Busch to take security precautions but did not know whether Zeman had been given similar advice.
>
> Officials at both publications said they were taking steps to protect their reporters.[24]

Also, that same day, in anticipation of Zeman's upcoming article about Seagal and Nasso, columnists George Rush & Joanna Molloy of *New York Daily News* added:

> Zeman is now said to have a 24-hour bodyguard. A *Vanity Fair* spokeswoman would say only he 'is taking the necessary security precautions.' . . .
>
> Writer John Connolly, who worked with Zeman on the *Vanity Fair* story, says he received threats in 1996, when he was reporting a *Time* magazine story on Seagal and Nasso.
>
> Reps for Seagal . . . deny any intimidation. Nasso tells us he himself has full-time security. The Staten Island moviemaker adds that he's "horrified" by "this terrorism" against Zeman, "a fine gentleman."[25]

Anita's problems with the *Los Angeles Times* began the day after the vandalism to her car when she reported for work. In the midst of her conversations with several top staffers, including executive editor John Carroll and an attorney for the newspaper, Karlene Goller, Anita was in the midst of a near emotional breakdown. "I'm a slobbering mess," she wrote in her notes.

According to Anita, Goller wanted to hire a private investigator to assist the *Times* with its probe. However, Carroll vetoed that suggestion, saying that this matter would be best handled by the law-enforcement community. At that point, the LAPD's Organized Crime Intelligence Division and the FBI were called and invited to a meeting at the newspaper.

Anita continued in her notes:

> I see Karlene out in the hallway. . . . She said, you know I'm
> thinking that it might be a good idea to bring someone in on this.
> Do you know Anthony Pellicano?" I said, "boy, I don't know
> Karlene. He doesn't have the greatest reputation." She said, "no,
> he's done some work for us in the past and he's done pretty well.
> I'm thinking I'll call him." I said, "well, I don't know. It's up to
> you guys."

During the meeting with the LAPD and FBI, Anita told the group
that Goller had suggested that the newspaper bring in Pellicano, an
idea that Goller defended. But both Mike Howard of the LAPD and
Stan Ornellas of the FBI warned against that. Ornellas specifically
said, "Stay away from that guy."

In early September, *Vanity Fair* published the Zeman-Connolly
article about Seagal and Nasso. Describing a key moment during a
tour of Nasso's Staten Island home, Zeman wrote:

> "It's not what it is," Nasso explains, speaking about the house in
> general. "It's what it gives off. It's Zen. It's chi. Like Mike Ovitz
> does it. It's Ovitzean."
>
> Nasso traces both his chi and his "celebrityness" back to
> Hollywood's fallen Zen master. "Real gentleman, Ovitz," Nasso
> says. "Knows his Zen. Stand-up guy." After all, Ovitz discovered
> and groomed Nasso's former meal ticket, the swaggering action star
> Steven Seagal. [26]

Zeman added:

> Seagal seems to respond to accusations with his own accusations
> followed by shadowy recriminations against the accusers, be they
> private individuals or professional journalists, whom Seagal routinely
> calls "scumbags" and "cocksuckers." Often, Seagal's wrath comes
> courtesy of his attorney Martin Singer, who once took the tack of
> suing a journalist before his story was even written.

Indeed, on behalf of Seagal, the feared and respected Singer had
filed a defamation suit against John Connolly in 1993—just before
Spy published Connolly's article about Seagal. However, after this
preemptive action and publication of the story, Seagal and Singer
dropped their complaint.

In a 1996 article for *Variety*, journalist John Brodie published a story about Connolly, saying:

> So far the threat of litigation and bodily harm are the hardest shots Hollywood has fired back at this white-haired shamus. . . . Seagal sued Connolly even before he wrote the *Spy* piece. In response, Connolly has subpoenaed CAA's Mike Ovitz and Warner Bros. And Connolly said he has even received the fledgling Hollywood journalist's badge of honor: a threatening phone call from private investigator Anthony Pellicano.
>
> Boasted Connolly, "He threatened to beat me up the next time I was in L.A. So I told him, 'Anthony, I'll be at Ma Maison Monday night. Bring your Louisville Slugger.' Guess what. He didn't show."[27]

A solid man of medium height with a ruddy complexion and a rapid cadence in his speech, Connolly had attended Brooklyn Law School but did not graduate. He joined the New York Police Department instead and worked out of a Brooklyn precinct. When he left the police force for reasons unknown, he became a stockbroker and later a journalist.

John called me in 1992 while he was working on a major story for *Spy* about the late freelance journalist, Danny Casolaro. I believed the official version that Danny had committed suicide, based on my own interviews after his death. However, John, based on his own information, insisted that someone had murdered him.

John and I met for the first time in Los Angeles in March 1993 at a dinner at Musso & Frank Grill on Hollywood Boulevard for reporters and prosecutors who had investigated MCA. John and I had been friends ever since.[28]

On the morning of September 23, I took the train to New York for a meeting near Union Square that afternoon at the headquarters of the National Writers Union. I had recently been elected as one of its three national vice presidents.

John and I arranged to attend a memorial service together at City University that night for a mutual friend, journalist Robert I. Friedman, who had died after being stricken with a rare blood disease while covering a political-corruption story in India.

During our dinner prior to the service, John told me that he and
Anita Busch had been in regular contact, adding that he had fed
George Rush of the Rush & Molloy column at the *New York Daily
News* the first story about the threat against her which had been
published on July 11, 2002.

In addition, John told me that he had discovered the identity
of the person who vandalized Anita's car and that he had already
revealed the name to Anita: Alexander Proctor, a local drug dealer in
L.A. I had never heard of the guy.

John did not tell me for whom Proctor was working or how he
knew this to be true. And I did not ask.

Also, John alleged that the FBI was protecting Steven Seagal—
because he was slated as a key witness in the upcoming trial of the
recently indicted Gambino crime family members, as well as that of
Seagal's former producer, Jules Nasso, and Nasso's brother, Vincent,
who was also a defendant.

During our time together in New York, John and I, having always
talked about working together, agreed that we should look for a
collaborative book project.

On October 8, Anita published an article in the *Los Angeles
Times* about Michael Ovitz and his ongoing legal battle with a
former employee. Seemingly a follow-up story to her earlier series
in the *New York Times*, Anita revealed:

> Onetime super-agent Michael Ovitz is being sued again by a
> former top executive.
> Cathy Schulman, the former president of Ovitz's film production
> division at now-defunct Artists Management Group, said in court
> papers that her former boss flew into a "rage" and fired her for telling
> auditors that she suspected Ovitz of "improperly allocating" film
> company funds.
> The lawsuit, which seeks more than $4 million in damages for
> wrongful termination and breach of contract, also accuses Ovitz of
> denying her producing credits and fees.[29]

Then, nine days later, a big break occurred.

On October 17, just as John Connolly had predicted at our dinner on September 23, federal agents arrested five-feet-six-inch, 130-pound Alexander Proctor for threatening Anita on June 20. He was held without bail until his arraignment on October 21.

A Reuters wire story added:

> For months, a top Los Angeles show business reporter has been slammed in the alternative press for her claims that she was being harassed by someone intent on stopping her from writing about an alleged shakedown plot against action star Steven Seagal.
>
> *Los Angeles Times* reporter Anita Busch was vindicated Wednesday. . . .
>
> Busch said: "I am particularly thankful to the FBI and the LAPD for investigating this."[30]

On October 18, I sent Anita a brief email, saying: "I was obviously pleased to see that Alexander Proctor was arrested, and I am looking forward to future arrests.

"I hope these bastards fry for messing with your life."

She replied later that day: "Yeah, me too. I hope and pray they get the other two guys. It freaks me out that they are still out there and it freaks me out even more that I would be asked to identify one of them. I don't think I have the balls to do that."

To that, I responded, "Lady, in my opinion, you have demonstrated that you have the balls to do anything you want."

The following day, Anita emailed me the story in the *New York Times* about Proctor's arrest. The article stated:

> The private detective, Alexander Proctor, 58, was arrested outside his home in Los Angeles on Wednesday morning, the police said. He was being held without bail at the Metropolitan Detention Center on charges of extortion. . . . The F.B.I., which is also involved in the investigation, declined to identify Mr. Proctor's employer, but said more arrests were forthcoming.[31]

In early November, Anita emailed another story from *Newsday* to me. The article suggested that Steven Seagal had been behind

the threats against both her and Ned Zeman. Attorney Barry
Levin of New York, who represented Vincent Nasso, Jules
Nasso's brother, appeared to be the source for the story. The
article added:

> Levin . . . made public his claim about the actor in a letter dated
> Oct. 31 to federal judge Frederic Block. Levin responded in the
> letter to an earlier prosecution claim that the defense was trying to
> "assassinate the character of the extortion victim," who sources and
> court records say is Seagal. . . .
>
> Brooklyn assistant U.S. attorney Andrew Genser said that he was
> aware of the West Coast probe about the threats but that Levin is not
> privy to what federal prosecutors may or may not be investigating.[32]

Then, in another turn of events on Thursday, November 21,
the FBI raided the Sunset Boulevard offices of private investigator
Anthony Pellicano as a prelude to his arrest. Widely known as a
tough and pragmatic detective, Pellicano—the same man whom
Karlene Goller, the counsel at the *Los Angeles Times*, had innocently
suggested they hire to get to the bottom of the threat against Anita—
was both feared and hated by some but admired and respected by
others, especially those he helped.

Directly or indirectly, usually working through a stable of
prominent Los Angeles attorneys, Pellicano had represented a
wide range of Hollywood celebrities, including, among many
others:

> *** Rosanne Barr-Arnold (actress-comedian):** Just ahead of an
> article in the *National Enquirer*, Pellicano found Arnold's seventeen-
> year old daughter whom Arnold had given up for adoption at birth,
> and reunited them, taking the sting out of the tabloid's exclusive.

> *** Kevin Costner (actor):** Pellicano challenged the veracity of
> a woman who had reportedly received $30,000 from a British tabloid
> for the story about her alleged eleven-year "friendship" with Costner.

> *** Tom Cruise (actor):** Attorney Dennis Wasser hired Pellicano
> to investigate Cruise's estranged wife, actress Nicole Kidman, during
> their divorce proceedings.

* **Farrah Fawcett (actress):** Pellicano received an assignment to probe the background of James Orr, a film producer whom Fawcett had dated and later accused of battering her. Pellicano cooperated with the police, providing them with photographs of bruises on Fawcett's body. Orr, who was convicted, received probation.

* **George Harrison (lead guitarist, The Beatles):** Pellicano helped the musician deal with a serious problem with two stalkers.

* **Mike Meyers (actor-comedian):** Imagine Entertainment sued former *Saturday Night Live* star Myers for his film project revolving around his character, "Dieter." Bert Fields of Los Angeles, the well-known attorney, represented Imagine in this case. Martin Singer, who hired Pellicano for the defense, represented Myers.

* **Adam Sender (New York investment manager):** Bert Fields's law firm represented Sender, who sued film producer Aaron Russo. Pellicano was allegedly retained by Fields; Pellicano collected information about Russo.

* **Don Simpson (television producer):** Pellicano accumulated damning information against Monica Harmon, Simpson's receptionist, who had sued her ex-boss for wrongful termination, derailing the litigation.

* **Jerry Springer (talk-show host):** After being filmed with a porn star and another woman in a hotel room, Springer hired Pellicano to discover who had set him up.

* **Kenneth Starr (business manager):** Pellicano was hired by Starr's attorney, Bert Fields, after actor Sylvester Stallone sued Starr, who advised him to keep his stock in Planet Hollywood, which was spiraling into bankruptcy. The case was settled.

* **James Woods (actor):** Allegedly stalked and threatened by actress Sean Young after an affair, Woods asked Pellicano to assist him in his harassment suit against her. Later, Woods dropped the suit.

Speaking of his work, Pellicano had once reportedly said, "My clients are like members of my family. Nobody messes with my family."[33]

Anita, Dave, John Connolly, and I, along with just about everyone else in the entertainment industry, fully recognized that if Pellicano were to be involved in this case, then this scandal was going to be huge.

On November 25, while on the web, I came across a popular website which had obtained and posted a remarkable document three days earlier. In his introduction, editor Bill Bastone of *The Smoking Gun* wrote:

> Actor Steven Seagal has been linked to threats directed at a *Los Angeles Times* reporter investigating the action star's relationship to a Mafia figure, according to federal court records. The explosive allegation is contained in an October 17 FBI affidavit filed in support of a government bid to search the Los Angeles home of Alexander Proctor, a 59-year-old ex-con who has been charged with threatening *Times* writer Anita Busch.[34]

Federal agents justified the raid in an October 17 affidavit prepared by FBI Special Agent Stanley E. Ornellas, the lead investigator on Anita's case, who quoted Proctor as saying that he had received $10,000 from Pellicano on behalf of Seagal to threaten Anita. In this chilling document that helped break the investigation wide open, Ornellas, who referred to government informant Dan Patterson as "CW," reported:

> 9. On June 20, 2002, I interviewed Anita Busch ("Busch") who told me the following:
>
>> a. Busch was working as a contract employee for the *Los Angeles Times*.
>> b. Busch arrived at home at approximately 8:45 p.m. on June 19, 2002, and parked her car across the street from her residence.
>> c. At approximately 8:00 a.m. on June 20, 2002, Busch was informed by her neighbor that her car window had been "punctured." Busch walked to her car to assess the damage and noticed: (1) a note taped to the windshield which said "STOP"; (2) a shatter mark just below the note; and (3) a tin foil backing tray turned upside down on the windshield.

Busch called the LAPD, which treated the baking tray as a suspicious package. After rendering the package safe, the LAPD determined that it contained a dead fish and a rose.

d. Busch believed that the incident was related to her investigative work for the *Los Angeles Times* on an as-yet unpublished article regarding Julius Nasso and actor Steven Seagal. Busch began her work for the *Times* on June 3, 2002, and was contracted through October 15, 2002.

10. On June 21, 2002, I again interviewed Busch, who told me the following:

a. An individual, whose name Busch provided to me and who shall be referred to herein as "CW," had left her six messages on her voice mail at her *Los Angeles Times* office during the morning hours of June 21, 2002. CW had indicated that it was "urgent" that he speak to Busch in person concerning the article she was writing about actor Steven Seagal.

b. At approximately 11:45 a.m. on June 21, 2002, Busch telephoned CW. CW stated that he had run into a guy a few days ago by the name of "Alex," and that Alex had told CW that he had been hired by a detective agency to blow up Busch's car. Alex was aware that Busch had been doing a series of articles concerning actor Steven Seagal.

11. On June 21, 2002, I interviewed CW, who told me the following:

a. He had left messages for Busch because he did not want to see anyone get hurt.

b. He has known an individual named "Alex" for approximately a year. Approximately four or five days earlier, CW met Alex at a car repair business. Alex told CW that he had been recently hired by a detective agency that had been contacted by "some people back east" to set fire to the car of a female reporter who had written a series of articles concerning actor Steven Seagal. Alex said that this was to serve as a warning because "they" wanted the reporter to stop writing the article. Alex stated that he had been by the reporter's residence and noted the difficulty in setting her car on fire because of the close proximity of an apartment building.

Alex was also concerned about an individual who lived in an apartment above the reporter's parked vehicle who stayed up late at night walking from room to room. Alex said that this was going to be a "tough job." Alex told CW that he was going to decline the job, but that the people back east were "ruthless" and would "get somebody to do it."

      c. Alex is involved in the distribution of cocaine and heroin and was currently on a "drug run." Alex normally receives $10,000 for each drug run.

      d. Alex was described as a white male, U.S. citizen, in his 40's or 50's, 5'6", 130 pounds, light brown hair, balding, blue eyes, no facial hair, tattoos or glasses. . . .

14. On July 3, 2002, CW met with Proctor at CW's residence. CW recorded the conversation with a digital recording device that I provided to him. I have reviewed the recording of the conversation, which revealed the following:

      a. Proctor stated that actor Steven Seagal had hired a private investigative firm to threaten the reporter [Anita Busch] who was preparing an article on Seagal. Proctor said that the private investigator is very famous and a big investigator in Los Angeles. Proctor identified the investigator as "Anthony," and Seagal as Anthony's "client."

      b. Proctor acknowledged that he had been hired to set the reporter's car on fire. Uncomfortable with that idea, Proctor had purchased a fish and a rose and placed them on the reporter's car. Proctor stated that he also placed a cardboard sign on the windshield with the word "stop" and put a bullet hole in the windshield. Proctor emphasized that "They wanted . . . he [Anthony] wanted to make it look like the Italians were putting the hit on her so it wouldn't reflect on Seagal." . . .

17. On August 13, 2002, CW met with Proctor at CW's residence. CW recorded the conversation with a digital recording device that I provided to him. I have reviewed the recording of the conversation, which revealed the following:

      a. Proctor acknowledged that the "Anthony" who had hired him was private investigator Anthony Pellicano.

      b. Proctor stated that he had owed Pellicano $14,000 as a debt. Proctor further stated that "they" had agreed to pay Proctor $10,000 for the job involving the reporter, but that

"they" were so pleased with Proctor's work that Pellicano
wiped out the entire debt and told Proctor they were even.

Using the recorded conversation that Dan Patterson, aka
"CW," gave the FBI as evidence, Agent Ornellas participated in
the arrest of Alexander Proctor and obtained the search warrant
for Pellicano's office. According to Ornellas's affidavit in the
wake of the Pellicano search, federal agents found "two metal
combination safes . . . in the rear of the subject premises. Pellicano
told [Special Agent Annette] Freihon that he was the only one with
the combinations to the safes. At SA Freihon's request, Pellicano
opened the safes."

In the first, Freihon found "two black plastic Pelican cases. . . .
One case contained a quantity of what appeared to be [C-4] plastic
explosive, wrapped in plastic wrap, along with a detonation cord and
blasting cap. The second case contained what appeared to him to
be two military anti-personnel grenades. SA Freihon also observed
in the same safe approximately 15-20 bundles of cash, the majority
of which bore $10,000 wrappers, as well as a number of pieces of
jewelry in assorted boxes and pouches."

A thirty-year veteran of the FBI, Ornellas was widely respected.
According to the *L.A. Weekly*:

> If the call ever came in to Central Casting for an FBI agent, no
> one would fit the bill more perfectly. He's the G-man who helped
> indict seven people, including former Bell city administrator John
> Pitts and Mayor Pete Werrlein Jr., on felony charges of racketeering
> and conducting an illegal gambling business in connection with the
> Bell Club, billed as the world's largest card casino when it opened
> back in 1980. Since being given the organized-crime beat 10 years
> ago, Ornellas tracked down cyber-criminals.[35]

On November 22, the *Los Angeles Times* reported:

> A man charged with threatening a *Los Angeles Times* reporter
> who was researching the relationship between Steven Seagal and an
> alleged Mafia associate told an informant for the FBI that Seagal was
> behind the threat, according to court documents.
>   Alexander Proctor, a 59-year-old ex-convict charged with
> threatening reporter Anita Busch, allegedly told the informant during

secretly recorded conversations that he had been hired to carry out the threat by Anthony Pellicano, known as the private detective to the stars.[36]

Reuters ran a wire story which was picked up by the *New York Times*, saying:

> Seagal's attorney Martin Pollner denied that the *Out for Justice* star had any involvement in the threats against Busch. He said Pellicano had been retained as an investigator in a civil lawsuit against Seagal, but the two were not "on speaking terms." . . .
> "This uncorroborated allegation by someone arrested is pure fiction and is nothing more than a transparent attempt to divert attention from himself and the real perpetrators,' Pollner said. 'This is part of an unrelenting campaign to disparage Mr. Seagal and reads like a bad screenplay."[37]

The following day, the attention shifted from Seagal to Pellicano, as the *Los Angeles Times* reported:

> Celebrated private investigator Anthony Pellicano was charged Friday with possession of two unregistered hand grenades discovered as federal agents searched his office for evidence his alleged involvement in a plot to threaten a *Los Angeles Times* reporter who was investigating actor Steven Seagal. . . .
> Attorney Donald M. Re said Pellicano had a "legitimate reason" for possessing the explosive, and denied that his client played any role in threatening the *Times* reporter.[38]

The shocking implication that Pellicano had played some role in the threat against Anita had done nothing less than supercharge this federal investigation.

3. *"Sleuth to the Stars."*

A Mafia associate in the Federal Witness Protection Program had first clued me in about Anthony Pellicano in 1992. William Jahoda, a former soldier in the Chicago Outfit and once one of the biggest bookmakers in the United States, had already turned state's evidence when I met him. His earlier appearance before a federal grand jury had led to the indictments of twenty of his colleagues in the mob. His trial testimony helped convict nineteen of them with the twentieth dying prior to his trial.

After the convictions, Jahoda, in violation of Wit-Sec procedures, invited me to visit him at his secret location in Boise, Idaho.[39] During our interviews, he discussed an incident in which Anthony Pellicano had allegedly masterminded the theft of producer Michael Todd's body from his grave in the Jewish Waldheim Cemetery in Forest Park, Illinois, and then the subsequent discovery of the body in 1977.[40]

Jahoda added that Pellicano, allegedly in concert with local mobsters, had conspired to steal a ten-carat diamond ring which Todd's wife, actress Elizabeth Taylor, had supposedly buried with him after his death in a plane crash on March 22, 1958. Pellicano, who said he found the body after receiving a tip from an informant and then reported his discovery to the police, always denied any wrongdoing.

According to the *New York Times*, "[T]he episode endeared Mr. Pellicano to Ms. Taylor, who introduced him to her Hollywood friends."[41]

Born on March 22, 1944 in Chicago and raised by his mother in Cicero, an Italian and Czechoslovakian community just west of the city, Pellicano left high school after a suspension for fighting.

Pellicano once told a reporter: "My mother was a working lady and never made more than $150 a week. I had to fend for myself. . . . Still I always had an inquiring mind. I was always looking for answers to things. I spent a short time in a Catholic School where they taught [that] Mary was a virgin and Jesus died for our sins.

"I always wondered why. I was never one to take information as truth without investigation."[42]

He joined the Army's Signal Corps, working as a specialist in cryptology, enciphering and deciphering coded messages. While in the military, he earned his GED. When he returned to civilian life, he received a job with the Spiegel Company in Chicago. He worked in its collections department, running down debtors who were in the midst of default on their Spiegel credit-card accounts.

In 1969, at twenty-five, Pellicano left Spiegel and went on his own, setting up a private-detective firm at first under the alias of "Tony Fortune." He became successful enough to earn a coveted seat on the Illinois Law Enforcement Commission, which allocated federal anti-crime grants.

However, Pellicano's winning streak was short-lived. He developed daunting financial problems that forced him into bankruptcy. Then, in the midst of the legal proceedings that followed, Pellicano disclosed a $30,000 loan he had accepted from the son of the notorious Paul "The Waiter" DeLucia, aka Paul Ricca, the former boss of the Chicago Outfit and a long-time business associate of former Teamsters boss Jimmy Hoffa, who had disappeared in 1975. Immediately, Pellicano's financial relationship with the DeLucia family was revealed by the Chicago press. Consequently, he was forced to resign from his seat on the commission.

In the aftermath of that scandal, Pellicano's tactics appeared to change.

In a *GQ* profile, Pellicano boasted that he used a baseball bat to beat up someone, adding, "I'm an expert with a knife. I can shred your face with a knife."[43]

In a first-person story about Pellicano for *Los Angeles Magazine*, writer Rod Lurie recalled:

> It was about 8 in the morning when the phone rang on my unlisted number. On the other end was a man who said his name was Anthony Pellicano. He said he was a private detective representing the *National Enquirer*. In fact, he said, "I am the *Enquirer*."
>
> He told me the owners knew about the story I was working on and that they were "very, very upset."
>
> His voice was measured and low. What he wanted to know, what the owners, he said, were paying him lots of money to find out, was which of the *Enquirer* employees were talking to me and who had given me a set of *Enquirer* documents.
>
> "I want you to understand this," he said, each word fully and clearly punctuated. "I am relentless. I will find this person. Tell me, and it will be confidential. Then I don't have to call you anymore."[44]

Shortly after the publication of his story, Lurie, while riding his bicycle, was hit from behind by a car. His collarbone was broken and so were a couple of ribs. The day after the incident, according to Lurie, "Pellicano called and asked, 'How are you feeling?'"[45]

Also, in my friend John Connolly's 1994 article about Pellicano for *Los Angeles* magazine, he wrote:

> Early last summer, I received a telephone call from Anthony Pellicano, who informed me that he was working for Steven Seagal, about whom I had just written an unflattering article for *Spy* magazine. Pellicano said he was "going to get" me and then began a tirade, calling me every name in the book and linking some curse words in couplets I had never heard before. I interrupted him long enough to ask if he always spoke to people he'd never met in such an obnoxious manner. He responded by screaming that I was a "cockroach" and went on to say I should be glad I was in New York and not on his turf. . . . I asked Pellicano if he was always a tough guy. "I'm not only a tough guy," he said, "I'm connected to the right people, you asshole."[46]

Pellicano, reinventing himself as an electronic-surveillance expert, left Illinois for California after Los Angeles attorney Howard Weitzman hired him as an investigator for car manufacturer John DeLorean's defense team. On behalf of DeLorean, who was facing federal charges for cocaine trafficking, Weitzman used Pellicano to undermine the government's case that had revolved around an allegedly incriminating surveillance videotape of the automaker.

In the end, the jury acquitted DeLorean. And Weitzman, suddenly viewed as a magician in the world of lawyers, credited Pellicano with playing a key role in his victory.

Weitzman and another high-profile Los Angeles attorney, Bertram "Bert" Fields of Greenberg Glusker Fields Claman & Machtinger, LLP, began introducing Pellicano to the local legal community. After becoming the president of the Forensic Lab in Los Angeles, Pellicano quickly became known as the "Sleuth to the Stars."[47]

Pellicano's fame increased as he made appearances in the television series *Crime Story* and in the 1988 motion picture *Illegally Yours*. He was a technical advisor for the movie *Enemy of the State*, and received a "special thanks" credit for the 1993 film, *The Firm*, which featured Tom Cruise as an unwitting associate of a law firm controlled by the Chicago underworld.

In 1993, Fields solicited the services of Weitzman to handle a criminal complaint against pop icon Michael Jackson, who had allegedly molested a thirteen-year old boy.[48] Pellicano worked as the legal team's investigator, soon alleging that the molestation charges had followed an effort by the young boy's father to extort $20 million from Jackson. The father denied the charge, and the case did finally settle after Jackson paid the boy's family an undisclosed sum of money.

Then, in 1995, Pellicano attempted to perform damage control for the racist, perjuring, Fifth-Amendment-taking Mark Fuhrman, the disgraced LAPD detective, in the midst of O.J. Simpson's murder trial.[49]

Also, in cooperation with the National Archives, Pellicano examined the infamous eighteen-and-a-half-minute gap in the Watergate tapes, supposedly resulting from an accidental erasure by Rose Mary Woods, the loyal secretary of President Richard Nixon. In addition, he reviewed the shocking videotape of the murder of President John Kennedy made by amateur cameraman Abraham Zapruder, among other items related to that controversial case.[50]

To be sure, Pellicano's special gift was his ability to make problems go away for those who had the cash and the right connections to certain attorneys who retained him.

During a 1978 interview with reporter Debbe Jonak, Pellicano told her an Oriental proverb, saying, "A man who knows how to live can walk abroad without fear of Rhinoceros or Tiger. . . . For in him the Rhinoceros can find no place to use its horn nor the Tiger a place to use its claws. And he will not die, because there is no place for Death to enter."

When Jonak asked Pellicano what this meant, he replied, "It means absolute confidence can conquer death. That's what I have. That's why I've been able to accomplish what I've accomplished."[51]

On November 24, 2002, John Carman, the Secret Service agent-turned-San Diego private investigator who knew Seagal, sent me a second email after the one I received on September 1, saying:

> What do you think of [the accusation that Seagal was behind the threat against Anita]?
> I know Seagal personally and I know he wouldn't do such a thing.
> It sounds like Nasso is trying to discredit Seagal before court.

To this, I replied:

> Anita is a good friend of mine, so I'll be very curious to know what happened. If you hear any rumors about any past, present, or future attempts to harm her, please pass that information along to me. She is a good and decent person, as well as a talented journalist.
> It's hard for me to believe that Seagal was involved, too. But, if he was, I hope he goes down hard—along with anyone else who tried to intimidate her. Because you have a strong sense of fairness from your experiences in law enforcement, I'm sure that you agree with me.

The private investigator came back with:

> Maybe you can put me in touch with Anita so I can help?
> I think Nasso is just trying to discredit Steven before his trial. This is typical don't you think?
> I am still very curious to know any details. Maybe I can feed some information to you or Anita.
> Maybe I can communicate with Steven something for Anita?
> Just to let you know, if he did do something wrong, I will be the first to tell him he is wrong and he gets what he deserves.
> I have seen Steven in situations that most people would not get involved in. I know Steven to be a considerate person and has a real heart. He may be the type of person that is easily misunderstood or taken advantage of. There are a lot of people that would love to bring him down at any cost.

In the wake of Pellicano's indictment, I cut-and-pasted my correspondence with the investigator and emailed it to Anita.

She responded:

> Just so you know, I was contacted by someone on behalf of the other guys who are basically saying the same thing. I said no. I have to say no now, too. There is a game being played by someone. If there is one thing I've learned over the years dealing with people like this, it is: Nothing is [as] it seems.
>
> There are many sides . . . and all sides are contacting me wanting to "help," but, I know the agenda . . . to talk to me to try and extract information about what I know and who I spoke with. And if it's not that, it's to see if I'll meet. To see if I'll keep going.
>
> Only I know what I did and who I spoke with before I got the drive-by on that Friday morning.[52] Proctor on tape allegedly says that Pellicano was complaining that what Proctor had done "didn't really help, she's back at it again." I wasn't, but he thought I was.
>
> I wasn't getting or giving any information to anyone, but someone was afraid that I was. And that was enough for someone to tell Pellicano to send those guys out again. I feel fortunate I wasn't pulled out of my car and raped and beaten (or worse) that day.
>
> Look. You know this: Everyone has an agenda. No one does anything out of the kindness of their heart . . . except you and Dave. I think that this guy . . . like all the rest before him . . . just wants information. I have no information to give.
>
> My people . . . my sources . . . even though I believe that one of them may either have told one of the sides the questions I was asking . . . OR . . . did it themselves as a favor for one side or the other, I can't betray them. Period. End of story.
>
> This guy might be the most honest guy in the world, but I don't want to know anything from him, and I have nothing to say to him. Steven and Jules are in a world of shit, and I just accidentally stepped in it. I'm trying to scrape the whole thing off my shoe . . .
>
> Tell him as politely and respectfully as you can that while I appreciate his concern, I just want to put this all behind me.
>
> Thanks for passing it on, Dan. Hope you are well.

On November 27, a federal magistrate set Pellicano's bond at $400,000. That same day, the private detective's then-girlfriend, Sandra Will Carradine, the ex-wife of actor and Academy Award-winning songwriter Keith Carradine, put up her home for bail and arranged for Pellicano to be released. Simultaneously, Pellicano was in the midst of ending his eighteen-year marriage to his fourth wife and the mother of four of his nine children, Katherine "Kat" Pellicano.[53]

On November 30, I sent Anita and Dave a story that appeared on the front page of the Style section of the *Washington Post*, written by entertainment writer Sharon Waxman, who declared:

> Then there's Busch, a former editor of trade paper the *Hollywood Reporter* who's now under contract with the *Los Angeles Times*, who spent the summer holed up in fancy hotels at *Times* expense, saying she feared for her life and couldn't live at home. Her actions earned snickers in Hollywood, where she is seen as something of a drama queen, and eye-rolls at the *Times*, where she became known as "the Tawana Brawley of the newsroom"—at least until police made an arrest.[54]

Legitimately upset about any number of things in Waxman's story, Anita demanded corrections from the *Washington Post* but only received a clarification that stated: "An article in the Nov. 30 Style section about a Los Angeles criminal case involving a prominent private investigator, said *Los Angeles Times* reporter Anita Busch had 'spent the summer holed up in fancy hotels at *Times* expense' after receiving a threat against her. Busch and her editor at the *Times* say she spent only one night at a hotel, and stayed at other locations afterwards."[55]

———

Later that same day, Dave Robb sent me an email, saying: "Dan: Why don't you write a book about this? I know a key figure who will cooperate."

Because of the relationship between Dave and Anita, this was my blessing.

4. *"Seagal is the only suspect who makes sense"*

After Dave Robb's suggestion that I write a book about the Pellicano case with Anita, which I knew he had already discussed with her, I felt nothing but excitement. In the wake of the arrests of Proctor and Pellicano, I sensed that this would be a very, very big story, and that Anita would be at the center of the storm.

On November 30, 2002, I sent Anita a basic confidentiality agreement which I copied to Dave. I pledged to keep it in force until we signed a collaboration contract.

When I spoke with Anita a few days later, she told me that she was planning to speak with Joni Evans, a top agent at the William Morris Agency, who, she said, had already approached her about writing a book. The one concern Anita expressed to me was the fact that William Morris also represented Steven Seagal.

Anita and I agreed to a working title for our book: *Woman at Risk*. We decided to work out the details of our collaboration contract at a later date.

Although perfectly capable of writing a book on her own, Anita did not want to write this particular book. She felt so traumatized by her recent experiences that she had no interest in writing her own story, even though she did appear to want her ordeal chronicled. In fact, both Dave and I sensed that she would not return to her former self until Pellicano was safely behind bars, along with the person who had allegedly hired him to threaten her.

On December 10, the Seagal part of the story continued with an article in the *New York Post* in which Jules Nasso's attorney flat-out denied that his client had anything to do with the attacks against Anita and Ned Zeman. The story stated:

> Russell Gioiella, the lawyer for Jules Nasso, wants to make one thing perfectly clear: Nasso, the former movie producing partner of Steven Seagal, isn't responsible for the death threats made last summer against two reporters. . . . "Ned Zeman interviewed Jules Nasso at length at Nasso's house," Gioiella says. "They got along fine. Why would Nasso have him threatened? It makes no sense whatsoever. Seagal is the only suspect who makes sense."[56]

On December 17, a federal grand jury indicted Pellicano on one felony count—not for threatening Anita, but for possession of unregistered firearms. (At the time of the November 21 raid on his office, federal agents found two live MK26 military grenades. Also, he faced one misdemeanor count for the illegal storage of the explosive materials, including C-4 plastic explosives, found in his office safe.)

At his arraignment the following week, Pellicano pleaded not guilty. To mark the occasion, his attorney, Donald Re, told a reporter for the Associated Press that Pellicano had *not* hired the now-imprisoned Alexander Proctor to attack Anita, adding: "There are no links to the Anita Busch case. You can investigate 'til you are blue in the face. They would not find anything because there is nothing."[57]

———

Back east in Brooklyn on January 14, 2003, jury selection began in the RICO case against the seven members of the Gambino crime family, including Peter Gotti and Anthony "Sonny" Ciccone. Through much of their investigation, federal investigators had tape recorded many of Sonny Ciccone's conversations as part of their probe of corruption on the East Coast waterfront. With the help of this surveillance, they had supposedly discovered the dispute between Seagal and Nasso.

Seagal's upcoming testimony for the prosecution was widely anticipated by those watching developments in the Pellicano case—even though Jules and Vincent Nasso would be tried apart from the other defendants.

Covering the opening of the trial, the *New York Times* published an article, saying:

> Steven Seagal, the martial arts movie star, is expected Tuesday at the Mafia racketeering trial of Peter Gotti and six other men who prosecutors say are members of the Gambino crime family. For weeks, judges, cleaning ladies and just about everyone else at the court have been fretting about getting a seat.
>
> Mr. Seagal, who is 6-foot-4 but looks much larger in posters, is to testify that he was frightened after being threatened by mobsters and extorted for hundreds of thousands of dollars.
>
> From the start, Mr. Seagal's account of extortion has given a dash of glitter to an otherwise grim trial concerning waterfront corruption and gambling deals.[58]

On February 12, Paul Lieberman of the *Los Angeles Times* described Seagal on the witness stand, saying:

> [Seagal was in a] silk shirt, though a brown silk jacket mostly covered it. Whereas other witnesses have come through the public part of the courtroom, he entered from the back, through the door used by jurors, near the judge's seat.
>
> He was in blue jeans and had a red beaded bracelet wound around his left wrist. His jet-black hair was pulled back in his trademark style.
>
> He spoke so softly at first, [U.S. District Judge Frederic] Block had to tell him to speak up. "Just sit back, relax," the judge said."[59]

Specifically, Seagal testified about his long association with Jules Nasso. According to the action-adventure star, the Seagal-Nasso partnership started to collapse during the divorce of Nasso and his wife. He claimed that, in a desperate effort to salvage their business relationship, Nasso allegedly sent Gambino *caporegime* Sonny Ciccone, also a former international vice president of the longshoremen's union, to speak with Seagal in Toronto during the filming of *Exit Wounds*, which was being produced without Nasso. According to Seagal, Ciccone instructed him to end all hostilities with Nasso and to continue making motion pictures with him.

Later, in January 2001, Ciccone met with Seagal and Nasso at a Brooklyn steak house. During this conversation, Seagal stated in his testimony, Ciccone tried to shake him down. According to Seagal, Nasso allegedly confirmed his own complicity in the threat by saying to his former partner, "If you would have said the wrong thing, they were going to kill you."[60]

In a third meeting on the West Coast, Seagal alleged that Ciccone and his associates instructed him to pay $3 million to Nasso even though Seagal insisted that he did not owe that money to his former partner.

Consequently, supposedly fearing reprisals, Seagal contacted an imprisoned Genovese capo, Angelo Prisco. In return for serving as his intermediary with the Gambinos, Seagal contributed $10,000 to Prisco's legal-defense fund.[61]

Subsequently, Seagal appeared before a federal grand jury where he took the Fifth against self-incrimination before receiving immunity.

Oddly enough, the prosecution had tried to suppress any questioning of Seagal about Anita Busch and Ned Zeman. In a letter from U.S. Attorney Roslynn R. Mauskopf to the presiding trial judge, Frederic Block, Mauskopf wrote:

> The defense should be precluded from cross-examining Mr. Seagal concerning these incidents. Mr. Seagal has unequivocally denied any involvement to the FBI and the government. Moreover, despite an investigation by the Federal Bureau of Investigation and the United States [Attorney's] Office for the Central District of California, including a search of the private investigator's offices who was implicated by Proctor, there has been no evidence linking Mr. Seagal to any of these incidents. In addition, Proctor's statement to the confidential source that Mr. Seagal was behind the threat was in the nature of speculation or belief, not of first-hand knowledge. . . . Any recorded statement by Proctor is hearsay and would be inadmissible in this trial.[62]

The trial judge concurred, insisting, "I'm going to keep some restraints on this so it doesn't turn into a media circus."[63]

Paul Lieberman wrote in his story:

> Defense lawyers in the case had pledged to expose Seagal as a "pathological liar." But the prosecutor brought up one matter the defense had threatened to use. He asked Seagal whether he was behind the June 2002 vandalism of the car of a *Los Angeles Times* reporter investigating his ties to Nasso and the mob. "No," Seagal said.[64]

In the end, the jury in the Gambino-crime family case in Brooklyn returned guilty verdicts against Peter Gotti, Anthony Ciccone, and their five co-defendants on the RICO case presented by federal prosecutors, including the attempted shakedown of Steven Seagal.[65]

On February 28, I took the train to New York for a two-day board meeting of the National Writers Union which began on Saturday morning. On Friday night, I had dinner at Vincent's on Mott Street in Little Italy with John Connolly and his girlfriend, Dorothy, who, remarkably enough, resembled Anita. John said that he had not yet met Anita but added that they were in regular contact about the Pellicano case.

I said nothing to John about my discussions with Anita regarding our proposed book project primarily because we still had not signed a contract.

In the March 2003 issue of *GQ*, John Brodie published a fascinating story about the link between Pellicano and Seagal. Brodie had actually interviewed Pellicano, who told the reporter: "First of all, Steven Seagal is an enemy of mine and has been for seven years. I can't stand the piece of shit. He's a rat cocksucker. Nobody's going to believe that I did this for Seagal. . . . Number two, if I was going to intimidate somebody, I'm not gonna put a fish on their car. I'm going to be in their face like I've been all my life. My whole career!"[66]

Brodie's story also provided previously undisclosed details about Dan Patterson, the confidential witness who had tape-recorded Alexander Proctor. Among other things, he revealed that Patterson had approached Barry Levin, Vincent Nasso's attorney, and tried to cut a deal. Brodie wrote:

> In late June, CW tried to sell Levin information about Seagal and Pellicano for $30,000. Knowing that paying for testimony was an expressway to being disbarred, Levin declined, but the two kept talking. In a conversation on August 29, which Levin recorded, the attorney finally pressed CW to tell him where the FBI investigation was headed.
>
> "I know, as a matter of fact, that they feel like Seagal's behind [the attack on Anita Busch]," CW says.
>
> Levin asks, "Who feels like Seagal's behind it? The FBI?"
>
> "Yeah," CW responds. "They now feel that's the whole case."

Confirming the Pellicano-Seagal falling out was Seagal's attorney, Martin Singer, who told Brodie, "The last person Steven Seagal would ever hire would be Anthony Pellicano."

Also, in early March, another gossip column in the *New York Post* featured a story about the Pellicano case. This time, Cindy Adams, who also interviewed Pellicano, published a celebration of the private detective, calling him the "man who's taken a silver bullet for the world's most famous [people]" and reporting: "[Pellicano's attorney] Donald Re explained it to me, "The United States attorney won't dismiss those weapons charges despite these items being found in a search for evidence which *now is a crime that didn't exist.*" . . . [Adams's emphasis]

Pellicano told Adams: "The thing is, many times the U.S. attorney has sent me tapes. I've cleaned them up. I've helped these guys. I've done things for the government. . . . So, one way I get the government asking for my help, on the other hand they're f---ing me. . . . I'm pissed. But I don't want anybody feeling sorry for me. I'm a big boy."

Adams added somewhat melodramatically, "In the Sodom and Gomorrah hills of Hollywood, those special talents of Lone Ranger Anthony Pellicano will be missed."[67]

On March 5, I flew to Los Angeles to discuss a prospective book deal about the "unofficial enforcers" of the Bush Administration— right-wing media people including, among others, Bill Bennett, Rush Limbaugh, and Bill O'Reilly, as well as the right-wing Internet websites—with porn king Larry Flynt.

During the final ten weeks of the Clinton impeachment drama between November 23, 1998, and February 12, 1999, I had worked as an investigative consultant for Flynt as part of his campaign to expose Republican hypocrisy in the midst of the GOP's shoddy endgame for the Monica Lewinsky scandal. I conducted the investigation of, among others, Speaker-designate Bob Livingston (R-Louisiana), collecting and handling the information that led to his resignation from the U.S. House of Representatives on December 19, 1998, perhaps the most dramatic moment on the day that the U.S. House impeached President Clinton.[68]

Even though Flynt had offered me a room at a local hotel, I preferred to stay with Dave Robb during my three-day visit and to sleep on his sofa. As always, he and I would play head-to-head poker and talk about our lives, our work, our girlfriends, and our colleagues into the early morning hours.

On my first evening in L.A., Dave and I had dinner with Flynt and his wife, Liz, at Flynt's card club in Gardena, just south of Los Angeles. After dinner, we went into the casino where Flynt introduced us to Johnny Chan, a legendary poker player whom many still consider to be the greatest in the world. Flynt and Chan were playing at the same table.

On Friday afternoon, during my meeting with Flynt in his office, he told me that he had re-read his contract with Kensington Books for another book he was completing which legally prevented him from writing the book about the right-wing media with me.

I was disappointed, but I still hoped that my prospective deal with Anita would come together.

That night, Dave and I had dinner with Anita, with whom I had had very little recent contact, and one of her girlfriends at Jerry's in West Hollywood. I mentioned our proposed book project, but Anita was clearly not ready to make a decision. So, once again, I backed off, assuming that, like the Flynt deal, the project with Anita might be a nonstarter.

Having not published a book since 1998, with the release of *A Washington Tragedy,* my work about the 1993 suicide of Clinton White House attorney Vincent Foster, I was really hungry to get back into publishing. I continued to be very excited about Anita's story, and I knew that I would be very disappointed if it did not happen.

After dinner, all four of us wound up at Anita's apartment. During our brief stay, she gave me a tour of her home, which included the walk-in closet in her bedroom. She said that, on at least one occasion, she had slept on the floor of that closet because of the overwhelming fear she felt lying in her bed.

After hearing that story, I couldn't quite understand the mixed message she was sending me. Did she want the book written or not?

Dave advised me to remain patient and to continue helping him keep Anita upbeat.

The following day, before I left Los Angeles, I sent Anita and Dave several pictures I had taken the night before at dinner and thanked them for a pleasant evening.

When I returned to Washington, I sent Anita another photo via email, saying on the subject line, "Here's my favorite from the other night." She replied, "Oh, dear God! I look dazed. But I'm glad you think I don't look so awful."

And, to that, I responded with, "[I]n my view, you are always looking good and standing tall. Now, get out there, and grab everything you've ever wanted!"

When I left L.A. without a collaboration agreement, I thought the book project with Anita was dead.

———

Meantime, federal prosecutors, in an attempt to revoke Pellicano's bail, filed papers with U.S. District Judge Dickran Tevrizian, saying, "On February 13, 2003, [Pellicano] telephoned the father of a former employee and potential witness in order to intimidate and dissuade the former employee from testifying before a federal grand jury conducting an ongoing inquiry into defendant's suspected criminal conduct."[69]

On March 13, David Rosenzweig of the *Los Angeles Times* published a remarkable, even sensational news story. Unknown to just about everyone, federal agents had conducted a *second* raid on Pellicano's office on January 15, 2003. The bounty received from that foray had led to a treasure trove of spectacular evidence.

Foreshadowing events to come, Rosenzweig wrote:

> Hollywood private detective Anthony Pellicano, who has represented some of the biggest stars in show business, faces possible indictment on charges of widespread illegal wiretapping and witness intimidation, backed by threats and occasional violence, a federal prosecutor said in court Wednesday.
>
> What began as an investigation into a threat against a *Los Angeles Times* reporter has grown into a large-scale probe involving other potential victims, said Assistant U.S. Atty. Daniel Saunders.

> Saunders said FBI agents have obtained the names of a number of people, including some lawyers, who hired Pellicano to conduct illicit wiretaps or secure the silence of potential witnesses.
>
> He said the FBI has also identified the computer software Pellicano allegedly used to tap into telephones, his contact at the telephone company and a corrupt law enforcement officer who assisted him.[70]

The allegation of widespread illegal wiretapping had now entered the growing Pellicano scandal.

5. *"I had no idea how serious this guy was"*

Because of procedural issues in the aftermath of a complicated Supreme Court ruling at the end of February 2003, federal prosecutors were forced to drop their indictment against Alexander Proctor for his attack on Anita.[71] But, at the same time, the prosecution filed federal drug-trafficking charges against Proctor and kept him in jail.

On March 17, the District Attorney's Office for Los Angeles County, picking up the case dropped by the local U.S. Attorney's Office in the wake of the Supreme Court decision, charged Proctor with threatening Anita. In the indictment, the DA's office stated:

> [Proctor] did willfully and unlawfully threaten to commit a crime which would result in death and great bodily injury to Anita Busch, with the specific intent that the statement be taken as a threat. It is further alleged that the threatened crime, on its face and under the circumstances in which it was made, was so unequivocal, unconditional, immediate and specific as to convey to Anita Busch a gravity of purpose and an immediate prospect of execution.

Reporter Matt Lait of the *Los Angeles Times* added in his article:

> Proctor, 59, faces up to three years in prison if convicted on the charge. . . . The charge filed against Proctor marks the latest development in that case, which began last summer and has taken authorities in several different directions, resulting in two criminal

prosecutions so far. . . . Proctor remains in federal custody on charges of conspiracy to distribute cocaine. His attorney was not available for comment. . . .

Deputy Dist. Atty. Ronald Goudy, who is prosecuting Proctor, said he does not anticipate filing charges against Pellicano and Seagal at this point.

"We filed against who we can file on at this time," he said, adding that the FBI is in charge of any further investigation into the matter. [72]

In one of her rare public comments, Anita told Lait, "I am very pleased the district attorney's office is pursuing the case because it is ultimately about the right of a reporter to freely and vigorously pursue a story without being subjected to intimidation."

After I read all of this material, I sent a message to Anita about Proctor, simply saying, "I had no idea how serious this guy was. . . . Call or write if you need anything."

On April 4, Bill Bastone, the editor of *The Smoking Gun*, who had already published the FBI affidavit that led to the search of Proctor's home, now placed online the actual transcripts of Dan Patterson's secretly recorded conversations with Proctor.

Specifically, Bastone reported that Patterson was "a 60-year old California man who began cooperating with FBI agents after his arrest in an unrelated fraud scheme.[73] In February, during a closed hearing, Patterson pleaded guilty to three felony counts. Presumably, Patterson's hoping that his cooperation in the Pellicano/Proctor investigation will result in a lesser sentence when he appears for sentencing, now scheduled for July 9."[74]

When I read the transcript, I was simply blown away by Proctor's boast that he was prepared to make another "hit" attempt on Anita, who, during my conversations with her, was already shaken up by Proctor's arrogance and bravado—and rightfully so.

In the frightening transcript, Proctor was referred to as "AP" and Patterson was simply "CW." Patterson told Proctor that Ned Zeman's article in *Vanity Fair* had referred to the first attack on Anita.

AP: And does it say what was happened to her?

CW: Oh, yeah, and it also says. . .

AP: About the fish?

CW: Yeah. . . .

AP: It says about her window getting shot up?

CW: Yeah, and [unintelligible] I think it says it was hit with a hammer or something.

AP: All right. And it says the fish?

CW: Yeah. It talks about, you know, everything, you know . . . and "Stop," and all that shit. . . .

AP: I'm famous.

CW: You're famous?

AP: No. You know what, I shouldn't, you know what, but it just, it just makes me laugh.

CW: I'm sorry.

AP: Because, because, no, no, no, no, because Pellicano, listen, that fucking guy, [unintelligible] that guy made me, makes, you know, he tried to make me think, at first he said it was such a good job, and then he comes back and says it really didn't do anything. And then he calls me up, that day that I called you, and says that he got a telephone call that says that somebody called him up and says to him on the phone, he doesn't wanna hurt him, but he knows through a phone conversation that he hired somebody to do this thing.

Later in the same conversation, while discussing the same article, Proctor stated:

AP: I think Pellicano's fucking with me and I think he wasn't straight with me and I think he uh, he's uh, trying to get out, I don't know why, he's nervous, and so he didn't want me to do any other jobs, so he pulls this prank as an excuse not to do any more work. Because when I got out of the car with him, I said, "Listen, I'm ready to attack, you know, whatever else you need done." [Pellicano] goes, "Oh, not with all this heat." I said, "'Listen, that's got nothing to do with anything. They don't have you and I together, nobody fucking knows, and even if they knew," I said, "they can't prove it because nobody saw, I don't give a fuck, it's not an issue, so . . . you're safe. So let's attack."

CW: Yeah.

AP: He hasn't called me back since. Nothing. And I called him up and helped him on another issue, I gave him some advice on something, I [unintelligible] some information, he has [unintelligible] problem. And I went and I talked to some people who happen to know about it, and I don't think he has a problem. So, I don't know what's with [unintelligible]. I think, you know what I think? I think, I think Anthony is losing it. I think he's losing it. I think he's getting to an age, quite frankly, that I think he just, there's deterioration. I see it.

CW: How old is that fucker?

AP: He's my age, 58.

During the afternoon of Tuesday, April 8, Anita sent an email, asking me to find an article that appeared in the *Bergen County Record* in New Jersey about "Steven Seagal and his 'friends,'" especially mobster Angelo Prisco. Because I was busy that day, making preparations to host a dinner for more than forty fellow Washington authors that night at The Old Europe, a restaurant just north of Georgetown on Wisconsin Avenue, I did not get around to performing the search until the following day.

I found two articles and faxed them to Anita.[75] I had no idea what she planned to do with the information contained in them. She was not writing an article about either Seagal or Prisco for her newspaper. I assumed that she was not writing a book without telling me. And I knew that she was not "lawyered up" to mount a legal attack against anyone.

However, our recent exchange did resurrect our discussions about a possible book project.

On Monday, April 14, the trial judge in the Pellicano case slapped down a motion by defense lawyer Donald Re to dismiss all charges against the private detective—based on what he considered the illegal search of Pellicano's office by federal agents.

As Re announced that he would appeal the decision, Judge Tevrizian ruled that jury selection would begin on April 29.

Interestingly, in a sworn affidavit filed as part of the prosecution's written response to defense attorney Re, Special Agent Ornellas wrote: "The data storage devices seized from Anthony Pellicano's offices during the November 21, 2002, and January 15, 2003, searches have a capacity of approximately 3.686 terabytes. This is the equivalent of nearly two billion double-spaced pages of text—enough to completely fill approximately 245 rooms measuring 10' X 12' X 10' to the ceiling."[76]

Once again, that was *two-billion pages* of material, much of it in the form of illegal wiretap transcripts.

The obvious questions were: If Pellicano had recorded these conversations, then who had authorized them? And who were the targets of these recordings?

On April 28, Anita sent an email, notifying me that Pellicano's trial had been postponed until July 8.

Responding to Anita's message, I wrote:

> Thanks for the update. With your cooperation, I could have the manuscript drafted before this asshole goes on trial.
>
> In my continuing view, you have no choice: You must do this book—with me or without me. But, knowing how smart you are, you are going to want to do it with me. I am loyal and know how to keep my mouth shut. I am fast and accurate. I am generally familiar with the cast. I can take a complicated story and make it easy to read. I know the publishing process. I am fun to work with. And— oh, yes—despite my advancing age, I am still fearless. . . .
>
> As I told Dave, you will regret it in six months if you don't do this.

Anita replied, saying: "Those guys are fucking assholes. You ARE fearless. I'll call you tomorrow one way or the other. I promise." (Anita's emphasis)

"There is nothing magical about tomorrow," I wrote back. "Take as much time as you need."

Anita added, "I just need to get the advice of someone first."

I had no idea whom she had in mind, and I did not ask. I did know that it could not be Dave Robb—because she fully understood that he wanted us to do the book together.

The following day, April 29, Anita sent another email, saying to me: "I need one more day. I can't reach the person I need to reach.

"[B]y the way, you should look at lukeford.net. I'm almost positive it's John Connolly or someone Connolly is talking to or working with who is doing it. I just told Connolly that as well."

Clearly, Anita was in the midst of some dispute with my old friend and her new friend, John Connolly, after she had read on Hollywood blogger and celebrity profiler Luke Ford's website: "Anita Busch greenlighted journalist John Connolly" to leak the first story about the June 20, 2002, attack against her to Rush & Molloy's "Daily Dish" column for the *New York Daily News* July 11, 2002.

During my conversation with John on September 23, he had told me that he had fed that story to George Rush. However, he never mentioned that Anita had "greenlighted" him to do so.

Also, Luke Ford had reported that "Journalist John Connolly is working on a book on Anthony Pellicano called *The Bad Detective*."

I think, more than anything else, Anita just simply hated Luke Ford. He had posted an extremely harsh profile about her which stated:

> Rageaholic Anita Busch is one of those journalists who can dish it out but not take it. She loves to whine and scream and threaten and cry to get her own way.
>
> "Anita is smart and talented, has great sources and knows everything going on in the industry," an entertainment journalist who's worked with Anita told me near the end of 2002. "She needs to learn to play well with others.
>
> "Over the years, Anita's gotten increasingly paranoid. The great irony is what we all thought was the crème-de-la-crème of her paranoia turned out to be real." . . .
>
> Many people who've worked with Busch say she believes in conspiracy theories and likes to trash people in print. Busch is

known around town for screaming obscenities, as in first thing in the
morning to a source, "You fucked me!" (*Salon* 10/3/97) . . .

Busch has a history of sucking up to powerful men she later
betrays. Busch worked for *Variety* editor Peter Bart and *Hollywood
Reporter* publisher Bob Dowling and later quit each, accusing them
of unethical journalism. [77]

At that time, nothing that Ford had written applied to the Anita
Busch I knew. Thus, I could certainly understand her objection to
John Connolly communicating with Ford about her—if, in fact, he
was.[78]

If John did provide Ford with any favors, the online blogger
certainly did not reciprocate his goodwill. In a profile of Connolly,
Ford wrote:

> Journalist John Connolly wrote stories about Danny Casolaro,
> Steven Seagal and "Inside the CIA" for *SPY* magazine. He's a
> complex, intelligent, troubling and sometimes unreliable reporter not
> afraid to use methods that would make many of his peers blanch.
>
> Though a bulldog on the job, he's sensitive towards any criticism
> directed his way, and cuts people out of his life with the greatest of
> ease.
>
> Calculating, John thinks himself much smarter than his sources,
> and this gets him into trouble. He will make grandiose claims that he
> can't back up and then he will claim he never said what he said. He's
> willing to lie to get a story, or simply to save face. . . .
>
> Some of his former clients viewed him as a "consummate liar."[79]

In my experience with him, John was incapable of double-
crossing a friend, and I told that to Anita.

With regard to Ford's mention of John's proposed book about
Pellicano, I simply shrugged that news off. As much as I liked John,
I knew that he was an excellent researcher but had difficulty actually
completing a book.

For instance, according to media critic Ken Auletta of the *New
Yorker*, "In 1999, [Harvey] Weinstein succeeded in persuading
[Miramax's] publishing house to give a book contract to John
Connolly, a *Premiere* contributor who had been working on a piece
about Miramax."[80]

As was widely known, John's book—which was to be published by Tina Brown, the executive editor of Talk Miramax Books—concentrated on the alleged sexual hypocrisy among the principals in Kenneth Starr's Office of Independent Counsel. Cheering on John's project, I had cooperated with his investigation, giving him a memorandum which provided never-before-revealed details about my investigation of Speaker-designate Bob Livingston in December 1998, including the circumstances revolving around his dramatic resignation on the day the U.S. House impeached President Clinton.

However, a research aide whom John had hired, supposedly betrayed him, giving portions of his manuscript—titled, *The Insane Clown Posse*—to internet gossip reporter Matt Drudge.

Time magazine reported: "According to Drudge's copy of the manuscript, Clinton's inquisitors included 'at least six gays.' Literary agent Lucianne Goldberg was branded a 'fag hag,' Ken Starr 'effeminate,' and the love life of political pundit Anne Coulter was also delved into. . . . *Talk* Miramax had First Amendment lawyer Floyd Abrams warn Drudge that he, not Miramax, would bear responsibility for airing [sic] the manuscript. But on Friday an embarrassed Brown issued a terse press release canceling the book. Connolly, a true believer in the right wing-conspiracy theory of Clinton's impeachment, called Brown 'a coward' for abandoning it. Brown insisted it would have been axed anyway."[81]

6. *"Only one person makes sense . . . Michael Ovitz"*

On May 1, 2003, Anita called while I was at my Thursday night poker game and formally offered me the opportunity to co-author the book with her. To my surprise, although we would share the copyright and she would have final say on its content—in other words, "editorial control"—she still insisted that I be the book's sole author.

I told her that I would write a collaboration contract that would allow her to be my co-author just in case she had a change of heart down the road. In addition, she agreed with my suggestion that we would split all advances and royalties 60-40 in her favor.

Frankly, I could not have been happier. The Pellicano case was going to be a huge story, and we had the inside track on it all.

Recognizing that no one knew Anita's story better than Anita, I suggested a process from the outset whereby I could get her information, flesh out the details of her experiences, and ensure that the final product was accurate. This is how I viewed *The Process*:

> 1. Anita would provide me with her printed documents—emails and other correspondence, as well as newspaper and magazine clippings, among other records, including whatever I could obtain on my own. Upon receipt, I would log all of these materials into a "Catalogue of Documents," which I would update periodically and share with Anita.
>
> 2. Anita would write rough notes of her story and provide them to me.
>
> 3. I would then take her rough notes and the printed materials, using them to organize the storyline and to create the flow of the narrative. From the outset, I chose to write the manuscript in a straight chronology and in the present tense. Through this, I believed that I could create a sense of immediacy—the drama inherent with the unfolding history.
>
> 4. I would provide each draft manuscript, fully footnoted, to Anita. (Just to be clear, to me, a manuscript is a living document that goes through several incarnations before achieving its permanent state, beginning with the rough drafts in which the author focuses on the organization and style of the book. Along with creating a structure based on true and accurate facts, early drafts are also repositories for speculation and theory—with the understanding that in the final draft all speculation and theory will be removed unless they serve some legitimate and agreed upon purpose.)
>
> 5. Anita would make whatever additions, corrections, and/or amplifications she wanted in the draft manuscripts and then return them to me. I would then make the necessary changes for the next draft, which she would review and approve. This is how I thought Anita would exercise her editorial control.[82]
>
> 6. Before completing the final draft, I wanted Anita and me to read the entire manuscript aloud, in person or over the phone, so that we could hear the flow of the narrative and make whatever adjustments were necessary. (I did this with my co-authors,

Tom Lange and Phil Vannatter, in our bestselling book, *Evidence Dismissed*, about the O.J. Simpson case.)

7. Both Anita and I agreed that we wanted the finished product to be completely accurate and truthful.

On or about May 14, trying to formalize what we had discussed about our book deal, I sent Anita the proposed collaboration contract.

The following day, Anita testified before the federal grand jury which had continued its probe of Pellicano's activities. She told me that federal prosecutor Dan Saunders, an assistant U.S. attorney in Los Angeles, was extremely interested in her telephone records in the midst of his questions about the problems with her phone and computer. In the aftermath of the questioning, she now had no doubts. Her phone had been wiretapped.

Anita shared the details of this truly remarkable situation revolving around her telephone with me, as well as with FBI Special Agent Stan Ornellas, who wrote in a sworn affidavit:

23. On November 25 and November 29, 2002, following the initial search of Pellicano's office, I again interviewed Anita Busch, who told me the following:

a. After receiving the threat on June 20, 2002, Busch did not live in her residence for a period of time.

b. A few days after receiving the threat, Busch began having problems retrieving messages from her home telephone. Following the replacement of her answering machine, Busch continued to have problems.

c. Upon returning to her residence, Busch discovered that she was missing e-mails on her primary account for the period June 17, 2002, to approximately July 12, 2002, and e-mails on her secondary account for the period June 20, 2002, to approximately July 9, 2002.

d. Over the next couple of months, Busch discovered that her computer hard drive had a virus identified as W32/magistr.b@mm. Busch was informed that this virus intercepted passwords and Busch's [W]ord files and sent the information via e-mail to an unknown location. Busch's hard drive "crashed" following deletion of the virus.

e. On November 5, 2002, still unable to get her answering machine to function, Busch contacted Pacific Bell to arrange for a technician to examine her home phone lines. Clifford Shillingford, a Pacific Bell service technician, examined Busch's phone lines for approximately two hours. Shillingford told Busch that the problem was at Pacific Bell's central station and that he had never seen a problem like hers. Busch asked Shillingford if she should contact the FBI or LAPD, and Shillingford said they probably already knew about it. Shillingford then told Busch that he could not discuss the matter further.

[f.] On November 18, 2002, still having problems with her phone lines, Busch spoke with Pacific Bell employee Sandra LNU (Last Name Unknown), #531, North Hollywood Station. Sandra told Busch that a "half-tap" had been placed on her second home telephone line. Sandra asked Busch if anything had occurred between June and November 2002, and Busch said that she had been the victim of a crime in June 2002. Sandra said that would explain why there was a "half-tap" on her line. Sandra said that no Pacific Bell employee had the authorization to place a half-tap on her line and that the tap could only be authorized by law enforcement authorities. Busch asked Sandra if the purpose of a half-tap was to identify telephone numbers, and Sandra replied that the purpose of the half-tap was to monitor phone conversations.

[g.] On November 20, 2002, Busch attempted to reach Sandra at Pacific Bell, and spoke to an unidentified female operator. Busch told the operator that she was attempting to determine the problem on her phone lines. The operator told Busch that a half-tap was on her line with "two wires" and a "RCmac" with a computer program at the "central office." The operator said that was equipment placed on her first phone line in June, removed by Pacific Bell's central office on November 5, and placed back on her other phone line. The operator told Busch that the equipment had been removed again on November 18, 2002.

24. On November 26, 2002, I spoke with FBI Special Agent Joe Carolla and Supervisory Special Agent Brian Tepper, who are knowledgeable in the area of interception of telephone communications. They informed me that a "half tap" is identical to a wiretap. . . .

28. On December 12, 2002, I spoke with Dave Lopes, Manager-Asset Protection, SBC (formerly known as Pacific Bell). . . . When Lopes first became aware of the half-tap on November 5, 2002, he verified that the three telephone lines subscribed to Anita Busch were not the subject of any authorized court orders to monitor conversations.[83]

But what had scared Anita—and really concerned Dave Robb and me—was that whoever had allegedly paid Pellicano for the threats against her on June 20 and August 16, as well as the wiretapping operation, was still at large. If he/she/they believed that Anita had possession of evidence against him/her/them, then Anita might still be at risk and could be attacked again.

Reporter Paul Pringle of the *Los Angeles Times* published a story about Pellicano on May 20. The journalist asked the private detective about the attack on Anita, writing: "'I would never do that,' Pellicano said, waving a hand as if to dispel a bad odor. 'Is there any evidence that I ever physically threatened a journalist?' . . . Pellicano would not discuss his relationship with Proctor, but he denied hiring him. 'I don't hire people to do anything,' he said. 'I do it myself.'" [84]

The following day, Anita called and told me that an old acquaintance had just telephoned her, someone she had not seen or heard from in several years. Noting that he was an associate of the Chicago Outfit, she added that he wanted to have lunch with her. She code-named him, "The Poet."

"Jesus, Anita," I said, knowing his name from my interviews with Bill Jahoda, the Chicago bookmaker who had landed in the Federal Witness Protection Program. "Don't you think it's kind of strange that this mob guy is suddenly reaching out to you only a week after you've testified before a federal grand jury?"

Anita insisted that she wasn't afraid of him and that she even liked him.

Challenging this and concerned for her safety, I continued, "So you think this *is* a coincidence—so soon after your testimony?"

Anita declined to heed my advice, saying that she had already decided to have lunch with him.

This was the first real disagreement that Anita and I had had. However, I quickly relented, assuming that Anita was simply looking for situations through which she could prove her courage and regain the confidence she had lost since her decision to leave the Seagal-Nasso story.

In the end, though, Anita, for whatever reason, did not meet with this mob guy.

In my view, Anita's redemption as a journalist would be manifested in our book project. Our book in which she had the opportunity to articulate what had really happened, warts and all, would set her free. She would have a sterling opportunity to tell her side of the story and what she had really been put through by this byzantine ordeal.

By this time, Anita no longer liked working for the *Los Angeles Times*, referring to it as "a snake pit." Although there were still reporters and editors there whom she liked and trusted, she held a grudge against Karlene Goller, the newspaper's deputy general counsel, who had suggested—seemingly with the best of intentions—that they bring in Anthony Pellicano to investigate the initial vandalism to Anita's car. Hearing that, Anita told me that she and the law-enforcement people immediately recoiled from that idea, having no idea that Pellicano would later be implicated in this crime.

Goller's husband was Jim Newton, an editor at the *Times* with whom I was acquainted. I respected him.[85]

Anita did not share my enthusiasm for Newton, sending me her notes where she wrote about what she was supposedly hearing from other reporters at the newspaper:

> [A Metro reporter] tells me about Jim Newton's baseball from Anthony Pellicano on his desk. He says this is all going to explode. He says, "We've been told to beg off stories." He says 'none of us know why.'
>
> I tell him that I think I might know why. I say that there is a conflict at the paper. That Karlene has hired Pellicano in the past. He says that makes sense with what is going on. He said that it's getting really strange around here. He said everyone knows that something is up. We've never been told to beg off stories in the past. He doesn't understand why they aren't telling the editors or the reporters this. He asks if [assistant Metro editor John] Spano knows about the conflict. I said [I] didn't tell him but did relay what happened the day Pellicano was arrested and then Jim Newton calling Spano after I called Karlene. I say that I've only told reporters working on this story. He is angry that they haven't been told. He said that this whole thing is a big mess. He says that Jim Newton will do anything to protect his wife, and that is what they are witnessing now. He asks if John Carroll knows and says he can't believe he knows this. I tell him about my emails with [deputy managing editor John] Montorio prior to the grand jury so I would think that he does.[86] He says that he is really angry over this. Really angry.

> I go up and tell Montorio that people are saying that they've
> been told to beg off stories involving Pellicano. I say Newton has a
> gift on his desk from Pellicano that he still displays. He tells me that
> Newton is going to take a leave of absence in three weeks. I tell him
> that I'm glad he is for the reporters' sake.[87]

The following day, June 4, I sent Anita an email which contained only one word: "WOW!!!" I was referring to an article in the *Los Angeles Times* that day, revealing that Pellicano's secret police connection was a twenty-nine-year veteran of the LAPD, Detective-Sergeant Mark Arneson.

The *Times* reported: "Police sources said FBI and LAPD investigators had checked the 50-year-old Arneson's department computer logs. The logs demonstrated a pattern of connections with people the 59-year-old Pellicano was investigating, law enforcement sources said. Among the systems Arneson accessed was the California Law Enforcement Telecommunications System, which contains records of arrests and convictions, sources said." Unauthorized use of this system was prohibited by law.

Then came the "WOW."

> The logs indicated that Arneson had accessed personal
> information about Anita Busch, a *Los Angeles Times* reporter who
> was investigating actor Steven Seagal and his ties to an alleged Mafia
> associate. The records Arneson had access to included Busch's
> driver's license, car registration and driving record, police sources
> said. . . .
> During a March bail hearing, a federal prosecutor alleged that
> Pellicano had been assisted by a corrupt law enforcement officer.
> Assistant U.S. Atty. Daniel Saunders said the investigations into the
> threat against the reporter [Anita] had grown into a large-scale probe
> involving other potential victims.[88]

In her reply to me, Anita wrote: "[Y]ep. [H]ere's a guy who put a 29-year career on the line to supplement his income. It's just amazing to me. When it comes to money, people lose all sense of themselves and what's important in their lives."

On June 12, during a telephone call between Anita and me, she said that her mind had been blown by some information she had just received.

Someone from the law-enforcement community—she did not say specifically whom at that time—had told her that the database information LAPD Detective-Sergeant Arneson had given to Pellicano about her was dated May 16, 2002.

Knowing that she had not joined the *Los Angeles Times* until June 3, I immediately recognized the significance of this revelation: This was nearly three weeks *before* she started investigating Steven Seagal and Jules Nasso—but just nine days *after* the final installation of her seven-part series for the *New York Times* on Michael Ovitz.

"Ovitz?" I asked, shocked by this news. "Was it Ovitz who hired Pellicano to attack you?"

Very upset, Anita said that she was now sure that it was Ovitz.

Shortly after that, Anita sent me her personal journal from that same day in which she wrote of her immediate reaction to receiving the news about the May 16, 2002, date from FBI Special Agent Tom Ballard on June 12, 2003—while she was visiting her sister at her home. Anita stated:

> I call the FBI and ask for Tom Ballard.
>
> He asks me about a few restaurants. If I ever visited any particular restaurants. . . .
>
> Then he asks me, "[D]id Stan tell you about the date that your information was run on the police database?"
>
> "No."
>
> "Do you want to know?"
>
> "Yeah."
>
> "May 16."
>
> I have to sit down. I sit down on her front step. Stunned.
>
> That was before the Seagal stories. That was before I even joined the L.A. Times. Dear God . . . **it could have only been one person . . . only one person makes sense and that is Michael Ovitz.** I tell him that I wasn't at the L.A. Times yet. I tell him that I must go home and get all the dates for you of what I was doing when.
>
> I go inside my sister's house and just sit on the edge of the bed. I get up and get undressed and take a shower. It is all I can think to do. **Ovitz. Who else would care about me during that time?** (Emphasis added.)

Anita also wrote about her second conversation that same day with FBI Special Agent Ballard:

> Ballard then asks me if I know some names. I don't know any of them. He asks the name of my writing partner at NYT. It's Weinraub. He said can you spell that? I do. He says, "[T]hat's a positive ID." I'm shell shocked at this moment. I say nothing. I pull off the road. I just sit there. **If Bernie Weinraub is on that list, which it appears that he is, then it is definitely Ovitz.**
>
> I feel whiplashed. My thinking was only one way on this . . . then boom, I'm thrown across the room. I get home and call my counselor. I need to see her. We schedule an appt.[89] (Emphasis added.)

She followed up these two conversations with Special Agent Ballard with three communications about Ovitz with Special Agent Ornellas.[90]

* In a one-page, single-spaced letter that Anita wrote on June 18, 2003, she provided Ornellas with an overview of her past association with Ovitz, saying:

> Enclosed are the Ovitz articles I wrote with Bernie Weinraub— and one I did alone—while I was working under a freelance contract at The New York Times. Bernie did one other article on Mr. Ovitz under his own byline (not included). . . .
>
> I've reported on Mr. Ovitz for many years. He and I sometimes bumped heads over articles I wrote or questions I've asked him, but in the end we've always continued to talk and remained cordial. We lunched together. He sent me Christmas cards over the years. I've been to his house and he invited me to his son's Bar Mitzvah (I declined the invite).
>
> After the series of articles in The New York Times, he retreated from everything. We haven't spoken since.

* In a handwritten note by Anita about her phone conversation with Ornellas on June 23, 2003, she stated:

> They are looking in [sic] Ovitz—3rd time. I've heard this—but not sure of the links. Having a hard time linking Ovitz to Seagal.

* Writing in her July 23, 2003, notes, referring to Ovitz by her code name for him, "ed" or "Ed," Anita wrote of Ornellas:

We talk for the longest time. The longest talk we've ever had. I tell him about Brad Grey trying to be like Mike Ovitz. . . . . He asks me if I'm writing a book, I said no. I've been asked several times, but no. He said about what? I said about everything that has happened to me. He said, "this?" I say yeah. . . .

He said he's trying to link Pellicano to "ed" right now, specifically when they first started working together.

I tell him that I can find that out in one phone [sic]. He said you can do that? I say yes.

July 27—I call XX. He tells me that "ed" hired Pellicano three years ago. The person who tells me this asks me why I am asking about it. I say for obvious reasons. He is stunned. He tells me that he used to use Gavin DeBecker. He might still use Gavin DeBecker. Now, I am stunned.

He also tells me that a good friend of his said "ed" told him that he was going to get even with everyone someday—and he was going to do it one by one. He told me many other things as well. I ask him if I could please tell the FBI this information. He says he doesn't want to get involved.

I tell him that can I at least tell him these parts (above). He says yes. So, I got permission to tell Stan only the part I'm telling you.

7/28—I tell Stan [Ornellas]. He also asks how my source knew. I told him that he was told by Pellicano himself. He says, thank [sic], Anita. I really appreciate it.

I hang up. I realize that he now has a timeline on which to work. I close my eyes and say a prayer for him and for me. I think now maybe, just maybe, they will be able to go back three years and find out. Please allow Stan to get this monster, and if you won't allow it, please cleanse his (ed's) blackened soul. . . .

Ed brought Seagal into Warner Bros. through Semel. Miller set up foreign sales with Nasso, Janus watched the investment. Nasso babysat. Ed made the deals. Semel told me once over dinner that he and Ed made a lot of money together so although he was great friends with Ron Meyer, he will always be friendly with Ed.

Later, in a fax to me, dated October 19, 2003, Anita detailed her run-ins with Ovitz, as well as the series that she and Bernie Weinraub had done about Ovitz for the *New York Times* between March 22 and May 7, 2002.

Based on what Anita had told me, I wrote in my personal notes, "Don't print: On October 27, 2003, Stan [Ornellas] told Anita that he was convinced that it was Ovitz."

In fact, since June 12, 2003, Anita and I were convinced, too.

———

Michael Ovitz was born in Chicago on December 14, 1946. He graduated from UCLA in 1968 with a BA in psychology. He started his career in show business as a tour guide for Universal Studios. In 1969, he took a job in the mailroom of the William Morris Agency. Eventually, he became an agent.

After a major disagreement with the William Morris brass, Ovitz, along with four other veterans of the agency, left William Morris and founded Creative Artists Agency in 1975.[91] CAA's client list quickly grew to include such celebrities as Alec Baldwin, Warren Beatty, Mariah Carey, Glenn Close, Sean Connery, Kevin Costner, Michael Crichton, Tom Cruise, Robert De Niro, Jonathan Demme, Herbie Hancock, Ron Howard, Lauren Hutton, Michael and Janet Jackson, Stephen King, David Letterman, Madonna, Paul Newman, Al Pacino, Martin Scorsese, Neil Simon, Wesley Snipes and Steven Spielberg.

In June 1995, Ovitz was the subject of a *Newsweek* cover story that identified him as, "Doc Hollywood . . . the Most Powerful Man in the Movie Business."[92]

Two months later, Ovitz left CAA to take a job as president of the Walt Disney Company, offered by his long-time friend, Michael Eisner, Disney's chairman of the board. Ovitz, whose duties were ambiguous and largely undefined from the outset, frequently clashed with Eisner, who soon fired him.

However, after only fourteen months on the job, Ovitz left with a huge severance package worth nearly $140 million.

He took his new money and eventually opened the Artist Management Group which appeared to be operating in high gear until Anita Busch and Bernie Weinraub published their seven-part series in the *New York Times* about Ovitz, based on a damaging audit report.

In the aftermath, Ovitz's world appeared to fall apart.

In an article for the August 2002 edition of *Vanity Fair*, journalist Bryan Burrough wrote about the "meltdown" of Michael Ovitz, stating:

> The man sitting across the conference table is on the verge of tears. A mist has fallen across his eyes. He begins to sniffle. He is a rolling mass of emotions. Anger. Self-pity. Contrition. Regret. He has been through so much. He never thought it would end like this. . . . Michael Ovitz is ruined. . . .
>
> "I didn't kill anybody; I'm not a murderer," Ovitz says. "I didn't set off a bomb in a shopping center. I didn't take off in a white Bronco. I'm an entrepreneur. The money I lost was mine. My money, my gamble, my mistake. And still they hate me. Everyone."
>
> Appropriately for a town that makes money from tragedy and comedy of grand proportions, the word Hollywood used to describe Ovitz's fall was "Shakespearean."[93]

Ovitz specifically named two people as part of a plot to get him: Anita Busch and Bernard Weinraub.[94] In addition, Ovitz suggested that the damning audit that served as the basis for the *New York Times* series had been leaked to Anita by Ron Meyer, the president of Universal Studios and Ovitz's former partner at CAA. Ovitz had alleged to Burrough, "Anita Busch plays pool with Ron Meyer three nights a week," a claim that Anita flatly denied.

Surprisingly, the most prominent public defense of Ovitz came from Cynthia Cotts, the media critic for the *Village Voice*. In her column, Cotts suggested that Weinraub was trying to "bring Ovitz down," adding: "Enter Anita M. Busch, who teamed up with Weinraub to write a series of *New York Times* stories this spring, publicizing every detail of Ovitz's 'Shakespearean' fall. . . . Some people in Hollywood actually started to feel sorry for Ovitz, because the *Times* stories felt like overkill. . . . The allegation of *Times* bias first reached me in March, when an Ovitz-watcher called to say that 'Weinraub and Busch is the most conflicted byline.' . . .

"According to two people who have worked with her, Busch is willing to trash people she doesn't like—and she hates Ovitz."[95]

In 1994, Anita had a notorious run-in with Ovitz.

During an interview over breakfast with Ovitz, Anita fell ill after consuming monosodium glutamate, which caused her to suffer heart palpitations. When she returned to the meeting after a trip to the bathroom, Ovitz asked her what had happened. She replied that she was allergic to MSG.

In the aftermath of the interview, Anita published her story. Predictably, Ovitz was less than thrilled with what she had written. Then, shortly after publication, she received a "gift-wrapped [present] . . . with a big white bow" from Ovitz, according to a newspaper report.

Inside was a container of MSG "and a wry note from Ovitz that said, 'Enjoy!'"[96]

———

For the three-month period from the end of June until late September, in the aftermath of Judge Tevrizian's decision to postpone Pellicano's trial, Anita and I had very little contact. The early flow of information she sent to me now trickled. I knew that she was traveling, visiting members of her family in Missouri, Texas, and Wisconsin. Simultaneously during this hiatus, I tried to find some short-term assignments while wrapping up my work with the National Writers Union.

Still, I remained very concerned that Anita had not yet signed our collaboration agreement and was giving me no reason why even though I had already started working on our project. Dave Robb, as always, instructed me to be patient and so I was.

During the interim, news continued to break.

Page Six of the *New York Post* ran a piece about Pellicano, "L.A. Private Eye's No Canary," which revealed: "Assistant U.S. Attorney Daniel Saunders confirmed to PAGE SIX that the feds had seized Pellicano's computer, but declined to say they had tapes of phone conversations. Asked if any of Pellicano's clients could be in trouble, Saunders said, 'No comment.'

"One insider said: 'The case keeps growing. [Pellicano's] computer had the whole history of who he worked for and what he did for them. The lawyers who hired him could be in trouble.'"[97]

Then, returning to the Nasso case, Paul Lieberman published an article in the *Los Angeles Times* on August 7, reporting:

> Julius R. Nasso, the pharmacist-turned-movie-producer who was described by federal prosecutors as an associate of a powerful Mafia family, announced Wednesday that he will plead guilty to a charge that he participated in an extortion plot targeting his former partner, movie action star Steven Seagal. . . .
>
> Nasso . . . complained that he had loaned the actor hundreds of thousands of dollars only to have Seagal renege on an agreement to perform in four more films for him. But prosecutors alleged that Nasso turned to friends in the Mafia for help after Seagal stopped working with him in 2000, leading to the plot to extort $150,000 per film from the actor. . . .
>
> Nasso and his brother had been scheduled to go to trial next month, and Seagal was again lined up to be a prosecution witness.[98]

Indeed, on August 13 in a Brooklyn courtroom, Nasso pled guilty to one count of extortion for his alleged role in the Seagal shakedown scheme.

7. *"I have no regrets for making this stupid decision"*

I flew to Las Vegas for the annual convention of the National Writers Union at Circus-Circus on Tuesday, September 16, 2003, during which I decided against seeking a second term as one of the three national vice presidents, all volunteer positions. I was starting to run low on funds and needed the time to focus on a new project, preferably Anita's book about the Pellicano case. But, if not that venture, then something else.

On Sunday, September 21, I flew to Los Angeles and rented a car at LAX, hoping to move the book along with Anita. I had reservations to return to Washington, D.C., the following Saturday,

September 27. Although I was still concerned and even a little upset that Anita had not signed our collaboration agreement, I simply assumed that I would leave town with the contract in my pocket.

As usual, I stayed with Dave Robb, who was busy preparing for his long-time girlfriend, Eileen Kelly, to move in with him.

I had brought along about eighty or so pages of notes, based on some of the materials Anita had sent me. After dinner on my first night in town, she and I worked on her home computer, making additions and corrections to the general timeline I had created.

On Monday night, Anita and I had dinner with her sister and brother-in-law, both of whom were talented lawyers. Her sister's husband, Paul Suzuki, and I immediately hit it off, and we wound up having dinner without the sisters on Wednesday night at his favorite sushi restaurant. Like Dave, he was extremely protective of Anita.

Simultaneously, while editing our materials, Anita was working on a story about California gubernatorial candidate Arnold Schwarzenegger. John Connolly, who had also written about this action-adventure star several years earlier, was assisting her.

On Thursday, Anita cancelled our work plans for the day, saying that she was not feeling well. She told me this after we had had a brief argument about our collaboration agreement. When I asked why she was not signing the contract, she replied that she didn't like the pressure that I was placing on her. When I noted that I had been waiting for her to sign this agreement—and remaining loyal to this project and her—since the previous May, she insisted, like Dave Robb, that I remain patient.

When she was still sick the following day, I decided to postpone my return flight to Washington until the following Saturday. I couldn't do anything else but send her some flowers with a note to "get well soon."

With Anita out of commission, I arranged to have dinner that night with retired detective Tom Lange, who, along with his partner, Phil Vannatter, had directed the LAPD's 1994-1995 probe of the murders of Nicole Brown-Simpson and Ron Goldman. I had written Tom and Phil's 1997 book, *Evidence Dismissed: The Inside Story of the Police Investigation of O.J. Simpson*, which had made every major best-seller list in the country, including the *New York Times*.

Tom and I, along with his wife, Linda, discussed Anthony Pellicano, whom Tom knew was used by many law-enforcement agencies—"because his equipment was often better than what the police had," he told me.

On Sunday, Monday, and Tuesday—with Anita still sick—I visited with family and friends in the Los Angeles metropolitan area. I did not want to take time off from work, but I had to find other things to do. Frustrated by this situation, I had no choice but to remain patient.

On Tuesday morning, September 30, Alexander Proctor pleaded guilty in a Los Angeles courtroom to trafficking narcotics. As an indication of the lack of communication between Anita and me while she was still out of commission, at least as it pertained to me while I was reluctantly sightseeing in L.A., I did not even know about the hearing.

The Los Angeles Times reported: "Alexander Proctor, 59, will be subject to a mandatory minimum sentence of 10 years behind bars when he is sentenced in federal court Jan. 12 for transporting a kilogram of cut heroin from Los Angeles to Atlanta in a secret compartment of his car.

"Proctor is also awaiting prosecution in Los Angeles County Superior Court for allegedly making a criminal threat last year against *Times* reporter Anita Busch."[99]

On Tuesday night, after helping Dave move his fiancé's belongings into his Beverly Hills apartment, I attended a surprise birthday party that Dave threw for Kelly at a local restaurant.

Despite their invitation, I simply refused to spend Dave and Kelly's first night together on their sofa, so I accepted an invitation to stay with other friends who refused to allow me to check into a hotel.

The following day, Wednesday, October 1, Anita felt a little better. Dave and I tried to drag her to a fun lunch with a group of journalist-friends at Musso & Frank's. She refused to show up—although she did say that she would have dinner with me that night.

Later, when I picked her up, I gave her a sweatshirt that I had bought at one of those tacky gift shops near Musso's on Hollywood

Boulevard which featured the embroidered words, "DRAMA QUEEN."

If looks could kill, she would have struck me dead right there. She saw absolutely nothing funny about my little passive-aggressive gift.

Anita and I had dinner at Fromin's, a delicatessen on Wilshire Boulevard in Santa Monica. Inasmuch as I wasn't looking for a fight, we didn't even discuss our contract situation. Then, in lieu of staying at a hotel, I accepted Anita's invitation to sleep on the sofa in her living room. While at her place, Anita showed me her voluminous file of documents and notes.

In the midst of leafing through her materials, Anita told me that, even though she understood my frustrations, she was still not ready to sign our collaboration contract. She didn't give me any reason for her reticence, and I did not press her. But I did feel that she was hiding something from me.

On Thursday, the same day that Anita's work on Schwarzenegger's alleged history of sexual harassment appeared in the *Los Angeles Times*, I spoke with Dave and told him that, if I didn't have a signed agreement by the time I left town on Saturday, I was walking away from this project. Dave, with whom I had stayed on Thursday and Friday, again advised me be patient with Anita, even if it meant returning to Washington without a contract.

By the time I had lunch with Anita and her sister on Friday, I had hit the wall over the collaboration issue. There was no argument. There were no harsh words. I just had had it with the nonsense.

After I dropped Anita off at her home, I called Mimi, my significant other since January 1988, who agreed with Dave, reminding me that I already had five months invested in this project. She insisted that before I left town I should give Anita at least one more chance. Mimi, who had spoken to Anita a few times on the phone, liked and respected her. Understanding the importance of this story, Mimi, a teacher and an internationally known art dealer, wanted me to do this project.

That night, I planned to play poker in Dave's regular Friday night game. Anita and I had made no plans to get together before

I left Los Angeles the following day. But, after dinner with Dave, I begged off on the poker game and called Anita, asking to see her. After she agreed, I drove to her home, hoping for closure—one way or the other.

While we were sitting at her dining room table, I told Anita that if I didn't fly home with a signed contract that I was walking away from our arrangement. Once again, Anita, still defiant, refused to sign.

At that moment, I took out a pen and paper, then dated and timed the following message: *"I have no regrets for making this stupid decision."* It was nothing more than a message to myself, noting what I had decided.

I said to Anita, "You and John Connolly have become close during the Pellicano and Schwarzenegger investigations, no?"

When Anita nodded that they had, I replied, "What if we asked John to join our team on the Pellicano book? Would you agree to sign the collaboration contract then?"

"You'd agree to that?" She asked.

"Reluctantly, but yes," I replied.

Anita asked how the money would be divided. I told her that if she would agree to reduce her split from 60 percent to 50 percent, then I would agree to cut my end from 40 percent to 25 percent and give John the same amount.

Also, instead of owning the solo byline, I agreed to share it with John.

I could not help but recall my earlier conversations with John in New York—about working together on a book project. And I sincerely did want to work with him on a book—just not on *this* book project.

As I sat at her dining-room table, experiencing mixed emotions in the wake of completely debasing myself with this idiotic suggestion, Anita jumped at my offer. In fact, after we agreed to bring Connolly in, Anita proposed that we drive to a local Kinko's and photocopy her documents—so that I could take them with me back to D.C.

Shortly after we got into Anita's infamous silver Audi to copy the files, she suggested that we call John and give him the news. We pulled onto a side street and parked the car. I called John in New York where it was nearly 12:30 A.M.

Putting John, whom we had just awakened, on the speakerphone so that Anita could participate, I told him that Anita and I had decided to write a book together about the Pellicano case.

Not surprisingly, John seemed confused, trying to figure out why we just woke him up to tell him that.

He quickly came to life when I told him that we wanted him as the third member of our team.

Then, to add to the drama of the moment, we revealed our deepest and darkest secret to him—that Michael Ovitz was our top suspect as the person who had allegedly paid Pellicano to pursue Anita.

John was aghast, even speechless. He had never suspected Ovitz.

When I arrived at Dave's home that night, my final night in Los Angeles, I told him what Anita and I had decided.

"John Connolly?" Dave asked, shaking his head. "Do you trust him?"

"Yeah, I do trust him, plus I like him as a person," I replied. "But, more to the point, Anita trusts him. She wouldn't sign the collaboration contract unless he was involved. So now, I have to share the byline and reduce my split from forty to twenty-five percent. Anita gave me no choice if I really want to do this book."

When I arrived back in Washington, I waited to tell Mimi until she was in a particularly good mood. And, when that moment came, she asked me the same question that Dave asked, "Do you trust John?"

Living by the philosophy, "If you can't get out of it, then get into it," I started to look for the bright side of this scenario. To my surprise, I quickly found it. And it wasn't any more complicated than this: I admired and trusted Anita and John, both of whom I viewed as good friends. Considering our backgrounds, we comprised an ideal team for this project which we would, no doubt, complete very quickly.

In other words, I decided to make the best of this situation.

On October 7, I sent a memorandum titled, "Our project," to Anita and John, proposing a possible scenario with regard to process, scheduling, and strategy. In this memo, I wrote:

> As we have agreed, Anita's story is not just another true-crime saga. It's not just another tale about Hollywood and its conniptions. And it's not just another reporter's memoir of adventure and peril. Few of those projects sell particularly well in today's market.
>
> Instead, Anita's story—which, indeed, incorporates all of the above—is an "in-your-face" *women's* story about an accomplished and respected woman journalist in grave danger, as well as how she handles her deadly situation and how the law-enforcement community and the media help and complicate her predicament.
>
> The parallels between our story and the upcoming movie, *Veronica Guerin*, slated for release on October 17, are stunning. And we must find ways to exploit these parallels with the timing of the sale of our book—especially since the movie will appear in the midst of Pellicano's scheduled first trial, which will, hopefully, feature Proctor's testimony.
>
> With our LA-NY-DC team, we have the best of all worlds—the full cooperation of the attractive heroine and the inside dope on the evil villains who tried to tie her to the railroad tracks.
>
> If there is any drawback to our alliance, it is the simple fact that all three of us have long histories of maintaining uncanny abilities to piss people off—and a lot of agents and editors in the publishing industry know it. Somehow, we need to turn this into an advantage, especially when we get around to promoting our project.
>
> **Process, schedule, and strategy:**
>
> Coinciding with her very legitimate concerns for her personal safety, Anita doesn't want our arrangement getting out before she wants it out. . . . Nevertheless, we should proceed with our work, even if that means completing the book on spec. Thus, I suggest that each of us moves ahead with performing the following tasks:
>
>> **Anita:** Continues to update her story and to send everything to me. Also, she should put together a list of the people she wants John and me to interview.
>>
>> **John:** Provides me with as much information—on disk—about Pellicano, Ovitz, Nasso, Seagal, etc. as possible.
>>
>> **Dan:** Catalogues all of the materials and writes the first draft of the manuscript—with the knowledge that both of you will amend, correct, and expand upon what I write, along with the understanding that Anita has final editorial control.

If acceptable to you, the book, which features Anita as our central character, will be written in third-person, *present tense*, and told in a straight chronology. The drama will be inherent with the unfolding history. Information is revealed to the reader as Anita learns it. If she doesn't know something, then it doesn't become a fact until she is either given that information by another character or discovers it herself. (This was our strategy for the Lange and Vannatter book about OJ—which I completed in about two months—and the results were spectacular.)

Here are the predictable incarnations of the manuscript—once again, with the understanding that Anita has editorial control:

    1. The final draft.

    2. The edits by my personal editor, Nancy Nolte, who has reviewed the manuscripts of all seven of my previous books—*before* I submitted them to my publishers. (She will be my responsibility. Her money will come exclusively from my cut.)

    3. The overview work by our principal editor.

    4. The line-by-line review by our copy editor.

    5. All versions of the galleys—and there could be as many as three.

    6. The page proofs.

    7. The blues.

    8. The final bound copy.

Simultaneously, while working on the manuscript, we should be drafting a formal book proposal—which can be sent immediately to a literary agent when Anita decides that she is comfortable with the timing.

Once again, I'll be happy to take the first whack at the draft proposal, which you are free to amend, correct, and expand upon. Please be thinking about what information you want the two sample chapters to contain. . . .

I would like the draft manuscript completed—regardless of whether we have a contract or not—by the end of the year. (My emphasis)

Connolly sent me an email, saying: "I've made preliminary calls to a number of repositories of information on Pellicano, *et. al*. This is going to be great fun to work with you and Anita."

As scheduled, Pellicano went on trial to face the explosives charges against him on Wednesday, October 8.

The Associated Press reported on the day's key testimony:

> Celebrity private eye Anthony Pellicano told an FBI agent that he had decided against turning over the two hand grenades and explosives found at his office, the agent testified on the first day of the investigator's trial. Pellicano told Special Agent Elizabeth Stevens that he didn't turn over the weapons to a bomb squad because he knew he'd be asked how he got them, and didn't want to say, Stevens testified Wednesday before U.S. District Judge Dickran Tevrizian.[100]

On Thursday, the *Los Angeles Times* continued:

> The only hint of who that client might be has come from Assistant U.S. Atty. Daniel Saunders. In July, he filed a motion to prevent Pellicano from basing his defense on a claim that he had taken the grenades and explosives from 'a former client (who died of a drug overdose in 1996) in order to prevent that client, whom defendant believed to be unstable, from causing harm to himself or others.' The defense never asserted any such claim, however. . . .
>
> Pellicano's defense team contends that he placed the grenades and C-4 explosives in an office safe and simply forgot about them.[101]

That afternoon, in the midst of the second day of his trial, Pellicano shocked everyone by suddenly accepting a deal offered by federal prosecutors. In return for pleading guilty to two of the three felonies for which he was charged, Pellicano would receive a lesser sentence than he faced if convicted on all three felony counts. Judge Tevrizian, after consultation with both prosecutors and Pellicano's defense team, announced that he would sentence the now-convicted private detective in January 2004.

Dave Robb, as a favor to Anita, John, and me, attended this courtroom drama and reported the details to us.

In his description of Pellicano, Dave wrote that he has "a birdlike face—a sharp nose, no chin and a pink face that looks like he's been out in the sun too much."

Also, he described Daniel Saunders, the relatively unknown prosecutor, as "a strikingly handsome guy who looks quite a bit like John F. Kennedy Jr. (only with male pattern balding)."

Actually, Saunders had been with the U.S. Attorney's Office in Los Angeles since 1997. His first assignment was with its Terrorism and Organized Crime Section. Before the Pellicano caper, his biggest case revolved around a Ukrainian prostitution-and-smuggling operation.

A likely reason why Saunders received the assignment to prosecute Pellicano was his connection to Dan Patterson, the confidential witness who broke open this caper. He was the prosecutor on one of Patterson's earlier cases.[102]

After graduating from Princeton, Saunders had moved to Los Angeles, hoping to find a career in show business. His first outing as a playwright, penning a play based on his senior thesis, closed quickly, prompting him to seek acting roles. Deciding to do more with his life, he went to law school at Berkeley. Upon graduation, he joined a law firm in Century City before becoming a federal prosecutor.[103]

As the Pellicano case moved forward, Saunders earned his best reviews to date—from FBI agents, fellow prosecutors, and even defense attorneys. He quickly became known as a real professional whose office did not leak information to the press.

————

On or about October 11, Anita called and told me that one of her sources had just informed her that John Connolly was in the midst of writing an article about Pellicano for *Vanity Fair*. Over the phone, she sounded like she was in shock.

My initial reaction was that her source must be mistaken.

When she replied that her source would not make a mistake like that, I volunteered to confront John, advising her to remain in "The Garden," which was my way of saying that we would "good-cop, bad-cop" John with me playing the role as the bad cop.

If things fell apart between John and me, Anita could step out of "The Garden" and negotiate a peace between us.

I immediately called John and told him what I had just heard from Anita. Tongue-tied, John started talking in circles. I knew at that moment that this allegation was true, and I was really ticked off about it. He finally confessed that he was, indeed, doing a story for *Vanity Fair*. However, he added that he planned to take whatever money he made from the article and use it to help finance the research for our book.

When I asked specifically for the subject of his article, John claimed that his story was *not* about Pellicano. Instead, it was about Judge Tevrizian, the trial judge in Pellicano's case, as well as a handful of the judge's attorney-friends, some of whom allegedly had ties to Pellicano.

When I asked for the names of the lawyers, he gave me three.

The following day, October 12, I sent John an email, giving him the results of my own cursory research into the alleged connections between the judge and each of the three attorneys. In short, I could not find any.

After Anita and I discussed the situation over the phone, we reluctantly agreed to accept John's word and allow him to write his story for *Vanity Fair*, hoping that his plan would be good for our book project.

Two days later, John sparked another problem among the three of us when he declared, based upon information he had received from one of his confidential sources, that he no longer trusted either Dan Saunders, the lead prosecutor in the Pellicano case, or FBI special agent Stan Ornellas, the lead investigator. Essentially, he suggested that the entire Pellicano investigation had been corrupted which could have a tremendous impact on our book project.

Once again, I disagreed with John in writing, echoing Anita's own sentiments. She had learned from experience to trust both Saunders and Ornellas.[104]

Despite our internal troubles, Anita, John, and I signed our collaboration contract, dated October 17, 2003.

While all of this was happening, gossip columnist Cindy Adams of the *New York Post* published another article about Anthony Pellicano, saying:

> Anthony Pellicano gets sentenced Jan. 20. He's turning himself in early, Nov. 17. Tough guy, he won't cry, won't take pity, won't squeal so the feds go easy on him, accepts the punishment although he doesn't believe he deserves it.
>
> "Morally I did the right thing," [Pellicano told Adams.] "Ethically I did the right thing. Legally I did the wrong thing. . . . I could have helped myself if I named names. But that's not me. Me, I protect my people. . . .
>
> "Hey, I could do a whole volume on Michael Jackson alone. But I'm a stand-up guy."[105]

On October 23, I overnighted Anita a rough 80-plus-page working draft of the proposed manuscript which incorporated the changes made while I had been in Los Angeles. In addition, I gave Anita a very rough first draft of the next forty pages. They were loosely based on the notes and documents she had given me, as well as an updated catalogue of all the documents I had collected.

In my cover letter to her, I told her that I would not send John what I had written until she had given me whatever additions and corrections she wanted to make. Also, I reminded her, "You are going to have many, many more opportunities to edit this manuscript. . . . Remember that we're hoping to have a completed manuscript by the end of the year—which is only about nine weeks away."

On October 28, I emailed a list of literary agents to Anita and John.

All three of us wanted a woman to represent what we agreed was to be billed as a "women's book," which was still titled, *Woman at Risk.* And, in addition to a woman agent, we preferred a woman editor, as well.[106]

Referring to the well-connected agent from the William Morris Agency she had talked to in December 2002, Anita replied: "We could do Joni Evans . . . this is the one problem I foresee . . . she will have to tell Jim Wiatt [the president of William Morris] and Wiatt will tell his great friend Brad Grey who will tell his lawyer and great friend Bert Fields who will tell his great friend Pellicano."

Wiatt was the head of the William Morris Agency. Brad Grey, who packaged such programs as *The Sopranos* and *The Larry Sanders Show*, was one of the agency's prized clients. And Pellicano had reportedly done work for Grey on at least two recent lawsuits that were handled by Fields.

Also, Pellicano had a relationship with Wiatt. According to Ken Auletta of the *New Yorker*:

> Pellicano even interested HBO in a series based on his work as a private investigator. He enlisted the director William Friedkin and the head of the William Morris agency, Jim Wiatt, who persuaded Brad Grey, the executive producer of *The Sopranos*, to take the idea to HBO, which eventually decided against developing it.[107]

From the outset, Anita had concocted code names for some of the higher-profile people in our manuscript. For instance, she described Steven Seagal as "The Baby." She gave Jules Nasso the name, "The Babysitter." She called Anthony Pellicano, "The Bird," and Michael Ovitz, "ED," Anita's acronym for "Evil-Doer" or "Evil Dude."

Just to be clear, among our team, "ED" was a reference to Ovitz and no one else.

On October 30, Anita sent me an email, writing:

> I spoke to John this morning about Ed and the babysitter. He thought he might confront the babysitter about Ed next week. I told him be careful. I don't want anything to screw anything up. He said he's been talking constantly to the babysitter. (I've known that for a year.)
>
> Dan, I don't think it's good to let the babysitter know anything at all. Your opinion, please?

I called Anita with my answer, saying that I agreed with her in the short term although I appreciated the wisdom of John speaking to

Nasso just before he went to prison which could be several months away. At the very least, I wanted a draft manuscript before we approached Nasso, Ovitz, or anyone else for interviews, hoping to get their versions of this story on the record.

8. *"So Hollywood is spying on Hollywood"*

On Wednesday, November 5, 2003, Janet Shprintz of *Variety* published a major news story, saying that federal agents had questioned prominent Los Angeles attorney Bert Fields about Pellicano's allegedly illegal wiretapping activities. Shprintz reported:

> Fields is believed to be one of several well-known entertainment attorneys who have been questioned in connection with the wiretapping investigation. . . .
> Fields hired Pellicano to help out his then-client Michael Jackson when the pop star was accused of child molestation. . . . Fields also represented Brad Grey when he was sued by Garry Shandling over profits on *The Larry Sanders Show*, advised him during negotiations with James Gandolfini on *The Sopranos* and represented him at trial last year in a breach of contract suit brought by Bo Zenga over *Scary Movie*. That trial ended in a directed verdict for Grey, which was affirmed on appeal earlier this week. It is not clear what role, if any, Pellicano played in any of these cases.[108]

Shprintz also stated that Image Entertainment had retained Fields in its suit against comedian Mike Myers over one of the characters he played on NBC's *Saturday Night Live*. Representing Myers was Marty Singer, the attorney who had also represented Steven Seagal. According to Shprintz, Singer hired Pellicano to help Myers.

In the aftermath of the *Variety* story, similar stories, with little new information, about the FBI's questioning of Bert Fields appeared in the *New York Times* and the *Los Angeles Times* on Friday, November 7.

However, the *New York Times* did report: "F.B.I. officials and criminal lawyers close to the grand jury investigation said they had been told they could expect indictments of people involved in the suspected wiretapping to be issued early in 2004."[109]

That prediction moved Anita, John, and me into high gear to get our book proposal ready for New York.

Unimpressed with these new allegations, Nikke Finke, the popular, must-read "Deadline Hollywood" columnist for the *LA Weekly*, wrote almost tongue-in-cheek: "*The New York Times*, the *Los Angeles Times* and *Variety et al.* would have us believe in their oh-so-serious recent articles that rampant paranoia is sweeping Tinseltown. . . So Hollywood is spying on Hollywood. Talk about an almost victimless crime. Good luck finding more than a few sympathetic characters who were 'done wrong.' . . .

"It's the most insidery of insider cases imaginable, from the moguls talking about it, to the media reporting on it, to the threatened *L.A. Times* writer, Anita Busch, who started it all."[110]

Also on Friday, the day after I sent John the first 86 pages of the Anita-approved rough draft manuscript, Anita said that she wanted us to approach Robert Gottlieb, the chairman of Trident Media Group, to represent our book. When we checked out Gottlieb, John and I agreed that he would be ideal, even though he was obviously not a female agent, our initial preference—a woman agent to sell a book to a woman editor about a woman at risk.

Gottlieb, a former top agent and executive vice president at the William Morris Agency, was widely credited with discovering author Tom Clancy after he had published *The Hunt for Red October* with Naval Institute Press, a small publisher in Annapolis, Maryland.

I found a 2002 article about Clancy in *Forbes*, which stated:

> [Clancy's] career had been carefully nurtured by his longtime agent, Robert Gottlieb, but two years ago Clancy ditched Gottlieb for Michael Ovitz—and now Ovitz has been forced to sell his Artists Management Group to another talent agency. Clancy remains listed as an Ovitz client. . . . [even though] Ovitz's career as a powerbroker seems to have stalled."[111]

The obviously strained relationship between Gottlieb and Ovitz made Gottlieb the ideal prospect to be our representative—unless, for whatever reason, he didn't want to get involved in a project where Ovitz was potentially a principal target.

On November 8, the *Los Angeles Times* published an overview of what was already known about the Pellicano case, featuring the significance of the threat to Anita, saying:

> What began with a crude attempt to intimidate a reporter has grown into a federal wiretapping investigation that has rattled Hollywood's legal elite. . . .
>
> The probe has its unlikely roots in an incident involving *Los Angeles Times* reporter Anita Busch, who was investigating the connection between action star Steven Seagal and alleged mafia associate Julius Nasso.[112]

In another major news report on November 11, the *New York Times* stated that the threat against Anita had "unleashed a chain of events that has suddenly entwined many of the Hollywood elite and threatens to turn into the kind of scandal that the show-business world has not faced in decades. Managers, actors, businessmen and lawyers are being questioned, and in some cases subpoenaed, by the federal government in a widening grand-jury investigation of suspected illegal wiretapping that has moved beyond Los Angeles to New York, according to entertainers, producers, lawyers and others involved in the inquiry. . . .

"What set off the growing investigation was the threat against Ms. Busch, an entertainment reporter for *The Los Angeles Times* who has also written for *The New York Times.*"[113]

The article was so spectacular for our book project that we decided to feature it in our proposal.

With everything starting to break wide open, Anita still remained very unhappy at the *Los Angeles Times* and wanted to resign as soon as possible.

I advised her that leaving the *Times* would be unwise. Just as when she left the *Hollywood Reporter*, she would have no institutional base.

Recognizing how much pain Anita was in, I suggested that she "lawyer up," so that she could reasonably consider her legal options.

Early on November 12, I emailed her a 1988 story I had written about Marvin Rudnick, a former federal prosecutor for the U.S. Strike Force Against Organized Crime who was now in private practice.[114] In my description of Marvin, I told Anita that he "is a totally honest and principled guy. Totally. Completely."

Actually, my persistent fear of a *Chinatown* ending to the Pellicano case was based, in part, upon my knowledge of what had happened to Marvin who had become a trusted friend of mine. In 1985, while working in President Ronald Reagan's Department of Justice, Marvin successfully prosecuted a reputed member of the Gambino crime family for criminal-tax fraud. During the sentencing phase of the case, Marvin learned that this Mafia figure had a business relationship with MCA, the chairman of which, Lew Wasserman, had served as Reagan's talent agent since 1939.

For Marvin Rudnick and those of us who knew of his dedicated service as a federal prosecutor, this was a real-life *Chinatown* ending, brought about by the rich and powerful in Hollywood who refused to be held accountable for their corrupt behavior.

When Marvin refused to relent in his legitimate pursuit of the mobster and his business ties to MCA, his superiors at DOJ suspended and then later fired him. And the instrument for the spiking of Marvin's case was the U.S. Attorney's Office in Los Angeles which was now handling the Pellicano wiretapping case years later.

Shortly after Anita read my story, she retained Marvin as her attorney to help her navigate through her legal options.

———

Also on November 12, with our book proposal in hand, I took the train to New York for lunch with John Connolly and our afternoon meeting with superagent Robert Gottlieb at his Madison Avenue office.

From all indications at the scene, our meeting with Gottlieb and Daniel Strone, the CEO of his company, went well. During our forty-five-minute discussion, they were very respectful to us, shaking hands at the end of our pitch and promising a quick answer. But, keeping our best secret, we only mentioned in passing that Ovitz was "of interest" to federal prosecutors.

On the train back to D.C., I wrote John an email, referring to Gottlieb as "the G-man," and copied it to Anita, saying:

> Thanks for a fun and interesting day, Big John!
> Here's my prediction. I think that the G-man will say he wants the job. However, he is going to insist that we rewrite the thing we gave him today, concentrating on what will happen in the future. He's going to want us to use Anita to get to the Big Picture—which, I think, is already pretty well spelled out in the thing we gave him. So, John, get out your crystal ball, and prepare to do your soothsaying number.
> Also, John came up with the idea of concluding "our thing" with the anticipated drama in January. I think that is the ideal conclusion—with Anita achieving complete vindication and the bad guys being brought to justice. A happy, upbeat ending: Just what we wanted. All subsequent news can be reported in the Epilogue and, later, the Afterward. . . .
> For the moment, let's not worry about the number. I just want to secure the G-man and then a house we respect and trust. If we receive a "go" tomorrow or Friday, I also predict that everything will be resolved within the next two weeks. [115]

Blinded by hope and optimism, I could not have read the situation worse. Gottlieb quickly blew us off, along with our project, with no reason given. We received the word from an assistant in his office. And, adding injury to insult, the assistant said that Gottlieb had lost our proposal.

But we were still in the game. In the wake of the *New York Times* article on November 11, an avalanche of reporting followed, featuring Anita's role.

Also, several new names in the Pellicano drama were introduced in an article published by the *Los Angeles Times*: Jude Green, who had survived the divorce from Leonard Green, her ex-husband and the former head of the Los Angeles Opera; and nanny Pamela Miller, who sued her boss in the wake of being discharged from her job by Taylor Thomson, a Canadian newspaper heiress. In addition, there was additional information about Bo Zenga and Garry Shandling, both of whom had sued their management representative, Brad Grey, in the midst of a contract dispute.

The *Times* noted that all of the defendants in these cases had retained Bert Fields as their attorney and that Pellicano had performed his investigative services for him.

Another lawyer mentioned in the *Times* article was Ed Masry who became famous for his portrayal by Albert Finney as Julia Roberts's boss in the 2000 film, *Erin Brockovich*. Masry had hired Pellicano to help him with his defense of a $6.6 million sexual-harassment and defamation suit against him filed by Kissandra Cohen, a former employee. In 2002, a jury cleared Masry of sexual harassment but ordered him to pay Cohen a year's salary, $120,000, for defamatory statements he made about her during a television interview.[116]

Even more new names entered the Pellicano case, stemming from the investigation of telemarketing executive John Gordon Jones, who had been charged but found not guilty of rape and kidnapping. Jones's attorney was Richard G. Sherman who also did legal work for Pellicano. Examining court records, the *Los Angeles Times* learned that "from late 1998 through an unknown date in 1999, Pellicano, without the knowledge of Jones, caused the conversations that took place over the home telephone(s) of Jones, both incoming and outgoing, to be intercepted and recorded. . . .

"Sherman and his partners, in preparing Jones' defense, came across documents that suggested to them that Pellicano had made the surreptitious recordings. Sherman said in the court papers that neither [of Jones's previous attorneys, Daniel] Davis nor [Ronald] Richards nor Pellicano would provide him with any information about the tapes."[117]

According to the *Times's* report, Davis and Richards claimed that, although they authorized nothing, they did hear one or more of Pellicano's secret tapes.

———

Still trying to remain upbeat after Robert Gottlieb's rejection of our pitch to represent us, I sent an email to Anita and John on November 14 in anticipation of the wiretapping indictments against Pellicano and his co-conspirators from the U.S. Attorney's Office. I wrote:

> There is one other possible route, which I have advocated before: Finish the job. And then go in January when the news breaks [about the anticipated wiretapping indictments]—and, as John suggests, we have our ending: Maximum exposure for a completed project in the midst of the predictable feeding frenzy—which should yield maximum rewards.
>
> This will give us plenty of time to find the right advocates—without a big goddamn rush, during which we could make a fatal mistake.
>
> Once again, I believe that there is no risk with this strategy—unless the *Chinatown* scenario is on the horizon. The only immediate downside is that Anita will remain in a holding pattern, absorbing the slings and arrows of the *LAT*. Then again, what will she face if she leaves?
>
> Also, I'm hip to Big John's itchy trigger finger in the midst of his righteous efforts to help us along. The only problem I have with that scenario is that we will lose control of the action before we finish our work.

Also that week, news reports confirmed that Pellicano, who surrendered to federal authorities on November 17, had married for the fifth time—to a 42-year-old bartender, Teresa Ann DeLucio of Las Vegas.[118]

9. *"ED is the property of the entire team."*

There was no shortage of news revolving around Pellicano's last day of freedom on November 17, 2003. For instance, the *New York Times* reported:

> Diane Dimond, an anchor on Court TV, said Thursday that while she was a senior correspondent on *Hard Copy* in 1993, she was harassed when she was broadcasting accounts about the accusations involving Mr. [Michael] Jackson. Ms. Dimond told *Vanity Fair* recently that her home was broken into and that documents were

stolen regarding the case. Mr. Pellicano has denied that he sought to intimidate her. . . .[119]

Paul Barresi, a private investigator, said in an interview on Friday that he worked for Mr. Pellicano and that he was questioned late last year by two F.B.I. agents. A spokeswoman for the F.B.I. would not comment on the investigation. But Mr. Barresi said that he was asked by Mr. Pellicano to find "derogatory information' on Sylvester Stallone and Arnold Schwarzenegger." [120]

Prior to this, Barresi's biggest claim to fame was his reported receipt of $100,000 from the *National Enquirer* in return for a story about his alleged two-year gay relationship with actor John Travolta. The article appeared in the tabloid in May 1990. However, Barresi, a former porn-film star who had filmed sex with both men and women, later retracted this claim about Travolta—and then later retracted the retraction.

In the *Los Angeles Times*, Chuck Philips, the reporter who interviewed Pellicano the night before he went to prison, published an article, allowing Pellicano to assure his friends and clients who were at risk that he would never cooperate with federal investigators. Pellicano told Philips: "My clients and lawyers who hired me are completely innocent. . . . They did nothing wrong. The government should leave them alone. And me, I'm going to take this punishment like a man. I will not participate in any way, shape or form with this investigation."[121]

Apart from Pellicano's message, Philips also reported that a former Pacific Bell employee named Rayford Turner was under federal investigation for his role in Pellicano's illegal activities. Philips wrote:

[O]fficials suspect that Pellicano paid employees at Pacific Bell to access telephone transmission boxes, locate specific phone lines and install devices that could record conversations. Pellicano would then dump data collected from those devices into a computer program and organize it to decipher conversations, the sources said.

The FBI recovered checks paid to Turner in Pellicano's bookkeeping records, and agents are investigating whether he assisted Pellicano in wiretapping conversations . . . .

Turner could not be reached for comment, but he has denied wrongdoing.

In addition, Philips's reporting included a fairly dark assessment of the FBI's investigation which one of his quoted sources described as "overly aggressive, unprofessional and bordering on dishonest."

———

On the day after Pellicano entered prison, Michael Jackson's Neverland ranch in Santa Barbara County was raided and searched. Had Pellicano provided investigators with inside information about this former client? Probably not, but Roger Friedman of the Fox News Channel later reported:

> My sources say Pellicano very likely may have set aside information about the Jackson case for a rainy day. It's possible— although no one will say for sure—that Pellicano gave material about Jackson from 1993 to the FBI.
> One source who's an expert on the subject of Pellicano tells me, ". . . It's too much of a coincidence that Pellicano went to prison and the next day the police were at Neverland."[122]

On November 20, the *Los Angeles Times* published another story, declaring:

> When FBI agents searched Pellicano's office last year, they found a folder labeled "Seagal" and other documents with the actor's name lying on a desk. They also found a "call list" with the name Alex Proctor. . . .
> In addition to the evidence recovered during the search of Pellicano's office, authorities have obtained telephone records that appear to show calls between Pellicano and Proctor. . . . [A] recently retired LAPD officer is suspected of providing Pellicano with information from [Anita] Busch's driver's license shortly before her car was vandalized and the threat was made."[123]

Clearly, our secret about Michael Ovitz's alleged role with Pellicano in their efforts against Anita was holding. Everyone in the media was still chasing Steven Seagal—whom I now believed was completely innocent of any role in the attacks on Anita.

However, like Anita, I wasn't so sure about Jules Nasso.

———

On November 17, Anita, John, and I returned to our original plan to seek a female literary agent to represent our book project. Through one of my closest friends, I received an introduction to his high-powered agent who, conveniently, was a woman. During our first communication, I asked her our team's stock question: "Before I send you the proposal, I'd like to ask you—with great respect— whether you have a personal or professional conflict of interest with any of the following people: Bert Fields, Brad Grey, Jules Nasso, Michael Ovitz, Anthony Pellicano, and/or Steve Seagal?"

When she replied that she had no conflicts with any of those people, I immediately emailed the proposal to her.

The following day, my friend's woman agent followed Robert Gottlieb and became the second agent to reject us, simply saying "something [is] not sparking for me here." Although Anita and John were supportive, I felt bad, saying to them: "All I can tell you is what you already know: We have the right project at the right time."

Then, in the wake of her rejection, we were rebuffed by three more agents.

Five agents had now turned down our project. No publishers had even seen it yet. Certainly during my career, I faced situations where I had difficulty getting publishers for my true-crime books. But I had never had a problem getting an agent. This was something new. I couldn't explain it.

With my tail between my legs, I once again had to report the bad news to Anita and John. Still, we agreed to stand by our strategy.

In fact, John declared: "The proposal is beautifully written. My only concern is the possibility that we (all of us) may have been too familiar with the subject to consider other ways of presenting the book. That is why I wanted us to get an agent we trusted as quickly as possible. Hopefully that person can direct us to the best way to market this incredible story."

———

While all of this was going on, John was in Los Angeles, staying at the Sunset Marquis Hotel and working with Anita.

On Saturday, December 6, Anita called me. She was very upset, explaining that she and John had just finished breakfast at a local restaurant. On their way out, they ran into Bryan Lourd, Michael Ovitz's former associate at CAA. By coincidence, Anita and John had been discussing Lourd just a few minutes earlier.

When Anita did not immediately introduce John to Lourd, he stepped forward and introduced himself, saying that he was writing an article for *Vanity Fair* about the Anthony Pellicano case.

When I asked Anita whether she had heard right, that John did not simply say he was writing a story about the judge in the Pellicano case, Anita snapped back that she had heard exactly what she had just told me.

Once again, I suggested to Anita—who, like me, was absolutely furious with John—to sit in "The Garden" and allow me, once again, to play my now-familiar role as the "bad cop."

I sent a restrained email to John, noting my concerns and referring to Ovitz by Anita's code name for him, "ED":

> Respectfully, I ask you to forget about ED's inclusion in your *Vanity Fair* article. You wouldn't even know about his significance to this case if we hadn't told you. ED is the property of the entire team. And, in the end, I don't want our grand finale to be viewed as cold coffee.
>
> *Vanity Fair*: I'm still baffled by what this article is about and why you are doing it without us, especially since you made your deal with the magazine after we signed our collaboration contract. At first, you said that it was about The Judge in the Pellicano case and a handful of lawyers who were his pals. My reaction to that idea was, "Go, John, Go!" However—correct me if I'm wrong—your story now appears to have morphed into a detailed synopsis of our book project, minus the inside specifics of Anita's personal adventure. Candidly, I fear that you are going to lose control of the action—if pushed by *Vanity Fair* to give up more than you had intended. From what I know—and I don't know very much about what you're doing—I believe that everything you're collecting on Pellicano should be used exclusively for our book, as well as for our first-serial potential, which we will share. The [exceptions], of course, are those matters in which you find yourself in a "use it or lose it" predicament. Furthermore—once again, with all respect to you—I think you should give Anita and me the opportunity to read your draft

manuscript before submission. I believe that you would make the same request if this situation was reversed.

John, I trust your instincts and talent. I know that you are totally loyal to our team and our project—and I am your biggest fan and defender. I know that you are trying to act in our best interests. I also know that you would never, ever do anything that would hurt Anita and/or me. However, I am concerned with all of the unilateral moves you're making in your dogged efforts to produce the best article possible. I know that you are not a punch-puller. And, unwittingly, you could be making mistakes.

For instance, Anita told me yesterday—quite innocently and without being at all accusatory—that after leaving a restaurant, you guys ran into [Bryan Lourd], a player whom, by coincidence, you had discussed over [breakfast]. As I understand what happened, Anita failed to introduce you, so you made your own introduction, identifying yourself as a reporter doing an article about Pellicano for *Vanity Fair*. . . .

I don't think that it stretches reality to assume that he might tell people that he ran into Anita, who was with a reporter from *Vanity Fair*, who was writing a story about Pellicano. Potentially, despite your best intentions, that could put her right back on the firing line. Remember, she's been warned, "Stop means stop." And, to date, she hasn't granted a single interview about her adventures since June 2002.

For your information, I fear that I might be doing the same thing—because of the difficulties I've experienced trying to get us a top-shelf agent. The more people I'm forced to go to, the greater the chance that our project will be revealed before we're fully prepared—which would also put Anita back on the firing line. For that reason, I am reporting everything I do to you and Anita.

Bottomline, as we already know, we must remain accountable to each other. That's the only way "our thing" is going to work.

Like I said, I now have over eight months invested in this project—on spec. I'm "all in."

The following day, December 8, John replied, saying:

Whew! Dan, [l]et's sell this as soon as possible with or without the information Anita owes you. I'm sure that you and Anita will feel much better when this is done. I do not share Anita's paranoia. I would never do or write anything to hurt any of us. But, as I told you repeatedly, we must get this book sold. If we have the wrong approach to make agents/publishers happy and excited, then let's

stop pussy footing around about conflicts, this, that whatever [sic]?
[Among] the three of us we own this story!

I am very underwhelmed by the law enforcement people. They
[are] not bad people, but I do not feel that these are major players like
we both know from the east coast. Consequently, we should move
expeditiously to get this sold. Then we can all relax and get on with it.

Essentially, John had neither admitted nor denied anything. But
acting as if he had done nothing wrong, he simply wanted us to sell
our book proposal as quickly as possible.

After hearing from John, I spoke with Anita. Remarkably, we
agreed, very grudgingly, to allow John to proceed with his article
for *Vanity Fair*, permitting him to take all the credit and keep all the
money with his co-author, Howard Blum, an honest reporter who
appeared to know nothing about the ongoing drama Anita and I were
playing out with John.

However, we gave John specific conditions during a conference
call among the three of us: 1) he could not use any material that he
learned from us; 2) he could not use Michael Ovitz as a character
in his story; and 3) he must allow Anita to read the draft manuscript
before he submitted it to his editor. Also, we were taking him at his
word that he would use the money he made from the *Vanity Fair*
article, perhaps as much as $20,000, and contribute much of it to our
book project.

John agreed to all of our terms which kept the now-uneasy
partnership together.

Also, Anita had found us an agent—a man, not a woman—who
expressed great enthusiasm for our project.

The person Anita had in mind was Mickey "The Cowboy"
Freiberg, a prominent Hollywood literary agent who was also
a close friend of hers. My biggest problem with him was that
he had represented mobster Salvatore "Bill" Bonanno's 1999
autobiography, *Bound by Honor: A Mafioso's Story*. To me,
Bonanno, reputedly the model for the Michael Corleone character
in *The Godfather*, was a vicious criminal, and I wasn't crazy about
sharing an agent with him. But, because I had failed to come up
with an agent for our project, I accepted Freiberg without protest, as
did John Connolly.

On December 19, 2003, Anita sent me a copy of the detailed transcript of a conversation she told me that she had secretly tape-recorded with Freiberg two months earlier on October 17. Because of a conversation she had with him the previous January, in which he had discussed the possibility that Ovitz was behind Pellicano's investigation of her, Anita was feeling skittish about her old friend.

Anita typed the transcript, but the references to "A," aka Anita, and "M," aka Mickey, were handwritten. The ellipses were all inserted by Anita in this excerpt:

> **A:** [H]ey, let me ask you something. When we met in January, you asked me if I thought Bert Fields or Michael Ovitz was involved in this thing.
>
> **M:** Yeah.
>
> **A:** Why did you ask me that?
>
> **M.** I don't remember why. Why?
>
> **A:** Because I keep hearing Bert's name now again and again.
>
> **M:** I guess I'm a good guesser.
>
> **A:** No, it's not that.
>
> **M:** Oh, honey, maybe I just know more than you think I know.
>
> **A:** Yeah. I think you do.
>
> **M:** Someone sold you out, honey.
>
> **A:** Who sold me out?
>
> **M:** Probably at your paper there. Let me tell you a story. Lew Wasserman himself called someone pretty high up over there to try and get his book review killed a few years ago. They published it, but something happened after that so . . .
>
> **A:** So . . . what? What happened?

M: I think it was someone at your paper there.

A: Who?

M: I don't know. Someone who read your notes, probably. It's just a guess. I'm a good guesser. I had a little run in with those same folks awhile back when I was working on a project.

A: Yeah. I know about that.

M: Man of Honor?

M: You mean the east coast? I don't know anything.

A: Well, no. What I want to know is why you brought up Bert and Ovitz. I want to you [sic] know why you would even ask about Bert? It's driving me nuts.

A: Do you think I was sold out by someone at the newspaper? [sic]

M: Well . . . who else knew about your notes?

A: Uh, nobody. But they did get into the computer. But I had all the stuff at the office.

The New York agency through which Freiberg worked was The Literary Group—whose president, Frank Weimann, was the agent I had pitched to Anita and John two weeks earlier. Frank had done a great job representing my 1997 best-selling book, which I coauthored with the two lead detectives of the O.J. Simpson case: Tom Lange and Phil Vannatter.

In effect, Freiberg would defer to Frank to sell our book to the publishing houses in Manhattan. Freiberg and Weimann would work out a split of their fifteen-percent commission.

When I called Frank to welcome him to the team, he gave me some good-natured grief, complaining that I hadn't come to him in the first place—so that he would not have to split the commission with Freiberg. But when I forwarded the pitch for him that I had emailed to Anita and John on December 8, Frank thanked me for the kind words.

Finally, we now had an agent—in fact, two of them, one on each coast.

Although the hard feelings that Anita and I held for John over his upcoming *Vanity Fair* story continued—though mostly left unspoken—we tried to get through the holiday season as a team. I sent Christmas cards to both of them, as well as to the agents.

John's card to me read:

> *Dan—*
>
> *It is an honor & a privilege to work with you.*
>
> *Your pal,*
> *John.*

Anita also sent a card to me that said:

> *Dan—*
>
> *I'm blessed to have you in my life.*
> *Merry Christmas!*
>
> *Love,*
> *Anita.*

10. *"I think you are a Godsend"*

Relieved that we finally had agents, I sent the most recent draft of the book proposal to Frank and Mickey, as well as to Anita and John, and asked for their comments. I also asked that we schedule a conference call among the members of our team.

Although Frank wrote, "I like this a great deal," he did suggest that I consider modeling the book after Nicholas Pileggi's *Wiseguy* about the mobster Henry Hill, which featured Pileggi's excellent third-person reporting with heavy doses of Hill's first-person narrative. The book was the basis for the 1990 motion picture, *Goodfellas*, one of the most popular Mafia movies ever produced. Nick co-wrote the screenplay with director Martin Scorsese.

In his response to my latest proposal, John added: "Considering how beautifully you write, from my perspective, we don't need a conference call. Just go do your magic."

I did not know exactly what to make of these remarks from John who was still skating on thin ice with Anita and me over his *Vanity Fair* article, so I sent John's email to Anita, saying:

> Please see John's message below. Aside from the fact that he's giving me far more credit than I deserve, he appears to be opting out of the conference call—which, as I wrote in my note to Frank and Mickey, will be about "our strategy" for selling the book.
>
> On its face, I have no problem with his decision. But, below the surface, how do we interpret this? What is he thinking now?

Anita replied to me, saying:

> Who the hell knows? It's John.
>
> Sounds like to me that he doesn't want to be involved in the decision making. That last response sounds like he's just along for the ride, and he doesn't want to suffer details.
>
> But, if you ask me, I think he knows damn well that he can trust the crew.

Concerned that John was already concealing material he collected for his *Vanity Fair* article, which supposedly had a January 5, 2004, deadline and a February 1 publication date, from Anita and me, I responded to her, saying:

> It also shows that—while you, Frank, and Mickey have made helpful additions and corrections—John still hasn't offered a single contribution to the proposal (or the manuscript) in the aftermath of all the talk and bluster about the importance of his trip to LA.
>
> Even though we appear destined to receive table scraps from the *Vanity Fair* story, I am not going to say a word—until after January 5.

The exchange over our mutual concern about John's unknown intentions and motives led to another exchange in which Anita wanted to reveal to FBI Special Agent Stan Ornellas, the lead investigator on the Pellicano case, that we were, indeed, writing a book. Specifically, she wrote: "I really want to tell Stan asap. I don't like keeping anything from him. It makes me uncomfortable."

To that, I replied:

> Wait to tell Stan until the pitch to the NY houses is thrown. Remember, as soon as you make this revelation, he will be required to write and file a 302 report—which, no doubt, will be widely distributed. In other words: Once you tell Stan, everyone in the federal law-enforcement bureaucracy will know shortly thereafter. It will be big news within the G.
>
> Some might not share our enthusiasm for this project. And we don't need any interference, real or imagined. That's one of the principal reasons why I prefer to approach one [publishing] house for a quick buyout—in order to prevent any unwanted publicity or interference.

In the midst of all of our troubles with John, Dave Robb constantly admonished me to be completely deferential to Anita and to keep her spirits up, saying that John's betrayal revolving around the concealment of his *Vanity Fair* article had hit her extremely hard. More to the point, Dave told me that she had really liked and trusted John and had difficulty coming to terms with the fact that she had been double-crossed by a good friend.

Thus, I took any opportunity I could to build up Anita when she was down and to inspire her when she needed a spiritual boost. For instance, I sent her a list of life-affirming quotes from the Dalai Lama after she had sent me the lyrics to a terribly depressing tune, *I've Changed*, by folk-rocker Josh Joplin, which she declared was now "my song." Part of the refrain lamented, "I've laid the barrel in my mouth."

Later, I wrote to Anita that her song should be Tom Petty's, *I Won't Back Down*. Also, I sent her an email with a link to Sting's *If I Ever Lose My Faith in You*, which I signed, "Your friend and partner."

Meantime, John's deadline of January 5 came and went—without him giving Anita the text of his story, as promised. John, who did give us some raw notes, said that his deadline had been extended.

On January 8, Anita forwarded an email that reporter Diane Dimond sent her—with the subject, "Pellicano—first me—then YOU!" (Diane's emphasis)

Actually, Diane, a well-known journalist, was not trying to one-up Anita. Instead, she was trying to get her to cooperate with an upcoming *Dateline NBC* segment about the Pellicano case, which was being reported by her friend, Josh Mankiewicz. But Anita had no interest in participating.

What really did gall Anita was the last sentence in Diane's message: "Good luck on your book. I'm a [definite] sale!"

How did Diane know that Anita was writing a book?

After I received this message from Anita, I immediately called John with Anita on the line, knowing that he knew Diane. When I asked him whether he had told her that we were writing a book with Anita, John denied it, insisting that he had no idea how Diane found out about the project.

During a subsequent telephone conversation with Anita, she suggested that we had to explain our deteriorating relationship with John to our agents.

I drew up a proposed draft for Anita's approval, suggesting what we might want to tell them:

> Playing the hand that John has unfortunately dealt us, I suggest that we wait until the publication of his *Vanity Fair* story to sell our fabulous book—thereby using *Vanity Fair* for our own public-relations purposes. As I understand the contents of this upcoming article, Anita is clearly the heroine, accurately portrayed as the genesis and lynchpin of the Pellicano investigation. We should have final confirmation of this within the next few days.
>
> Turning lemons into lemonade, with the help of this misbegotten *Vanity Fair* article, we should appear to the publishing houses as savvy and well connected—with a keen sense of timing.
>
> What say you?

To be sure, Anita saw how the Connolly situation was also getting to me, and so she also gave me some much appreciated support, writing on January 9:

> I'm so sorry this is so stressful for you.
>
> For what it is worth, I am glad you have been there through this. . . . I think you are a Godsend. Thank you. Thank you. Thank you.

> Don't worry, Dan. This will all work to everyone's advantage.
> I've no doubt.
>   PLEASE don't worry. EVERYTHING right now is in the
> garden. Relax. The *Vanity Fair* piece is only moments away. Then
> we can breathe a sigh of relief. (Anita's emphasis)

Anita, accompanied by Dave Robb, went to the federal courthouse in downtown Los Angeles on January 12 and watched as Alexander Proctor was sentenced to ten years in a federal prison. Once again, Dave sent me a copy of his report, which included a description of Proctor, saying: "Short, balding and with a receding chin, Proctor, at 59, looks remarkably like an aging Lee Harvey Oswald. They'd even be about the same age if Oswald had lived."

David Rosenzweig of the *Los Angeles Times* reported on January 13: "Proctor, who now has three drug-trafficking convictions on his record, still faces prosecution by the Los Angeles County district attorney's office in connection with the threat against Busch, who attended Monday's sentencing.

"If convicted of making a criminal threat, Proctor could face another three years behind bars."[124]

In the midst of all this, John sent Anita—who had given the Connolly-Blum writing team a short quote, lauding Stan Ornellas and the law-enforcement community for their work—only those portions of the *Vanity Fair* manuscript which referred to her. He did not, contrary to his promise, send her the entire text of his story.

Anita quickly replied to John, noting several errors in what he had written—and that even the one brief quote she had given "was taken out of context and is inaccurate."

Then, on the morning of January 14, John emailed the "Daily Dish" column in the *New York Daily News* to Anita and me. Columnist George Rush of Rush & Molloy, a friend of John, wrote:

> [S]ources tell us that [Michael Ovitz] still matters to federal prosecutors investigating wiretapping allegations against jailed private eye Anthony Pellicano.
>   According to insiders, the FBI wants to ask Ovitz about snooping Pellicano is said to have done for him in the past.[125]

Because of this revelation, which completely blew our biggest secret out of the water, John insisted that we must sell our book immediately.

When I actually saw this in print, I was really angry with John whom I believed had planted this story with Rush in order to justify his use of Ovitz, aka "Evil-Doer," aka "ED," in his *Vanity Fair* article, which violated our agreement.

John even had the audacity to fax Anita and me the article, saying in a handwritten note: "I'm sure that some reporters are going to be all over this. We should tell Mickey today. Agree?"

Specifically, John told us that Ross Johnson, a well-known Hollywood freelance journalist, was preparing a story about Ovitz and Pellicano.

Now absolutely livid with John's latest betrayal, Anita shouted at me over the phone that she wanted to handle this, personally. I had never heard her so angry. However, after convincing her to continue sitting in "The Garden," I wrote to John, saying in the subject line, "We are on hold," adding: "To hell with George Rush and his little note in today's paper, based on his anonymous 'sources.'

"I don't care whether ED is on the front page of the *New York Times*, kissing Pellicano on the mouth. We are not doing anything until you clear that goddamn *Vanity Fair* story with Anita."

John must have been shocked when he received my email since this was the first time I had ever expressed disrespect towards him. In his response, he only wrote, "Anita has already cleared all the stuff on her."

I shot back at John: "Anita hasn't cleared the stuff on her. To date, all she's done is point out several blatant errors in the piece. From what I understand, she's waiting for those corrections to be made—and to see the material about her in context with everything else in your story."

Defending his work, John came back with: "[They] were what can only be described as minor corrections that were [adjusted] or taken out completely. As to anything that Anita did not want in the story, they are not in the story. I don't really know your problem with this, but since the beginning there has been one reason or another why we are not [aggressively] getting the proposal out there. I will say it again, that is an error."

Bringing the agents into this argument, I replied: "Frank and Mickey insist that we need to know the contents of your *Vanity Fair* story before we proceed—so that they have all the necessary information before going to the publishing houses.

"Also, the agreement you made with us was that Anita would see the entire article—not just the stuff about her."

Still refusing to admit his latest breach of trust, John wrote to me in an email:

> With all due respect to Anita, some of her objections were a tad much, nevertheless I had *VF* make those changes. I will not do that to the whole story. There is nothing in it that should be a concern to her or you or Mickey. If you don't trust me then we have all made a big mistake. Additionally, without her help, because she did not want to be involved, I moved Howard [Blum], without his knowing that I was talking to her, to structure the story to highlight Anita as a hero who is responsible for all that has and, hopefully is about to occur. It is a great promo for the book. No one could have done more.
>
> I have been gently pressing for months for us to move quickly and was repeatedly pooh-poohed! Yesterday, I learned that Kat Pellicano is shopping a book/movie deal proposal that she wrote with the help of a woman named Ellen Feigen.[126] Kat Pellicano has also been repeatedly approached by *48 Hours*, *Dateline* and *Primetime*. Dan Saunders has let it be known that he plans on writing a book and leaving the US Attorney's office after this case. I'm also sure that there are others out waiting in the wings.
>
> We had the Pellicano/Ovitz/Berkle story weeks ago and now Rush is out there first. Instead of publishers reading it today and laughing that they knew about it weeks ago, they will see in our proposal and wonder if we got it after Rush?
>
> I'd really like to personally hear from Mickey and or Frank as to their [hesitancy]?

Knowing that I had the support of everyone else on our team, I responded to John with: "I'll have plenty to say about all of this after you have cleared your entire story with Anita, as you promised.

"With regard to Frank and Mickey, feel to free to call them."

John then brought Anita into the battle, writing to her:

> I'm taking a day to chill out after some of the difficult
> conversations I have had with Dan in the last few days. Be that as it
> may, you and Dan are very important to me. Minutes ago, I was told
> by Dan Saunders that he is releasing documents in open court today (It
> has to do with Pellicano's sentencing) that clearly link him and I believe
> others to the attack on you. I have alerted Frank [Weimann] so that
> he can get the documents and get going on the selling of the proposal.
> More importantly, I wanted to be sure that you knew so that you can
> protect [yourself] from the media onslaught following the release of this
> information. Saunders did not offer, nor did I ask for specifics. The
> fireworks are beginning and they're not from *Vanity Fair*.

Anita, who was still more upset than I was but had strategically
decided to play it cool, simply replied: "I hope you and Dan work
out the problems you're having. I'm very concerned about this.
Thanks much for the head's up. I really appreciate it."

Simultaneously, Anita encouraged me to pump up the volume with
John and ask him the home-run questions. Obedient to Anita while
remaining in my continuing role as the "bad cop," I wrote to him:

> Once again, I'll have more to say about all of this later. But for
> right now, I would appreciate answers to the following questions:
>   1. Is Ovitz's name going to be mentioned in the *Vanity Fair*
> article?
>   2. Have you offered *Vanity Fair* any material from our
> manuscript?
>   3. Are you going to allow Anita to read your entire draft
> article—as you promised?
>   I will be looking forward to what Saunders releases in court
> today. However, we are still not going to consider pitching our book
> proposal until the *Vanity Fair* [situation] is resolved.
>   Finally, despite our current troubles, you continue to mean a lot
> to me, too.

John never replied to my email or to any of my questions.
However, on January 15, John did send an email to Anita which
he copied to me, saying:

> I'm sure you know by now, but in the event you haven't been
> told, the documents put into evidence today by Dan Saunders state on
> page 8, "The information about Anita Busch obtained by defendant's

> sources on May 16, 2002 was contained in a file found on defendant's office computer. . . . The file was created on June 3, 2002."
>
> The PR person at Saunder's [sic] office is sending me the documents. I'll let you know more as I [learn more].

This was a clear reference to LAPD Detective Mark Arneson's May 16, 2002, background check on Anita for Pellicano, which he had done more than two weeks before Anita joined the *Los Angeles Times* and began to investigate Steven Seagal and Jules Nasso—*but just a week after her New York Times series on Michael Ovitz had concluded.* Similar to the gossip piece in Rush & Molloy, I viewed this as John's way of telling Anita and me that Ovitz was now fair game for his article in *Vanity Fair*.

11. *"Even the Garden of Eden had a snake"*

As John Connolly had predicted, the federal prosecutors handling the Pellicano case did release a cache of documents on Thursday, January 15, 2004. They hoped to persuade Judge Tevrizian to come down hard on the former private detective and to give him the maximum 33-month prison stretch at his upcoming sentencing hearing.

Assistant U.S. Attorney Dan Saunders stated in the government's brief, which Anita and I obtained through a source other than Connolly:

> It is no secret to this court, which reviewed the affidavit for the initial search of defendant's office, . .that the government has collected evidence strongly indicating that defendant hired a man named Alex Proctor to burn the car of *Los Angeles Times* contract reporter Anita Busch in order to intimidate her on behalf of one of the defendant's clients. . . .
>
> The initial evidence of defendant's involvement in the threat against Busch stemmed from Proctor's recorded conversations with a government cooperating witness, in which he claimed responsibility for the threat and repeatedly stated that he had been hired by defendant to silence Busch's reporting. . . .

Proctor's . . . statements in the recorded conversations are
thoroughly consistent with and corroborated by other evidence. For
example, his description of his actions against Busch fully comport
with the manner in which the threat was in fact carried out. . . .
There is [also] objectively verifiable confirmation of Proctor's
relationship with defendant during the time frame of the threat
against Busch . . . and of Proctor's recorded conversations with
the cooperating witness. An address book seized from Proctor's
residence upon his arrest in October 2002 contained the entry
"Anthony P." with home and office telephone numbers listed to the
defendant. . . . Toll records for Proctor's cellular telephone . . . reflect
31 calls from Proctor to defendant's home or office from July 1,
2002, to September 4, 2002, two calls from Proctor to defendant's
office on June 17 and June 18, 2002, . . . two calls from defendant's
office to Proctor on August 27, 2002, and a call from defendant's
residence to Proctor on June 17, 2002. . . .
The information about Anita Busch obtained by defendant's
sources on May 16, 2002, was contained in a file found on
defendant's office computer pursuant to a search warrant. That
file, which was created on June 3, 2002 (approximately two
weeks before the threat), contained Busch's personal information,
including her descriptive data, residence address, and vehicle
information relating to the vehicle on which Proctor left the dead
fish, rose, and note.[127]

However, Donald Re, Pellicano's lawyer, continued his
aggressive defense of Pellicano, insisting that he played no role
in the threats against Anita whose former partner at the *New York
Times*, Bernard Weinraub, added in his story:

"It's garbage," Mr. Re said. "First of all, they're relying on
Alexander Proctor, someone sentenced to 10 years on a drug job.
They wouldn't rely on anything Proctor said if it hurt them."
. . . A transcript of the recorded conversation between Mr.
Proctor and [an] F.B.I. informant accompanied the government's
court filing. . . . It reads like outtakes from *The Sopranos*. At one
point, Mr. Proctor is quoted as talking about the threat against Ms.
Busch.[128]

As with the earlier transcripts of Proctor and confidential witness
Dan Patterson, which were uncovered and released by Bill Bastone
of *The Smoking Gun* website, the newly released transcripts revealed
additional discussions about Anita.

On July 3, 2002, two weeks after the attack on her car, Proctor told Patterson:

> Yeah, I put a sign pasted in the window. "Stop." I put a bullet hole so that . . . bullet hole, shot the car up, you know, so that she sees the bullet right there. And then I put a dead fish with a rose in its mouth by the window. (laughs) Dead fish. Because I wanted her to think it was Italians. I don't know if it worked or didn't work. I haven't heard from him. But that's what [unintelligible] bullet hole right in the fucking windows and put a dead. . . . I said, "Oh, this is really creative." I bought this beautiful rose and stuck it in through its mouth. . . dead fish. It was about this big, the fish. (laughing) . . .
>
> It was a nice big fucking fish right out of the market. Gutted and everything. And I buy a beautiful red flower . . . a rose 'cause if nothing else you'd think the guy is psycho, you know to put a fucking bullet through her window, you know, right [unintelligible] she's driving she can look right at it.[129]

On January 17, 2004, after reading the available documents, Anita wrote an email to me, saying: "[B]y the way . . . I find it odd that John didn't immediately send us the documents that he got from the U.S. attorney's office. Doesn't matter. Sounds like he may have already made the decision to leave."

Giving her my opinion about all of this, I wrote back:

> The questions are: How is he going to leave—and how much damage will he cause on his way out? That's why I have insisted that you stay in The Garden. In the end, I don't think that he'll try to hurt the book if he feels that he still has your respect. . .
>
> [A]s he flails away, desperately searching for an exit strategy, he is actively seeking a fall guy for his troubles. By this time, I would imagine that even he is in disbelief as to the depths of his betrayals to people who were his loyal friends.

Anita had more to say and wrote:

> The Garden. Yeah, well. Even the Garden of Eden had a snake.
>
> We need to move past this insidious jungle and get to the other side. Let's just figure out the best way to navigate around the snake and leave him behind. He will always be there, but he will be coiled up into himself. If we move past him with grace, he will not attack us.

On January 18, John Connolly sent an email to Anita, resigning from our book project.   She then copied his message to me. Connolly wrote:

> Let me make it official, I am withdrawing from the project effectively immediately. If Mickey or Frank want me to sign something they can Fax it to my home. I'll be back late Monday and will sign and return it. So that I do not contribute to the [paranoia], let me state that I have NO, repeat NO intention of writing a book about anything to do with any of this. Now that the supposed God Awful threat of the VF story has been eliminated, go out and sell the story now. I truly wish that you make a ton of money from the grief that Pellicano brought to your life. You and I will still be friends and as always I will always be available to assist you. Good luck with the book. (John's emphasis)

Anita and I were relieved to hear that Connolly had no intention to write a competing book about the Pellicano case, which would have placed all of the information we gave him at risk.

Also, Anita notified the literary agents about Connolly's resignation, asking us to accept his offer and get him to sign something official, adding that she had to work out some personal problems. "I will do that," Anita wrote, "after John signs off and Dan and I come to a new agreement."

Sensing that Connolly would not respond to me and still wanting Anita to appear neutral, I asked our New York agent, Frank Weimann, to handle the unpleasant job of getting Connolly to put his resignation formally in writing, saying in my email to him:

> Here is John's letter of resignation. After over two months of screwing up, he finally appears to have done something right, even though he is strapping himself to the cross in the process, portraying himself as a hero misunderstood—while using me as his foil and fall guy.
>
> Considering that his email address is on this document—and that he has confirmed his action in a telephone call to Anita—do we really need to ask him to sign something? Frankly, I don't want to give him another bite of the apple. But, if you think it's necessary, please move forward.

Frank sent a letter to Connolly on January 20 which simply stated:

> This letter is to confirm that Anita Busch and Dan E. Moldea have accepted your resignation from *A WOMAN AT RISK: Anita Busch and the Hollywood Mafia* (working title). The collaboration agreement that was signed by all parties on October 17, 2003 is hereby void and you have no financial interest whatsoever in this project.
>
> Please sign and return this letter by fax and general mail. I will have Anita and Dan sign it and I will forward an executed copy to you.

Connolly signed the letter, but no one on our team thought for a second that this would be the last time we would hear from him.

Still, Anita appeared almost giddy that our gnawing problem with Connolly had finally been resolved. With the tension relieved, she joked in an email to me: "[T]oday is [the] international day of the very good looking, beautiful and damn attractive people, so send this message to someone you think fits this description.

"[P]lease do not send it back to me as [I] have already received over fifty thousand messages and my inbox is jammed."

PART TWO:
Anger

12. *"Woman at Risk"*

On January 23, 2004, in the wake of Pellicano's plea
agreement with federal prosecutors on the explosives charge,
Judge Dickran Tevrizian sentenced the "Sleuth to the Stars,"
shackled and garbed in prison-issued clothing, to thirty months
in a federal prison and fined him $6,000. Earlier in the hearing,
Pellicano's attorneys had tried to recant his guilty plea, a motion
the judge quickly denied.

Unlike the Proctor sentencing, Anita did not attend this public
event, mostly because she did not want to deal with the media. But,
once again, Dave Robb witnessed the hearing and reported back to
us what he saw and heard.

The following day, the *Los Angeles Times* noted in its story:
"But that does not mark the end of Pellicano's legal woes. He
remains the target of a wide-ranging federal investigation into illicit
wiretapping and a separate probe of a criminal threat made against a
Los Angeles Times reporter."[130]

With Pellicano safely tucked away in jail, Anita called me on
January 29, saying that she had just received a copy *Vanity Fair*,
the one that contained the dreaded story by John Connolly and
Howard Blum. But, instead of being furious, she simply appeared
deeply hurt by the "many inaccuracies in this piece," as well as the
fact that her only quote, which she had placed in writing, had been
"blundered." In addition, she was upset that *Vanity Fair* had run

a photograph of her, a picture that the magazine appeared to have obtained through a photography service.

Already in violation of our three-point agreement, Connolly had failed to allow Anita to see his manuscript before publication. Now, he had also breached the agreement about naming Ovitz, writing:

> Pellicano, a former employee of his told *Vanity Fair*, began to wiretap the phones of Ron Burkle, a billionaire grocery tycoon who claimed he was owed money by Ovitz, as well as the phones of two agents who were managing partners at Creative Artists Agency, the talent agency Ovitz had founded and then left.
>
> Burkle, as things worked out, received a tip that Pellicano was tapping his phone and boldly set up a meeting with the detective, according to someone familiar with the events. Pellicano immediately asked the tycoon why Ovitz was after him. When, this source continued, Burkle explained that the attention was motivated by Ovitz's attempt to renege on the money he owed Burkle, Pellicano burst into an indignant rage.[131]

The article added that Pellicano revealed to Berkle that he would no longer target the billionaire on Ovitz's behalf. However, Pellicano's electronic surveillance on Ovitz's two former associates at CAA continued. One of those associates was Bryan Lourd, to whom Connolly had made his indiscreet comment the previous December while he was at breakfast with Anita in Los Angeles. It was that remark that ignited Connolly's falling out with Anita and me.

Also, the story contained an anecdote about Dave Robb on the day of the initial threat against Anita that seemed to come directly from us, violating the third proviso of our agreement. When I asked Dave whether he had shared the story with John, he replied that John had called and asked him to recount the incident which, according to Anita, he could only have learned from us.

In return for betraying two loyal friends and partners with his long-concealed article in *Vanity Fair*, Connolly reportedly received a big payday, along with a shared byline with Howard Blum, a respected reporter who had no connection to the deal among Anita, Connolly, and me.

In the Rush & Molloy column of the *New York Daily News*, George Rush boasted that he had earlier predicted that "onetime

Hollywood powerbroker Michael Ovitz would be dragged into the scandal surrounding Pellicano."[132] Simultaneously, he promoted Connolly's article in *Vanity Fair*.

Anita and I continued to believe that Connolly had leaked the original story to Rush. And there was little doubt that he was behind this one, too.

Lamenting the denouement of the Connolly betrayal, I sent an email to Anita and our agents, saying: "Well . . . clearly Big John lied to us. ED is front and center in his upcoming article in *Vanity Fair*. See Rush's column today."

"ED," aka Michael Ovitz—as Anita had dubbed him—had now been introduced into the Pellicano scandal. And the exclusive story that Anita and I had wanted to save for our book was now gone.

Ovitz was now public property.

———

In a stunning development, the *Los Angeles Times* published a story on February 1 about Pellicano's work with numerous law-enforcement organizations, stating:

> [F]or three decades, prosecutors across the country had no hesitation about using [Pellicano] as an expert witness in dozens of cases. Despite his unsavory image and win-at-all costs reputation, Pellicano built a lucrative career as an 'audio forensics' expert, analyzing and enhancing tape recordings.
>
> Interviews and court documents show that prosecutors often turned to Pellicano to examine disputed evidence in troubled cases. In some instances, he vouched for the authenticity of tape recordings that defendants claimed had been altered.
>
> In others, he enhanced garbled or faint recordings after other experts, including those at the FBI, were unable to do so.

Prosecutors had retained Pellicano in Birmingham, Alabama; Tampa, Florida; and Houston, Texas, as well as the district attorneys' offices in Los Angeles and Orange counties, along with the

California attorney general's office and the U.S. Attorney's Office in San Francisco. And, from all indications, he had performed admirably and effectively for each of these clients.

Several of the prosecutors with whom he had worked had even written letters to the court, supporting Pellicano's request for bail in the aftermath of his ongoing legal problems.

Of course, most of Pellicano's work focused on his expert analyses of tape recordings. In numerous cases, Pellicano's expertise helped prosecutors gain unlikely convictions.

Further discussing Pellicano's important work on behalf of the government, the *Los Angeles Times* added:

> Pellicano also served as a prosecution expert in the high-profile trial of Thomas Blanton Jr., accused in a 1963 church bombing in Alabama that killed four African American girls. Pellicano produced enhanced tape recordings and a transcript that bolstered the government's case.
>
> Then-U.S. Atty. G. Douglas Jones said Pellicano's analysis was instrumental in convicting Blanton in 2001.[133]

———

With Connolly now gone from our team, Anita and I signed our new collaboration agreement in which we returned to what we had originally discussed. Anita received sixty percent, and I accepted the remaining forty percent. Of course, Anita kept her editorial control. But, according to our contract, the byline would read, "By Dan E. Moldea, in cooperation with Anita M. Busch," which was a change that I had asked for in lieu of having a solo byline. I knew that Anita's name—not mine—would sell this book.

Further, the contract designated Frank Weimann and Mickey Freiberg as our agents.

On February 3, 2004, my friend, former federal prosecutor Marvin Rudnick, reluctantly told Anita that due to financial considerations he could not handle her possible civil case against Pellicano, et al. on a contingent-fee basis.

Consequently, Anita, in consideration of Rudnick's advice, decided to meet with Matt Geragos of the law firm Geragos & Geragos, which had represented, among other high-profile clients, Michael Jackson in his most recent child-molestation prosecution.

Anita wrote to me on February 4: "I'm going [to] see Geragos tomorrow. I have one concern which I'm going to share with them immediately upfront and that is this—what will happen, if as part of the indictment, that they have evidence that Michael Jackson, through an attorney, hired Pellicano and may have been complicit in some kind of illegal activity? What would your law firm do then?"

Addressing her consideration of Matt Geragos, the brother of Mark Geragos, I replied: "Regarding the [Geragos] litmus test, I yield to Marvin's good judgment. I have always admired [Mark Geragos's] representation of Susan McDougal, the Whitewater figure who went to jail rather than be forced by Kenneth Starr to lie about Bill and Hillary Clinton's role in that matter."

Soon after, Anita retained the Geragos firm which also brought in another excellent attorney, Brian Kabateck, to help with the case.

On Friday, February 6, Frank Weimann gave our book proposal to Mauro DiPreta at William Morrow, hoping that he would give us a preemptive bid so that we would not have to shop our work to any other publisher and risk further exposure.

Our proposal, which had been approved by Anita and me, as well as the two agents, stated, in part:

> *Woman at Risk* is the gripping drama of an accomplished journalist who braved death threats while in the midst of investigating organized crime's reach into Hollywood. This real-life whodunit follows the story of Anita Busch, a reporter who sharpened her skills at the Hollywood trades before working for such publications as *Vanity Fair* and the *New York Times*.
>
> In June 2002, Busch was forced to leave her home for nearly six weeks while the FBI and Los Angeles Police Department's organized crime unit investigated the threat against her life.
>
> Though fearing for her life, she continued to file news stories for the *Los Angeles Times*. Busch did not relent from her duties as

a reporter even as some of her journalist colleagues turned on her, alleging that she had fabricated the attacks to gain public attention.

She fought relentlessly to defend her life and reputation while, unbeknown to her own friends and co-workers, the FBI was closing in on a suspect. With the help of an FBI informant who surreptitiously recorded conversations of an ex-con, drug dealer named Alexander Proctor, the FBI made an arrest.

In taped conversations, Proctor unwittingly boasted of his role in the crime against Busch and confessed that he was originally hired to blow up her car. The felon then named Anthony Pellicano, a private investigator in Los Angeles, as his employer.

Pellicano, known as "the sleuth to the stars," has worked for such celebrities as Elizabeth Taylor, Kevin Costner, Michael Jackson, and attorneys Bert Fields and Ed Masry of *Erin Brockovich* fame, to name a few. Also, Pellicano has good friends in the Mafia.

The FBI raided Pellicano's office and in the search discovered military-grade C4 explosives, enough to blow up an airliner. The FBI seized Pellicano's computer hard-drives, which yielded over 2 billion pages of information.

Included in the haul were numerous illegal wiretapped conversations with Hollywood figures, high-priced lawyers and media organizations going back two decades.

Having opened Pandora's Box, the FBI and the U.S. Attorney's offices in Los Angeles and New York have now descended on Hollywood's newest organized crime syndicate—crooked lawyers, dirty cops and the wealthy elite who hire them to threaten, defame and destroy lives.

Proctor is currently serving 10 years in federal prison. Pellicano is also in federal lock-up, serving 33 months for illegal explosives. However, Hollywood powerbrokers are nervously awaiting the next act—federal indictments of illegal wiretapping and witness tampering that will no doubt involve well-known names.

Busch, who has repeatedly rebuffed numerous interview requests from the national media, reveals for the first time to author and investigative journalist Dan E. Moldea how she handled her deadly situation during a time when the media, law enforcement, and organized crime figures both helped and complicated her predicament.

And, in managing this complicated role as journalist and victim, this courageous woman unflinchingly raised the curtain on Hollywood's criminal elite.

On Saturday, February 7, I flew to Los Angeles to appear in a documentary about the murder of Senator Robert Kennedy, the subject of my fifth book in 1995. Of course, while in town, I wanted to spend as much time working with Anita as possible.

That first night in L.A., I took Anita, her attorney-sister and attorney-brother-in-law, as well as Dave and Kelly, to dinner at Todai, a sushi-buffet restaurant, just outside the Beverly Center. I stayed with Dave and Kelly on Saturday and Sunday night. After that, I checked into a room at the Beverly Garland Hotel on Vineland Avenue in North Hollywood, which was offered by the producers of the documentary.

On Sunday, Anita and I drove to a suburban town to have lunch with her parents who were very kind to me and extremely supportive of their daughter's book project. During the late afternoon, we met with a mutual friend who had a unique perspective on the local underworld at Du-Par's on Ventura Boulevard in Studio City. Later that night, Anita and I had dinner with former LAPD Detective Tom Lange and his wife, Linda, at The Smoke House Restaurant in Burbank.

On Monday, February 9, George Rush ran yet another item, saying: "CAA is selling the rights to Howard Blum and John Connolly's *Vanity Fair* story" about Pellicano. Rush continued, "Studio interest is said to be strong."[134]

Anita and I believed that Connolly did this for our benefit, trying to rub our faces in his newfound glory and financial gain in the wake of us forcing this double-crosser off our team.

That afternoon, Anita and I had lunch in Pasadena with Marvin Rudnick, who could not have felt worse about withdrawing as Anita's attorney.

On Tuesday, Anita and I had dinner at Orso on West Third Street with Mickey Freiberg, one of our two new agents. I liked Mickey immediately. He appeared very knowledgeable about the Pellicano scandal. And more than anything else, he seemed to adore Anita. To me, that was the real litmus test.

Was anything else going on between Anita and me besides work? To my knowledge, nothing else was happening, except that by seeing Anita in her element with her family and friends, I had developed a healthier respect for her as a person and had become even more protective of her in the midst of this ongoing ordeal.

And that's the place where Dave Robb wanted me to be. Like him, he wanted me to be one of the pillars in her life—solid and trusted, like a big brother.

After passing through the Connolly gauntlet, I now viewed my friendship with Anita as being even stronger having survived some rough patches. Through the writings she sent me, as well as the content of our verbal communications, I knew that she genuinely trusted me. And that trust was well placed.

I returned to Washington, D.C. on February 12. When I arrived home, I opened a Valentine's Day card that she had sent me, which she signed, "Love, Anita."

Once again, this was friendship, nothing else. And I was happy that the rough waters were finally settling down.

Now knowing how sensitive Anita was to any photographs taken of her, I sent her a note after emailing the photographs that I had taken of her and her parents, saying: "Just for the record, I consider any and every picture I take of you to be your property. Feel free to use or destroy them at will—since you own 'em." (My emphasis)

Also on February 12, some tapes of conversations with Pellicano, recorded by the late tabloid reporter Jim Mitteager, the bureau chief of the *Globe* in Los Angeles, were made public by television station KCBS in L.A. During one conversation with Mitteager, Pellicano addressed how a "woman reporter" was at odds with one of his clients, foreshadowing what later happened to Anita Busch.

Pellicano: Where is she now?

Mitteager: She's in L.A.

Pellicano: She still work for the *Enquirer*?

Mitteager: She's a stringer. I mean she's a nobody.
Pellicano: She was a go-fer.

Mitteager: Yeah, she's a go-fer, an empty suit.

Pellicano: I could probably terrorize her, can't I?

Mitteager: You could probably terrorize her, yeah (laughing). You probably could.[135]

———

In Brooklyn on February 17, Jules Nasso, after pleading guilty in August 2003 for his role in an alleged shakedown scheme against his former partner, Steven Seagal, received a one-year-and-one-day prison sentence.

The Associated Press reported: "Nasso . . . also will pay a $75,000 fine and receive mental-health counseling after his release from prison. . . . The plea agreement between Nasso and Assistant U.S. Attorney Andrew Genser took into account what prosecutors called Nasso's law-abiding past and a history of acute depression and anxiety that affected his mental stability."[136]

That same day, the judge, Frederic Block, doubled the sentence for Nasso's younger brother, Vincent, slapping him with a two-year prison sentence. He had pleaded guilty to two felonies—for his role in the alleged Seagal shakedown scheme and for supposedly forcing Sonny Ciccone and the longshoremen's union to use the Nasso family's pharmaceutical company.

The *Staten Island Advance* added:

> After the sentencing hearing, there was some evidence of bad blood between the Nasso brothers, as the two men almost came to blows in the hallway outside the courtroom.
> When Julius addressed Vincent's wife, the young brother lunged at Julius—and had to be restrained—as he shouted, "You don't talk about my wife. You pulled a fast one, big boy. You coughed me up."[137]

Anita still believed that Jules Nasso, in concert with Michael Ovitz, might have engineered the threat against her via Pellicano. And I simply accepted whatever Anita told me. After all, no one knew as much about what had happened to Anita as Anita Busch.

What I did know was that, inasmuch as Ovitz was now at the hub of Anita's conspiracy theory, this was now a Hollywood thing—not a Mafia thing, which was why I had gotten involved in this project in the first place. Ideally, I had wanted to investigate the Mafia's influence in Hollywood just as I had in my previous book, *Dark Victory*, not Michael Ovitz's alleged personal vendetta against Anita Busch.

13. *"Tell us what you want, and we'll deliver."*

Michael Ovitz was in the midst of his own problems. In Delaware, a lawsuit was filed by Disney stockholders, protesting the extraordinary payout Ovitz had received from the Disney board after company chairman Michael Eisner fired him as Disney's president. In return for his fourteen months on the job, which ended in December 1996, Ovitz received a whopping $140-million severance package. And, now, the stockholders, led by Walt Disney's nephew, Roy Disney, wanted that money back.

On February 25, 2004, the presiding judge in the case released a letter, written by Eisner to Ovitz, which stated:

> [M]y biggest problem was that you played the angles too much, exaggerated the truth too far, manipulated me and others too much. I told you 98% of the problem was that I did not know when you were telling the truth, about the big things, about small things. And while you telling me that those dishonest days were over, you were deceiving me on a specific matter. . . .
>
> I want it to end as soon as possible. I want you to direct your energies to how to exit, not how to cure. We are beyond the curing stage. We are now in salvation. I would like to remain friends, to end this so it looks like you decided it, and to be positive and supportive.[138]

Another document made public during the discovery process revealed that Eisner had considered letting Ovitz go shortly after he accepted the job. However, Eisner decided against releasing

Ovitz, adding, "More specifically, Mr. Eisner believed that, if fired, Mr. Ovitz would commit suicide."[139]

On another front, attorney Ed Masry of *Erin Brockovich* fame had retained Pellicano years earlier to help with his defense against his former paralegal, Kissandra Cohen, who had lost a sexual-harassment case against him but won damages for defamation. And now, Cohen had filed another suit against him, charging that Masry had hired Pellicano to wiretap her telephone.

On or about February 27, my 54th birthday, I received a "one-of-a-kind-brother" card from Anita, in which she wrote:

> *I'm glad I know you—I feel honored to know you.*
>
> *Love,*
> *Anita.*

On March 3, my girlfriend, Mimi, and I broke up. Since we had become a couple in January 1988, we had separated only once before—from the spring of 1993 to the fall of 1995. Prior to 1993, Mimi found it difficult to withstand the highs and lows of my career. However, since 1998 and the publication of my last book, she had watched me trying without success to return to the game, which essentially meant publishing a new book. For reasons I could not explain, my earlier proposed true-crime book projects had not been selling in New York.

When Anita refused to sign our collaboration agreement before John Connolly came on board, Mimi, like Dave Robb, appealed to me for patience. However, Mimi now viewed the circumstances of the falling out with Connolly and the publication of his article in *Vanity Fair* as the death knell for our book project. She did not believe for a second that John wasn't going to try to write a book of his own, even though he had said, in writing, that he would not. In the wake of his article, she believed that John had all the momentum. And she now feared that my project with Anita could wind up becoming nothing more than a monumental waste of time.

Considering how much I had invested in the Anita project, I did not take Mimi's prediction very well. And that caused problems between us across the board.

When Mimi and I first started going out, I was a month shy of my 38th birthday. I had most of my hair. I had my weight under tight control, and I was in fairly good shape. In the world of romance, I was still in a sellers' market.

Now, a week after my 54th birthday, those days were far behind me. And I knew it.

———

For several weeks, I had difficulty reaching our New York agent, Frank Weimann. My emails bounced back to me, and he wasn't returning my calls. Anita and I had no idea if and how William Morrow had responded to our proposal.

Consequently, Mickey Freiberg, our Los Angeles agent, pushed the process forward, making contact with Frank. He had to be in New York on other business at the end of the month, so he arranged for us to pitch our book while he was there.

Everyone agreed to rendezvous with Weimann in New York from Tuesday, March 23, to Friday, March 26. "Between now and then," according to Mickey, Frank would arrange meetings for us with interested publishers—unless William Morrow came in with a preemptive bid.

Anita and I both were ready to receive our monetary payoff for our efforts. Unintentionally, we had taken a vow of poverty to complete this project.

She and I agreed to get a couple of rooms at The Roosevelt Hotel at Madison Avenue and East 45th Street in midtown Manhattan. Also, I offered to treat her to a Broadway play on Wednesday night, allowing her to choose whatever she wanted to see. She selected *The Boy from Oz* at the Imperial Theater on West 45th Street.

On March 10, Weimann sent Anita and me an email, notifying us that David Highfill, a senior editor at G. P. Putnam's Sons, a subsidiary of Penguin, wanted to meet with us, as did Denise Oswald of Faber and Faber, a subsidiary of Farrar, Straus and Giroux.

When Anita learned that a publishing house under the Penguin umbrella was in the mix, she notified Frank that a friend of hers was the former chairman of Penguin. She told Frank to tell her when he wanted her to make the call.

Although the separation agreement with John Connolly had already been executed, Anita suddenly wanted him to return all of the materials we had given to him, including the pages of the Anita-approved manuscript, the three catalogues of documents, and whatever drafts of the proposal he still had in his possession. I warned Anita that this would probably be futile—since he could just photocopy anything he wanted. After all, a confidentiality agreement was not part of the resignation letter that Connolly had signed.

She remained adamant about getting everything back, and she personally wanted to handle the exchange of documents with Connolly.

I sensed that Anita was less interested in getting back the files and more interested in confronting Connolly, face-to-face. Once again, I asked her to appear neutral.

Assuming that Connolly would refuse to deal with me, I asked Frank Weimann to be our intermediary once again. It was a terrible thing to do to Frank especially after Connolly requested that we return *his* documents, but Frank agreed to broker the deal between Connolly and us.

In the end, Connolly simply insisted that he had already returned any of our documents that he had not already destroyed. He claimed that he had nothing left.

I didn't know what he had or had not destroyed, but I did know that he never gave anything back to me.

Because of Connolly's poor track record with honesty, at least with Anita and me, no one on our team doubted what I said, especially after I gave Connolly, via Frank, a detailed list of what materials we had of his. Soon after, we returned everything via Federal Express.

Of course, Connolly reached out to Anita and, according to her, blamed everything on me, adding, "I'd just like to forget I ever met him."

In that same message, he pleaded with her, saying, "I have never nor would I ever do anything on either a personal or professional level to cause you unhappiness."

After Connolly's monumental betrayal during the *Vanity Fair* debacle, Anita could barely contain her feelings about him. But, wisely, she remained neutral. No doubt, Connolly was ready to cut my throat, but he would not try to sabotage our project as long as Anita did not treat him with disrespect.

On the morning of March 18, I flew to Long Beach, California, for a writers' conference at which I agreed to lead a seminar on investigative journalism. Anita picked me up at the airport. We had breakfast together at Café Latte on West Olympic in Los Angeles and discussed our upcoming strategy in New York, as well as the new draft chapters I had brought with me. That night, we had dinner with Anita's sister and brother-in-law, along with Dave and Kelly at Jerry's Deli in West Hollywood. As usual, I stayed at Dave's apartment.

The following day, I asked Dave to run the seminar with me. Dave agreed and drove us to the conference at the Marriott in Manhattan Beach where I was booked to stay on Friday and Saturday night.

That evening, I went out to dinner at a nearby Daily Grill with several reporter-friends who were at the conference and stayed out late with them, swapping war stories.

On Saturday afternoon, Anita came to the hotel to work on our book. We had lunch and then returned to my room where we went through the latest rough draft of the manuscript, page-by-page. In the midst of this editing session, I excused myself to attend the banquet for the writers' conference, ordering room service for Anita who did not want to go to the dinner.

When I returned, we continued working until well after midnight and then went out for an early breakfast at a nearby Denny's. She dropped me back at the hotel and returned to her home in L.A.

The next day, Anita arranged for Paul Suzuki, her brother-in-law, to pick me up at the hotel and take me to his home for lunch with her, as well as with his wife and children. After a few hours of pleasant conversation, Paul drove me back to the airport in Long Beach. He treated me to dinner at the Todai's sushi franchise near the airport before I returned to Washington.

Two days later, on Tuesday, March 23, I took an early train from Union Station to New York, checking in to The Roosevelt during the early afternoon and then trying to connect with Frank Weimann whom I could not reach. However, I did speak with Frank's assistant who told me that our first meeting on Wednesday had been cancelled.

Anita and Mickey Freiberg had flown in together from the West Coast. Mickey was staying with friends. Anita came to The Roosevelt where I broke the bad news to her: We had no meetings scheduled for the next day.

Then, according to Frank's assistant, Mauro DiPreta of William Morrow, Mark Resnick of St. Martin's, Kristen Kaiser of Random House, and David Highfill of Putnam had all either passed at the last minute or cancelled our scheduled meetings on Wednesday, leaving us with only one appointment on Thursday and another on Friday.

Very upset, Anita and I had dinner at Café Centro in the MetLife Building near Grand Central Station, and then we went uptown for drinks at the Warwick Hotel, at the corner of West 54th Street and the Avenue of the Americas. We were safely in our separate rooms by midnight, alone with our thoughts.

On Wednesday, with all of our meetings cancelled, Anita and I just went sightseeing. We took the subway at Grand Central to the construction site that was once the World Trade Center—and, since September 11, 2001, had become hallowed ground. Also, we walked to Battery Park and saw the Statue of Liberty in the distance. After lunch and stops at a couple of department stores Anita wanted to see, we returned to the hotel.

Because I felt so badly about this disastrous situation, which I knew that Anita could not afford, I wrote her a check for $1,000, covering both her flight and her three-night stay at The Roosevelt. Also, I picked up all of our expenses.

During the early evening, we walked to the Imperial Theater. While we were crossing traffic-cluttered Fifth Avenue, I took Anita's arm, something I would do for my grandmother.

Anita recoiled, saying that she didn't like a man to take her arm unless she was "involved with him."

I was completely stunned by this reaction, laughing, "Are you kidding me?"

The stern look on her face confirmed that she was quite serious.

After an early dinner at The Celebrity Deli near the theater, we went to see *The Boy from Oz*, a musical about singer-songwriter Peter Allen, which featured the major film star Hugh Jackman. I certainly enjoyed the show, and she seemed to, as well.

After the theater, we returned to the hotel. Anita told me that she had a late date with the new chairman and CEO of Sony Pictures Entertainment, Michael Lynton, an old friend and business associate.

Alone, I went back into the Midtown evening for a late dinner at a small sushi bar near the hotel. When I returned to my room, I started preparing notes for our scheduled meeting the following day.

On Thursday morning, Frank called me. This was the first time I had spoken to him since I arrived in New York. He told me that the only meeting scheduled for that day—with Bruce Nichols of Free Press—had been cancelled, too. Frank added, though, that our meeting for Friday with Faber and Faber had been confirmed.

I tried to get an explanation from Frank as to what was going on, but he was short on time and said he was not feeling well. Thus, I did not get an answer.

"This is a goddamn nightmare," I thought to myself.

Anita appeared as devastated by this news as I was. We went our separate ways that day, agreeing to meet for dinner with my old friend, author Laurence Leamer, who was in town to promote his big new book about Arnold Schwarzenegger, *Fantastic*.

At dinner with Larry that night, Anita and I vented our frustrations. He was a trusted friend of mine who knew the publishing industry well. I took the blame for everything, lamenting that, if I was still in the game, the publishers would be clamoring to meet with me and to discuss my next work.

To my great surprise, Anita appeared to be very supportive of me, refusing to allow me to accept responsibility for this fiasco.

As much as I liked Larry, I had to control my temper because he kept suggesting, over and over again, that Anita write the book in the first person, which would cast me in either an "as told to" or "with" credit line.

Anita continued to side with me, saying that she didn't want a byline, but Larry refused to relent.

Clearly agitated with one of my closest friends, I told him that, if a publisher came to us with a serious offer, along with the proviso that Anita must write the book in first person, then we would consider making an adjustment. I insisted, "Why should I give up the solo byline before anyone has offered us anything—or even made that suggestion?"

When Anita and I returned to The Roosevelt, Anita invited me to her room. We had a good time, watching a movie on television and playing cards on the bed. At about 11:00, I told her that I was going to back to my room. She said that she was having fun and asked me to stay a little longer.

"You know," I replied, "I don't have to leave at all."

Anita looked at me, shaking her head playfully, saying, "That wouldn't be a very good idea."

Recognizing that what I had just said was more of a reflexive reaction to a trusted friend rather than an actual proposition, I laughed, "You've got that right, Lady!"

She laughed, too.

We played cards for another hour, and I left at a little after midnight with no further drama or awkward moments.

On Friday morning, I checked out of my room and arranged to have my luggage held by the hotel's concierge.

When I sat down with Anita in the hotel's dining room for breakfast, she snapped, "I wish you'd stop hitting on me."

Stunned by this latest reaction, I laughed, "I didn't say a word."

When she did not reply, I got serious, "Hey, what's wrong? What's up?"

"Sorry," she added. "I'm in a bad mood this morning."

"Have I said or done anything to make you feel uncomfortable? I've certainly never laid a hand on you, except when I took your arm when we crossed the street the other day."

Anita simply replied, "Forget about it. Everything's okay."

Shortly thereafter, Mickey Freiberg joined us in the dining room. Mickey said that Frank would not accompany us to our meeting.

Trying to process that news, my mind was still reeling over this "hitting on me" thing that Anita had just dropped which I immediately viewed as nothing more than a cheap shot. In fact, I even believed that she had set me up for this the night before.

By this time, I knew how Anita operated. If she was upset with a man and needed an edge, she often accused him of "hitting" on her. Two others about whom she had made this charge were Terry Semel, the CEO of Yahoo!, and John Montorio, a top editor at the *Los Angeles Times*. She also accused one of her sources—whom she code named "Lambchop"—of "hitting" on her, too.

I had never been anything but a gentleman, as well as a loyal friend to her. Indeed, just a few weeks earlier, she had described me "a godsend." And her recent cards and letters were laudatory towards me and signed, "Love, Anita."

After breakfast, the three of us took a cab to Union Square for our one meeting with our one prospective publisher. We arrived early, so we walked around an open-air bazaar. As Anita purchased presents for her family and friends in Los Angeles, she bought me one, too—a pre-September 11th wide-angle photograph of the Manhattan skyline with the Statue of Liberty and Battery Park in the foreground, along with the World Trade Center.

Still shaken, I viewed this gift as an apology for her cutting allegation against me at breakfast.

At 11:00 A.M., Anita, Mickey, and I met with Denise Oswald at Faber and Faber. Denise asked good questions and seemed to connect with Anita. The meeting went very well. When Denise asked why I was writing the book in the third person and not Anita in the first person, I replied, "We're flexible about that. Tell us what you want, and we'll deliver."

I knew that Larry Leamer would have approved of that response.

Afterward, I took the three of us to lunch at the Blue Water Grille, which was also in Union Square. We were upbeat, believing that we might have a deal.

When we left the restaurant, Mickey peeled off as Anita and I grabbed a cab uptown to head back to The Roosevelt. I carried Anita's luggage to the front of the hotel and hailed a cab for her. She thanked me again for the $1,000 check, and we kissed on the cheek. Then, a moment later, she was gone.

I would not see her again—until I saw her in court nine-and-a-half years later.

I returned to Washington later that day. The entire four-day-three night trip to New York, including the thousand dollars I gave to Anita, had cost me over $2,500—all for one meeting with one publisher. But, if that publisher made a legitimate bid, it would have been worthwhile.

On Saturday, I called Anita to make sure that she had arrived home safely. While we were on the telephone, I repeated that I had always tried to be a gentleman with her, even when we were kidding around as friends, and apologized if I had ever said or done anything to offend her. She repeated that there was no problem between us and told me to forget about it.

14. *"It is absolute heresy to write an entire book on spec"*

On Saturday, March 27, 2004, I sent Frank Weimann an email, saying: "Everything appeared to go well with Denise Oswald, who struck us as a first-rate person and editor. Obviously, we are hoping that she makes an offer. However, if she lowballs us or simply doesn't bid, let's put everything on hold and reevaluate our situation."

Anita, Mickey, and I had already agreed on that.

I still hadn't spoken to Frank since our brief phone conversation the previous Wednesday morning. And Anita did not speak with him at all while we were in New York.

After Mickey asked me the following Tuesday if I had heard anything about Denise Oswald, I called Frank. When I didn't reach him, I left a message.

The next Friday, still hearing nothing from Frank, I sent Anita and Mickey an email, saying:

> Tomorrow will be the one-week anniversary of our meeting with
> Denise Oswald in New York. So far, she has not made an offer. . . . .

> [W]e need to make some decisions about our next move—who
> should make it and when.
>
> Also, we need to know exactly who has received our proposal,
> who has passed and why (along with any rejection letters), and who
> rejected a meeting with us while we were in New York. In other
> words, we need a status report on the state of our ship—which, to
> date, we have not received from Frank.

In early April, while we were still waiting for Denise Oswald's
decision, Anita notified me that she had begun writing a novel and
sent me a few chapters, saying in an email: "I'm writing down
stories I've heard over the years and just filling in the blanks . . .
total creative license. (I have to do something with my mind or I'll
go crazy)."

As the author of several nonfiction books, I had little interest
in the world of fiction, but what she sent me read very well. I
encouraged her to continue writing her novel, noting that I had
plenty of work to do on our nonfiction project, adding: "As you
might or might not know, it is absolute heresy to write an entire book
on spec. But, in this case, I view it as money in the bank."

Meantime, Marvin Rudnick sent me an email on April 3, asking:
"Is Anita doing ok? I hope I was of some help. Please let me know."

I responded, saying:

> From my perspective, Anita has experienced a catharsis over
> the past few weeks. And she has done it all on her own. She
> has been eating well, sleeping more with fewer nightmares, and
> exercising. She appears to have more confidence and simply
> refuses to accept any grief without a fight. In short, she seems
> determined to get beyond her very legitimate fears and to regain
> control of her life. . . .
>
> Anita loves and respects you. You guys will always be good
> friends.

On April 17, prompted by me, Anita began communicating with
Marvin again—consulting him, along with her new attorneys, about
her intention to leave the *Los Angeles Times*.

Once again, she asked for my opinion about that subject, too.
From the outset, I had opposed her decision to leave the newspaper,
because she would wind up alone as an independent writer, like me.
However, this time, she had cause, a very legitimate but unresolved

complaint with the newspaper about which the top brass had been unresponsive. Consequently, for the first time, I supported her decision to leave, knowing that her soon-to-be-filed lawsuit against Pellicano would keep her in the spotlight—and that the spotlight would keep her safe.

On Thursday, April 22, Anita gave John Carroll, the executive editor of the *Los Angeles Times*, who had been very supportive of Anita throughout her tenure, her thirty-day notice.

Shortly after she submitted her resignation, Anita and I learned from Mickey, who was in touch with Frank, that Denise Oswald had passed on our book project.

As much as I liked and appreciated Frank, I did not feel that he had the necessary enthusiasm for this project, especially after what had happened in New York. Frank, who was still upset that Anita and I had gone to Mickey before him, put up no fight and, with his usual class, walked away from our project. However, to my disappointment, Mickey, whom I felt had failed to motivate Frank to be more enthusiastic and assertive, remained.

I now wanted him gone, too.

After agreeing, at first, to allow me to cut Mickey loose, Anita, who still considered him a friend, changed her mind, saying: "I slept on this and I don't want to fire Mickey. I don't see that he's done anything to warrant it."

So we argued about Mickey.

Anita became so upset over this situation that she called Dave Robb to complain about me, throwing yet a new issue into the fray.

Of course, Dave called and ordered me to back down to her immediately. Disputing Anita's sudden claim that I was unhappy playing the second-fiddle role on this project, I reminded Dave that I happily played that same role when I had written Tom Lange and Phil Vannatter's book about the O.J. Simpson case. Even though Dave remembered that project, as well as how enthusiastically I played my backseat role, he still instructed me to give in to Anita.

Reluctantly, out of respect for Dave, I caved in to Anita and agreed to keep Freiberg as our agent.

On May 17, Anita forwarded to me an email response she had sent to John Connolly three days earlier, in which she referred him, along with "all media calls," to her attorney. Also, she sent John's response, in which he wrote: "I had no intention of asking you anything about what happened to you or anything whatsoever about the Pellicano case. I wish you well and am quite saddened that you would think that I had an ulterior motive."

On May 22, her final day at the *Los Angeles Times*, Anita sent a package to me via regular mail, saying in the cover letter, "Thought you might want to see this."

Attached was an article about Connolly, "Other People's Money," written by reporter Christopher Byron and published in *New York* magazine in 1990. I had never seen the article, and I could not have been more shocked when I read it.

Byron cited a series of alleged ethical lapses Connolly had engaged while working as a Wall Street broker—a job he had landed *after* he left the NYPD and *before* he became an investigative reporter. Summing up his story, Byron wrote that a legal dispute with one of Connolly's clients served as the impetus for his problems. Byron stated:

> Thus began the unraveling of a bizarre tale of Wall Street intrigue: the three-year saga of a Wall Street stockbroker who, acting under a government grant of immunity from prosecution, used his yuppie clients to spy on organized crime's alleged involvement in the stock market. At the same time, the stockbroker was working part-time as a financial journalist, writing exposés of the very people he was secretly informing on for the government. Some of the spying led to his biggest story of all: a *Forbes* magazine cover article deflating Donald Trump's wealth.[140]

All I could think was: How could I have been a good friend to John for so many years without knowing any of this?

On May 27, I returned to Washington after a speaking engagement in Spokane, Washington. That same day, Dave Robb and his fiancé, Kelly, arrived, too, just as D.C. came under siege by swarms of harmless but large and ugly deafeningly noisy cicadas, an event that occurred every seventeen years.

While in Washington, Dave and Kelly stayed with me.

On their first night in town, I took them to a party at the Marco Polo restaurant in Rosslyn, Virginia, for Ishaq Shahryar, the former ambassador from Afghanistan to the United States, who was a close friend of Janet Donovan, one of my best friends in Washington. Shortly after being introduced by Janet, Dave and Ambassador Shahryar, who also lived in Los Angeles, began discussing a book they might want to co-author.

15. *"This should not be shopped until charges come down"*

On Friday, May 28, 2004, Anita's attorneys filed a civil lawsuit against Anthony Pellicano, Alexander Proctor, LAPD Detective Mark Arneson and the City of Los Angeles, and SBC Telecommunications (formerly Pacific Bell), along with "Client Doe, Law Firm Doe, and Does 1 through 100."

The complaint, written by Mathew Geragos and Brian Kabateck who did not specify a dollar amount for damages, stated:

> 17. The claims against known Defendants and the presently unknown Defendants described herein arise out of the Defendants Pellicano, Proctor, Arneson and Does 1 through 100, intentionally and maliciously engaged in a scheme and course of conduct of threats, intimidation, harassment and invasion of privacy for the purpose of deterring, hindering, preventing and retaliating against Plaintiff for investigating and writing articles about the entertainment business.
>
> 18. The ongoing pattern and course of conduct engaged in by Defendants and each of them, at the instigation of CLIENT DOE, LAW FIRM DOE and Does 1 through 31, includes the following:
>
> > (a) Wiretapping of Plaintiff's telephone lines. The date of commencement of said illegal wiretapping is not yet known; however, Plaintiff only became aware of illegal wiretapping within the past two years;
> >
> > (b) On or about June 20, 2002, at Plaintiff's residence in Los Angeles, California, Plaintiff was threatened, harassed and intimidated when she discovered her car windshield had

been smashed. A note taped next to the hold in the windshield contained the [word] "Stop;" on the cracked window was an upside down tray with a dead fish and a red rose hidden underneath;

(c) On or about June 21, 2002, Plaintiff began receiving urgent telephone messages with a male voice on the other end, who asserted that there was a plan to blow up Plaintiff's car;

(d) In July 2002, two unknown males, apparently tracking Plaintiff's whereabouts, arrived at Plaintiff's parents' home, where Plaintiff had been staying, and threatened Plaintiff by their physical appearance;

(e) In August 2002, Plaintiff discovered that her computer had been hacked into and two months later her hard drive was destroyed by this tampering;

(f) On or about August 16, 2002, two males, driving a Mercedes with tinted windows and no license plate, drove at an excessive rate of speed in an attempt to run over Plaintiff who barely escaped. The vehicle then pulled up right next to Plaintiff and one occupant then leaned out of the window and made menacing gestures in an apparent effort to assault and terrorize Plaintiff;

(g) In or about March 2003, Plaintiff's car was broken into and a small hole was drilled near the driver's visor.

19. The above conduct frightened, terrified and devastated Plaintiff. Having her telephones wiretapped, her computer hacked into and her life threatened, Plaintiff was severely impacted in her ability to fully perform as a journalist.

20. Plaintiff also suffered monetary losses due to the damage to her property, to wit, her vehicle and computers.[141]

In a draft letter to her attorneys that Anita asked me to edit, she wrote:

I finally find out the date that LAPD detective Mark Arneson ran my name illegally in the police database. It is May 16th, 2002. I am stunned. . . . I hadn't joined the L.A. Times until June 3. The Gambino sweep in New York [in the midst of which Jules Nasso was arrested] happened on June 4. I wasn't even assigned the longer story on Nasso and Seagal until later in the week. There is only one person who would have been interested in me at that time: Michael Ovitz.

Writing of Anita's litigation, the *Los Angeles Times* reported:

> "She's trying to get on with her life in terms of a new career," her attorney, Matthew Geragos, said. He declined to identify that career.[142]

Management representative Brad Grey's nemesis, Bo Zenga, filed a similar suit against Pellicano on June 2—the third such case, following those by Anita and Kissandra Cohen, the paralegal who had sued attorney Ed Masry.[143]

———

On June 5, I did a seminar on investigative reporting at the Spring Writers Conference, sponsored annually by Washington Independent Writers, the largest local organization of independent writers in the United States. While at the conference, I ran into Deborah Grosvenor, a respected local attorney who was also a literary agent. In her previous career as the director of book acquisitions and subsidiary rights for Naval Institute Press, she had purchased Tom Clancy's first book, *The Hunt for Red October*. Of course, that work had made Clancy a superstar.

I had also seen Deborah at a book party for a friend the previous month and mentioned my project with Anita. During our conversation, Deborah had said that she had no relationship with either Robert Gottlieb, the agent who represented Clancy, or Michael Ovitz, the agent who lured Clancy away from Gottlieb.

That same afternoon, hoping that we would finally have our woman agent, I arranged a conversation between Anita and Deborah, and they immediately appeared to hit it off. Ironically, Deborah was the agent for Susan McDougal who was also represented by the attorneys at Anita's law firm, Geragos & Geragos.

When we got down to discussing money, Deborah insisted that she would not split a commission. Understandably, she wanted her entire fifteen percent.

On Monday afternoon, Deborah and I in Washington had a conference call with Anita and Mickey Freiberg in Los Angeles.

When we told Mickey that Deborah did not want to split the commission, Mickey, who now had over six months invested in this project, predictably balked.

But Mickey had no real concern. Anita and I had already agreed to give Deborah the fifteen percent she wanted, as well as the 7.5-percent commission that Mickey expected. In other words, so that Anita could keep Mickey on board, I agreed to pay 22.5 percent in agents' commissions, which, in my experience, was completely ridiculous, especially since I still wanted Mickey gone.

At this point, I had over a year invested in Anita's book project, and I was determined to see it to the finish line, even if I had to keep Mickey on board.

After Deborah answered all of our questions and exited the conference call, Anita, Mickey, and I continued talking. Mickey opposed bringing on Deborah, saying that he had another agent in New York who would split the usual fifteen-percent commission.

The agent's name was Jay Acton whom I had met during a party at the home of another close friend, author Mark Olshaker. Jay represented Mark, along with the co-author of their best-selling nonfiction books, former FBI profiler John Douglas.

Knowing that Jay, a hugely successful agent, specialized on true-crime books and had good contacts in the law-enforcement community, Anita and I agreed to go along with Mickey's choice with the general understanding that we would return to Deborah if things did not work out.

Simultaneously, all of us agreed that we should not re-pitch our proposal until the U.S. Attorney's Office in Los Angeles released the Pellicano wiretapping indictments that the federal grand jury had already handed up and were reportedly under seal. From everything we were hearing, those indictments could come any day.

After we showed Jay, for whom I had enormous respect, our proposal, he sent me an email, saying: "You've done another great job on an incredibly fascinating story—congratulations! I do agree with Mickey that this should not be shopped until charges come down. Let's keep in touch on this one. You have my admiration for a job well done."

On June 18, I sent Anita the next draft of the first two parts of the manuscript via overnight mail. For the next five days, Anita faxed me specific pages which contained her handwritten additions and corrections.

The next day, I received an email from John Connolly, the first time I had heard from him since mid-January. Appearing to believe that my book project with Anita had collapsed, Connolly wrote:

> I recently spoke with Anita and was saddened to learn that she/ she and you are no longer writing the Pellicano [book]. Anita has told me [that] she is moving on with her life and in my brief conversations with her, she sounds very much like the "old" Anita Busch we all know and respect. Despite the rumor mill, I am not now, nor have I even [contemplated] writing a book on Pellicano. Nor do I have any film or production deal. You and I have been friends for too long to let anything come between us. I'm still not sure what sparked all the [unpleasantness] that transpired, but neither one of us profited from it.
>
> Someone has come to me with [devastating] information about Pellicano, a studio head, and Ovitz. I have also been sent a script for a pilot written by Pellicano which was commissioned by Brad Grey. I am considering doing a newspaper story on what I have learned, but if you are writing a book or for that matter anything on this subject, I'll not write this piece.
>
> The last thing I want is for you and I to be driven further apart. We have too much common ground for that. I would hope that someday, in the not too distant future, we can have a cup of coffee and put this behind us. Please let me know your thoughts.

Assuming that he was just fishing with his "saddened-to-learn" comment about Anita and me ending our partnership on the Pellicano project, I replied to Connolly:

> I'm glad to hear from you, but I really don't want to get into what I agree and disagree with about your letter. In fact, I just don't know what to say. As you know, our friend, Anita, is in the midst of litigation and isn't in a position to say very much. And, as you probably realize, your story in *Vanity Fair*—which I thought you profited from—caused enormous problems.
>
> Of course, I would like to patch things up with you at some point in the future. However, since you asked, continuing to write about this matter wouldn't be a step in the right direction.
>
> I hope you're well and kicking ass.

Connolly only responded with, "I'm well. Thanks for asking.
Hope you are also doing well."

———

On July 6, Anita told me that her attorney had received a
message from Jules Nasso's legal team, which was seeking whatever
cooperation they could get in what appeared to be a desperate effort
to keep their client out of jail. Nasso was scheduled to enter a
federal prison the following month to serve his one-year-and-one-
day sentence.

Anita still believed and so I believed, too, that Nasso, whom
Anita code had named "The Babysitter," could be indicted as a co-
conspirator in the threat against her.

Anita asked for my opinion on how she should deal with her
attorney with whom she was furious for opening the door to Nasso's
lawyers. I put my response in writing, saying:

> Your attorney had the best of intentions—especially after
> hearing that a key figure in this drama wanted to provide
> information helpful to your case. No doubt, he is on a constant
> search for any and all advantages he can accumulate in this legal
> battle, and he viewed this as nothing less than a potentially huge
> break. His worst sin is that he spoke to the Babysitter's attorney
> before speaking with you. . . .
>
> In short, I see no downside to what has happened—and nothing
> but great promise for what can result. . . . My advice is to see what
> [Nasso and his attorneys] have, evaluate it after receipt, and then
> decide what you and your team want to do next. . . .
>
> I think you might've just received a lucky break. Once again,
> there is no downside to playing out your hand.

The following week, Robert J. Hantman, Nasso's lead attorney,
submitted a brief to the trial judge in the case, claiming that his client
had provided "substantial assistance" to the U.S. Attorney's Office in
Los Angeles during its investigation of Pellicano. Hantman wrote:

> Mr. Nasso's information materially assisted in the preparation of
> the government's application for a search warrant . . . for the offices
> of Anthony Pellicano. . . .

> Mr. Nasso's involvement began when he started hearing rumors that Steven Seagal was "going to get him arrested," in May 2002 following Mr. Nasso's filing of a lawsuit still pending against Mr. Seagal. Mr. Nasso asked former law enforcement agent William McMullan to look into the matter, because Mr. Nasso was aware of Mr. Seagal's "star power" and friendship with the F.B.I. in Los Angeles.[144]

Also, I could not help but notice a statement that Hantman quoted from federal prosecutor Dan Saunders's January 15 brief to the court regarding Pellicano's sentencing:

> The information about Anita Busch **obtained by defendant's sources on May 16, 2002**, was contained in a file found on defendant's office computer pursuant to a search warrant. That file, **which was created on June 3, 2002** (approximately two weeks before the threat), contained Busch's personal information, including her descriptive data, residence address, and vehicle information relating to the vehicle on which Proctor left the dead fish, rose, and note.[145] (My emphasis)

Clearly, Nasso's legal team had not grasped the significance of the dates referred to by Saunders. These events were *prior* to Nasso's indictment—and, thus, *before* Anita received the assignment to report on Nasso and Seagal on June 4, 2002. With regard to the threat against Anita, that should have been viewed by all as exculpatory for both Nasso and Seagal.

Meantime, despite the impassioned claims of Nasso's legal team, the court refused to reduce his prison sentence.

16. *"Wish you were here!"*

For most of the summer of 2004, Anita and I were either busy with other interests or traveling. *The New York Times*'s sources who predicted that the Pellicano wiretapping indictments would be handed up "in early in 2004" were obviously wrong. A lull had descended over the news coverage of the scandal.

With more free time, Anita finished her novel and was preparing to sell it—via her agent, Mickey Freiberg. I had an investigative consulting assignment, which took up a considerable amount of time, but it helped clear much of the debt that I had accumulated since Anita invited me to be her coauthor on May 1, 2003.[146]

Until federal prosecutors handed up the long-anticipated Pellicano wiretapping indictments, Anita and I had to be patient. We stayed in touch by phone and email, sending each other articles about politics, particularly about the upcoming presidential election, and any number of funny anecdotes found on the Internet. I tried to keep Anita well informed, and she tried to do the same for me.

Even in the midst of our arguments about Mickey Freiberg, I often playfully began my emails to her with the innocuous salutation, "Dear Anita Chiquita," and I usually signed them, "Your friend, Dan."

After making Anita's corrections to the June 18 draft manuscript which she had faxed to me, I really did nothing more on the book during the summer than collect information and update our catalogue of documents.

Anita did ask for my opinion after she received an invitation to appear in a Sky-TV documentary in the United Kingdom.

I replied in an email: "My advice? Be nice but blow them off. As you already know, you are only going to have one chance to tell your story for the first time. You might as well pick the biggest and the best in the US market after the book is released. Regarding their request for someone to talk about the Seagal case, give them [Los Angeles Times reporter] Paul Lieberman. He will probably appreciate the thought."

Anita responded: "[Y]ep, you are right. I think that is a good idea."

From the outset, Anita had problems selling her novel, and, to my surprise, she blamed Mickey Freiberg. She told me that she was thinking about firing him and going to the William Morris Agency.

I advised her to do what was best for her. However, acting with circumspection because of my respect for Mickey's partner, Jay Acton, I asked her not to do anything that would jeopardize *our* book project.

Seeing that I was suddenly defending Mickey, Anita revealed to me that he had said to her the previous spring, "Instead of getting rid of Frank, we should've gotten rid of Dan."

After hearing that, I immediately returned to my former position. Now, I really wanted Mickey gone, which unfortunately meant that we would lose Jay Acton, as well.

Needless to say, I was very upset with Anita when she finally did fire Mickey as the agent for *her* novel on September 24, but she allowed him to remain as the agent for *our* nonfiction book project.

From that point on, I didn't miss any opportunity to criticize Anita, personally, for allowing Mickey to remain on our team. To me, this was a totally unfair situation that she was forcing me to accept.

———

That summer, Dave Robb and his long-time girlfriend, Ellen Kelly, were married in Reno. But, for a variety of reasons, neither Anita nor I could get to Nevada for the wedding.

At the same time, Mimi and I had just gotten back together, even though she still had reservations about my line of work. I was just happy and relieved that we had found our way back to one another.

On October 19, Anita, whom I had not seen since our disastrous trip to New York the previous March, sent me a postcard from Oklahoma on which she handwrote:

> *Dan—*
>
> *Wish you were here!*
>
> *Love,*
> *Anita.*

———

Anita and I did follow with great interest the continuing trials and tribulations of Michael Ovitz which had subsided considerably after Cathy Schulman, the previous president of Ovitz's talent company, lost her $4 million arbitration against her former boss. In fact, the hearing over her alleged wrongful termination resulted in an order for her to pay Ovitz $3.6 million.[147]

Anita had written about the Schulman case in October 2002 for the *Los Angeles Times*.

The following month, Ovitz's winning streak continued as the court dismissed him from a portion of the stockholders' litigation against the Disney board.[148]

But the month after that, Ovitz took a huge hit when his win against Cathy Schulman in arbitration was thrown out.[149]

Later that fall, public attention again returned to Delaware where Ovitz took the witness stand during the Disney stockholders' trial and railed against his former boss, Michael Eisner.

Ovitz testified: "Now I'm not the smartest guy in the world, and I'm not the dumbest guy in the world. And I'm a fantastic loyal friend, and I am a horrible enemy. But I was this guy's friend. I'm not sitting here trying to play victim because I don't play that role very well."[150]

Reporting on Eisner's testimony about his former underling, the *New York Times* said:

> By May 1996, Mr. Eisner said there was a near open revolt among management. "[Ovitz] rubbed people the wrong way," Mr. Eisner said. "He was controversial and it got worse."
>
> Mr. Eisner said he told executives, including Mr. Ovitz, to relax.
>
> Mr. Eisner said Mr. Ovitz became upset when he was not asked to join a ribbon-cutting at the Disney Store on Fifth Avenue in New York. Mr. Eisner said he worried then that Mr. Ovitz had become depressed and that he might commit suicide, a notion he said he shared with the Disney investor Sid Bass in spring 1996.[151]

To our chagrin, Anita and I watched helplessly as the Ovitz-Pellicano story started to go wide. For instance, Roger Friedman of Fox News reported that his sources were telling him that the federal grand jury investigating Pellicano had Ovitz on their plate, asking questions about the possibility that he had used Pellicano to investigate Eisner. Friedman wrote:

> One reason, according to insiders: Pellicano, working for Ovitz, may have been scouring the landscape for any material that would cast Eisner in a bad light.

Indeed, there was some allusion made to this in the shareholders' trial back in November. When the plaintiffs' attorney, Steven G. Schulman, cross-examined Eisner, he questioned the Disney chief's characterization of Ovitz in notes from a phone call as "dangerous" and "a caged animal." He asked Eisner if he was worried that Ovitz represented a threat to him or to Disney.

Schulman, perhaps probing in an area that he may return to later, asked Eisner, "Did you consider him a danger to your privacy? Were you concerned that Mr. Ovitz had some way to harm you personally?"

Eisner vehemently replied, "No."[152]

———

Early on the morning of December 8, while working online, I found the docket in Anita's civil case on the Los Angeles County Superior Court's website. After setting up an account, I bought all of the records available and faxed them to Anita, who wrote to me: "Oh, and THANK YOU for doing this . . . incomprehensible that I have to find out about my case from you rather than my own lawyers." (Anita's emphasis)

As we had the previous year, Anita and I exchanged Christmas cards. In addition, she gave me the DVD of *Goldfinger*, my favorite James Bond film. I bought her a home-surveillance camera with a wireless receiver that she could hook up to her television set.

I had sent Frank Weimann a Christmas card, telling him in a handwritten note how sorry I was about what had happened earlier in the year. To my surprise, Frank called, and we discussed those events.

Frank explained that he was completely against the timing of our March trip to New York, saying that Mickey Freiberg had bullied him into it—only because he had already planned a trip there and did not want to spring for a return trip. Frank added that while we were in town and staying at The Roosevelt, he really was sick in bed with the flu.

Getting really serious, Frank warned that Freiberg wanted me gone from the project, saying I was the obstacle to getting a deal for Anita. I told him that Freiberg had said the exact same thing to

Anita, adding that I would be happy to be a mere ghostwriter if that would get us a deal.

Although I again redoubled my efforts to get rid of Mickey, Anita continued to protect him, even though I told her what Frank had said—and I reminded her that she had already fired him from her own project.

This situation with Freiberg continued to fester and take its toll on my friendship with Anita.

———

As the Pellicano case started to heat up again, few things in Hollywood shocked me more than the *Los Angeles Times* story on January 3, 2005, which reported that Brad Grey, whom we believed was either a possible witness or even a target of the Pellicano investigation, would soon be named as the new head of Paramount Pictures.[153] Anita, who knew Hollywood much better than I, took the news in stride.

My question was, "What did Viacom—Paramount's parent company, which also owned CBS—know that we didn't?"[154]

In the renewed anticipation of federal indictments in the Pellicano wiretapping case, the *Los Angeles Times* revealed:

> For the last two years, FBI computer specialists have been combing through the equivalent of nearly 2 billion double-spaced pages of text. . . . .
>
> Although the contents of the files have not been disclosed, they may be relevant to a pending federal wiretapping probe involving Pellicano, a number of rogue police officers and some big-name entertainment lawyers.
>
> If so, that investigation could be significantly affected when a three-judge panel . . . decides on a request by Pellicano's lawyers to declare the search illegal, suppress the seized evidence and overturn his conviction.[155]

On Thursday, January 13, the three-judge circuit court panel heard Pellicano's appeal in Pasadena. Once again, Dave Robb attended the hearing.

During one of my previous investigations, I had come across one of the judges, Stephen Reinhardt—a well-known civil libertarian appointed by President Jimmy Carter, whom I instinctively felt would rule on Pellicano's behalf. I predicted to Anita and Dave that the judges would vote, 2-1, in favor of the federal prosecutors.

————

The never-ending bad predictions by media organizations about the timing of the indictments had already become a chronic problem. Each time Anita passed on a rumor to me that the indictments were imminent, I dropped whatever I was doing, including my paid consulting work, and returned to the manuscript.

Usually these rumors were based on nothing more than bits and pieces of information Anita had received from her sources, such as the timing of a member of the prosecution team's vacation or the continuing postponement of one particular FBI agent's pending retirement. More often than not, "next month" turned into the month after that and then the month after that.

It almost became comical. But I had dug this trench, and I was in it for the long haul, I thought.

On January 28, I sent Anita a note, asking her whether she was in the midst of a catharsis in the wake of the recent death of a close friend, Bernie Ebbins, whose estate she was handling as his executrix: "Are you okay? You've been so quiet. Consequently, I'm more worried about you than usual."[156]

Anita replied: "Yes. It has taken up an inordinate amount of my time. I'm also deciding whether to change lawyers."

Anita told me that she resented the fact that her attorneys were trying to use her as a vehicle to collect new clients who were also alleged victims of Pellicano's handiwork for a potential class-action suit.

Always ready to defend good attorneys, I responded to this news, saying:

> With regard to the option of changing lawyers, I still believe
> that it is premature. I suggest that you draft a list of complaints and
> allow your attorneys the opportunity to respond before you take this

very harsh action—which could wind up causing you additional problems.

Until the feds pull the trigger, to my great distress, everything and everyone is on hold. Your lawyers haven't even had the opportunity yet to perform—with the exception of dealing with status conferences and stalling tactics. They fucked up badly in the manner in which they dealt with the [Nasso's] attorneys, but I was under the impression that they have atoned.

If there are still problems, then you should confront these matters by putting them in writing—and give your lawyers a chance to reply. If their response is unsatisfactory, then do what you have to do.

Demonstrating the consequences of the ongoing Freiberg unpleasantness, Anita came back to me with a quick, slap-down answer, stating: "I understand your opinion on this matter . . . I am going to do what's best for me in the long run, whatever that may be."

17. *"I just can't sign the truth away for money"*

On February 9, 2005, after an item about Brad Grey's joyful reaction to his new job as the chairman of Paramount Pictures appeared in the Rush & Molloy column of the *New York Daily News*, I nearly drove Anita crazy, wondering, once again, what the hell the Viacom board knew that we didn't know about the Pellicano probe.

Did they have inside information about the government's case against Pellicano and his alleged co-conspirators? Was the fix in?

In addition, Anita and I were still fighting over Mickey Freiberg—whom she still wanted to stay while I wanted him to go.

Somewhat frustrated with my concerns, Anita wrote to me: "All I can say is please stop freaking. Everything is going to work out. Have faith."

Shortly after that, Anita sent me an online birthday card in addition to the birthday card that she had sent by regular mail.

In response to her thoughtfulness, I responded with:

Thanks for the card(s) for my 55th birthday. Inasmuch as my great-grandfather, grandfather, and father all died at 64, I assume that I have only nine years left to torture you. I am hoping that the indictments will be announced before I die. But I do fear that, even then, I will still be stuck with Mickey as my agent.

Good-naturedly, Anita came back with: "I'm going to allow you to bitch about Mickey for the [umpteenth] time because it is your birthday today. But, ordinarily, I'd slap you silly. Ahem!"

Anita's decision to keep Mickey for *our* nonfiction project even though she fired him for *her* own fiction project was not my only concern. I now started to fear how Anita's attorneys who represented her pending civil case against Pellicano could jeopardize our book. I wrote a memo for my own files, which I titled "Man at Risk":

> My stated goal is to get back into the game.
> Anita's stated goal is to make money.
> Understanding this, here's how I can get fucked:
> 1. [Anita's] lawyers, who were unaware of the book project before they agreed to handle the case, insist that it not be published until the litigation is completed, fearing that information contained in the book will give the defendants free discovery.
> 2. During the course of litigation, other authors seize upon everything coming out on the public record and publish their own books, rendering our project cold coffee. . . .
> 3. The defendants [in Anita's civil case], individually or collectively, agree to settle their cases for a large amount of money. But in return, they insist that Anita sign a confidentiality agreement. If she refuses, they will proceed with the five-year legal battle.[157]
> 4. The attorneys allow the book to proceed—but insist that it be sanitized.
> [5.] Mickey Freiberg, without Anita's approval, goes to the publishers and sabotages my credit line, forcing me into a subordinate position, i.e. "as told to" or "with."

On March 2, I had lunch with my friend, author Mark Olshaker, with whom Anita had spoken a few months earlier about the agent Jay Acton. Because she appeared to respect Mark's opinion, I asked her to speak with him again during a conference call. All of us were on cell phones with Anita in Los Angeles and Mark just a few tables away from me at Krupin's, a popular delicatessen on Wisconsin Avenue in Washington.

The subject? Mickey Freiberg and how badly I wanted him gone.

When Anita continued to balk at getting rid of Freiberg, I got angry. I had finally had enough, and I barked at Anita, saying that she was "jeopardizing everything we had done" by keeping him on board.

Admittedly, I had placed Mark right in the middle of this dispute which should have only been between Anita and me. He tried to support my position while sympathizing with the complication of Anita's friendship with Freiberg.

But, still upset, I replied that their friendship had not stopped Anita from firing him from her own fiction project a few months earlier.

Finally, Anita had heard enough, and she abruptly ended the conversation.

A few seconds later, Anita, who was now angry, too, called me, saying that our project was finished. She would no longer work with me.

When I replied that she had no authority to do that under the terms of our contract, she asked, "What are you going to do? Sue me?"

Filled with remorse early the following morning for speaking so harshly to Anita and after talking with Dave who, once again, advised me to back down to this "fragile woman" who was actually as tough as anyone I knew, I wrote Anita a groveling hat-in-hand message, saying:

> I didn't want an entire day to pass without apologizing for upsetting you.
>
> I'm sorry that I tried—and have been trying—to bully you into making what I consider to be a very important and necessary decision.
>
> You deserve better than that from me.

A few hours later, without commenting on what I had sent her, she emailed an article to me from an unidentified and undated publication which discussed the fact the Mickey Freiberg and one of his partners were handling the print and television rights for Joey Buttafuoco's upcoming wedding in Las Vegas. Buttafuoco, of course, was the former Long Island lover of Amy Fisher, the so-called Long Island Lolita, who had tried to kill Buttafuoco's wife.

At least for the moment, all seemed forgiven, even though Anita still insisted that Freiberg stay and I still wanted him gone.

Regardless, I now found myself constantly walking on eggshells with my co-author who had a fish and a flower placed on the windshield of her car nearly three years earlier.

———

On March 7, with Anita's permission, I sent Dr. Nancy Nolte, my long-time writing coach, the latest version of our manuscript, *Woman at Risk: Anita Busch and the Hollywood Mafia*. A former instructor of mine at the University of Akron, "Mrs. Nolte," as I always respectfully called her, edited all of my previous manuscripts before I sent them to the publishing houses where I was under contract.[158] She always made my work much better.

In fact, I had dedicated my 1995 book about the murder of Senator Kennedy to Mrs. Nolte.[159]

In late March, Anita called and told me that her mother and father were going to be visiting her brother who lived in a Washington suburb. Because I liked her parents, I offered to take them to lunch.

Knowing that Anita's mom and dad were conservative Republicans, I decided to take them to a very special place.

On March 24, I called her parents at their son's home and made the arrangements to pick them up the following day. During our brief conversation, Anita's mom asked me how the book was going.

Laughing, I replied that Anita and I were not getting along very well, but that everything would be fine after we sold the book. When she asked what the problem was, I replied offhandedly that we disagreed on whether our current agent should stay or go.

After working out the details for the lunch, I sent Anita an email, saying: "I just got off the phone with your mom—who is such a nice person. Anyway, I want to take them to George Bush's favorite restaurant tomorrow for lunch, the Peking Gourmet Inn. The place is lousy with photographs of Republican elites, right-wing fanatics, and military-industrial-complex types. They will be in heaven."

Indeed, Mr. and Mrs. Busch were very charming and great company. I did bring along the draft manuscript which was now over 350 pages in length. And I let them skim through it. I wanted them to see that this project was for real. Other than that, I discussed nothing else about my business with Anita, except to laud their daughter and to say how much I appreciated having her as a friend. During our visit, I did not even mention the dispute over our agent.

When I returned home, I sent Anita an email, along with a photograph I took of her parents at the restaurant. I wrote: "We had a lot of fun at lunch. Your folks, of course, think the world of you—although they are worried. I told them that [you] will be fine. You are loyal, very smart, and a hard worker. You are a woman of destiny. . . ."

The following day, Anita sent me an online thank-you card.

But, then later in the day, Anita called, screaming at the top of her lungs. When I asked her what was wrong, she yelled that I had tried to manipulate her parents into convincing her to fire Mickey Freiberg as our agent.

The charge was so utterly ridiculous that I could only laugh about it, which fueled her strident outburst even more. When Anita asked me if I had brought up the disagreement over our agent, I replied that we had no discussion about the specifics of our book project while I was with her parents.

Anita demanded to know when the issue of the agent was discussed. I told her that during my telephone conversation with her mother the day before the lunch she asked me how that book was going. And I told her, honestly, that we were not getting along very well. When Mrs. Busch asked why, I replied that we had a disagreement over our agent.

I repeated that we discussed nothing of substance over lunch, inviting her to ask her father if she did not believe me.

After Anita hung up on me yet again, I wrote her an email, saying:

I can assure you that—if I really wanted to "manipulate" you—I would've first tried to do it through Dave. I wouldn't try to use your parents, whom I care for very much but who know even less about the book-publishing industry than you do. They are hardly qualified to carry the message I'd want you to hear—from someone who has published seven previous books. Dave is qualified and could deliver it with force—but ask Dave if I've ever tried to recruit him to do it. The answer is no, I haven't.

Soon after, I received a nice thank-you card in the mail from Anita's parents, thanking me for showing them a wonderful time. They appeared to be oblivious to this most recent dispute between their daughter and me.

Suddenly, even the most innocent communications I had with Anita became a potential flashpoint.

Seeing me battle financially, Dave Robb offered to loan some money to me, adding that my credit was good. In the past, he had played my banker in similar situations. And, of course, I always repaid him. Thus, I had no problem with accepting his generous offer.

On April 7, I received Mrs. Nolte's notes about our manuscript. My writing coach's primary concern was Anita's portrayal in the book as overly sensitive, highly emotional, erratic, secretive, fearful, and paranoid. Specifically, she thought that Anita seemed unduly suspicious of some of her colleagues at the Los Angeles Times. Simply speaking, Mrs. Nolte feared that the book critics would take my head off for the manner in which I had depicted Anita.

Through our earlier conversations, Mrs. Nolte knew how much I thought of Anita whom I had always described as a very good person. Mrs. Nolte did not recognize the Anita I described in our manuscript, which was exactly how Anita wanted to be viewed.

Indeed, Anita wanted to be portrayed as dark, wounded, and diminished because of Pellicano's actions against her.

I immediately agreed with Mrs. Nolte, but Anita had complete editorial control over the book and had already cleared much of the existing draft manuscript. Nevertheless, taking Mrs. Nolte's advice, I called Anita and talked about what appeared to be her unpleasant image in our book. I added that, in the next draft, I wanted to soften some of Anita's harder edges and to make her more sympathetic to the reader. On top of that, I wanted to help her leave the door open for a future return to journalism—should she choose to take that route.

From the outset, I had advised Anita to broaden her options, not to limit them.

Anita responded harshly, saying that she wanted to be portrayed as written and approved. In fact, she sent me an email, insisting:

> [Y]our editor doesn't understand this because she hasn't experienced it or anything like it. In fact, very few people have experienced anything like this. [Y]ou experienced part of it yourself so you understand a bit about it. [I] think [D]r. [J]effrey [W]igand [the tobacco-company whistleblower] experienced something very similar. [I] think [K]aren [S]ilkwood experienced something similar. [I] even think that people in Watergate experienced something very similar. [T]he point is, you can change words here and there, but you can't change the truth of what happened. No matter how distasteful it is on your palate.
>
> Do you think Karen Silkwood (if alive) would work in a nuclear plant ever again? Or that Jeffrey Wigand would work at a tobacco company ever again? Or even those innocents with principles who watched their president in action through Watergate would want to work with Nixon again?
>
> I mean, even Paul Rusesabagina who loved his country so much he was willing to die for his beliefs can't live in Rwanda anymore.
>
> Why? Because when you go through something like this ... it strips you down until you bleed from the bone. It pummels you to an inch of your life.
>
> I mean, get real. Life is fucking ugly at times, man. It's ugly. I've seen the worst of human nature. Corruption is human nature's cancer. It's decaying and bloodied. It smells of rotting chicken. It's as disgusting as it gets.
>
> Why do you think that Dave Robb and I were looked on in such awe when we walked away from the corruption? Because very few people have the guts. Most people [choose] to swallow the cancer and let it eat inside of them until their insides swell and ooze as their moral fiber [hemorrhages] out of their rectum. That's why.
>
> Going through something like this opens your eyes to your [naiveté] and your ridiculous idealism. It takes you out of Disneyland and dumps you into the middle of a gang rape in the Bronx. It's violent and [unconscionable].

It's unimaginable. And it's fucking dangerous ground when you expose it. That's why she is scared for you. That's why.

You can go the safe route, or you can stand up.

"The hottest place in Hell is reserved for those who remain neutral in times of great moral conflict."

I know for a fact that I'll never be in the company of the Devil. How 'bout you?

Sensing that Anita's question wasn't simply rhetorical—and that she really wanted an answer—I replied:

I would never be "in the company of the Devil." Never. And I have spent my entire career—31 years—fearlessly standing up against the bad guys as an independent writer and author. Mrs. Nolte, who is also one of my closest friends, has seen and heard everything that has happened to me. Rest assured: I am not afraid of anything—including anything or anyone in this book about you. And she doesn't fear for me because I'm doing this book.

Mrs. Nolte and I are not trying to change the truth about anything. However, we are trying to protect you while placing you in the best possible light. We are trying to explain, effectively and truthfully, how your very legitimate complaints against two people at the *LAT* has [evolved] into your complete and total disdain for the profession of journalism.

If that's how you really feel, that's how I'll write it. But I want this book to help put you back in the game if that's what you want—not alienate you from everyone in your former profession. Journalists have an uncanny knack of taking any attack on journalism, personally—regardless of how legitimate.

BTW: Whenever I was beaten up, had a gun rammed down my throat, had a shot fired at me, or had a knife pulled on me, these situations always made me stronger and more determined to finish my work. I have never left a job while under fire.

You are not alone here. (My emphasis)

Anita remained defiant, responding, in part:

I don't need protection. It was never only two people. You are the one who wanted to pare it down to two people. The truth is it was a handful of people in management who were trying to protect their collective asses. . . .

Give me a fucking break. Yeah, me go back to journalism. It doesn't stand for shit anymore to me. Don't you get it? It doesn't

stand for shit. It's pathetic joke. I don't respect it. I want no part of
it. It is over for me.

After receiving Anita's veto of Mrs. Nolte's suggestion to soften
her image, I called Mrs. Nolte and discussed the situation with her.
Mrs. Nolte's biggest concern revolved around Anita's transparent
tactic of alternating roles between the crusading journalist and the
wounded victim and playing them to whatever suited her purposes at
any given moment.

Still predicting that the current portrayal of Anita would be
raw psychological meat for book critics, Mrs. Nolte advised me to
emphasize Anita's editorial control over the entire manuscript and
simply say in the book's prologue that this is her side of the story,
authorized and approved by her.

In a follow-up message that Mrs. Nolte sent to me, she wrote:
"If she is satisfied with her depiction in the book as it now stands,
I am not concerned about it—I questioned it because I couldn't
believe she would want it that way."

18. *"My attorneys first must read it"*

On April 11, 2005, after applying Mrs. Nolte's edits to the text, I
sent the manuscript to Anita via overnight mail. In my cover letter,
I wrote: "My principal concerns at this point continue to be getting
a) the chronology down, b) the facts right, and c) the documentation
together."

This would be the third time that Anita saw Part One of the book,
the second time she saw Part Two, and the first time she saw Part
Three. I assumed that Part One would now be close to completion,
Part Two would need some editing, and Part Three would require a
considerable amount of work.

In addition, I noted my ongoing problem with the fact that we
had so many people in the book to whom she had given code names,
even to some of those who had already been identified publicly,
like the now-famous "Confidential Witness," Dan Patterson. In lieu
of naming him, Anita insisted that I call him, "The Mystery Man,"

throughout the manuscript. She continued to feel loyal to Patterson because of his warning to her on the day after her car was vandalized.

On April 12, Anita, after receiving the manuscript, sent an email, rejecting my appeal to name the unnamed in our book.

———

Later that day, Anita gave me some shocking news, saying, almost off-handedly, that she had just fired Mickey Freiberg as the agent for *Woman at Risk*. After all of the fighting and ill-will that had been caused by the Freiberg dispute, his sudden dismissal by Anita was a complete anticlimax.

She did not give me any reason, and I didn't ask for one. I was just grateful that Freiberg was finally gone. Despite the temptation, I did not gloat or say, "I told you so." Knowing how much damage this matter had done between us, I did not want to spend another moment dealing with it. And, right or wrong, I viewed this action by Anita as an act of good faith, as well as a new beginning.

On April 13, Anita authorized me to call Deborah Grosvenor, the agent I had seen at the WIW writers' conference the previous June. I called Deborah immediately and arranged to take her to lunch. She was a real pro and would be perfect for our project.

At the lunch with Deborah at the Cafe Deluxe in Bethesda, I gave her a copy of the proposal. In addition, Anita had asked me to reveal to Deborah that our top suspect in the June 2002 threat against her was Michael Ovitz—which was really a shock to Deborah.

Also, I recounted to Deborah the difficulty we had trying to get an agent for what we thought would be a much sought after book project.

I followed up the lunch with a note to Deborah, saying that Anita and I hoped that she would accept the offer to become our agent.

———

On April 15, I received a telephone call from another former Mafia figure I knew who had flipped and turned state's evidence.

A few months earlier, after he told me that his wife was dying of cancer, Anita had suggested that I give him the details about a little known experimental cancer treatment.

After I finished this latest conversation with the ex-mobster, I wrote Anita a message, saying:

> [The Mafia guy] and I tried to conference you on your home and mobile lines but received no answer on either.
>
> He said that his wife is alive today because of the treatment you introduced her to. Delivery is by three different means: injection, oral liquid, and pill. His wife takes the pill.
>
> Remarkably, there have been no side effects. At its worst, the tumor was the size of an orange. At the moment, it is the size of a pea.
>
> Prior to this treatment, she rarely went out of the house. Now, she goes out every day.
>
> You should be very proud for what you've done.[160]

To be sure, Anita had probably helped to save this woman's life—or, at the very least, extended it.

———

On Tuesday, April 19, Dave Robb called, saying that both he and Anita really liked Part One of the April 11 manuscript. Specifically, Dave told me, "It sings," adding that Anita had spent several hours on the phone with him, reading it aloud—"laughing and giggling" throughout.

Later, I received Anita's handwritten edits for the first two parts of the manuscript—in which she wrote "I think this really moves well so far. Pretty good job, DAN!" (Anita's emphasis).

That was the best review I could have received. In other words, after the third draft of Part One, she was finally starting to enjoy the manuscript. Our system of drafting and editing and then re-drafting and re-editing was working.

———

On April 21, Anita told me that Joni Evans had called, asking to be her agent. Evans was the prominent agent at the William Morris Agency with whom Anita had discussed a possible book project way back in December 2002.

I replied that we had already selected Deborah Grosvenor as our agent. I suggested that Anita use Evans to represent her other work. After her failure to sell her earlier novel, Anita had already started work on a new one.[161]

Early Friday morning, after I returned home from my Thursday-night poker game, I received a message from Anita:

> It's a little after midnight. I just finished the additions. I hope I don't have nightmares tonight. Reliving this is really horrible stuff. Would like to forget that it all happened.
> I'm going to give the new pages to Paul [Suzuki, Anita's attorney-brother-in-law,] tomorrow night and hopefully send the first section out to you Saturday instead of Monday. Started on the second section already. Hope to have that completed by the weekend. . .
> Talk to you tomorrow. I'm exhausted.

However, the big news was that Anita had learned from one of her sources that the Los Angeles County District Attorney's Office would soon indict Pellicano and no fewer than five other people for the June 2002 threats against her. In response, I faxed a memorandum to Anita, anticipating how this could affect our book project, saying, in part:

> The news is a lucky break for us. The beauty about the DA indicting first is that we will not be entering the anticipated fray in traffic. With Anita at the epicenter of this action, we will be running in open field. No one else . . . will even consider writing a book about Anita's case. . . .
> Deborah wants to see the manuscript—so that she can help strengthen the proposal. Thus, after Anita finishes her review, I will make the corrections and print out a [clean] draft—for Deborah and Anita's lawyers.

In her handwritten response, which Anita immediately faxed back to me, she agreed that we should give Deborah, as well as her lawyers, the next version of the manuscript.

Anita declared that our proposal was "in fairly good shape now." However, she added: "You [are] getting a little ahead of things. Deborah hasn't even agreed to anything yet. We don't know who [the] state will charge or arrest yet."

Despite my previous concession that we had to send the manuscript to her lawyers, Anita felt the need to emphasize this point three times. In her first handwritten note, she said: "[N]othing can be done, obviously, w/o the approval of my lawyers. My lawsuit is my future and I deserve to benefit from that reimbursement unhampered."

Then, in a follow-up page to her notes on the faxed memo I had sent her, she handwrote: "OH—my attorneys first must read it. Not Deborah & attorneys at the same time. My attorneys take precedent." She signed and dated the statement, "4/22/05."

In addition to those statements, she followed up with yet another email, stating: "Things will happen as they are supposed to. We can make decisions as they arise. My attorneys must get anything first, you know that as well as I do. I know you are anxious but you must just know that everything will work out. Just ease back a bit, okay? Everything will be fine."

Of course, I agreed to Anita's demand about her lawyers, saying:

> Well, I guess that the attorneys-thing trumps everything. And I can certainly understand that.
>
> If that's the strategy, then I guess there is nothing more for me to do until I receive your corrections—then make a clean copy for them. But I can tell you that once Deborah hears the news, she will go into overdrive. We want to be ready to spring into action. Once the trigger is pulled, there is no way that everyone isn't going to make the connection to the larger issue.

Anita replied:

> I stayed up late last night so I could mail everything in section one out today, minus the additions that [her brother in law, attorney Paul Suzuki,] has to approve. I will try to get him to do that tonight. It is two (or three) pages which I will fax over to you after I work with him on it. I made a notation with the thing where the addition should be.

Then it will be on its way today instead of tomorrow. You should get it tomorrow. I'm going to mail it express mail. You can tackle that this weekend, while I tackle the next section. Sound good?

19. *"She has editorial control"*

On the evening of April 22, 2005, Anita and I spoke on the phone, dealing with specific items in the draft manuscript. In one section, I had written a description of Alexander Proctor in which I wrote: "Tough and wiry, he is five-feet-six and 130 pounds. He dresses like a professional golfer, a throwback to the early-sixties when Frankie, Dino, and Sammy set the standard for cool."

Little did I know that when I wrote the phrase, "dresses like a professional golfer," it would ignite a shooting war between Anita and me.

The problem was that I had seen a photograph of Pellicano dressed in a black golf shirt and black slacks similar to the attire worn by Gary Player, the great professional golfer also known as "The Black Knight," and I had mistakenly thought it was a picture of Proctor whom I proceeded to say "dresses like a professional golfer."

When I discovered my own mistake, I decided to let the description of Proctor stand—primarily because I liked the way I had described him. If it later turned out that he was not among those millions of men who wore black golf shirts and black slacks, then I would delete the description from the manuscript.

After hearing this, Anita went ballistic, accusing me fabricating information and adding, "I will not work with someone who makes things up."

Even though I offered to take the passage out of our draft manuscript immediately, Anita decided to make a stand against me. She also noted a scene in an earlier draft where I depicted her swimming at the YMCA, which had been based on her own statements.[162] She also complained about a recreated conversation between Pellicano and Proctor that I had in that same earlier manuscript, based on Proctor's own tape-recorded statements to confidential witness Dan Patterson.[163]

In the both of those cases, with no prompting from Anita, I had already and unilaterally deleted these passages from the draft manuscript. But, still, Anita used them all these months later to portray me as a dishonest person.

Clearly, Anita now wanted me out, and she was using these flimsy excuses to get out of our contract. I believed that all of this had been provoked either by her conversation with the agent from the William Morris Agency or her abrupt insistence that her attorneys must approve the manuscript that I was in the midst of drafting—or both.

In the immediate aftermath of our two-day email battle, I received the now-expected call from Dave Robb, our mediator and her protector. I told Dave that Anita was being completely unreasonable.

In a tone more serious than ever before, Dave replied that Anita was on the verge of walking away from this entire project. I replied that the current battle was about nothing more than whether or not Proctor dressed like a golfer.

When Dave asked about the scene where Anita was swimming at the YMCA and the other where I had recreated the conversation between Pellicano and Proctor, I replied that I had removed those scenes on my own. They were not even in the April 11th version Anita was reading.

Dave said that he was under the impression that those scenes were still in the existing manuscript.

"They're not. . . . Dave, I haven't done a goddamn thing wrong," I said with exasperation. "She has editorial control."

"This is *her* story!" Dave replied before giving me his mantra: "Just shut the fuck up, and do what she wants!"

Dave's solution? I was now Anita's stenographer, even though my name was on the cover of the book. In effect, with all of the self-destructive material that she insisted appear in the manuscript, Anita was committing political suicide and forcing me to help pull the trigger.

After my trip to the woodshed with Dave, Anita faxed two lengthy additions to the manuscript, which she also emailed to me without any further comment about the dispute.

Upon receipt, I replied: "Thank you for emailing the text to me. I'll add them to the materials I received yesterday. Please call or write if you need anything else.

"As I reconfirmed to Dave yesterday—and as I have said all along—I am going to give you everything you want in this book."

I hoped that I could appeal to our eventual publishing house to overturn some of her more ill-advised decisions. In the end, the publisher would have a major influence on the book's final content.

Later that morning, Anita responded to the first draft of the third part of the manuscript which she had never seen before. Admittedly, it was very rough, primarily because Anita had kept such a low profile during the period covered. Other than the news about the filing of her civil suit, she was barely a character in this part of her own story.

Anita complained that I had omitted a handful of anecdotes that she had shared with me. In one, Anita noted that a nurse she had met in the hospital had the name "Gambino" tattooed on her arm, suggesting that somehow she had a connection to the Carlo Gambino crime family.[164] In another, she and a friend saw a suspicious car and followed it. But nothing was learned and nothing was ever proven.

In other words, both of these stories, along with the others she wanted added to the book, went absolutely nowhere and did absolutely nothing but add to her image as a paranoid and narcissistic drama queen.

Also, she complained that I did not publish nine pages on why she had decided to leave journalism, which I considered a completely and totally self-righteous and self-serving diatribe, filled with ill-advised, self-destructive statements.

In this letter, she clearly fixed blame on Michael Ovitz, aka "Mr. O," for her predicament. Specifically, she wrote:

> Who did it? The bad guys, of course. Private investigator Anthony Pellicano and the thugs he hired at the behest of Mr. Big, the ultimate bad guy whom I will call Mr. O. . . .

> You find some relief in knowing that Mr. O's ultimate justice is going to be harder than any prison sentence. His blackened soul will eventually be judged by the heavens.
>
> Then you forgive Pellicano, his hired thugs and even the evil Mr. O.

On April 26, I stumbled across an article on the MSNBC website, indicating that John Connolly was peddling a book proposal about the Pellicano case. Immediately, I sent the link to Anita.

She replied: "[Y]eah, so. [W]e already knew that he was working with [a private detective in Los Angeles before Anita and I approached him to join our team in October 2003] and then trying to work with Kat [Pellicano's fourth wife]. It is nothing we already didn't know."

Actually, this was *not* something that I knew. In fact, in all communications that Connolly had sent to Anita and that Anita then sent to me, he appeared to be doing back flips in his efforts to convince her that he was *not* writing a book about the Pellicano case.

———

The next day, I received the corrected manuscript from Anita who emphasized, once again, that her attorneys must see the manuscript before anyone else, including Deborah who agreed to represent us a few days later.

On May 2, the day after the second anniversary of Anita's invitation for me to participate in our now godforsaken book project, I finished the next draft of the first two parts of the manuscript, based upon Anita's edits for the first 289 pages of the April 11 version.

Once again, I agreed that Anita should know any and all changes I made in the manuscript. Also, I guaranteed that her changes would be made. If I disagreed with something, I would say so in writing and explain why.

Along with the manuscript, I added a seventeen-page memorandum, "Additions, corrections, amplifications," which addressed every single substantive comment that Anita made on the manuscript along with the continuing issue over all the fake names we were using at her insistence.[165]

There was another problem. In this latest draft manuscript, Anita had greatly watered down the nature of her complicated relationship with a former boyfriend, an ex-convict and fringe organized-crime figure whom she had given the code name, "The Car Guy." A former associate of the notorious Mafia figure and reputed contract killer Anthony Spilotro of Chicago and Las Vegas, "The Car Guy" was actually listed in "Nevada's Black Book" of undesirables who are barred from the state's casinos.[166]

Anita had told me about "The Car Guy" in May 2003, within days after she asked me to be her co-author. She wrote:

> Dan, I need to tell you one thing that I'm not proud of, but it is what it is.
> A few years ago, I went down to Louisiana to see this illegal gambling operation. I went down as a journalist and they knew I was there.
> In this den of thieves (which is what it was), I met a guy . . . who was legendary in this world. I was told to stay away from him because he was ruthless. So, I thought, that was as a [sic] good reason as any for me to crack him. . . .
> I decided to try and get the ruthless guy's life rights and do a book on him. He didn't want any part of it. When I showed up a second time, he took me outside in back of the place and pulled out a gun. First he said that he could kill me and thrown me in the marsh and no one would ever know. . . . I said that I wanted his life rights and I wasn't leaving until he agreed.

Without a collaboration agreement with this "nefarious" character, as she described him to me, Anita returned to Los Angeles. Then, about a month later, this "ruthless guy," aka "The Car Guy," called from LAX, asking for a ride to a meeting. During the next few days, he and Anita began writing portions of their book about his life and times. In her letter to me, Anita continued:

> The guy really liked me. . . in a more than a friend way, but I just wasn't into him at all. He wasn't much to look at and was

uneducated. He actually looked like Sinatra in the 1950s—scrawny, you know—and with really bad teeth. He was nice and all. Treated me really like a princess, but I just had no interest whatsoever.

Eventually, though, he broke me down. He was an amazing cook. During this time, he began to stay in my house when he would come to town and we would write together.[167] One of these times, in a moment of weakness, we ended up together. . . It was just that he was not only an amazing cook, but an amazing lover. . . .

I found out 3 weeks later that there WAS someone after him . . . he got arrested at my house . . . picked up by the feds. I still am not sure what for but it had to do with something about skipping out on a hearing. . . . He was also doing some illegal gambling operation in Vegas.

It didn't matter. I stuck by him as a friend. He was impressed with the loyalty and to be loyal back, he continued to write the book in prison. When he got out of prison, I allowed him to parole to my house. . . .

At this point, he was telling me that he was in love with me. For my part, I was in love with his cooking and the sex and didn't give a rat's ass about him otherwise. . . .

He said I had too much integrity to be with him. So, after a few really painful months, . . . he ended up splitting after his parole was finished. I was very, very happy; he wasn't.

I truly regret it more than anyone could ever know, and I'm totally embarrassed about the whole thing. . . .

I know he worked as a personal courier for [Tony] Spilatro [sic] . . . taking money from Vegas to Chicago to New York to Florida and he mentioned Detroit once or twice, but I didn't know anymore and didn't ask. I did ask him if he ever killed anyone and when he hesitated with me, I told him that I didn't want to know. (Anita's emphasis)

In Anita's corrections to our April 2005 manuscript, "The Car Guy," once a key character in our manuscript, went from her "lover" in a previous draft to nothing more than "a close friend" in the most recent version.

In other words, Anita's demand for Absolute Truth with no punch-pulling rang hollow after she forced me to dilute the real details of this important relationship with a man she had told me was associated with organized crime.

Just to be clear, I did not know, at first, the identity of "The Car Guy." Anita did not tell me. However, I discovered his identify before we became convinced that Michael Ovitz had hired Pellicano to investigate Anita.

Wondering if "The Car Guy" might have played some role in the attack on her, I had earlier run a background check on him. After Ovitz's role came to our attention on June 12, 2003, we were both convinced that "The Car Guy" was not involved.

On May 8, 2005, Anita returned the May 2 draft manuscript to me, which included the diminished role of "The Car Guy." This replaced the April 11 version. And I returned the new draft to her on May 10. Once again, I accompanied this version with another challenge to Anita's edits, "Additions, corrections, amplifications II." As before, when I did not make a change, I explained why in writing.

It was clear that Anita was prepared to challenge me on anything and everything—even though she now had conflicting standards on her use of The Truth.

In her handwritten notes, Anita declared that she "would not send forward" the first two parts of the manuscript to her attorneys unless I added a single quote from a colleague of hers at the *Los Angeles Times*.

Doing what she asked, I simply went to the designated page and added the quote. Then I emailed that single page to Anita on Wednesday, May 11, asking her to use it as a replacement page.

After receiving the one-page replacement on May 11, Anita replied: "got it. will send to the attorney on friday. tomorrow. i'll be busy from 8 a.m. to 9 p.m."

Sending the first two parts of the manuscript to her attorneys—after all the hoops she required me to jump through, including the May 11 change on a single page—indicated that Anita had approved the first two parts of the manuscript.

However, she had placed the first rough draft of Part Three on hold indefinitely.

20. *"Why give out free information that can have holes poked into it?"*

On the morning of May 12, 2005, Anita wrote me a brief message, saying that she was ill. Trying to lighten things up, I replied, "Then, may I do something to torture you today?"

Anita did not respond.

On May 15, I rewrote the pitch letter to our book proposal and faxed it to Anita her for approval. She included some handwritten comments and sent it back to me. I made the changes and gave this document to our new agent, Deborah Grosvenor, the following day. During my meeting with Deborah, I advised her of Anita's decision—that she wanted her attorneys to read the manuscript before our agent. Deborah, who is an attorney, had no problem with this strategy.

That same day, the *New York Times* published another story about Bert Fields, noting again that he had been questioned by FBI agents in November 2003. However, Fields told the *Times* reporter, "It's been over two years and I haven't heard a thing. I'm not worried, since I didn't wiretap or use anything that had the slightest indication of being from a wiretap."[168]

On May 17, I accompanied Mimi to a book party for a friend of hers at Cada Vez restaurant on U Street in northwest Washington. At the party, I saw one of my best friends, Danny Wexler, who had worked at the White House for President Bill Clinton. Danny introduced me to Senator Hillary Clinton, who was also present. During my thirty-second encounter with Senator Clinton, I handed Danny the digital camera in my pocket, and he snapped a picture of us.

When I arrived home that night, I sent the photograph in an email to Anita and Dave. Knowing how much I admired Senator Clinton, Anita wrote back: "A fine looking couple. I bet you already have that framed on your wall. hee hee."

Then, moments later she sent another message, saying: "[I]s that the Devil wearing Prada?

"You know I think she is one of the evildoers."

Clearly influenced by the spin placed on the Pellicano scandal by the right-wing media, Anita appeared to have bought into the allegation that the private detective had worked for Bill Clinton's presidential campaign in 1992.

For the moment, we avoided that discussion. To my knowledge, other than making a $500 contribution, Pellicano had played no role in any of the Clinton's campaigns.

———

On May 24, Anita had a meeting with one of her attorneys at the Geragos firm. During our subsequent telephone call, Anita told me that the lawyer was alarmed by the manuscript, because it could potentially give too much information—free discovery—to the defense in her civil case.

Consistent with the worst-case scenario that I had written to myself on February 27, Anita dropped the bomb on me, saying that our book could not go forward.

Anita did tell me that her attorney added that if she and I really needed money that the attorney might be willing to go through the manuscript and make the necessary changes, so that it could be sold and published when the indictments were handed up.

Although Anita had told me after retaining her attorneys the previous year that she had fully informed them about our book project, I began to wonder *what* she really told her attorneys—and *when* she had actually told them.

Later that night, I sent an email to Anita, saying:

> Because the lawyer has possibly left the door open for us when the trigger is pulled, I've decided not to say anything to Deborah right now.
>
> From what I understand, the attorney has three basic problems with the manuscript: 1) the identification of certain unnamed sources, 2) the use of some of your personal writings, and 3) the needed change of the text about your FOIA request.
>
> In short, I have no problem with making any of these adjustments/changes.

If the lawyer still refuses to allow us to move forward after the trigger pulling, then I'll explain the situation to Deborah.

What really puzzles me is that your attorneys knew that we were writing a book. What did they think it was going to contain—poetry and [recipes]? Why didn't they express their concerns earlier?

Anita replied:

The attorneys [sic] main concern, as I told you before, is **why give out free information that can have holes poked into it?** Those things I told you were some of the top concerns of what would need to change and why it would be hurtful to me and my case, but there were others as well which I have not discussed with you. So, as I said earlier today, **we cannot do this now. It is non-negotiable. I cannot go against my own attorneys. Perhaps we can revisit this project at a future date.** First and foremost, they need to see where this is all headed.

I think you should be straight with Deborah and tell her what my attorneys said to me about the situation. Tell her it cannot move forward now. [Emphasis added]

With the reality of the situation starting to sink in, I responded:

I am fully aware of the attorneys' concerns—even though just about everything is going to come out in written interrogatories and in depositions.

However, I thought you also told me that the attorney was willing to revisit this situation *when the trigger is pulled.* I am willing to make any and all changes that are necessary.

Are you going to ask her to do that—or is this now a *fait accompli*? If it is, I'll call Deborah later today. But I don't know why you are taking the hard line when the attorney has left the door open.

Should I continue to have faith? (My emphasis)

The final sentence in my message referred to a February 9, 2005, email Anita sent me, which I attached and in which she wrote: "All I can say is please stop freaking. Everything is going to work out. Have faith."

In lieu of having faith, I now believed that she viewed our manuscript as a cudgel, nothing more than a bargaining tool in her lawsuit.

Sensing that she had me checkmated, she wrote: "Give it all a rest, Dan. Please. For Crissakes. I spoke to Dave tonight and he had an idea for us. You can talk to him about it. I hate it that you are even emailing me about this stuff that should never be written. Please PLEASE just give it a rest." (Anita's emphasis)

Later that day, I wrote to Dave Robb: "Anita wrote that you wanted to discuss something with me. If possible, please call me before you go to work."

During my conversation with Dave, I asked him what his idea was.

He replied that he did not know what Anita was talking about. He told me to stay by my phone while he called Anita.

When Dave called back, he simply said that Anita told him that she would go back to her attorney and inquire about the changes she offered to make—so that we could sell the book. Dave instructed me to give her some time to make good on her offer. He ordered me not to say or do anything until June 1.

After our conversation, I sent Dave an email where I attached the recent emails between Anita and me that led to this situation. I added:

> As promised, below is the exchange between Anita and me after she used her lawyers to pull the rug out from under me on Tuesday.
>
> For id-purposes, Deborah is Deborah Grosvenor, our agent. The references to "trigger pulling" refer to the anticipated indictments.
>
> Bottomline, she was wrong about John Connolly—and caused us huge problems over that. She was wrong about Mickey Freiberg— which caused eight months of fighting between Anita and me before she finally fired him. Last month, she flat-out fabricated a slew of false and unfair charges about me, stemming from my "on-spec" first-draft manuscript. And now she is causing huge problems over her decision to take an even harder line than her lawyers about the future of the book.
>
> Ironically, just a few months ago, she wrote to me, saying that she was seriously thinking about firing her lawyers—for what she claimed was their unethical behavior. And, in a move I now regret, I helped to convince her not to fire them.
>
> As agreed, I will not [say] anything further at least until June 1.
>
> Once again, I really appreciate you being here for us. Without you, I have no idea what would've happened.

The following day, May 26, Anita sent me a story about Michael Ovitz and film producer Brian Grazer, without any other comment. Keeping my promise to Dave, I did not reply. However, I did send a card to Anita for her May 31st birthday.

Anita called on her birthday to thank me, saying that she had received the card in the mail. Our only real topic of conversation was the recent admission by former FBI agent W. Mark Felt that he was "Deep Throat," *Washington Post* reporter Bob Woodward's secret source during the Watergate investigation.

On June 3, after keeping my promise not to confront Anita but still hearing nothing, I concluded that Anita was clearly in breach of our collaboration agreement. But in lieu of taking legal action against her, I decided to give Dave the opportunity to work this out peacefully.

I sent Dave an email, saying:

> It is now June 3, and, as promised, I haven't said 1 word about the dispute. Anita called me on her birthday to thank me for the card I sent her. Other than the disclosure of Deep Throat, nothing else was discussed.
>
> To business, I am wondering whether Anita has acted on the idea you came up with on May 24. . . . I think she told you that she planned to approach her attorneys to discuss it either the next day or the day after. I'm wondering if that ever happened.
>
> By the way, I have looked over the collaboration contract that she and I signed. There is absolutely nothing contained in that document which justifies what she has done. She has no power to stop this project unless I agree to it. . . .
>
> Once again, I apologize for keeping you in the middle of this situation. But Anita and I need you. We both appreciate your fairness and integrity.

Dave replied: "I would like you to sit tight for a few more weeks. We should know by then whether more criminal charges are going to be filed, and how that will impact Anita's civil suit. I have [an] idea, but let me keep it in reserve right now."

In response, I wrote to Dave:

> Okay, I'll sit tight while you try to work things out,
> understanding that you are not making any promises or giving any

guarantees. If your best efforts can't work this out, then nobody else's can either. I'll trust your secret plan. . . .

Respectfully, I will not agree to anything that places me at Anita's mercy or makes me [dependent] on her goodwill and best intentions. Her behavior during the past six weeks has been nothing more than an abomination. What Anita has done to me is worse than what John Connolly did to us. In the wake of his blatant double-cross after just a few weeks on our team, Connolly was kind enough to leave Anita and me with our book project. At the moment, Anita has left me with nothing after my two years on the job—and shamelessly acts like she had the right to do it.

On June 8, Anita emailed that she had received some bad news: The district attorney was not going to indict Pellicano and his co-conspirators for the threat against her. She sent me an email, lamenting: "*[C]hinatown* is getting ready to play out here on the small screen."

A few minutes later, before I had a chance to respond, she added: "[A]nd it's not something I care to watch play out . . . I haven't been pummeled into the ground enough apparently."

Sensing that she was reaching out for a friend, I decided to reply as the loyal friend I continued to be, simply writing: "You have no choice but to stay strong."

"[Y]es," she replied. "I have no control over the situation . . . I've been daisy-chained to death."

I responded, trying to refocus her attention on our book project, "If this is a simple lament, then fine. I understand your frustration. But you are surely not dead and certainly not helpless—far from it."

Once again, our written and verbal communications were friendly and cordial. I believed that, with the potential bad news on the law-enforcement front, Anita had returned to the option of publishing our book.

21. *"I really have nothing more to say to you"*

On June 9, 2005, Anita called and told me that the U.S. Court of Appeals for the Ninth Circuit had refused to reverse Pellicano's conviction and upheld the FBI's search warrant of the private detective's office. She had not yet seen the 2-1 opinion or the dissent by Judge Stephen Reinhardt, which was exactly what I had earlier predicted. I went online, obtained it, and sent it to her.[169]

Anita told me that, because of the appellate court's decision, the DA's office might now indict before the statute of limitations expired on June 20.

I sent a message about the breaking news to our agent, Deborah Grosvenor, along with the links to the opinion and dissent. In my message to Deborah, I added:

> The District Attorney's Office in Los Angeles County appears to have been stalling in issuing its indictments—primarily because they had earlier retained Pellicano to do some work on several criminal cases. Obviously, they feared that prosecuting Pellicano could force the convictions in those earlier cases to be overturned. County prosecutors are facing a June 20 statute of limitations—three years to the day after the attack on Anita. We'll know what the DA's office will do within the next eleven days.
>
> With this important decision by the Ninth Circuit, the U.S. Attorney's Office in LA, which has already issued two sets of sealed indictments, should not have any other impediments to pulling its trigger—finally and at long last.

———

Exploiting the Ninth Circuit's decision upholding Pellicano's conviction, *NewsMax.com*, a right-wing online publication, published an article on June 10, 2005, repeating the old charge that Pellicano had been hired by the Clintons to investigate and attack their enemies, an allegation publicly denied by Bill Clinton's attorney, David Kendall. Specifically, *NewsMax* stated:

> Senior Bush White House advisor Mary Matalin . . . says that Pellicano played a critical role in Mr. Clinton's 1992 presidential campaign by suppressing inconvenient accounts from several women who had alleged affairs with Mr. Clinton.
>
> During a 1997 stint as a talk radio host on CBS's Washington, D.C. affiliate, Matalin explained: "I got the letters from Pellicano

to these women intimidating them. I had tapes of conversations from Pellicano to the women. I got handwritten letters from the women. . . .

The notorious Hollywood sleuth also performed an audio analysis on Gennifer Flowers' tapes, where he concluded that they had been "doctored." Pellicano's finding was soon discredited, but his conclusions were still cited by top Clinton aides George Stephanopoulos and James Carville. [170]

In fact, Pellicano had performed an "audio analysis on Gennifer Flowers' tapes." However, he did this task for KCBS, the CBS affiliate in Los Angeles, not for the Clintons or their political campaign. Pellicano concluded, "I don't know that it was 'doctored,' but it was selectively edited."[171]

In my reply to Anita who raised this issue over the phone, I wrote to her on June 11, already aware that she thought Hillary Clinton was an "evildoer":

Given the choice between believing *NewsMax*—which is owned by Christopher Ruddy, who made a fortune by falsely claiming that Vince Foster was murdered by the Clintons—and David Kendall, one of the finest attorneys in D.C., there is no choice. I know as a fact that Terry Lenzner was the private investigator hired by the Clintons. I never heard of Pellicano being involved with them—and I know a lot about what was going on. As you can attest, the only inside information I knew about Pellicano when we began our thing came from protected-witness Bill Jahoda.

Obviously, I'll be very curious to see what the feds come up with about this. If I'm proven wrong, so be it.

Recognizing that she had struck a nerve with me by attacking Bill and Hillary Clinton, Anita came back swinging, saying:

[T]hey wouldn't touch the Clintons. Are you kiddin' me? And, to be honest, neither of us know anything.

The only ones who know are the Clintons, whomever did the hiring and the employee himself.

To say otherwise is absolutely [ludicrous]. If there is one thing I've learned from everything that has happened to me ... and you should know this as well ... that unless you got something from the horse's mouth ... you got nothing. You got third hand bullshit that doesn't mean diddly squat.

Sensing that Anita was just itching for an argument, I gritted my teeth and decided to back off, refusing to give it to her over this issue.

When I didn't engage that battle, Anita wrote back to me: "I would like to know why you haven't told Deborah that everything is on hold when we've known about that for a few weeks now. I think it is very unfair to her."

Knowing that Anita had never even called Deborah and really could not care less about her, I sensed that Anita was, yet again, just looking for a fight.

Still trying not to give it to her, I replied, trying to be completely accommodating:

> I really appreciated that you broke the ice and shared your concerns about "the small screen" with me last Wednesday. And I am so happy that the Ninth Circuit delivered such great news and, hopefully, eliminated your concerns on Thursday.
>
> To business, I'm going to copy this exchange to Dave because—as part of his admirable efforts to keep the peace between us—he didn't want me to address these matters prior to the indictments. But yours is a reasonable question that deserves a prompt answer.
>
> As agreed, nobody, including Deborah, is doing anything until the indictments. Like the rest of us, she has been and continues to be "on hold," so we are certainly not wasting any of her time. As I've said before, I see no reason for us to concern Deborah with your preliminary dealings about this issue with your attorneys.
>
> Significantly, I remember that you told me on May 24 that one of your lawyers had left the door open for a possible compromise. Also, without being specific, you mentioned Dave's "idea for us" in your May 25 email to me, which you appeared to believe could help solve our problem. (By the way, I still don't know what Dave's idea is. He has asked me to allow him to keep it "in reserve," and I've agreed.)
>
> To be sure, I have always made the importance of your lawyers and their role in your civil case very clear to Deborah from the outset. She is also well aware that I have not yet given her the manuscript out of respect for your attorneys and your legal position. However, I think that it would be truly unfair to start jerking Deborah around over the minutia of a complicated situation that we are trying to work out. When this scenario stabilizes, she will be among the first to know the result.

Nevertheless, I still have full faith and confidence that everyone—including Dave, Deborah, your lawyers, you, and me— will be on the same page when the indictments are finally returned.

As it turned out, Anita really was on the warpath.

In her response to my conciliatory message, Anita fired back:

I have been trying to keep you in the information loop out of respect, but obviously I have made an egregious error by doing so. *I think it's best that we no longer talk.* I understand clearly what you are doing here and it is for legal reasons. You clearly reminded me yesterday that we have a signed contract. Hence, you made your intentions known. *Anything more you have to say, you can speak to Dave and he can relay. I really have nothing more to say to you.*" [Emphasis added)

———•———

In the aftermath of Anita having ended our direct communications, Dave called and explained his idea to me, which I immediately believed was the best solution to this now-ludicrous situation. He did warn me from the outset that Anita had already rejected his plan, but she did so while she was very angry. I told Dave that he should try to sell the idea to her again at a later date.

Dave's idea was simple: Anita would allow me to proceed with the sale of the book after the indictments. In return, she could retain her sixty-percent cut of the royalties, as well as her editorial control over the manuscript. Meantime, she would tell her attorneys to stand down and allow the collaboration contract to define our professional relationship.

Knowing that I could live with that, I also considered placing an officially registered U.S. copyright on the manuscript—in compliance with the terms of my signed agreement with Anita. But I decided to hold off at least until the statute of limitations in the criminal case had passed on June 20.

During the late afternoon of June 17, while I was checking the website of the Los Angeles County District Attorney's Office, I saw that county prosecutors had indicted Pellicano and Proctor for their roles in the June 20, 2002, attack on Anita—just before the statute of limitations expired. However, they had not indicted anyone else.

I sent a link to the DA's press release to Dave at 5:00 P.M.

Two hours later, Anita sent a note to Dave and me, attaching the initial news story by the *Los Angeles Times*, which had not reported anything that was not already widely known.

In response, I sent a note to both Anita and Robb, saying: "Well, this is the moment we've been waiting for. Are you prepared to move forward with our book project or not?

"Of course, I am hoping that you are."

Not waiting for Anita to reply, I sent a message to our agent, Deborah, saying:

> There is good news and bad news.
> The good news is that the District Attorney's Office in Los Angeles County today indicted Pellicano and Proctor for their June 2002 attack on Anita—just as the statute of limitations were about to expire. . . .
> The bad news is that the crooked cop, the corrupt phone-company employee, and Mister Big were not indicted—although I am assuming that the anticipated indictments by the U.S. Attorney's Office will clarify the roles of these three guys.
> Also, Anita's attorneys, who are handling her civil case, are apparently—and suddenly—concerned about the extent of the revelations in our manuscript. Anita and I are at odds about this, but there are efforts to bring about a lasting peace.

Hearing nothing from Anita, I sent the following letter to her the next morning, which I copied to Dave:

> I'm surprised that I haven't received a response to my return message to you last night. As you know, time is of the essence now that the trigger has been pulled.
> Once again, I am really pleased that the District Attorney indicted Anthony Pellicano and Alexander Proctor for their terrible attack on you. As you clearly remember, we had mutually agreed that the timing of the indictments would initiate efforts to sell our book—much of which, with your guidance and cooperation, I have already written on spec during my association with you over the past two years. (In your corrected version of the draft manuscript on

April 20, you wrote, among other things, "I think this really moves well so far. Pretty good job, Dan!")

As I have repeatedly stated, verbally and in writing, I am prepared to move forward with our project and to make whatever changes are still necessary in the manuscript. Nevertheless, in written communications to me on May 25 and again on June 11, you declared that our book project has been postponed indefinitely or is "on hold." You explained that one of your attorneys was concerned that the manuscript might give too much information to the defendants in your civil suit. You added that your decision is "non-negotiable," even though you had already told me that your attorney had indicated that careful editing could solve the problem.

I do not know exactly what is going on. I do not know exactly what you told your attorneys—whom you were . . . so critical of and wanted to fire just a few months ago—about our project. And I am completely baffled as to why they were so shocked by the contents of our manuscript if, as you have always represented to me, they were fully aware of our project from the moment you retained them. In addition, I do not understand why my mere mention of the fact that you and I have a signed collaboration contract would suddenly provoke you to write on June 12, "I think it's best that we no longer talk. . . . I really have nothing more to say to you."

Regardless, under the terms of our signed collaboration contract, you have no unilateral right to stop, to postpone, or to place our book project on hold.

I would like to begin pitching our book proposal as early as Monday, June 20. Any significant delay could harm the economic value of this project for both of us. Obviously, I would like you on board with this. I want to finish what I've started and then be done with this project.

If I haven't received your written statement to the contrary by June 19 at 6:00 P.M., your time, I will assume that you have agreed to comply with our contract, and that I may proceed with the sale of our book with your full cooperation. (Emphasis added)

Predictably, Anita returned to her attack mode, refusing to deny that she was in possible breach of our contract, instead lashing out with:

I have my brother and my parents in town for Father's Day. I have to meet with the prosecutors next week. I have not spoken to my lawyers since this has been filed. I find your threatening emails and manner towards me thoroughly reprehensible. Let me remind you how unprofessional you have been throughout this entire matter, starting with you trying to hit on me repeatedly for months and continuing with you writing things in the manuscript that were completely false and fabricated. You have also not made changes or corrections that I ordered. I have told you for over a year and a half to go do something else. The bottom line is this is my life and you may not go forward under any circumstances without my written consent.

Without waiting for my reply, Anita immediately came back with a second message: "I have been out of town until last night enjoying my family. How dare you start bullying me again."

And then she wrote a third: "You have also dragged my parents into this in an obscene and manipulative way. You should be ashamed of yourself . . . as I am ashamed for you."

Seeing that Anita had taken off the gloves with these new false charges, I wrote a message to Dave Robb, saying:

> You have been heroic in your efforts. Short of a performing a miracle, there is nothing more you can do now.
> You and I have done everything we can to salvage this project. Anita has done everything she can to sabotage it.
> Just let this play out.

Remarkably, Dave refused to stay out of this renewed fray, still hoping he could keep the deal together. He called, and we spoke for nearly an hour. I described the substance of our conversation in a message to myself: "Dave . . . called me, and he did something he has never done before. He asked me to trust him completely and without question. He has asked me not to do anything—not to sell the book and even not to copyright the book. Nothing. He said his plan could take months, but he is asking for my patience. . . .

"So I have no choice. I must back off and see what happens."

On June 19, I responded to Dave, saying:

> From the outset, let me say that I will remain faithful to our understanding of yesterday afternoon—even though I can't think of anyone else I'd do this for. Anita's behavior has been and continues to be despicable. She deserves a concerted legal challenge for

what she has done. But you are my brother, one of my most trusted friends, and I will do anything for you. . . .

Although you will not allow me to respond directly to Anita for her latest barrage of false charges yesterday, [I want] to give you my defense in writing. Keeping this explanation short, let me say that in response to the contents of her emails yesterday:

> * I have operated under the terms of our contract. Anita has not. Thus, Anita is the one who has been unprofessional.

> * I have attempted to salvage and move forward with our book project. Anita has unilaterally tried to sabotage the project, using her attorneys as a blackjack. Thus, Anita is the one trying to bully me.

> * With regard to Anita's bogus but never-ending complaints about the manuscript, there is a very simple story about what happened. I can now trace Anita's ham-fisted attempts to sabotage our book project to her April 21 conversation with superagent Joni Evans, senior vice president of the William Morris Agency, whom she boasted had called and wanted to represent her on her own first-person book. After that date, Anita treated the agent we had already selected and [me] with undeserved disdain and disrespect.

> * In addition, Anita believed that I had destroyed the June 18, 2004, version of the draft manuscript, which included her handwritten corrections. She used this opportunity—beginning after her conversation with superagent Joni Evans of the William Morris Agency on April 21—to complain about the intentional mistakes and omissions I had allegedly made in the April 11, 2005, draft manuscript. However, she was understandably upset when I told her that I had found the June 2004 manuscript. Why? Because it proved that most of her complaints were the only fabrications and lies that actually existed [in] this situation. If you want my point-by-point defense, I will give it to you. In short, I can defend everything that I did.

> * As promised, I did make all of the changes she asked me to make up to page 280. In fact, she refused to forward those pages to her attorneys until I did so. (As you might recall, I had to send her a single addition to page 230 on May 11 before she would approve the manuscript, which she had received earlier that day. Then, she gave it to her lawyers.)

> * I have surely never threatened Anita. However, she is threatening me by denying me my contractual right to profit from our book project and my two years of work.

* With regard to her blatant personal attack on me, I flatly deny ever acting improperly or inappropriately towards her. I have always been a gentleman, and I have always shown her nothing but respect. Would I risk my friendship with you by acting in any other manner? Of course, I wouldn't.

* With regard to Anita's ridiculous allegation that I tried to manipulate her parents, the story is simple. Anita told me that they were in a nearby Virginia suburb. I called them and invited them to lunch. Because they love George Bush, I took them to his family's favorite restaurant, the Peking Gourmet Inn. Can you imagine me saying anything but wonderful things about their daughter while we were having lunch? If you ever want to read the email exchanges over this particular Anita fantasy, I'll be happy to give them to you.

* Finally, I will take responsibility for my own decisions, but Anita told me on nearly a month-to-month basis that the indictments were imminent. This certainly goes back to last September when she insisted that the trigger would be pulled by the U.S. Attorney's office in October. Based on that information, I gave up a $7,500 a month consultancy, so that I could concentrate on writing the manuscript. When no indictments were handed up in October, she then claimed that they would be announced in December, then January, February, and March. In April, Anita received information that the District Attorney's office was going to indict five people for their roles in the attack on Anita. As you know, the DA's office filed two indictments on Friday, just as the statute of limitations [was] running out.

Dave, I am so tired of this. But I really appreciate your willingness to remain in this fray—even after I gave you a graceful means of exit in my note to you yesterday morning.

Dave responded: "If this has a chance of working out, and I still believe it does, I firmly believe that this is the only way to go. I have your best interests at heart."

He signed the email, "Your brother—Dave Robb."

I told Dave over the phone that the only way I would continue to work on this project was if he came on board and became our third partner. With Anita already approving as much as two-thirds of the manuscript, I told Dave that I would give him an equal split for just working with her to finish the final third of the book.

In other words, I offered Dave the same terms that Anita and I had given to John Connolly, which reduced my split from forty to twenty-five percent.

Now burned out from this horrific experience, I wanted no further contact with Anita Busch.

Simultaneously, with my two-year-plus deal in ruins, Dave extended my credit. As of June 22, I owed him $11,000.

Also that week, columnist Nikki Finke, whom Anita once described to me as "completely insane," published a remarkably cogent story in *LA Weekly*, "Requiem for Anita Busch," which stated, in part:

> She is gone and, worse, she is near-forgotten, an inconspicuous end to an esteemed career. . . .
>
> Busch also made enemies of almost every reporter who tried to write about her during this time by threatening libel suits and demanding top-to-bottom corrections. Then again, the high-strung journalist tended to come undone whenever anyone turned the tables and wrote about her. She was known as a wonderful friend to have, and a terrible foe; the only problem was that, somewhere during her career, the line blurred and she became increasingly combative. . . .
>
> Again and again, the rap on Anita was that she didn't play well with others, and complaints about her behavior from inside and outside the media mounted. A lot of this was just Anita being, well, Anita.[172]

PART THREE:
Bargaining

22. *"An interesting situation has developed"*

On Tuesday, July 12, 2005, I had dinner with a good friend, author Gus Russo, at Krupin's, the popular delicatessen in northwest Washington. During our conversation, Gus mentioned that he had been approached by screenwriter John Leekley, a close friend of Jules Nasso.

Leekley had told Gus that Nasso, who had just been released from prison, was looking for someone to write his memoir with his full cooperation. Because Nasso trusted Leekley and Leekley trusted Russo, Nasso wanted Gus, a respected crime reporter, to write his book.

Having heard about my book project with Anita from another author, and then hearing from me that it had just gone south, Gus asked if I was interested.

"Jesus," I asked, "what does Nasso want?"

Gus replied that he did not know for sure, adding that he was supposed to speak with him the following week.

Obviously fascinated, I advised Gus not to sign anything with or accept any money from Nasso. I did not say anything about Anita's suspicions that Nasso could have been behind the June 20, 2002, threat against her—with or without the participation of our principal suspect, Michael Ovitz.

Gus specialized in organized-crime investigations and had already published three true-crime books. I believed that his most important work would be his upcoming fourth book, *Supermob,* a groundbreaking biography of Hollywood attorney Sidney Korshak, the link between the legitimate business world and organized crime. In my 1986 book, *Dark Victory*, Korshak was one of its three principal characters, along with President Ronald Reagan and Lew Wasserman, the chairman of MCA.

While Gus was doing his research, I had tried to be very helpful to him, admiring the fact that he was doing something that no other crime writer had the tenacity to accomplish—to write an entire book about Sid Korshak. I had written a blurb for this book which Gus featured on the back cover:

> Nearly all of us who have written about the underworld's penetration of legitimate institutions have given considerable thought to authoring a book about Sidney Korshak. However, it took the courageous Gus Russo, with his groundbreaking research and his fabulous rock 'n' roll writing style, to accomplish that landmark feat. Simply speaking, *Supermob* is a grand-slam home run.[173]

A sort of Renaissance man, Gus, tall with a graying beard, was also an accomplished guitarist, as well as an ace tennis player. During his long career in music, sports, and journalism, he had earned a reputation as a hard worker, an honest man, and a nice guy.

On July 15, a month after our falling out, I received a package in the mail from Anita, which contained three videotapes: 1) a commencement address I had delivered to a school in 1997; 2) a television show on the murder of Robert Kennedy in which I was featured; and 3) the feature film, *The Conversation*, which I had given her as a present. She enclosed a note that simply said, "Thanks for letting me see these."

This was the first communication of any kind I had from Anita since June 18. Seeing no need to reply, I did not.

On Monday, July 18, Gus called, saying that he had spoken to Nasso on Saturday at his home in Staten Island. He shared his notes with me in which Nasso had told him:

> What I'm going to give you is backed up by witnesses and hard documents. I will not waste your time. I will not send you chasing rabbits. I want someone who is honest and let it all out. I still have

the lawsuit and all the depositions—and all on film. When you see them it will all be black and white. I'll not only give you the proof, but also first, second and third party witnesses—people who worked for us, with us.

And you want to know something, the little negatives about me—I'm fine with that."

When I asked Gus what kind of a deal Nasso was offering, he replied that Nasso wanted nothing—no collaboration contract, no money, no credit, and no editorial control. He felt that he had been treated totally unfairly and was completely misunderstood. He simply wanted an open-minded writer to sit down with him, go through all of his files, and "let the chips fall where they may." Also, Nasso would be available to answer any and all questions.

Because he did not know very much about the Pellicano case, Gus offered Nasso's story to me.

Catching my breath, I was incredulous. I told Gus that he would hate himself down the road if he just *gave* me the project. Adding that the Pellicano wiretapping scandal was going to be huge if and when the indictments were ever handed up, I suggested that we consider working on the project together.

Gus asked me when I wanted to speak with Nasso.

Before taking another step, I asked for Gus's permission to speak with Dave Robb, whom Anita had designated as my intermediary to her, about Gus's offer.

I recalled Anita's June 12, 2005, email to me saying: *"Anything more you have to say, you can speak to Dave and he can relay. I really have nothing more to say to you."* Recognizing potential complications, I decided that it would be best to be completely honest with everyone—from Anita via Dave Robb, to Gus, and even to Nasso.

Before speaking with Dave, I discussed the situation with a close friend who had warned me that Dave would tell Anita, who would, no doubt, interpret my good-faith notification as an act of intimidation: In other words, "Either let me publish my book about you or else. . . ."

I replied that Anita who had already turned minor skirmishes into major firestorms had become predictable.

I asked Gus for time, and he gave it to me, adding that Nasso did not expect an answer until the following week. Wanting this in writing, I started to draft an explanation for Dave.

On July 23, Dave called just to say hello. I took this opportunity to tell him the news about Nasso. In fact, I read him the draft email I had prepared for him, which stated:

> An interesting situation has developed—and fallen into my lap. A reporter/friend has been approached by Julius Nasso, who has offered him a "warehouse of information" with regard to the Mafia in Hollywood, as well as his relationships with Ovitz and Seagal—and what he knows about Pellicano and the attack on Anita. He has offered my reporter/friend this information unconditionally—and has agreed to cooperate fully.
>
> In other words, Nasso doesn't want any editorial control. He doesn't want any money or any kind of written/verbal contract. He just wants a book written about his life and times and is willing to allow the chips to fall where they may. Nasso, through the endorsement of a trusted friend of his, rightly has complete confidence in my reporter/friend's abilities. Nasso is even unconcerned about the effect that such a book might have on his continuing civil litigation with Seagal. He just wants this book done, accurately and quickly. (Nasso has offered my reporter/friend money for expenses. My reporter/friend, [preserving] his independence, has refused, saying that he will not accept any money from Nasso for any reason.)
>
> Remarkably, my reporter/friend has invited me to co-author the book with him. He now knows that I had been writing a book with Anita—and that the project is currently on hold. He doesn't know any of our secrets, like Ovitz's role in the attack. Of course, he is willing to agree that we will share anything we obtain about Anita's situation with her. Of course, both of us will do anything necessary to protect Anita from further harm. . . .
>
> I can do this book without violating my contract with Anita and while preserving my interest in our book, *Woman at Risk*. (And, of course, I still want you to be my partner on the Anita project.)
>
> My reporter/friend is going to do the Nasso book with or without me. Once again, if I am his co-author, I will have access to everything. Anita and our book will benefit. Despite my ongoing problems with Anita, I ultimately remain loyal to her and our book project. And, if there is any doubt about that, you already know that I am totally and completely loyal to you. As always, if I were to

> double-cross Anita, I would be double-crossing you, as well. And, as
> you already know, I would never ever do that.

During our phone conversation, Dave said that he wished I had
not told him about this new development, adding that my book with
Anita would never come out after she learned about this.

I repeated that I wanted him to join our team and finish the final
third of the manuscript. In other words, I now wanted to do *both*
books.

The following day, July 24, I emailed Dave the exact same
statement I had read to him, adding:

> I gave you this information in confidence. I leave it to you
> whether to tell Anita—who, as usual will place some nefarious spin
> on what's happening.
>
> My advice? I have trusted you to work out the problems that
> Anita has invented over our book. Now, trust me to work out the
> advantages we can gain as a result of the situation that has been given
> to me.

When I called Dave to discuss the situation further, he replied
that he would prefer that we agree that our conversations about this
subject had never happened. He knew nothing and did not want
to know anything further. He even said it like Sergeant Schultz
of the old television show, *Hogan's Heroes*, "I know NOTH-ing,
NOTH-ing!"

Refusing to agree to that and adding that, through him, Anita
had now been notified, I told Dave that the only reason that I was
not already taking legal action against Anita was because of my
continued loyalty to him.

But—regardless of what would happen to the Anita project in
the future—by doing the Nasso book, I would not be throwing away
two years of my professional life. The Nasso project would give me
something to show for all that time and work.

After my conversation with Dave, I called Gus. Trying to keep
my full-disclosure effort in full swing, I suggested to Gus that he
arrange a three-way conversation with Nasso during which time Gus
would introduce me. At that time, I would reveal to Nasso that Anita
and I had a now-collapsed book project.

On July 25, Gus called and told me that he had identified me, by name, as his co-author to Nasso who had never heard of me. Thus, it seemed unlikely that he had any knowledge of my book project with Anita.

My immediate concern was John Connolly whom I then believed in all likelihood had a cozy relationship with Nasso's legal team. I feared that he would find out about my involvement in this project and then try to sabotage me with Nasso, as well as with Anita, to whom he would, no doubt, gleefully report this news if Dave Robb had not already done so.

Also that day, Gus told me that screenwriter John Leekley had called him, saying that a producer-friend in Hollywood wanted to option the Nasso book immediately upon its sale to a book publisher.

On July 26, Jules Nasso and I spoke for the first time during a conference call that Gus had arranged. I immediately told Jules that Anita Busch and I had worked on a book about her situation, but that she had quit the project.

In short, Jules had no problem with my connection to Anita, even after I made it clear that I would never betray any of her secrets.

However, I did ask Jules to keep my association with Anita quiet, adding that I also wanted him to avoid mentioning my role to John Connolly. To my surprise, Jules said he could not stand Connolly, who, a year earlier, had informed him that Michael Ovitz was actually behind the attack against Anita. Further, Jules alleged that Connolly had also told Michael Eisner, the chairman of Disney and Ron Meyer, the head of Universal Studios (formerly MCA), that Ovitz was behind the Pellicano attack on Anita.

I nearly dropped the phone when I heard that shocking piece of information. But, after thinking for a moment, I realized, "Of course, John would tell him and anyone else about Ovitz. What was there to stop him?"

Indeed, I had already decided not to discuss anything with Nasso that I had learned exclusively from Anita. But now that I knew that Connolly had already revealed the big news about Ovitz, I felt free to discuss that particular subject with Gus immediately, as well as with Nasso down the road.

Because Anita still suspected that Nasso might have played a role in the threat against her, I really wanted to question him very thoroughly about his relationship with Ovitz, as well as with Steven Seagal and, most of all, with Anthony Pellicano. If I determined that Jules was involved in the June 2002 attack against Anita, I would do everything I could to jam him up legally.

As crazy as it sounds, I still remained very loyal to Anita, even though we were at war.

Jules invited Gus and me to his home on Staten Island on Thursday, August 4, saying that we could stay as long as we wanted to stay, see whatever we wanted to see, and ask whatever we wanted to ask.

After the conference call, Gus and I agreed to write the Nasso book together, saying that we would equally split all royalties and share both the byline and the copyright.

23. *"Stay away from my partner!"*

During the early morning of August 4, 2005, I drove to Baltimore and picked up Gus Russo. Together, we drove three hours-plus to Staten Island for the first of our two days of interviews with Jules Nasso. We checked into our rooms at the local Hilton and then went to a nearby diner for breakfast.

At 10:00 A.M., the time of our scheduled appointment, we arrived at Nasso's home which was a beautifully designed, gated beachfront estate he had named *Villa Terranova*. With large rooms, high ceilings, and ornate artwork, as well as celebrity photographs on the walls, an enormous collection of model boats, and large indoor and outdoor bars, the place was simply fabulous.

When we met and shook hands with Nasso, I gave him a Roman Catholic scapular, a gift from the two of us. According to the faith, *"Our Lady [of Mount Carmel] gave her Scapular as a sign of salvation, a protection in danger, and a pledge of peace."* The inscription on the small square of soft brown cloth read: *"Whosoever dies clothed in this Scapular shall never suffer the fires of Hell."*

Although Nasso, whom I assumed was a Roman Catholic, appeared moved by this gesture of good faith, I still believed everything Anita had told me about him. Therefore, I really did not expect to like this guy. In fact, I did not want to like him at all.

But, from the outset, it was impossible not to like and even respect Nasso. With his small frame and friendly demeanor, he reminded me of an Italian Dudley Moore. Five-feet-six, he had brown eyes and just enough gray in his brown hair to make him appear distinguished. Although he could get extremely intense when discussing his recent legal predicament, he also had a wonderful sense of humor. He was a funny guy.

Still, along with figuring out how Nasso's relationship with Steven Seagal affected the Pellicano wiretapping caper, Gus and I were determined to document Nasso's ties to the Mafia, assuming, of course, that they did exist. After all, his sister-in-law, the wife of his youngest brother, Frank, was the daughter of Johnny Gambino, the notorious boss of the southern Gambino crime family in Cherry Hill, New Jersey. And Nasso's maternal grandfather's name was Genovese—as in New York's Vito Genovese crime family—although we were not clear whether there was a family connection. Genovese is a common name.

When asked, Jules explained that his grandfather, a police official in Calabria, grew up as an orphan. He never knew his real name. His foster parents gave him the name *Genovese* because his orphanage was in Genoa.

Also, the Nassos on his father's side, just two generations earlier, were actually the *Nassaus*, a family of Sephardic Jews. And Nasso's father, Francesco, Jr. had spent the final months of World War II in a Nazi concentration camp.

Gus and I learned of Nasso's bloodline within the first ten minutes of our taped interview, begging the question, "How could Jules Nasso, with his orphaned grandfather on one side and Jewish heritage on the other, wind up as a made-member of the Mafia's Gambino crime family which consisted only of those with provable Italian-Sicilian bloodlines?"

From the outset, this information knocked us off track. And we now needed to discover who the real Jules Nasso was.

Born in 1952, Julius R. "Jules" Nasso had come to the United States with his parents who had lived in Terranova, Italy. The family settled in Bensonhurst where his father worked as a carpenter and his mother remained home with Jules and his two brothers. After the elder Nasso was badly injured in a serious accident at a construction site, Jules, still in his early teens, went to work in a local drug store, near the Brooklyn Piers.

Jules explained that, as fate would have it, he became a pharmacist, earned his doctorate, and bought that same drug store, among many others. By age thirty, he had become a multimillionaire and had married his college sweetheart.

His business brought him to the West Coast where he stayed with Jimmy and Scott Baio, two kids from the old neighborhood who had come to Hollywood and become television stars. Through them, he met other actors, including Danny DeVito, Tony Danza, Penny Marshall, and Robin Williams, among many others.

Back in Brooklyn, even though he was a successful businessman, he applied for and received a $35-a-day job, working as a translator for Sergio Leone, the Italian director who was working on *Once Upon a Time in America* which would become a classic gangster film.

Continuing with his story, Jules told Gus and me that in 1987, while attending a party in Beverly Hills, he met an Aikido martial-arts expert and aspiring actor, Steven Seagal, and his pregnant girlfriend, Kelly LeBrock, who was already a successful model and actress. At the time, Seagal was trying to get his first film, *Above the Law*, produced.

The two men immediately hit it off, especially after Seagal learned of Jules's connection to Sergio Leone, Seagal's favorite director.

Jules introduced Seagal to Steven Ross, the chairman of Warner Communications, whom Jules knew from his New York businesses. Ross introduced Seagal to Terry Semel, the president of Warner Brothers, who set up a demonstration for Seagal's Aikido talents. Jules and Semel attended the demonstration, along with several other executives at Warner. Also present was super-agent Michael Ovitz of CAA, whom Seagal had met through actor James Coburn, a student of Seagal's.

Seagal charmed and delighted the small crowd of Hollywood heavyweights, especially Ovitz and Semel. Soon after, Seagal received a deal to produce and distribute *Above the Law* in which he played a tough and honest cop with a bad attitude.

Jules told Gus and me that, on the basis of the success of that film, Warner financed a second Seagal film, *Hard to Kill*. That film made even more money than the first.

After the completion of *Hard to Kill*, Seagal and Jules created their own company, Seagal-Nasso Productions. Seagal purchased the home next door to Jules's estate on Staten Island for his visits to New York.

Now best friends, Seagal and Jules were inseparable. Jules was the best man at Seagal and Kelly LeBrock's wedding, and he served as godfather to two of the Seagals' three children.

Jules explained that, because of a complicated situation in the midst of a writers' strike in Hollywood, Seagal-Nasso Productions made the film, *Marked for Death*, with Twentieth Century Fox. But for their next film, *Out for Justice*, they returned to Warner Brothers.

Seagal's fifth film, *Under Siege*, was the biggest money-maker of all. After that, Jules declared that he and Steven Seagal were on top of the world.

But Jules added that after the release of their next film, *On Deadly Ground*, things began to change after Kelly LeBrock discovered her husband's affair with the family's babysitter. LeBrock had given the task of telling Seagal that she was divorcing him to Jules.

Although a misbehaving cad, Seagal felt crushed by the disintegration of his family, according to Jules.

Still, Seagal-Nasso Productions moved forward with their next film, *Under Siege 2*. But, after that film, they lost their agent, Michael Ovitz, who had assured them that he was not leaving his talent agency, CAA. Contrary to that promise, he wound up as the president of Disney, serving under his old friend, Michael Eisner, Disney's board chairman.

Nasso explained, "Nobody knew anything. There were rumors all over the place that he was leaving CAA. Throughout that whole process, I ran into him twice. Each time, Ovitz told me, 'Don't worry about it. Everything is going to be fine.' That last night we saw him, while we were at the premier of *Under Siege 2* at the Mann Chinese Theater on Hollywood Boulevard, we asked Ovitz if he was leaving CAA, and he, once again, said, 'No.'"

According to Nasso, Seagal, in particular, was absolutely furious when Ovitz left CAA on Monday, August 14, 1995. Nasso said that he told him, "Go find me an agent."

After a meeting with International Creative Management Chairman Jeff Berg and then-Vice Chairman Jim Wiatt at Seagal's home on Mandeville Canyon Road in Brentwood, Nasso selected their agency to represent Seagal.[174] Bill Block, who headed ICM's West Coast office, replaced Ovitz.

Asked what he said to Ovitz, Nasso told Gus and me, "I haven't seen or heard from Ovitz—not since that day in 1995 at the premier of *Under Siege 2*."[175]

In view of Anita Busch's Ovitz-Nasso conspiracy theory—that Nasso and Ovitz had conspired together to attack her via Pellicano—that information was pretty shocking to me.

In the midst of all of the Seagal-Nasso successes, according to Jules, Seagal began dealing with a fringe Buddhist cult which had proclaimed the actor as the reincarnation of a revered Tibetan lama. And his new religion had begun to affect his work. Seagal-Nasso's subsequent film, *Glimmer Man*, was changed during production to accommodate Seagal's personal spiritual beliefs.

Jules told us that Warner expressed deep concern about Seagal's religious conversion, which had resulted in his subsequent action film, *Fire Down Below*, having very little action. Soon after, Seagal-Nasso's next film, *The Patriot*, went independent and did very poorly at the box office.

Jules told Gus and me that, now needing to raise money from private investors, Seagal-Nasso tried to entice foreign-rights investors with a four-film package. However, after these deals were made, Seagal allegedly reneged, forcing Jules to repay millions of dollars to their investors.

Even though Jules was furious with Seagal, he still loaned the actor $500,000 to pay off a back-tax debt to the IRS. And because Seagal supposedly needed money, Nasso bought the house Seagal owned next to his, merging the two properties to expand his already huge estate.

Jules continued, telling us that although Seagal's debt to Jules was growing, Seagal unilaterally tried to bring a new partner into Seagal-Nasso Productions. His name was Danny Provenzano, an alleged Mafia figure in New Jersey and the grandnephew of the infamous labor racketeer Anthony Provenzano.[176] "Tony Pro" had been widely credited with engineering the 1975 murder of ex-Teamsters boss Jimmy Hoffa.

Jules met the younger Provenzano but did not like or trust him.

Consequently, Seagal told Jules that he was severing both his personal and professional relationship with Jules. To ensure a smooth breakup, Seagal did say that he was willing to accept Jules's younger brother, Vincent, as their intermediary.

Although Jules had gone on with his own career, making several successful films, including the highly praised movie, *Narc*, which he co-produced with actor Tom Cruise, Provenzano, Seagal's new partner, allegedly felt threatened.

According to Jules, during his next three face-to-face encounters with Provenzano, the alleged New Jersey mobster became physical, roughing him up and threatening his life.

Jules was terrified, especially after receiving information that Seagal had made a quiet trip to New Jersey—where he met with Provenzano and John "Sonny" Franzese, an aging but still notorious capo with the Joseph Colombo crime family in Brooklyn.

On September 13, 2000, Jules, going public with his acceptance of the break-up, bought an ad in *Daily Variety*, announcing the end of his partnership with Seagal.

Also, Jules went to see a detective with the New York Police Department who worked as Seagal's bodyguard when the actor was in New York. Responding to Nasso's concerns about Danny Provenzano, the police detective advised Jules to find a trusted middleman, besides his own brother, to deal with Seagal.

The intermediary Jules chose was Anthony "Sonny" Ciccone, a man whom Jules had known for years as a top official with the longshoremen's union. Ciccone was also a long-time customer at his waterfront drug store. Jules knew that Seagal had met Ciccone during the shooting of *Out for Justice*, and the two men immediately became friends. According to Jules, Ciccone had become a frequent visitor to Seagal's home in California.

Jules insisted to Gus and me that the principal reason for his talks with Ciccone was to get Seagal to order his attack dog, Danny Provenzano, to back off.

According to Jules, Seagal agreed to allow Ciccone to serve in this limited role, as long as Jules's younger brother, Vincent, remained as the go-between for Seagal and Jules who were still trying to settle their dispute over their company's finances.

Jules explained that the first meeting between Jules and Seagal, mediated by Ciccone and attended by Vincent, took place in Toronto in October—while Seagal was shooting *Exit Wounds*, his first film without Jules since they created their partnership.

Their second meeting was in January 2001 at Gage & Tollner, a venerable steakhouse in Brooklyn. Their third meeting was on February 2 at Brioso, Ciccone's own Brooklyn restaurant, which was also the location of the fourth meeting later that month.

In June, Jules called in the $500,000 loan he had made to Seagal for his back-tax debt. Seagal asked Jules to include the loan as part of a complicated payout plan within Seagal-Nasso Productions.

Jules refused.

Then, Jules pressed another issue. Seagal had possession of a handgun registered in Jules's name. Fearing that someone could commit a crime with that same gun and use it to frame Jules, Nasso asked for its return. When Seagal balked, Jules filed a report with the police department. During the follow-up investigation, a police detective called Seagal and questioned him about the gun.

According to Jules, that action caused a heated argument during a July 5, 2001, telephone call between Jules and Seagal which concluded when Nasso angrily hung up on him.

As of our interview with Nasso in August 2005, that was last time Nasso and Seagal had spoken to each other.

24. *"Levin rejected Mr. Patterson's demand for money"*

On March 20, 2002, Jules Nasso sued Seagal in a $60 million breach-of-contract litigation, revolving around Seagal's alleged default on his movie deals with Jules. Nasso noted in his complaint that during his twelve-year professional relationship with Seagal, he had never received more than union scale for any of their films. In all, he had made only $675,000, an average of a little over $56,000 annually.[177]

Also, Nasso had to repay investors $2.4 million for the four-movie package in which Seagal allegedly refused to participate. Nasso conservatively estimated that they could have earned between $21 million and $39 million in profits had Seagal fulfilled his alleged obligations to their production company.

On April 3, shortly after Nasso filed his lawsuit, Seagal had the first of his four secret meetings with the FBI. Loeb & Loeb, the law firm that already represented Seagal-Nasso Productions, as well as both Seagal and Nasso, individually, represented Seagal during these discussions—in which he accused Nasso of criminal behavior.[178]

Nasso alleged to Gus and me that he believed that Seagal had decided to turn to the federal government and use his connections in the law-enforcement community because of his lack of a legitimate defense against Jules's legal assault.

The following month, May 9, Seagal secretly testified before a federal grand jury in Brooklyn that was hearing evidence about corruption on the waterfront by members of the Gambino crime family. Much of the evidence was based on the government's court-authorized electronic surveillance, including that against reputed labor racketeer Sonny Ciccone and his trusted associate, Primo Cassarino. Once again, although not permitted in the grand-jury room during the prosecutor's questioning of Seagal, Loeb & Loeb represented the actor during this process, too.

In the first substantive question, Assistant U.S. Attorney Andrew Genser asked Seagal, "Sir, do you know an individual named Jules Nasso?"[179]

After Seagal took the Fifth Amendment, Genser, with the approval of the U.S. Department of Justice, provided Seagal with statutory immunity and directed him to answer his questions. Of course, that meant that Seagal could not be charged for anything he said, as long as he told the truth. If he lied, he could be charged with perjury, among other crimes.

On May 11, unsourced gossip reached Nasso, indicating that Seagal was "going to get me arrested," according to Jules.

Concerned with these rumors and looking for answers, Nasso immediately dispatched his trusted private investigators, former DEA and Customs agent William McMullan, who had worked for Universal Marine Medical Supply since 1995, and Tom Vinton, a twenty-seven-year veteran of the FBI who specialized in organized-crime investigations.

In the midst of their probe, McMullan and Vinton discovered Seagal's friendship with Robert Iden, the special agent-in-charge of the FBI's field office in Los Angeles. As a favor to Iden, Seagal was the guest speaker at a dinner on May 23, 2002, to honor FBI personnel who were killed in the line of duty.

In addition, law-enforcement officials told McMullan and Vinton that Jules Nasso was in big trouble. When Nasso's legal team offered to deliver their client to provide his side of the story in late May, federal prosecutors allegedly refused to take the time to hear it.

And that was when Anita Busch entered the picture after joining the *Los Angeles Times* on June 3, just hours before she received the assignment to report on the activities of Nasso and Seagal.

On June 4, federal agents arrested Nasso just sixty-five days after he filed his $60-million lawsuit against Seagal, as part of the 68-count RICO case against members of the Gambino crime family.

Arresting officers scaled Nasso's tall fence and, with guns drawn, entered his home. They stormed into his bedroom where he was sleeping and asked for his guns and licenses. Then, they handcuffed him and quickly took him into custody.

While sitting in a cage at the Waterfront Commission in downtown Brooklyn with Peter Gotti and other actual members of the Gambino crime family—who probably wondered who the hell he was—Nasso saw Primo Cassarino led into another cage, followed by Sonny Ciccone, and Jules's brother, Vincent. When Jules saw them together, he started to suspect that all of this had something to do with Seagal.

At the arraignment, the judge addressed the fifteen other defendants who were charged with the most counts. Jules, who faced two counts of extortion, and Vincent, who was charged with three counts, were the last to be arraigned. They were each held on a $1.5 million bond.

Jules's attorney for the arraignment was Robert Hantman, Nasso's civil attorney, even though Jack Litman, a criminal attorney, would later handle Jules's case.

Out on bail, Jules was released that afternoon and returned to his home.

Nasso told Gus and me, his voice rising, "It was all bullshit. I knew something was going to happen with Seagal. But I didn't think that, in my wildest dreams, I was going to be implicated with organized crime."

What really stung his pride, he said, was that his scruffy mug shot had appeared in the *Staten Island Advance* the following morning where his family, friends, neighbors, and business associates could see it.

———

During my questioning, Nasso said that he did receive requests for interviews from Paul Lieberman of the *Los Angeles Times*. Jules insisted, "Yes, I spoke with Paul. But I had no idea that he was working with a partner. And I certainly had no idea that his partner was Anita Busch whom I had never heard of before."

The threat against Anita occurred on June 20, 2002—after which time she dropped the Seagal-Nasso story and went into hiding for several weeks, immediately believing that Nasso and Seagal were behind the vandalism on her car.

On or about July 11, the same day that the *New York Daily News* broke the story about the threat to Anita, a man named, "Dan," telephoned Nasso's attorney, Jack Litman. "Dan" told Litman that he knew who had threatened Anita three weeks earlier.

Once again, Nasso and his attorneys sent Bill McMullan to investigate.

At this point in our interview with Nasso, I pulled out and read a portion of a brief that Nasso's attorneys later filed, which continued:

> Mr. McMullan directed an investigator in Los Angeles named Andy Catalan to conduct an investigation of the caller, who was identified as Dan Patterson.
>
> Mr. Patterson stated that he was working as a confidential witness for the F.B.I. and that an individual named Alex had committed the attack against Ms. Busch. He further stated that he had recorded conversations with Alex. Mr. Patterson also stated that he was working on the Anita Busch case with F.B.I. agent Stanley E. Ornellas. Mr. McMullan's investigation revealed that Alex was in fact Alex Proctor, who was eventually arrested for the assault by the F.B.I.
>
> On August 29, 2002, at approximately 6:15 p.m., a conversation took place between Dan Patterson and Barry Levin, Esq., at which Mr. McMullan was present. Mr. Patterson stated that the F.B.I. felt that Steven Seagal was behind the attack on Anita Busch. . . .
>
> Mr. Patterson said he had a copy of the tape of the conversation he had with Mr. Proctor in which Mr. Proctor claimed Mr. Seagal and the unnamed private investigator, later identified as Anthony Pellicano, hired him to assault Anita Busch.[180]

In his own sworn affidavit, McMullan picked up the story, saying:

> Mr. Patterson incorrectly believed that Mr. Levin was the attorney for Julius Nasso and asked him for money in exchange for information that Mr. Patterson had that would clear his (Mr. Levin's) client. . . .
>
> Levin rejected Mr. Patterson's demand for money.[181]

After Patterson's request for money in return for his taped conversation with Proctor in which Proctor alleged Seagal's involvement in the attack on Anita Busch, the Nasso legal team contacted Stan Ornellas at the FBI and gave him the details of their encounter with Patterson.[182]

During our interview with Nasso, he corroborated all of this information and provided Gus and me with all of the supporting documentation.

Nasso admitted to us that he had met Pellicano "a couple of times a long time ago," adding that Seagal had told him in or about 1990, "I don't want you talking to him." Nasso alleged that, directly or indirectly, Pellicano had done "a lot of the work for Seagal."

In addition, Nasso believed that federal prosecutors were protecting Seagal, one of their key witnesses in the upcoming trial of the Gambino crime family members.

When Gus and I asked Nasso why he felt it necessary to deny that he had threatened Anita Busch in a December 10, 2002, *New York Post* story, Nasso replied, "Dead fish? Italians back East? It looked as though I did it. . . . What would you do?"

25. *"Gimme five"*

On February 11, 2003, Seagal testified against the Gambino defendants at their extortion and racketeering trial. During his testimony, he discussed the now-infamous January 29, 2001, meeting among Sonny Ciccone, Primo Cassarino, and the Nasso brothers.

Almost from the outset, Seagal stated under oath, there was tension at the meeting. Ciccone, who explained that Seagal still owed Jules money, barked at the actor, "Look at me when you are talking. Look, we're proud people, and you work with Jules. . . . Jules is going to get a little and the pot will be split up. . . . We'll take a little."

In a private moment as they walked out of the restaurant, Seagal alleged that Jules told him, "You know, it's a good thing you said this—and didn't say that—because if you would have said the wrong thing, they were going to kill you."

Even though it was this alleged statement that would eventually help send him to jail, Jules insisted to Gus and me that he never said this or anything like that to Seagal, with whom he spent the rest of the evening at a couple of New York restaurants without any evidence of conflict or even hard feelings.

The U.S. Court of Appeals for the Second Circuit summarized Seagal's testimony with regard to Nasso, saying:

> At trial, Steven Seagal testified that he became good friends with Jules Nasso in the late 1980s. At Jules Nasso's request, Seagal brought him into the movie business, and the two men formed a production company called Seagal-Nasso. In the mid-1990s, however, Seagal grew to believe that Jules Nasso's personality had changed. He decided that he did not want to work with Jules Nasso any longer and severed the business relationship in the late 1990s. According to Seagal, Jules Nasso was unhappy about the end of the relationship, and told Seagal that Seagal owed him approximately one million dollars. Seagal's accountants and attorneys, however, disagreed, telling Seagal that Jules Nasso owed him money, rather than vice versa.[183]

Addressing the afternoon of the meeting at Gage & Tollner, the *New York Times* added: "Mr. Seagal . . . did not acknowledge that he was ever afraid, saying instead that he was 'uncomfortable' and 'increasingly uncomfortable' as the scheme that the government calls extortion unfolded. He did say he was licensed to carry a gun, and took one to the 2001 meeting with Mr. Ciccone. 'In New York, I always carry a gun,' he said."[184]

According to Nasso, Seagal's most memorable fiction revolved around his allegation that he was forced into the car with Jules and Vincent *en route* to Gage & Tollner on January 29, 2001. What was really amusing about this scenario was that Seagal, a martial-arts expert, and his police-detective bodyguard, were both carrying handguns. Jules and Vincent, who were half their size, were unarmed.

To Gus and me, this was exculpatory for both of the Nasso brothers.

Further, Bill McMullan, Nasso's investigator, interviewed the *maître d'* and chief of security at Gage & Tollner, as well as the waiter who serviced the Ciccone-Nasso-Seagal table.

> * The waiter, Mark Bermuda, told McMullan that "Steven Seagal did not appear to be uncomfortable or upset. On the contrary, Mr. Bermuda remembered Seagal as having a good time and interacting later with the patrons in the bar area of the restaurant signing

autographs. Mr. Bermuda stated that Seagal did not display any stress or fear or anger."[185]

* The maître d', Wade Sinclair, who had worked at the restaurant for twenty-five years, corroborated his waiter's observations, adding that Seagal had given him an autograph while he was working the crowd after the dinner.[186]

* The chief of security, Vincent Palumbo, actually observed the Ciccone-Nasso-Seagal dinner party on his closed-circuit-security camera. McMullan wrote: "Mr. Palumbo stated that Seagal appeared to be in a good mood; that Seagal never displayed any sign of stress, fear or anger; that he [Seagal] appeared to be enjoying himself and was amiable with everyone; that he [Palumbo] did not see any threatening gestures towards Seagal; that he [Palumbo] did not see any weapons and that he [Palumbo] did not hear any loud voices or threats."[187]

"We were celebrating," Jules said. "The only thing Seagal said about me was that I whispered his ear that day at Gage & Tollner's, 'It's a good thing you said this. Otherwise, they would've killed you.'

"But the truth is, I never said that."

Jules added that, because the trial judge in the racketeering case had severed Jules and his brother, Vincent, from the other fifteen defendants, their attorneys did not have the opportunity to cross-examine Seagal.

On April 11, U.S. District Judge Charles P. Sifton released a 31-page decision in the $60-million *Nasso v. Seagal* case. In short, he refused to grant the defense motion to dismiss, clearing the way for the case to go to trial, saying, in part: "Because [Seagal-Nasso] Productions was organized for the purpose of developing and producing films, Nasso may prove that Seagal failed to act in good faith and to deal fairly in its relations with the corporation. . . ."[188]

Four months later, the roof collapsed on Nasso.

Before U.S. Magistrate Judge Viktor V. Pohorelsky, Nasso reluctantly pleaded guilty to one count of extortion during a hearing on August 13, signing a statement, saying:

> Between approximately September 2000 and May 2002, I participated in conversations as recorded on surveillance tapes in regard to obtaining assistance involving a business dispute with my partner Steven Seagal. Such disputes stemmed from my claim that there was money owing to me from Steven Seagal.

An understanding was reached between myself and other
participants involved in the conversations. This understanding
was that one of the participants of the conversations would make
statements to Seagal that would be perceived by Steven Seagal as a
threat intended to induce payments of the monies that I claim are still
due me, your Honor. I plead guilty to Count 58 of the indictment. At
least one of these conversations took place in Brooklyn and another
one out of the State of New York. . . . I would like to put on the
record that I left Mr. Seagal September of 2000 and I have produced
four films after that, your Honor.[189]

Significantly, Nasso vehemently continued to insist that he was
not and had never been a member or an associate of the Mafia and
specifically the Gambino crime family.

Regarding his decision to plead guilty, Jules told Gus and me
that he really did not want to cop a plea, adding, "I looked at my
brother, who was pleading for me to sign—because he didn't want
to do twenty years. So I signed. My brother had nothing to do
with this. I destroyed his family. His three children will grow up,
knowing that their father went to jail for something he had nothing
to do with."

As part of the deal, Vincent Nasso did plead guilty to two counts,
one for his role in the alleged extortion scheme against Seagal and
the other for wire fraud for paying a $400,000 kickback to waterfront
mobsters in return for a prescription-pharmaceuticals service
contract related to the ILA's national-health plan.

The day of the Nassos' sentencing, during which harsh words were
exchanged between the two brothers, was, up until our interview with
Jules, the last time Jules and Vincent Nasso had spoken to each other.

On February 17, 2004, U.S. District Judge Frederic Block
sentenced Jules to one year and one day in prison and fined him
$75,000.[190] In handing down this punishment, Judge Block said for
the record: "I will say this: I don't recall any hard evidence that
would satisfy the Court that if I had to rule on the issue factually that
Jules Nasso is an associate of organized crime."[191]

In addition, contrary to the media taunts that Nasso had used Seagal
as his "meal ticket," Judge Block added: "Jules Nasso was a profound
business person. He has been involved in the entertainment business
for many, many years. By his own admission, he has produced four

films subsequent to the Steven [Seagal] split up. He had a long-standing relationship with [Seagal]. He was the engine behind his success in terms of the amount of movies that were produced."[192]

On July 13, Nasso's attorneys, in a last-ditch effort to keep their client out of jail, filed a remarkable memorandum to the court, asking the judge to force the government to file a 35(b) motion that could reduce Jules's prison sentence because of the assistance he provided to federal prosecutors during the Pellicano probe.

That was when Jules's attorneys attempted to solicit the cooperation of Anita Busch's lawyers. Nasso's attorneys made an interesting argument in which they claimed Nasso's investigators, like Bill McMullan and Andy Catalan, had helped with the FBI's preparation of its application for the first search warrant on Pellicano's office in November 2002.

Nasso's attorneys concluded their argument, saying: "Mr. Nasso's assistance allowed the government to secure the warrant to search the office of Mr. Pellicano, which led to the discovery of illegal explosives and other incriminating evidence, such as the Seagal file. Mr. Pellicano was arrested and is now incarcerated because of the evidence found in the search, which was premised on the warrant Mr. Nasso helped obtain."[193]

Even though Nasso and his attorneys were right, federal prosecutors rejected all of their arguments to the court. To do otherwise could jeopardize the credibility of Steven Seagal, their star witness in the RICO case against the recently convicted Gambino crime family members.

———

When Jules entered Elkton Federal Prison, a medium-security facility in Lisbon, Ohio, on August 20, 2004, as Prisoner #67923-053, he received greetings from no fewer than seven prison officials. They all assumed that Nasso was a major Mafia figure because his prison records mistakenly stated that he was "recognized as an associate of an organized crime family with a potential for violence."[194] Worse yet, Nasso had pleaded guilty to attempting to shake down Steven Seagal, the action-adventure film star who was widely admired by both prison officials and even prison inmates.

Indeed, there were several major organized-crime figures at the prison, including Carmine Agnello who was reality-TV star Victoria Gotti's husband; Salvatore "Solly D" DeLaurentis of Chicago; and Joseph Zito of the Genovese crime family, along with Salvatore Avellino of the Lucchese crime family.[195]

No doubt, all of these tough Mafia guys must have been wondering, "Who the hell is Jules Nasso?" And Avellino, in particular, believed that because Nasso's sentence was so short he must be a snitch who had cut a deal for a lesser sentence in return for information about his supposed mobster associates.

For the first seven days of his imprisonment, Nasso was thrown in "the hole"—a prison within the prison, a nine-by-seven cell with no window and where a florescent light remained on throughout the day and night. He had no mattress, only a pad of foam rubber on the floor. His prison garb was made of paper, a routine procedure to prevent suicides by hanging.

With this horrific experience fresh in his memory, Jules became emotional and told Gus and me that he cried through his first night in prison.

Once out of the hole, Nasso spent most of his time in the prison library which was usually empty.

To ease the pain, Nasso's family members, friends, and business associates visited him regularly. His long-time partner, John Rossi, protected Jules's interest in their pharmaceutical operation.[196]

Damian Lee, an associate of Nasso in the film business—who had been the executive producer of *One Eyed King*—protected Nasso's film-development work.

After nearly ten months in his own private hell, Jules Nasso was released from prison on Friday, July 1, 2005, fifteen days before Gus Russo's first conversation with him.

———

Accepting Jules's offer to download any files we wanted from his computer, I inserted a flash drive into his USB port, went to Windows Explorer, and tried to download his entire Word file onto the device.

Jules was just a little irritated for what I was attempting to do, and he had a legitimate beef. He interrupted me as I was downloading, saying that everything in his Word file was not relevant to his legal cases against Steven Seagal or the Pellicano matter. Proving his point, he started opening specific Word files that had to do with his family, his film-production business, and his personal finances.

In the end, Gus and I went through all of his files, noting those that were relevant to what we were doing. Because they were not in a single folder, we agreed that we would leave the flash drive with Jules who would have his assistant do the work and then send the device back to me.

In addition, Jules gave us the original of the *pro se* file that he had created while in prison, a legal action taken by someone who represents himself without an attorney. We promised to copy this file and send the original back to him.

In his key *pro se* document, Nasso attached Anita's civil suit as an exhibit, saying: "This exhibit shows Anthony Pellicano is named as a Defendant. . . . Future discovery will show Steven Seagal may have hired Mr. Pellicano to frame movant. By doing this, they believed the civil claim against Seagal would disappear."[197]

During our interviews with Nasso, he continued to insist that Seagal was responsible for the attack on Anita's car.

Through all the time that Gus and I spent with Jules, I never betrayed any of Anita's secrets. However, after Jules told us that John Connolly had alleged to him personally a year earlier that Michael Ovitz was behind the attack, I felt that this subject was fair game—even though Nasso clearly did not believe it.

When Jules directly confronted me, demanding evidence that Ovitz was working with Pellicano, I replied that the key piece of evidence was contained in the 35(b) motion that Nasso's own attorneys had filed in July 2004. But, somehow, they did not grasp the significance of what they had cited.

I asked Nasso, who appeared puzzled, to give me a copy of that document which he quickly found and handed to me.

"When were you indicted, Jules?" I asked.

Playing along with my Perry Mason moment, he replied, "June 4, 2002."

I noted that this was Anita's second day on the job at the *Los Angeles Times*.

"Right," he said.

"And were you on Anita's radar screen prior to your indictment? Was she writing articles about you?"

"Not that I know of. . . . So what does this have to do with my attorneys' 35(b) motion?"

Handing the document back to Jules, I said, "Please turn to page 13."

When Nasso flipped to that page, I continued, "Now read aloud the second paragraph cited from the U.S. Attorney's January 23, 2004, memorandum to the court regarding defendant Anthony Pellicano's sentencing."

Turning on a light to see the text and putting on his glasses, Jules read:

> The information about Anita Busch obtained by defendant's sources *on May 16, 2002,* was contained in a file found on defendant's office computer pursuant to a search warrant. That file . . . contained Busch's personal information, including her descriptive data, residence address, and vehicle information relating to the vehicle on which Proctor left the dead fish, rose, and note. (Emphasis added)

Still not getting the connection, Jules put down the document and asked, "So?"

"Well," I replied, "what's the key date in what you just read?"

Not waiting for him to re-read that section, I said, "May 16. . . . According to the prosecution, Pellicano obtained the information about Anita on May 16. Were you on Anita's radar screen on May 16? That was nearly three weeks before you were indicted."

Starting to get it, Jules picked up the document and re-read that section. Then, he asked, "So what was Anita Busch doing prior to May 16?"

"As the public record shows," I replied, "that was just nine days after she had finished her seven-part series for the *New York Times* about Michael Ovitz and his alleged financial improprieties."

Watching Jules as he mulled this new information over in his head, I stood up and shook Jules's hand, declaring, "Congratulations, Jules! You're off the hook!"

Jules quickly asked, "What about Seagal?"

"He's off the hook, too," I responded. "In fact, if anyone's been framed for the threat against Anita, it's Seagal. He's taken a pounding over this. Like you, he's completely innocent."

———

Before leaving for a meeting during the late afternoon, Jules asked Gus and me to have an early dinner with him at his home.

While I was sitting in the kitchen alone, a little boy came up to me. I put out my hand, asking for five, and the little boy slapped it with his little paw. Pretending that he had just hurt me, I shook my hand, feigning pain, which caused the little boy to start giggling.

At that moment, his mother entered the kitchen. She had seen what I did and was also laughing.

I stood and introduced myself. While we were shaking hands, she said that she was Jules's sister-in-law. Knowing that Vincent's family was not speaking to Jules, I asked if she was the wife of Frank Nasso, Jules's other brother. She replied that she was.

Struck by this moment, which I hoped my friendly poker face did not betray, I asked if her father was Johnny Gambino of Cherry Hill, New Jersey.

She replied that her father was, indeed, Johnny Gambino, the grandfather of the little boy with whom I was just playing "gimme five."

As Gus, Jules, and the others came into the kitchen for dinner, I wondered why—when Jules was in trouble and needed someone to reason with Seagal—he had not simply solicited the participation of Johnny Gambino, one of the most feared and influential Mafia figures in the country? Gambino could snap his fingers and make happen anything he wanted to happen.

When I asked Nasso that question out loud after Gambino's daughter left the kitchen, he shrugged and replied almost matter of factly, "I don't do business with Mafia guys. I never have."

26. *"Both Gus and I are long-time lone wolves"*

On August 24, 2005, while we were still waiting for Jules Nasso to send us the documents we asked to be downloaded onto my flash drive, I prepared a draft proposal which I sent to Gus for his approval. In my cover letter to him, I wrote of this document: "It is rough. It is incomplete. But it is something for us to play with while we wait for JRN to send us the stuff.

"After you make your additions and corrections, let's talk to our agents and solicit their advice."

Upon completion of the proposal, I planned to ask Deborah Grosvenor, my last agent with Anita Busch, to represent me. Gus said that he would use his long-time agent, Noah Lukeman.

The following day, I stumbled across an article in the *New York Daily News* that trumpeted a party Jules was throwing on September 8, celebrating the completion of his Cinema Nasso Film Studios, located on his Staten Island estate.[198]

I called Gus, who had just received an invitation, leading me to believe that, for whatever reason, I would not be invited. I wrote to Gus on August 27: "I'm so glad that you're going to that gala at his home on September 8. I'm sure you're thinking the same thing I am: It could be the centerpiece for the first or last chapter. While you're hustling all of those starlets and divas who will be in attendance, please take good notes."

On August 29, the *New York Times* published an article about Nasso's upcoming celebration, saying: "Mr. Nasso . . . is planning a party to celebrate his next business venture: about 500 guests have been invited to the groundbreaking on Sept. 8 of Cinema Nasso Film Studios in Staten Island.

"According to the invitation, the festivities include cocktails, dancing and fireworks on the beach."[199]

That same morning, I called Deborah Grosvenor and invited her to represent me on the Nasso project. She immediately agreed to be my agent. When she asked for the name of Gus's agent, I replied "Noah Lukeman." By coincidence, Deborah had dinner with Lukeman during their appearances together at a recent writers' conference.

She added that Lukeman had worked for Michael Ovitz.

When I heard that, I nearly had a heart attack. I confirmed this information via Google and called Gus whose reaction was similar to mine.

On his own website, Lukeman noted that he "worked as a Manager in the New York office of Artists Management Group [AMG], Michael Ovitz' multi-talent management company."

AMG was the target of Anita Busch and Bernard Weinraub's seven-part series in the *New York Times* from March 22 to May 7, 2002. Lukeman, now an accomplished literary agent, was not implicated in any wrongdoing.

Giving Gus whatever time he needed to work things out with Lukeman, who represented Gus's upcoming book on Sidney Korshak, I sent our proposal to Deborah.

A few hours later, along with an invitation to Nasso's party on September 8, I finally received the documents that Jules had sent. All of the files we had requested, without exception, were loaded on the 512 MB flash drive I had left him.

I downloaded all of the materials onto my computer and then overnighted the device to Gus, so that he, too, would have a set of these documents.

Also, I finished copying all of Jules's original *pro se* documents and overnighted them back to him.

On September 1, Deborah called, saying that she had not received the proposal. As it turned out, I had an old email address for her. She had obtained a new one since our last exchange during the Anita debacle.

However, since we now had Nasso's documents, Gus and I decided to use them to update the proposal, which we sent to our agents on September 6.

In the brief synopsis of our story, we wrote:

> This is the true story of actor Steven Seagal's self-destruction, a fast-spiraling freefall that led to two separate federal investigations of corruption in Hollywood. With scenes set in Los Angeles and New York, the plot unfolds through a remarkable cast of celebrities, attorneys, private investigators, crooked cops, and Mafia figures. Sorting the guilty from the innocent and the misunderstood supercharges the twists and turns in the narrative.

Also on September 6, I received a letter in the mail with a September 3 time-stamp from Los Angeles. The handwritten return address was "B Clinton," followed by Anita's post-office box.

I recognized Anita's handwriting. Inside the envelope was a postcard from the "Boyhood Home of Bill Clinton" and a leaflet, "Visit President Clinton's First Home."

She enclosed no note or message.

This was now the second communication I had received from Anita since June 18 when she had leveled all of those spurious charges against me via email. I mean, if she genuinely believed all those allegations she had hurled against me, why would she bother sending me something like this?

Since the collapse of our book project in June, I had not initiated a single contact with her—by phone, email, or regular mail. And I had not replied to either of her two mailings since then.

On the morning of September 8, Mimi and I picked up Gus in Baltimore, and we drove to Staten Island to attend Jules Nasso's gala affair.

Jules wanted to thank his family, friends, and supporters, over 300 in attendance, for standing by him throughout his ordeal, as well as to christen Cinema Nasso Film Studios, which was located in the house next door to Nasso's home, ironically the same place that Steven Seagal had once owned and resided.

On the invitation, Jules had written: "Cinema Nasso Film Studios is continuing in the tradition [of] my grandfather, Francesco Nasso, bringing quality film production to the industry. I am proud to be involved in the legacy of my family in opening Cinema Nasso Film Studios."

The party featured numerous open bars, high cuisine, fireworks by the famous Grucci family of Long Island, and music by Chuck Mangione.

The following day, Mimi, Gus, and I had breakfast with Nasso, screenwriter John Leekley, and Bill McMullan, Nasso's private detective. Gus had business with Nasso and Leekley, so Mimi and I walked around Nasso's estate and along the edge of the bay in Nasso's backyard. Fluent in Italian, Mimi spoke with Jules's Italian mother and with some men who were working on Jules's property.

After Gus's meeting, we drove home.

On September 12, Gus said that his agent, Noah Lukeman, did not like our book project and would not represent it. Deborah told me that she wanted to sleep on it.

The next day, Deborah really shocked me with her sudden withdrawal as my agent, writing:

> I'm having a hard time seeing the larger story here, and am not sure that the names of Seagal and Nasso are enough of a draw to carry the story. I think the project is problematic for a host of reasons, including legal liability. . . .
>
> Having said that, I would also like to say that should this project as currently conceived not work out for you, I'd love to talk about other ideas. I have a great deal of respect for you as a writer and

reporter, and would love to see you on something really big and
deserving of your talent.

Shaken by this news, I could only thank Deborah for her time
and wish her well. Through all of this—from Anita to Jules—she
had been fair-minded, honest, and professional.

But then, following Deborah's departure, four more agents turned
us down.

Gus and I were both clinically depressed over our agent situation.
In fact, for me, this was a total disaster. In the effort to sell the Anita
project, Anita and I had, directly or indirectly, approached nine
prospective agents. With the Nasso venture, Gus and I had been
turned down by five more.

On October 1, feeling completely dejected, I offered Gus the
right to publish an article about Jules, telling him he could take all
the credit and keep all of the money. In return, I asked him to allow
me to write about all of this in a first-person account one day. I
wanted Gus to get a payday after all we had been through—and I
wanted to be able to tell my own story.

However, Gus remained loyal and wanted to give our book about
Nasso another shot.

I told Gus about an agent who had contacted me a few months
earlier. His name was Carmen La Via, who was with the Fifi Oscard
Agency. I sent Gus the letter La Via had sent me, which said:

> I am a literary agent in New York and a big fan of *Dark Victory*,
> your book about the mob, MCA and Ronald Reagan. I had 2 copies
> that I lent out to two young agents that needless to say [were] never
> returned. I've tried all over to replace them to no avail. Is there an
> off chance that you would know where and how I could get a copy.
> I'd appreciate your help.

After receiving that message, I sent La Via an autographed
copy of my out-of-print 1986 book. Later, La Via sent me a thank-
you note, saying: "Received the book. Thank you for your quick
response and for the book which is now required reading for our
aspiring agents.

"As you know, I am an admirer of yours and a good agent. So
keep me in mind when in the market for new agency representation."

On October 10, after receiving Gus's permission, I wrote to La Via, saying: "May I ask you to tell me something about yourself? I'm under the impression that you represent big-time movie stars, not grunt crime reporters.

"Actually, if you liked *Dark Victory*, you're really going to love the new project that my partner, Gus Russo, and I are putting together."

La Via replied:

> Well, I started my career representing actors, some big name movies stars like Peter O'Toole, George Segal, Geraldine Chaplin and many not so big. The first book I sold was *Donnie Brasco*, the true story of FBI agent Joseph Pistone who was undercover in the mob for 6 1/2 years. The book was a *NY Times* best seller and became a successful feature film that starred Al Pacino and Johnny Depp. At about the same time I turned an actor client into a best selling author and that is William Shatner, who wrote about his experiences during and after the making of *Star Trek*, the series, and the subsequent feature films. He then wrote a science-fiction novel called *TekWar* for Putnam which eventually became a series of 10 titles.

Busy with work on his upcoming book about Sidney Korshak, Gus suggested that I speak with La Via and to make the decision on our behalf. In short, La Via and I had a pleasant conversation on October 12, so I sent him the proposal.

Carmen liked what he read and had a few ideas about how to make it better. So I called Gus, and we had a conference call with the agent.

Contrary to the previous advice we had received, La Via wanted more emphasis on Steven Seagal and less on Jules Nasso. Gus and I wanted to tell the story through Jules, which was the better story, but we also wanted to sell the book, so we did it Carmen's way.

On October 17, Carmen reacted to our updated proposal, writing: "I received your up-dated proposal and rightly or wrongly, it's exactly what I asked for and I certainly want to represent it and you. . . .

"I'm very excited about this."

La Via also wanted to know if Gus and I had any plans to remain partners after our book about Nasso and Seagal. I replied, saying:

> Both Gus and I are long-time lone wolves, who have a common interest in this subject. Although another subject could come along

for us, this is the only project we've agreed to. Also, after Gus's book on Sid Korshak comes out next year and achieves the great success we hope, he'll probably forget my name.

We couldn't be happier that you are on board with us. If you need anything, please call or write.

That same day, Carmen sent us his agency's standard representation agreement.

The following night, I hosted another authors' dinner at The Old Europe restaurant in Washington which Gus attended. After we shook hands when Gus walked in the dining room, he and I signed the representation agreement which I overnighted to Carmen the next day.

27. *"HOT HOT HOT"*

On October 19, the *New York Times* published a story that sent shock waves through the entertainment industry. It revealed that federal prosecutors would soon indict Pellicano on wiretapping charges as part of a broader federal racketeering/conspiracy case. The newspaper which the previous year predicted that the indictments would be handed up "early in 2004" now featured a prediction that the indictments could come in November 2005.

Bigger still was the latest implication of Michael Ovitz as a principal in the Pellicano caper. The newspaper stated:

> Mr. Ovitz referred questions to his lawyer, Bart H. Williams, who said Mr. Ovitz had cooperated fully with the F.B.I. over several interviews. He said Mr. Ovitz had engaged Mr. Pellicano through a law firm for three litigation matters but did not authorize or know of any wiretapping. But he said prosecutors had not even suggested to Mr. Ovitz or asked him if he had hired Mr. Pellicano to look into his former partners at Creative Artists.
>
> "In fact, it's come to our attention that Mr. Ovitz was taped by Anthony Pellicano," Mr. Williams said. "If one thing's become clear to me, it's that Anthony Pellicano consistently peddled information about Michael Ovitz to third parties."[200]

Obviously, I wanted to see some evidence of that.

Along with Ovitz, other top Hollywood executives questioned, according to the *Times*, included Paramount Chairman Brad Grey; Ron Meyer, the president of Universal Studios, and Ovitz's former partner at Creative Artists Agency, as well as Kevin Huvane and Bryan Lourd, two remaining CAA partners.

As soon as I saw the *Times* article, I emailed it to Dave Robb who replied: "It's a great story. Indictments are coming. Be patient."

Also, I sent the story to Gus and Carmen, telling them, "This should be a very, very good omen for us."

Carmen wrote back: "Our timing is special. I sent the proposal to HarperCollins and Bantam yesterday.

"HOT HOT HOT."

I just could not have agreed more. I now thought that Gus and I were golden, and that our book would sell immediately.

John Connolly's personal public-relations agency, the Rush & Molloy column in the *New York Daily News*, ran an item that same day, revealing that John was, indeed, still in the game, saying:

> Reporter John Connolly is shopping a bio titled, *Sin-Eater* (what Pellicano called himself). Connolly, who's repped by Lisa Queen, promises fresh info on Pellicano's ties to [Tom] Cruise, [Sylvester] Stallone, [Arnold] Schwarzenegger and the Hollywood player Connolly believes was behind Pellicano's alleged threatening of reporter Anita Busch.[201]

Clearly, Connolly planned to reveal Ovitz's alleged role in the June 20, 2002, threat against Anita.

On October 23, the Page Six column in the *New York Post* parroted the Rush & Molloy story, adding:

> John Connolly, who covered the Pellicano case for *Vanity Fair* and is writing a book about him, *Sin Eater* (a phrase the dick used to describe himself), says a retired LAPD cop will also be indicted, as well as Pac Bell employee.[202]

That same day, Carmen called and told me that, like Bantam and HarperCollins, St. Martin's had passed, saying that editors did not think that Seagal would make a very good central character for our book.

The next day, Putnam rejected us. Nevertheless, Carmen claimed to be optimistic.

Getting nervous again, Gus and I discussed our situation. We decided to stay the course.

On October 26, Carmen called and said that Random House had passed. Like St. Martin's, Random House had a problem with Seagal as the major character.

That same day, Carmen sent Gus and me a rejection from Star Lawrence, the executive editor of W. W. Norton, who wrote:

> I love Dan Moldea and always enjoy reading his stuff. But in this case I just think the material is too far from my own interests and expertise, and too far from what Norton wants to be publishing for me to get into this stuff. It is all quite tentative at this point, and, needless to say, fraught with potential legal difficulties. The publisher who jumps in here would have to be very savvy about Hollywood, and willing to assume very big exposure on the legal front. I just don't think I/we are up to this challenge.

The reaction from Star, who had been the editor of my 1995 book about the murder of Senator Robert Kennedy, was a very, very bad omen.

Carmen's cover note simply stated, "Not to worry, we'll find a home."

That night on CNN, anchorwoman Nancy Grace did a program about the upcoming Pellicano wiretapping scandal. Her guests for the segment were John Connolly and journalist Diane Dimond.

In one portion of the interview, Connolly suggested that Pellicano had already offered to turn state's evidence against Michael Jackson for child molestation and might do the same in the Hollywood wiretapping case.

> **Connolly:** Well, I think if I [were] any of the attorneys who did business with him, I'd be really concerned tonight. I would not want to stake my future on the fact that Anthony Pellicano is going to be a standup guy and not roll over. As Diane and I both know, Anthony tried to roll over on Michael Jackson, except certain people were not interested in what he had to say.
>
> **Grace:** What do you mean he tried to roll over?

> **Connolly:** He sent an emissary to get a message to [Santa Barbara District Attorney Tom] Sneddon that he wanted to cooperate and get him information about Michael Jackson.
>
> **Grace:** So why wouldn't he roll over now?
>
> **Connolly:** Well, I think he will. I think a lot of people are saying he's not going to roll over, but I think he will.[203]

After hearing nothing further from our agent by November 4, I wrote to Carmen, saying:

> We haven't heard from you during the past week, so we're assuming that nothing has happened. Thus, we assume that William Morrow and Viking are still in the hunt. Are there any others?
>
> Also, are you hearing anything about John Connolly's proposal, which is supposedly circulating New York via his agent, Lisa Queen? Have you heard of proposals by any other authors with regard to the Pellicano case?
>
> Obviously, we are interested in your expert opinion about what is happening. We have always believed that being in the right place at the right time—as we clearly are—was a bankable commodity.
>
> As always, we appreciate your fine representation.

La Via replied, "If it were easy we'd be in a different business."

———

On November 5, Anita Busch, whom I hadn't heard from since her "B Clinton" postcard of September 3, sent me an email about the former Mafia guy whose wife was probably saved by the experimental anti-cancer program Anita had arranged for her.

> If you would, please contact [the former Mafia guy] and ask him to call me. It's important. I'm meeting for the first time with the doctors whose therapy saved his wife's life. I contacted them out of the blue to see if I could help them in any way. We just spoke and now I'm meeting them tomorrow.

They said they are currently trying to cull together 42 patients for another clinical trial in Manila, this time helping victims of other kinds of cancer beyond pancreatic and colon cancer. I would like to try and help them do this, and in turn, help others possibly save their own lives of the lives of people they love.

I would like to talk to him or his wife before I meet with them tomorrow night.

After contacting the ex-mobster, I wrote back to her—my first response to her since June: "I just got off the phone with [the former Mafia guy]. I gave him your home number—not your cell phone since it's confidential. He said he'd call you immediately.

"I hope you're well and kicking ass."

She replied:

Thanks very much. Yeah, he called while I was out. I'm hoping that his wife is still doing well. I hope they she or they could help round up some others they might have met who have cancer who would be willing to take part in a clinical trial outside the U.S. . . .

I'm contacting everyone I know. I think [the former Mafia guy] and his wife could really help because they experienced the results first-hand. Perhaps they will help in rounding up as many people.

I think this is very important work. I believe wholeheartedly that these two doctors have found the cure for certain types of cancer.

By November 11, Gus and I hadn't received any answer to the questions lingering with our proposal, so we sent Carmen another message, asking him: "With respect and regardless of whether the news is good, bad, or ugly, could you please give us a detailed update as to what is happening with our book project?

"In anticipation of the upcoming indictments, we'd like to know exactly where we stand."

Later that same day, La Via's assistant wrote back to us: "Carmen has asked me to tell you that he will reply in detail on Monday with a list of editors he has sent this to and their replies.

"And of course, he remains very enthusiastic about the project."

To our chagrin, Monday came and went with nothing from Carmen or his assistant.

On Tuesday, November 15, I finally reached Carmen and asked him when he was going to send us the promised information from the editors. He replied that Fifi Oscard, the owner of his talent agency, had died the previous Friday, and that the office was experiencing a combination of grief and chaos. However, he said that the information was in his computer and that he simply had to "cut and paste it into an email." He added that he was going to send the proposal to Simon & Schuster, which was a subsidiary of the Viacom corporation. Viacom owned Paramount Pictures, whose new head, Brad Grey, was among the possible targets in the Pellicano caper.

Two days later, an Internet publication, *Radar Online*, alleged that CBS, another subsidiary of Viacom had "killed an in-depth investigative special on Pellicano. . . . We hear that CBS News show *48 Hours Mystery* signed documentary filmmaker Sarah Teale in June 2004 to do an hour-long segment." [204]

The story added that CBS was "all hyped about the story until Brad Grey was named head honcho at Paramount."

From this episode, I started to fear that even if we were able to publish our book, there was no guarantee that we could get on television to promote it.

On November 22, while I was in Ohio visiting my family for Thanksgiving, *Radar Online*, citing a "very high-level source close to the case," predicted:

> [T]he first round of "several indictments" will be issued this week or next and will focus on the Tinseltown attorneys who allegedly hired Pellicano to secretly bug and wiretap their clients' enemies and courtroom adversaries. . .
>
> [T]o guarantee maximum media impact, they will be arrested at their homes, offices, or favored power lunch spots and led away in cuffs in full view of their peers and the press. . . .
>
> The grand jury investigation is expected to have explosive ramifications in Hollywood. [205]

The following day, National Public Radio ran a story on *All Things Considered* which asked the key question that everyone in the entertainment industry still wanted to know—"What's on those tapes?" [206]

The next month came and went without any indictments and with no attorneys led away in handcuffs and with no word from our agent about the state of our ship.

After receiving a Christmas card from Anita, postmarked December 7, I sent her one. This was the fourth unsolicited communication that Anita had initiated since our falling out the previous June.

I did not know whether she was looking for a way to resurrect our book project while simultaneously saving face or whether she was just attempting to stay in touch, hoping that I would not sue her for breach of contract.

One thing for sure: Dave Robb had obviously decided not to tell her about my association with Jules Nasso.

On December 20, Gus sent me Cindy Adams's column in the *New York Post*, noting a letter that Pellicano had sent to his friends, saying:

> The day I am scheduled to be released in February, the State will either pick me up and take me to the County jail, or the Government will take me into their custody to await trial on these "new" indictments. They could have indicted me any time along the way I was incarcerated, but they wanted me to spend the maximum time in prison before starting the New Game.
>
> They continue to ask if I would be a RAT! I WILL NEVER INFORM ON ANYONE FOR ANY PURPOSE WHATSOEVER!! Notwithstanding the fact that all the lawyers I worked for and had "friendships" with have abandoned me. I am a man and will continue to be one until I am no longer alive, and beyond if that's possible. I cannot believe the amount of fear out there.[207] (Pellicano's emphasis)

On December 21, Gus and I met for dinner at Krupin's delicatessen in Washington prior to going to a nearby funeral home to pay our final respects to Pulitzer Prize-winning columnist Jack Anderson who had died a few days earlier.

We discussed the ongoing dilemma with regard to our book project and our agent. We agreed that we would probably have to wait until the indictments to re-pitch our book. However, that meant that our huge lead on the mainstream media would quickly evaporate and probably place us in direct competition with several other anticipated book proposals, including John Connolly's.

On December 30, Gus and I sent Carmen a message, noting: "With respect, when we last spoke on November 15, you said that you would send Gus Russo and me a list of the editors who have received the proposal for our Nasso-Seagal-Pellicano project, as well as their responses. Could you please send us that long-awaited information?"

———

Late on January 1, 2006, Anita sent me a peculiar email with all the words in the lower case, referring to two of her unnamed sources by her codes names for them, "lambchop" and "nighthawk," with "found out today" on the subject line.

Before responding to her fifth unsolicited communication with me since our falling out, I wrote Dave Robb a message on January 2, attached Anita's email and saying: "I received this message from Anita last night. It refers to two characters in our book. I'm assuming that this is a good thing—like the book is still in play.

"What do you think? And how should I respond?

"As you already know, if this book is still in play, I want you to come into the deal."

Dave called, and we had a long talk. He said that Anita now expected a quick settlement from the defendants in her civil suit against Pellicano, the LAPD, the phone company, and the others after the indictments. When I once again raised the probability that she would be forced to sign a non-disclosure agreement as part of a financial settlement, which would effectively kill our book, Dave said that he had recently discussed my concern with Anita. He said that she told him that she would never agree to that.

I told him that she was delusional. When confronted with a big payday in return for a non-disclosure agreement, she would sacrifice the book.

During our conversation, I did not give Dave an update about my relationship with Jules Nasso. And he did not ask for one. As he had made clear after receiving my email on July 24, 2005, he did not want to know. Still, I had left it to him in that email to tell Anita as she had instructed.

In my response to Anita's latest email to me, and afraid to say too much or to sound too presumptuous, I simply replied blandly on January 2: "Thanks for the news, Anita. I hope you have a fabulous 2006."

To my surprise, I received the sixth unsolicited correspondence from Anita on January 4, in which she said: "Go see *Munich* and watch carefully what happens to Eric Bana's character, belief system, sense of security, etc. It is astounding in the similarity of what happened to me."

That weekend, Mimi and I went to see *Munich*. Although I was not as enthusiastic about the similarities between the two experiences, I did not want to interfere with whatever progress that Anita and I were making. So I simply replied on January 8: "After seeing the film last night, I agree. The similarities—especially about the need to protect sources, family, and friends, the on-the-job pressures and whether to stay or go (and trust or not trust), as well as the threatening street scenes and horrible nightmares—were particularly chilling.

"Sooner or later, you will be rewarded for the sacrifices you made—and are still making—for your ordeal."

To that, Anita responded:

> I don't know if I will be compensated or not. What hit me is the scene when he was trying to sleep in the closet and going from room to room with a gun. It was exactly what I did, at one point.
>
> Also, the deterioration of the human condition and then the realization that home doesn't exist anymore. My home was journalism; his Israel. The ideals shattered for both of us and left us homeless.
>
> I still have nightmares on occasion. You know, they never really go away.

———

On January 10, I asked for Gus's permission to send Carmen La Via a very harsh letter. Upon receiving the go-ahead from Gus, I sent the message, saying:

Twelve days ago, I respectfully asked you to make good on a promise you made to Gus and me six weeks before that. We have received no response from you.

Your inexplicable decision not to send us the promised information—as well as the silent treatment you are now giving us—begs the question: *Do you want to continue as our agent or not?* We'd like to know as quickly as possible—in anticipation of the indictments which will presumably be handed up before Pellicano is released from jail on February 4.

Please show us the respect and courtesy that we have always shown to you. If you are still our agent, please send us the promised information. If you no longer want to represent us, please say so. (My emphasis)

28. *"Nasso did not have anything to do with the threat on my life"*

That same afternoon, I received a heads-up from a friend that two people had just pleaded guilty in the Pellicano case. When I went online, I found the press release on the website of the U.S. Attorney's Office in Los Angeles. The Department of Justice stated:

A 24-year veteran of the Beverly Hills Police Department pleaded guilty yesterday to seven felony counts, admitting that he accessed law enforcement databases for the purpose of supplying confidential information to Pellicano and employees of his now-defunct investigation agency.

Craig Stevens, 45, of Oak Park, appeared in federal court Monday afternoon and pleaded guilty to two counts of wire fraud for depriving the citizens of Beverly Hills of his honest services as a sworn police officer. Stevens also pleaded guilty to four counts of unauthorized access of protected computers to commit fraud. In pleading guilty to the unauthorized access counts, Stevens admitted that he used the Beverly Hills Police Department's computers to obtain information about four individuals from the Department of Motor Vehicles and sold that information to Pellicano and his employees. Stevens also pleaded guilty to lying to the Federal Bureau of Investigation when he denied that he had ever provided information to, or received

> payments from, Pellicano, when in fact he had repeatedly sold
> information to Pellicano. . . .
>
>   In the second case announced today, a former client of Pellicano,
> Sandra Will Carradine, a 58-year-old Carpenteria resident, pleaded
> guilty on Friday to two counts of perjury. Carradine, who hired
> Pellicano in relation to her divorce proceedings, admitted that
> during a grand jury appearance in October 2004 she lied when she
> denied having any knowledge that Pellicano had wiretapped her ex-
> husband's phone.[208]

Simultaneously, I saw that the *Los Angeles Times* had already published a story about this huge development on its website, calling it, "the first big break in a 3-year old federal investigation."[209]

In my first unsolicited communication to Anita since our falling out, I sent the link to her without comment, assuming that she did not know.

She replied curtly: "[Y]es, I know. [T]hanks."

Then, almost immediately after sending that reply, she sent me a second, commenting on the *Times* article, complaining about some error made in the story, which apparently had been repeated after being corrected in a previous edition: "[T]hey, by the way, apparently never read their own corrections. [J]eez."

Still afraid of saying the wrong thing, I did not reply to Anita, even after she included me in a group email which was nothing more than a cartoon about the Jack Abramoff lobbying scandal that was erupting in Washington.

Later that day, Gus and I spoke on the phone. We wondered aloud whether our agent, Carmen La Via, might be ill. Thus, we decided to call him for the first time since November 15.

After our conversation with La Via, who was well and even contrite, Gus and I sent him another email, memorializing what was discussed:

> We just finished our first conversation since November 15. I am
> relieved that you are well and safe.
>
>   Thank you for, once again, promising to [send] us the list of
> the editors who have received the proposal for our Nasso-Seagal-
> Pellicano project, as well as their responses.

> As we discussed, I am hoping that they reconsider after the indictments are handed up by the U.S. Attorney's Office in Los Angeles.

After three more days passed with no response from La Via, I sent him yet another message:

> It's now been several days since we spoke, and Gus and I are still waiting for the information you promised to send. During our telephone conversation, you said that it was in your computer, and that all you had to do was cut and paste it into an email. Please take a moment to do that.
>
> Things are starting to happen very quickly, and we need to know where we stand.
>
> BTW: Michael Ovitz's former nanny (from sometime between 1987-1993, thirteen years ago) has found a publisher for her book.[210]

After still hearing nothing from Carmen, Gus and I wondered whether we could get another agent to pitch our now-damaged goods book project after the indictments—without the list of editors who had received the initial pitch from Carmen, along with their responses.

In short, we agreed to leave the prom with the one who brought us. In other words, at least for the moment, we decided to stick with Carmen and wait for the indictments.

———

On January 18, Anita sent me an email in which she wrote: "I've knocked out a fictional account of what happened to me. Would you like to see it?

"If so, I will send it to you, but you must promise that you will not show it to anyone or talk about it to anyone except to Dave Robb—not even to Mimi or your Mom.

"What say you?"

Now fully recognizing that Dave Robb had not told Anita about my book project about Jules Nasso, I decided that, in all fairness, I had no choice but to tell her—before she sent me her fictionalized account.

I wrote back: "Thanks for the offer, Anita. Before you send me anything, I must tell you something—in writing.

"I'm really racing today, but I'll get it to you as soon as possible—certainly no later than this time tomorrow."

In her reply, Anita wrote, "[W]ell, out with it then . . . as you feel you must . . . in writing."

Before responding, I called Dave Robb and told him that I was going to reveal my Nasso book project to Anita.

Dave vehemently objected, saying that she would hit the roof and cease all communications with me.

I replied that, since he had not told her after my notification to him the previous summer, she would find out from someone, somewhere. After all, Gus and I were not operating in a vacuum. Not wanting to take advantage of her offer, I added that, before she sent me the manuscript of her novel, I wanted to show good faith by revealing the news about my relationship with Nasso.

Dave still did not think it was a good idea.

When I asked Dave why she was even offering to show me the manuscript, he replied that Anita was afraid I was going to launch a legal attack against her if she tried to sell it without my permission.

I told Dave that she was right. I would not even hesitate to do so, especially while she was in breach of our existing contract.

After speaking with Dave, I called Gus Russo and told him what was happening. Seeing how complicated this situation could become, Gus generously offered to withdraw from the Nasso book, allowing me to work with Anita and Dave to merge both books into one.

After all of the snakes I had been doing business with since I began this project, I simply could not believe what a truly noble gesture that was on Gus's part.

A half hour later, Dave called me back. He told me that he had just spoken to Anita and told her about my book project with Nasso.

When I asked for her reaction, he said that she was fine with it, adding that she had learned a lot over the past several months—and now knew that Nasso had no role in the attack against her.

Also, I told Dave about Gus's generous offer to walk away from the Nasso book, allowing Anita, Dave, and me to merge the information from the two books into one. Unimpressed with Gus's remarkable gesture, Dave told me that Anita would not want any information from Nasso in her book.

I replied that she would be crazy not to accept it—because she and I had made a lot of mistakes in our book that Nasso had cleared up during the interviews Gus and I had had with him.

The following day, January 19, I assumed that everything was fine, based on what Dave told me. Still identifying Michael Ovitz as "ED," I wrote Anita an email, saying:

> I'm glad that Dave, prompted by me, told you yesterday of my involvement with Gus Russo and Jules Nasso—which was the reason why I wanted to respond to your offer "in writing." In good faith, I wanted you to know about this before you sent me your novel. If you have any specific questions or concerns, please feel free to ask. As Dave told you, Gus and I tried but failed to make a publishing deal for Nasso's story.
>
> Just so you know: 1) Gus and I did not sign any agreement with Nasso, 2) Nasso had no financial stake in the book project, 3) Nasso had no control over the contents of the manuscript, and 4) Gus and I neither asked for nor received any money from him. Significantly, Nasso—whom I am convinced had no role in or any prior knowledge of the attacks on you—simply wanted a fair and accurate portrayal of his life and times, especially with regard to his turbulent relationship with Steven Seagal. He repeatedly said that he would supply us, exclusively, with whatever information we needed and then "let the chips fall where they may." *(FYI: Jules knows that ED was probably behind the first attack on you— because John Connolly told him two years ago* after *he broke from us. Remember that nightmare? You and I have been through a lot together.)*
>
> Just to be clear, despite our problems and unlike Connolly, I have always remained loyal to you and our book project. If I were to betray you, I would be jeopardizing my friendship with Dave, which I would never do.
>
> Obviously, I still want to complete our non-fiction project, *Woman at Risk*, in anticipation of the upcoming indictments. With regard to your fictionalization, please tell me what your intentions are. And then let's figure out some way that we can work this out peacefully. In the end, I want both of us to succeed, regardless of whether we do it together or separately.

I would prefer [to] handle all of this by email, copying everything to Dave. If you want to talk, I suggest that Dave or someone else you trust be invited to participate in the discussion as a mediator. I'll likely accept whomever you choose.

Meantime, I hope you are safe and well. (My emphasis)

To my surprise, Anita became almost unhinged in her response to me, also referring to Ovitz in her usual code name, "Ed," and saying:

If [John Connolly] told Jules Nasso about Ed, then he also told him about the book project between us and that is probably why you were approached by Jules. But you probably thought about that already. He's been trying to get to me for the past 3 1/2 years through various people. He came to you and you engaged him.

When you were first approached to do the Jules Nasso book, given the fact that this man was a suspect in my case, you should have told me.

If you were indeed "loyal," you would have told me that you were talking to him and thinking about going into business with him. In fact, you had an obligation to me as [your] partner to tell me that you were talking to a suspect in my case, let alone getting in business with one. I don't know how you could have, in good conscience, gone as far as to approach publishers about a book with him without telling me. That means that you had to write up a proposal and spent a great deal of time doing that. That is an incredible breach of trust.

There are things going on that you have and have had no knowledge of. How can you forget Nasso's comments about what a stand-up guy Ed was in the *Vanity Fair* piece immediately after I was threatened? Neither I nor you will know for sure if he was involved in the attacks against me until after ALL the indictments are released. It's not about what he <u>says</u> or what someone <u>thinks,</u> it's about what <u>is</u>.

I punched out a fictional account of this in 17 days time. The day I was finished with it (prior to an edit even), I wrote and told you about it. My intentions on the fictional account is to sell it. That is how you do the right thing, Dan.

You say, "If I were to betray you, I would be jeopardizing my friendship with Dave, which I would never do," but you obviously have already betrayed me.

We have very different definitions of loyalty and trust. To be honest, I don't trust you Dan. And you have given me even more reason not to with these latest moves. I would like a peaceful

> resolution as well, and the only way I see that happening is by
> dissolving our contract and parting ways. We both put a lot of work
> into that non-fiction account and I would also like to see it come out
> someday when it is <u>safe for me</u> to do so which you have, I might
> remind you, promised to me more than once.
>
> So maybe Dave and me and you should get on the phone and
> come to some kind of resolution. (Anita's emphasis)

Before I had a chance to reply, she came back with another
message, saying: "[O]h, and you can forget about dangling your
legal term 'good faith' in my face . . . you have shown no good faith,
only [flimsy] justifications for your actions of betrayal."

As soon as I recovered from the initial shock of Anita's reply,
I assumed the obvious: Dave had not really told Anita that I had
notified him—in his role as Anita's designated representative—the
previous July or any time since about the Nasso project before I
agreed to anything.

In fairness to Anita, she was completely in the dark about this
matter and responding as anyone else probably would, given the
same set of circumstances. She was operating only on the basis of
what Dave had or had not told her.

Immediately, I called Dave, complaining about Anita's over-
the-top reaction and her latest false accusations against me. When I
appealed to Dave to clear up this mess by revealing the timeline to
her, he refused and insisted that I not say anything about his role. He
said that he would work everything out.

Refusing to allow Anita to get away with what she had said but
reluctantly not giving up Dave's secret, I shot back an email to her,
saying:

> First of all, I wasn't approached by Nasso. Last July, I had
> dinner with Gus Russo—a good friend who has written three books
> about the Mafia, including a bestseller about the Chicago Outfit
> and a forthcoming, widely-anticipated book about Sidney Korshak.
> A screenwriter who was a mutual friend of Gus and Jules had
> recommended to Nasso, who had just been released from prison,
> that he [ask] Gus to write the book about his life and times. Gus and
> Jules connected and hit it off.
>
> At that time, Jules didn't even know my name.

Gus had already heard from [another author] that you and I were collaborating on a book with some overlapping themes. I have no idea how [the other author] knew this. He and I haven't spoken in several years.

In the midst of our dinner, after hearing that *Woman at Risk* was on hold indefinitely, Gus asked me if I was interested in the Nasso's project. Of course, I was, as long as 1) I didn't have to sign an agreement with Nasso, 2) Nasso had no financial stake in the project, 3) Nasso had no editorial control over the content, 4) I would never accept any money from Nasso for any reason, and 5) Everyone "understands that I am loyal to Anita Busch and will protect her at all costs."

During the first conference call among Gus, Jules, and me, I laid out my terms, all of which Nasso agreed to. He insisted that he simply wanted "the true and accurate story" to be published, and that he would "let the chips fall where they may." In return, he would give us anything we needed, exclusively. He had no problem with my loyalty to you. In fact, he has great admiration and respect for you. And I believe him.

In addition, I now know the entire story about the *Vanity Fair* piece (and the bedroom scene in particular[211]), as well as [John Connolly's] relationship with Nasso and his attorneys and investigators. I know the whole story about the Nasso-Seagal relationship with ED and Pellicano, as well as Nasso's relationship with your former partner at the *LAT*, among many other things that once troubled us.

In short, Nasso was not involved in either of the attacks on you. That is what it is. And I am willing to stake my reputation and career on that simple fact.

Trust me on this: You don't want to challenge my loyalty to you about this or anything else—because I have been and continue to be loyal. And I can flat-out prove it if it ever becomes necessary.

With regard to the trust issue, especially after the painful events of last May and June, the feeling is quite mutual. That's why I want everything in writing—and/or someone to witness any discussion we have. If you really want an agreement that will void our contract, I am now more than happy to discuss it.

Whether you want to believe it or not, I have always been a true and loyal friend to you. But, at the moment, I want you out of my life as badly as you foolishly want me out of yours.

I am too upset to discuss this any further today. If you want a conference call, pick a time tomorrow or Saturday when Dave is available.

Although I sympathized with the fact that Dave had not told Anita about my connection with Nasso, her reaction to my total honesty had just plain pissed me off. But, because Dave insisted that I not give him up, I was helpless and had become nothing more than target practice for Anita, who wrote:

> While I BELIEVE that Jules Nasso did not have anything to do with the threat on my life, I also have evidence that he has not told the truth on important matters, matters of which you are unaware. The fact—which you cannot dispute—is that the only ones who know for sure is law enforcement and the U.S. Attorney's office. So, you don't KNOW and neither do I for certain.
>
> When you put forth to him what you did about me, it was a natural response for him to say that he also has the same opinion. The man can't have the same opinion about me. He doesn't know me. . . .
>
> If he is officially cleared as a suspect, my opinions, of course, will change. Until that time, I want to steer clear of any and all suspects. And, as my partner, you should have the same thing as not to put me or my case into any jeopardy. I would have done that for you.
>
> The very sad fact is (and to me it truly saddens me), we just don't think the same way about very basic things in life, Dan. We also don't agree on what a non-fiction book is supposed to be.
>
> For the record, I don't know [the author who spoke with Gus Russo]; he is someone who has been in your circle in the past, not mine. I have no idea who told him this, but I believe sincerely that it did not come from you. I can guarantee you that it didn't come from my family or attorneys. I don't know if Marvin Rudnick, Mickey Freiberg or Frank [Weimann] or [John Connolly] know him or not. I can check with Mickey if you'd like, but I sincerely doubt he knows him.
>
> Saturday is my father's birthday, so unfortunately I will not be available, but please [think] about this as a possibility for us to disengage:
>
> 1). First we mutually agree to rescind our contract.
>
> 2). I will reimburse you the $1,000 you reimbursed me for in New York on what was for both of us (for different reasons) an unpleasant and unprofessional trip. I will pay you as soon as I am able to.
>
> 3). We will give the book to someone we both trust, love and respect: Dave Robb.

4). If Dave agrees, he will take what has been done so far from
both of us and write the book under his sole byline. We can both
help him complete it, and he can do whatever side financial deal he
wants to do with you.

I'm sorry this has not worked out as either of us had hoped.
(Anita's emphasis)

A few hours later, Anita sent another email, saying that her plans
had changed, and we could talk on Saturday.

Later that night, Anita sent me her third consecutive email
without any response from me, noting the earlier article about the
prison official who had challenged Jules Nasso's claim to have
witnessed a murder while he was in prison, which, of course,
Gus and I had already discussed with Jules. She added and
underscored, "One of many, many lies, Dan." (Anita's emphasis)

29. *"Make up with your brother"*

On Saturday, January 21, 2006, Dave Robb called me at my
home. I was out, but after checking my messages later that night
from Clyde's, a Washington restaurant where Mimi and I were
having dinner, I returned his call on my cell phone.

After speaking with Dave, I believed that he had worked out
everything. As I understood the deal, Anita had agreed that Dave
would enter our arrangement and help finish the book which he and I
would now co-author.

I could not have been happier about that. In fact, Dave asked
me to write a contract to that effect which would supersede the
agreement between Anita and me. I was going to use the deal with
John Connolly as my model, replacing Connolly with Dave and
noting that the execution of this new agreement would void the
previous contract between Anita and me.

On Sunday, January 22, without having responded to Anita's
meltdown three days earlier, I drove to Ohio to help my 83-year
old mother move from our family home into an apartment at an
independent-living facility which she had selected for her senior years.

I remained on top of what was happening in Los Angeles. But after the tentative agreement that Dave and I had made on Saturday night, Anita threw what appeared to be a knuckleball on Monday.

As it turned out, Dave still did not tell Anita that I had revealed the Nasso project to him before I agreed to proceed with it. Because he had not done this, Anita still falsely believed that I had betrayed her.

Consequently, undoing the agreement that Dave and I had made on Saturday night, Anita wrote: "I faxed you the [rescission] and cancellation. Please sign today and put in the overnight mail.

"Also, I still need to know what information you gave to Julius Nasso about me and/or my case."

Then, in her fifth straight email without having received any response from me, Anita added, "Before I forget, you might want to know that one of the investigators who worked for years for Anthony Pellicano has also been working for Jules Nasso."

Anita was referring to Paul Barresi, the former porn star and ex-Pellicano employee. Earlier, Nasso's attorney had allegedly tried to use Barresi in an effort to gather intelligence on Pellicano's relationship with Steven Seagal. As I told Jules when Gus and I interviewed him, any expenditure to prove that Seagal was behind the threat against Anita was a complete waste of time and money.

Seagal, like Nasso, was an innocent man, falsely accused.[212]

Because I was in Ohio and did not have access to my fax machine in Washington, I wrote back to Anita: "I don't know anything about the '[rescission] and cancellation' document to which you referred. And I won't return to DC for several days.

"Please send me the text of this document in an email."

Anita replied: "Will do. Let me know if there is anything you object to in it. In the meantime, please let me know what information you gave to Jules Nasso about me or my case. He is getting ready to go back into court against Steven Seagal and a former investigator of Anthony Pellicano's is helping him. I really need to know what information you gave to him."

Then, with her now-routine follow-up to her own email before I had a chance to respond, she added: "I need also to know what you told Jules Nasso about the book specifically? They are getting ready to start discovery on their lawsuit against each other."

She then emailed the mystery document to me, saying in her cover letter: "Please sign and put into the overnight mail tomorrow, January 24th.

"Also, please let me know ASAP what information Jules Nasso has received from you, [specifically] regarding the book project, and me, and my case."

This was the document Anita wanted me to sign:

[Rescission] and Cancellation of Agreement

Whereas, Dan Moldea and Anita Busch had previously entered into an agreement to co-author and sell publication and marketing rights to a literary manuscript entitled *A Woman at Risk: Anita Busch and the Hollywood Mafia* (working title) and

Whereas, Dan Moldea and Anita Busch now wish to amicably dissolve, rescind and cancel said agreement,

Therefore the undersigned parties for valuable consideration mutually agree to the following:

1. The parties hereby mutually agree to dissolve, rescind and cancel any and all oral and written contracts between themselves, including but not limited to any agreement to co-author and sell publication rights and any other marketable rights in and to a literary manuscript with a working title and based on or about *A Woman at Risk: Anita Busch and the Hollywood Mafia.*

2. Any and all contracts entered into previously by the undersigned parties in respect to this literary property are considered null and void. All financial claims based on previous contracts entered into by the below parties in respect to this literary property are likewise null and void.

3. David Robb shall serve as the arbitrator to any dispute to this agreement. If Dave Robb refuses to be the arbitrator or otherwise is unavailable to act as arbitrator, then the parties shall pursue the resolution of the dispute through binding arbitration through any other arbitration service used by the courts.

4. Moldea has no financial claims on any and all fictitious accounts authored by Busch.

5. Moldea will not disclose the contents of the manuscript to any individual or private or public agency and may not use the information he obtained from Busch to write, publish or market his own manuscript for the purpose of selling publication rights.

6. The undersigned parties represent and warrant to each other that he/she has not sold, assigned or transferred any rights to the

literary manuscript and the contents thereof, or any other intellectual rights to the manuscript entitled *A Woman at Risk: Anita Busch and the Hollywood Mafia.*

7. The Agreement shall be binding and inure to the benefit of the executors, administrators, successors, agents and employees of each of the undersigned.

8. Our respective signatures herein below shall constitute this to be a complete and binding agreement between the undersigned. The undersigned have read the above, understand its terms and agree to be bound by it.

She had spaces for our signatures, as well as for Dave Robb, whom she described as our "witness and mediator."

Then, she sent another email, "4th request," in which she wrote, "I need to know ASAP about what you told Jules Nasso about my own case, me and the book project."

When I read Anita's proposed contract, as well as her "4th request" email, I had reached the end of my rope with her, and I lost my temper, sending my response to Anita without speaking to Dave:

Once again, I am not in DC and only checking my emails sporadically. Late last night was the first time that I saw your proposed separation agreement—the theme of which ran totally contrary to what Dave had told me on Saturday night.

Since your attorney clearly wrote that document, I think it's only fair that my attorney, who is out of the country until next week, be permitted to read and analyze it before providing me with his sound legal advice.

In addition, you now seem to be using my innocent discussions with Jules Nasso as part of some grand legal strategy that you are concocting against me. My attorney needs to take the necessary time to consider this, as well.

Incidentally, although I can appreciate the importance of you trying to portray me as unresponsive—by saying that this is your "4th request"—please remember that you sent me your first request for this information only yesterday (2:17 A.M.) while I have been out of town and out of touch.

In short, when I am ready to respond to you, I will surely respond. Rest assured, though, that I won't tell Dave one thing—and then go off and do something else.

Still unaware of the heads up I had given to Dave six months earlier, Anita just continued her attack, writing:

1). How did it run contrary? I don't understand. I read the contract to Dave before I sent it to you. It is the same thing I read to him last night. It has not changed one iota from when I read it to him last night. Not one word.

2). I wrote the document and ran it past [my] brother in law and then I rewrote it. I haven't hired any lawyers.

3). I am not concocting any grand legal strategy against you. That is your paranoia.

[There was no point 4.]

5). You have orally agreed to dissolve this contract and now you are stalling. Why is that, Dan?

6). The fact that you didn't tell me about Jules Nasso is an incredible breach of trust. If you had come to me about it, I would have told you why it wasn't a good idea. You don't know everything Dan and now because of your naive and behind-my-back actions, you have a duty to try and clean up any fallout from it.

7). Once again, what did you tell Jules Nasso?

At or about 4:00 P.M. on January 24, Anita called me on my cell phone. Although the connection was bad, I heard her say something about having a problem. Before she finished whatever she was trying to say through the static, I replied that she was about to have a major *legal* problem—with me. And then I hung up on her.

A few hours later, I received a message from Dave Robb. When I returned his call, he advised me "to surrender" to Anita by signing the separation agreement. He promised me that Anita would reward me with the book "sometime in the future."

I told Dave that he was now as delusional as Anita, reminding him that she had told him to make a deal with me just the previous Saturday, and then recanted the agreed-upon deal the following Monday.

I was also upset that after eight months of serving as our intermediary, Dave could only advise me "to surrender" to Anita.

Getting a little upset with my "brother," Dave, for allowing this situation to spiral out of control, I suggested to him that he withdraw as middleman, adding that he had not done a very good job because he refused to crack down on Anita, allowing her to run roughshod over me since our falling out the previous spring.

I told Dave to allow my lawyer to work out my differences with Anita.

In the midst of our conversation, I mentioned that I planned to leave Ohio the next day and drive back to Washington, D.C., joking, "Maybe I'll get killed in a traffic accident on the way home."

"That would solve everyone's problems," Dave laughed without missing a beat, breaking a very tense moment. I laughed, too.

On January 25, Anita sent me another email, saying:

> I talked to Dave after he spoke to you. Maybe this would work:
> We'll come to a simple agreement to rescind the contract.
> Something like, "The contract is rescinded."
> Then you and Dave come to your own agreement and Dave and I will come to our own agreement.
> We will then go forward from there.

One minute later, Anita added in a separate message, "Dave thinks that the best thing for us to do is to think along constructive lines."

While I was at my poker game on Thursday night, Dave called and left a message at 11:47 P.M. When I returned home about an hour later, I returned his call.

Dave wanted me to accept Anita's most recent offer: That she and I would rescind our existing contract—and that she would then create a new contract with Dave, who would have a separate contract with me for the nonfiction book.

Dealing with the issue of control, I again reminded Dave of our tentative agreement the previous Saturday night, which Anita then unilaterally overturned the following Monday.

I added that, under this proposed arrangement, I would be powerless to stop Anita from signing a non-disclosure agreement with the defendants in her civil suit, which would, in effect, void our ability to publish her story.

During our conversation, I reminded Dave, yet again, that I had notified him about my prospective relationship with Nasso.

After saying that he did not remember what I had specifically told him in July, I re-sent him the email which I had read to him over the phone on July 23 and then sent to him, via email, on July 24—along with Anita's June 12, 2005, directive for me to go through Dave if

I wanted to communicate with her. I was on the phone with Dave when he received the copy.

In the body of the email, I wrote, "How can Anita get away with claiming that I plotted to conceal the Nasso project from her—and, thus, betrayed her?

Defiantly, he told me that he had just deleted this email without even looking at it.

On January 27, in a tough message to Anita, I wrote:

> After I spoke with Dave last Saturday night, I assumed that everything was fine. As I understood the deal, you had agreed that Dave would enter our arrangement and help finish the book which he and I would now co-author. In fact, Dave asked me to write a contract to that effect while formally ending the agreement between you and me. I was going to use our contract with John Connolly as my model, noting that the execution of this new deal would void our previous understanding.
>
> That's what I agreed to.
>
> However, your proposed separation agreement on Monday— asking me to surrender all of my rights to this project, to abandon over two years of work, and to keep quiet about it—blindsided both Dave and me.
>
> Thus, your latest proposal to void our contract in favor of a scenario in which you would forge a new contract with Dave—who would then create a separate deal with me—doesn't appear to be in my best interests. As you proved this past week, you obviously feel that you may either ignore or sabotage anything that Dave and I agree to do. And, under your proposed arrangement, there would be absolutely nothing I could do about it.
>
> Significantly, under our existing contract, I have a 40-percent interest in the authorship of your story, regardless of whether it is fiction or nonfiction. And, needless to say, I will aggressively defend my rights in that agreement. Because of all of the disrespect you have shown me since last April—for the bogus reasons you have concocted—I am in no mood to do you any favors.
>
> Furthermore, I repeat unequivocally that you are flat-out wrong when you claim that I plotted to conceal my relationship with the Nasso project and thereby "betrayed" you. Nothing could be further from the truth. And, once again, I can prove that I have always been totally loyal to you, even while you were busy trying to demonize and undercut me.
>
> In the wake of this and all of your other provably false charges against me—dating back to last April—I have no intention of signing

a statement that does nothing more than break our existing contract, which you unilaterally and unjustifiably breached last spring.

However, as stated above, I will consider signing an acceptable new agreement that clearly says therein that it supersedes our previous contract and protects all of the fine work I have done on this project, which you have already acknowledged both verbally and in writing.

Finally, your proposed separation agreement was so upsetting that I have now decided that I will not surrender any part of my 40-percent share of this project. If Dave or anyone else does become a party to our arrangement, his or her fee should come from your portion of any advances and royalties—not mine.

That, Anita, is the easy way out of this mess that you have created and continue to exacerbate.

In addition, I added a postscript to this message, addressing the issue of Dave as our mediator:

> PS: Dave quickly appears to be burning out as our intermediary. I don't want to subject him to any more of the pain we are inflicting. (In fact, I have not cc'd this email to him.) If Paul Suzuki, your brother-in-law and personal attorney, is willing to step in, I'll accept him as Dave's replacement. I've always liked and respected Paul, who will not have Dave's divided loyalties in this matter. If Paul and I can't work something out, then I'll ask my attorney, who will return from abroad next week, to deal with Paul or whomever you choose.

When Anita notified him about my reply, Dave was absolutely furious with me, calling back his loans from the previous year and adding: "Dan: I'd like my $11,000 back."

I'm not a very sensitive guy, but Dave's response hurt me to the core—because I knew that this situation was no longer just business. It was now personal and could cause long-term damage to my twenty-two-year friendship with Dave.

Later in the day, Anita, appearing conciliatory for the first time in a long time, wrote:

> Here is our common ground:
> Both of us want to complete the book. We both have chosen Dave to help complete the book, which he has agreed to. Moving from there, let's figure out how to do that.

I hope you can appreciate the continued fear and horrible nightmares these threats have caused me. I hope you can also appreciate that the people who have [caused] me so much pain and suffering and have also hurt other victims need to be brought to justice. That remains the most important thing to me. I don't want anything to harm the investigator's and [prosecutor's] efforts on this case. It's too important to me and to all the other victims of these insidious crimes. We <u>need</u> to see justice served. This has devastated my life and my career, as you know. You know, more than anyone else, how this has destroyed me. Because we have not spoken for such a long time, you have no idea how horribly this continues to affect me. I continue to be unable to sleep through the night, and I am fearful every time I leave the house and always look down the street to see if someone is going to try to come after me again. I know that others have suffered the same way at the hands of these horrible people. It is my intention to have my portion of any money from the sale of our book go to a charity for victims of crime. Let's figure out a way to do that together. (Anita's emphasis)

Appreciating what she said, I wrote back: "I agree, Anita."

The following day, January 29, Anita tried to patch things up between Dave and me, writing:

"You either get tired fighting for peace or you die" . . . John Lennon

In the spirit of Lennon, you and Dave have been friends way too long. Make up with your brother.

Fighting is not the best way to win an argument. If carried to its ultimate conclusions, the old idea of "an eye for an eye" eventually ends in making everybody blind.

To Anita's apparent peace-making attempt, I replied: "Dave might be upset with me, but, bottomline, I have no problems with Dave.

"You're right. He is my brother, as well as your best friend. And I'm willing to do just about anything to patch things up."

Anita underscored her peace-making efforts in her response to my message, saying: "Now, to paraphrase Jake Blues: I ran out of gas. I had a flat tire. I didn't have enough money for cab fare. Someone stole my car. Thank God I had my brother.

"Patch things up with him."

The irony of Anita now trying to resolve the problems between Dave and me was astonishing, especially since her breach of our contract, along with her growing list of false charges against me, had created this situation in the first place.

Shortly after receiving Anita's second email, I sent a note to Dave, attaching my recent exchanges with Anita and adding:

> Here are my conciliatory exchanges with Anita since Saturday. As you can see, you are the major topic of discussion.
>
> Let me ask you: Are you still upset with me? If so, what can I do to make peace?
>
> Regarding the loan, you have every right to be eager for its quick return. And, as you already know, I am doing everything I can to get it back to you.

I signed this message, "Your brother by choice not an accident of birth, Dan."

Dave gently admonished me, writing: "As you know, I feel very protective of Anita. Now I feel like I have to protect her from you, Dan. [Y]ou *are* my brother. But she is my sister. Which makes her your sister, too. (Dave's emphasis)

30. *"I never concealed anything from you"*

With the welcomed prospect of peace and harmony among Anita, Dave, and me, Anita suddenly decided to question the nature of my soul, sparking yet another outbreak of hostilities. She wrote:

> Dave told me once how he admired you. He said that you go after the murderers, extortionists, men who brutalized the working man and that you fight hard for [reporters'] rights. He said you would bump chests with these men and were fearless in your pursuit of these kinds of animals who pass for people. These are the same kinds of people who brutally raped me and others of peace of mind and who terrorized our families and friends. They stopped a reporter from reporting a story, destroyed her career and took her music away. They called a woman's father and told [him] his daughter wasn't going to be around very long. They tried to run down two

journalists in the street; they beat a man to a pulp. They may even have committed murder. These are people who tortured someone's mother who was suffering from cancer! These are the animals behind these threats. The enemies. But now, you are bumping chests with your "brother" and one of the victims of these hideous crimes. I know what fear can do. I, too, am broke and struggling, but during this horrible series of events, Dave held out his hand to you and put it with mine and I said, okay, I will take him with me. Larry Leamer's words in that New York restaurant that night were very true. I could easily have done this by myself, but I chose to help Dave's great friend—this crusader among men who slays the bad guys and protects the victimized. Have you really renamed the enemy? In the Talmud it says that traveling on the right path is "the highest good," but when that path becomes yourself, then a person is blind to all those around him. People are putting their hands out again for you now, but it seems that fear has renamed them.

The greatest battles you'll ever wage [are] within your own soul.

Realizing that Dave was still not coming clean about what he knew about my role in the Nasso project from the outset—thus the reason for Anita's existential riff—I replied, still without ratting out Dave:

For the most part, I am still a fearless man. And I have not "renamed" the enemy. I am still among the best for distinguishing the good guys from the bad. That's why I have recoiled so dramatically from the charge that I "betrayed" you. That could never happen. Obviously, you are one of the good guys. So is Dave. And so am I.

After receiving your last email, I sent Dave a message, and he has returned it. Now, I'm getting ready to send one back to him. The issues are a little more complicated than you might think.

In the end, Dave and I will work out our problems. I'm just hoping that you and I can do the same.

To me, the easiest way is a new agreement, generally based on our contract with John Connolly, in which we replace John's name with Dave's. And, just so you know, I continue to be open-minded about going the first-person route. As I have said before, that's always been a possible bargaining point with a publisher.

With regard to matters about my soul, I don't know exactly how to respond. But I have been sleeping well.

In her reply, Anita returned to the issue of Jules Nasso.

Earlier, on January 19, 2006, Anita had written to me "While I BELIEVE that Jules Nasso did not have anything to do with the threat on my life. . ." (Anita's emphasis)

However, she started posturing in her next message, leaving open a possible line of attack against me in the future:

> Are you aware that neither Jules Nasso nor his associates have been cleared as a suspect in my case? Are you aware that Jules Nasso is friends with the man who told me "as long as you don't write about it, you'll be okay?" Are you aware that he is friends with Lambchop? Those are two people who are connected, and I am absolutely terrified of them.
>
> Are you aware that Nasso hired a private investigator early on that interfered with my case so much so that [investigators] had to change the way they went about investigating my case?
>
> Are you aware that he is working with a former Anthony Pellicano investigator?
>
> Are you aware that he is preparing to sue the FBI in my case?

Trying to return our discussion back to the issue of reconciliation, I wrote to Anita, again referring to Ovitz by her code name for him: "ED":

> Nasso knows none of [the] secrets that you confided in me. Your confidences have been protected. He only knows about ED because Connolly told him after he split from us. If you have an upcoming deposition or something, you have nothing to fear. You will not be blindsided by anything that I told Nasso—because we didn't discuss anything about you that wasn't on the public record.
>
> My goal was to get information out of Nasso—not to give him anything about you. And, just to be clear, not once did he ever try to pry something out of me that I knew about you. He believes that he is a victim, and he was eager to tell his story, unvarnished.
>
> If you want me to ask him about these other matters, I will. More to the point, if Nasso is implicated in the attack on you, I will surrender any and all claims to the Anita project. That's a promise.

I just could not have put it more on the line than that: If Nasso were to be implicated in any way in the attacks against Anita, I would walk away from our contract and return all of my rights to the

book back to her. But still seemingly demanding a fight with me,
Anita continued:

> He got a valuable piece of information from you. It was hearsay
> until you confirmed to him that we were working on a book. Who
> knows who he has told that to. That is one of my major concerns.
>
> Now, did you get any assurances whatsoever from him that he
> wouldn't [subpoena] you or me or the manuscript? He is readying for
> discovery in his lawsuit against Seagal and he is also readying a lawsuit
> against the FBI. His investigator obstructed the investigation of my case.
>
> He was not and is not a source for this book. He was a possible
> subject for a book for you. I can have nothing to do with him. I was
> told to steer clear of him, and I've been abiding by that.

Trying to put her mind at ease, I declared:

> Anita, you have nothing to worry about in this regard. Jules
> Nasso has no legal standing with regard to my association with you.
> I have no written or verbal agreement with him. And, even if he
> does come after me—which he will not—he has to get through my
> attorney, who protects me like Dave protects you.
>
> I know just about everything about Nasso's case against Seagal.
> It has nothing to do with you. With regard to his investigator's
> alleged attempt to obstruct your case, I don't believe it. Why would
> he bother? If anyone jeopardized your case, it was CW, [aka Dan
> Patterson,] who tried to sell his information to Nasso's lawyer. The
> Nasso team immediately informed the FBI, which requested that they
> cease all contact with CW—and they did.
>
> With regard to being a source for our book, I'll play it any way
> you want. But he did shed light on several things that troubled us or
> helped to correct items that were just plain wrong.
>
> Also, give me a little credit here. I have put my money where
> my mouth is. If Nasso is implicated in the attack on you, I will
> surrender any claim to the Anita project. Once again, that's a
> promise.

Still refusing to get off my case, Anita said:

> You don't believe it? You think I'm lying to you then? Ask
> Nasso's own attorney [sic] Barry Levin if Nasso's investigator caused
> investigators to investigate my case differently. Go ahead and call
> him. Tell him you heard, but don't say it came from me.

I was told in no uncertain terms to steer clear of Nasso and I must abide by that. I cannot go against that.

What about if Nasso's investigator or other associates are implicated or charged? Also, Jules Nasso has not been cleared as a suspect in my case nor was he when you went to converse with him. We had previously agreed not to talk to anyone . . . in fact, I told you that you could talk to the bodyguard I had hired. You didn't even want to talk to him and he was a <u>good guy</u>. You then start talking to a man who is associated with people I am deathly afraid of, has conflicts up the wazoo in my case, and was not cleared as a suspect and didn't ask or inform me about it first? We were both alarmed that we found out that John Connolly was working for Nasso. Remember that? Yet, still, you went forward to talk to this man without talking to me? (Anita's emphasis)

Trying to quell Anita's concerns and fears, I responded:

Of course, I don't think that you're lying. I do think you are mistaken, just as you were innocently wrong about several things in our manuscript that had to do with Nasso.

With regard to Barry Levin, I have never spoken to him. And I don't want to complicate things further by communicating with him now—unless you really want me to get an answer to this.

You were told to stay clear of Nasso. And Nasso's people were told to stay clear of CW, whose request for money from Nasso's team and the circumstances of his tape-recorded conversations with that creep, Alex Proctor, caused the feds some real problems in their investigation. I think that's where the confusion is. Because CW approached Nasso's team—for the purpose of helping Nasso in his case against Seagal—Nasso became a peripheral character in the probe of the attack on you. . . .

With regard to the upcoming prosecutions, I am betting everything that Nasso was neither involved in nor had any prior knowledge of the attack(s) on you.

Finally, for the umpteenth time, it is not true that I attempted to conceal the Nasso project from you. (My emphasis)

Refusing to acknowledge that I was truly loyal to her throughout my association with Nasso who had nothing but respect for her, Anita continued her accusations against me, digging herself a deeper hole. Once again, Dave could have easily dispelled all of these charges by simply admitting to her that he knew about my prospective relationship with Nasso before there was an actual relationship. But once again, Dave said nothing to help my case. Anita replied:

> I have known about CW's actions with Barry Levin. And please, don't tell me one more word about what Nasso has said to you. I don't want to know. I am steering clear and I must abide by that on all levels. No more, please.
>
> On the other issue, you didn't you tell me you were approached for a book with him, you didn't tell me that you were thinking about talking to him, you didn't tell me that you had conversed with him and you didn't tell me that you were continuing to converse with him or tried to sell a book about him. What you did do is confirm to him that we had a book project. Do you have any assurances from him that he will not [subpoena] me or you or the manuscript?
>
> The fact is you told me nothing for 7 or 8 months, Dan. Not a word to a partner on a project about talking to a suspect who may or may not have been involved in the threat on your partner's life. If that's not wrong, I don't know what is. I couldn't even conceive of doing that to you. This man is connected to people I am terrified of, conflicted up the wahzoo and hired someone who [interfered] with my case. (Anita's emphasis)

One minute later, Anita completed her thought, adding, "not to mention . . . [Nasso] has plans or is already suing the very people who have been trying to help me . . . the FBI."

Four minutes after that, she continued, "and, by the way . . . I already know it to be true about Jules' investigator. It is a fact."

Still trying to allay her fears, I considered telling her about Dave. I assumed that, at some point, Anita would simply ask him the obvious question: What did Dave know and when did he know it?

> You are wrong, Anita. I have protected you every step of the way. And I will continue to protect you, even if our business situation goes south.
>
> With regard to my claim that I never concealed anything from you, I can fully document it.
>
> Let me put it this way: If the situation [was] reversed—and you had done what I did—I would be thanking you for the manner in which you handled it. And then I would apologize for wrongly

accusing you. But more than anything else, I would know, once and for all, that you were a true friend—which I have always been to you, even when I didn't like you very much.

I'm off to the Wizards-Pacers NBA game tonight. Then, leaving early in the morning, I'll be out of town until Thursday. I'll check my messages before I turn in tonight.

That afternoon, just as I sent Anita my most recent email response, she called me, asking me to do nothing more than to turn on my fax machine. As soon as I had, she faxed me a one-page receipt, showing that she had used a credit card to make a $4.04 purchase at a 99-Cents Only Store.

I took this as yet another mixed message in which, in the midst of our never-ending battles, she was expressing some degree of solidarity for our mutually dismal financial situations.

Anita confirmed this a few minutes after the fax arrived, writing in another email: "All I have is your word. All you have is mine. And Dave's. And that should be good enough.

"I hope at least you got a chuckle out of the 99 cent store thing. I'd be laughing, too, if it weren't so pathetically real.

"What a fucking mess."

Actually, I really could not have agreed more. Finally, Anita and I appeared to be on the same page. We were in the same foxhole.

Then, Anita wiped out that momentary feeling of goodwill by responding to something I had written earlier, which, once again, begged the question of what Dave knew and when he knew it.

I should thank you? Are you out of your mind?!

You got involved with a man without my knowledge who was a suspect in my case and is tied to two people I am TERRIFIED of. You didn't tell me what you were doing for 7 to 8 months. To tell me now that it was intentional, only makes it more unimaginable.

If you wanted to protect me, you would have come to me first and discussed it. I would have told you then what I was told . . . steer clear of this man. You knew he was a suspect in my case. You knew that he was friends with Lambchop.

What you have done is put me in a terrible, terrible position. (Anita's emphasis)

Later, Anita wrote under the subject of "please clear something up": "I'm very confused by something you keep insisting upon and that is that you didn't keep the information from me. How can that be when I didn't know about it until last week and you had been involved with him for months and months? It just doesn't make any logical sense to me."

At that point, I knew that I did not even have to respond. Knowing how clever Anita was, it seemed obvious, especially to her, that she needed to ask our mutual friend.

I had the feeling that I would be hearing from Dave very soon.

———

On February 3, the *Los Angeles Times* reported that federal prosecutors planned to return Pellicano to Los Angeles soon in anticipation of the beginning of his long-awaited wiretapping trial.

> In recent months, documents and interviews show, at least five local law firms have been subpoenaed for records of Pellicano's work for their attorneys. Though the firms turned over some of the records, others were withheld on grounds that the work was confidential or irrelevant.[213]

Also, the *Times* noted that Los Angeles U.S. Attorney Debra Wong Yang had "recused herself from the case because she had worked earlier in her career for Greenberg, Glusker," which was Bert Fields's law firm.

That same day, federal agents arrested music-industry executive Robert Joseph Pfeifer, alleging that he had participated in Pellicano's dirty-tricks campaign against Pfeifer's one-time girlfriend, Erin Finn. According to an email written by Pfeifer several months earlier, which was obtained by the *Los Angeles Times*, he stated that he expected to be indicted in the Pellicano case, adding: "Hypothetically, I am assuming I will not have the money to fight this if it escalates; I am not going to jail. You see me. I wouldn't last a night. I have two alternatives then to run or commit suicide."[214]

That same day, federal prosecutors ordered Pellicano rearrested upon his release from Taft Correctional Institution where he had completed his thirty-month sentence for possession of illegal explosives. Federal marshals escorted him to another jail in San Bernardino County.

The following day, February 4, both the *New York Times* and the *Los Angeles Times* published stories predicting that the Pellicano indictments would be handed up on Monday. According to the *New York Times*, Pellicano had dropped attorney Victor Sherman and retained Steven F. Gruel, a former Strike Force prosecutor in San Francisco, who had hired Pellicano "as a forensic audio analyst in 1996 while prosecuting an organized-crime case in San Jose."[215]

———

With the Pellicano indictments imminent, Gus Russo and I needed to figure out what to do with our phantom agent, Carmen La Via, whose inattention to our book project had been a source of massive frustration.

We decided to send Carmen another letter, asking him to stay or go. Still angry with how we had been treated, I wrote the first draft which Gus criticized for being a bit "over the top."

Gus wrote the final draft of the letter which was far more diplomatic than my first draft, stating:

> As you likely know, tomorrow is D-Day for Anthony Pellicano—he is to be arraigned on new indictments that will likely rock Hollywood. Obviously, time is of the essence regarding our book project, as we expect there to be a flurry of book proposals on the case in the coming weeks, albeit without the sources we have in our corner. That being said, we have reviewed our email traffic for the last three months (as well as phone records) and are at wits end regarding your seeming refusal to send us a list of editors who have seen the proposal, as well as their responses. Perhaps there are "acts of God" reasons for your unresponsiveness; we have no way of knowing. But as we hope you understand, we cannot allow this moment to pass. Thus, unless we hear from you in response to our numerous requests by Monday at 5:00 pm, we will regretfully be forced to terminate

our relationship and move on to other agents who continue to
approach us.

Perhaps someday, when you have time, we will learn why you
decided to drop all contact with us.

31. *"My cat is dying"*

At long last, the U.S. Attorney's Office unsealed an indictment
on Monday, February 6, 2006, charging Pellicano and six other
people with 110 counts of conspiracy and racketeering, along with
witness tampering, wiretapping, identity theft, and destruction of
evidence. Those indicted with Pellicano included LAPD Sergeant
Mark Arneson, former telephone-company employee Rayford
Turner, software designer Kevin Kachikian, and Las Vegas
businessmen Abner and Daniel Nicherie, who were brothers.

Kachikian, the new name among the targets, had created
Telesleuth, a computer program which helped facilitate the conversion
of audio recordings into digital signals that were then stored on
Pellicano's computer. This best explained how the two billion pages
of wiretap transcripts and related documents were generated.

According to the indictment, numerous people were targets
of Pellicano's wiretapping and/or background-check operations,
including but not limited to: Anita Busch and her partner on the
Ovitz series, Bernard Weinraub of the *New York Times*; CAA agent-
executives Kevin Huvane and Bryan Lourd; actors Keith Carradine
and Kevin Nealon, and Garry Shandling; Carradine's girlfriend
Hayley DuMond; producers Aaron Russo (no relation to Gus Russo)
and Bo Zenga. Other victims included Herbalife co-founder Mark
Hughes; real-estate developer Robert McGuire; Arthur Bernier, a
former employee of Ovitz; and James Casey, who had sued Ovitz's
company, as well as Kissandra Cohen and Bilal Baroody, both of
whom had sued attorney Ed Masry.

In its press release accompanying the indictments, the U.S.
Attorney's Office in Los Angeles stated:

> The wiretapping conspiracy charge alleges that Pellicano, with
> the help of Turner and Kachikian, illegally intercepted telephone

communications of a number of individuals. According to the indictment, Kachikian began developing the Telesleuth software program in 1995. As early as 1997, the indictment alleges, Pellicano—with the aid of Turner, who provided proprietary telephone company information that allowed the wiretapping— was illegally listening to phone calls of people such as real estate developer Robert McGuire, Herbalife co-founder Mark Hughes, actor Sylvester Stallone and journalist Anita Busch.[216]

Brian Sun, an associate of attorney Bert Fields, spoke to the *New York Times* about Telesleuth. According to the *Times*:

> Brian Sun, a lawyer for Mr. Fields's firm, Greenberg, Glusker, Fields, Claman, Machtinger & Kinsella, said its lawyers believed that Mr. Pellicano intended to use Telesleuth on behalf of his many law-enforcement clients. Mr. Sun said the firm also believed that Telesleuth could not be used as a wiretapping device, although the participant in a call could use it to record a conversation.
> "It would be ludicrous to suggest that the firm or any of its lawyers would ever have associated themselves with any wiretapping activity," Mr. Sun said.[217]

The New York Times became the first media organization to note Ovitz's importance with regard to the May 16, 2002, date, revealing but underplaying: "At the time, Bernard Weinraub, a *New York Times* reporter, and Ms. Busch, then a freelance writer, were collaborating on stories about Mr. Ovitz's troubles at Artists Management. On May 16, 2002, prosecutors say, Mr. Pellicano had his police informants run both Mr. Weinraub's and Ms. Busch's names through criminal databases."[218]

Buried as it was in the article, only those familiar with the minutiae of the case would have appreciated the significance of this information.

When the *Times* asked Ovitz's attorney, James Ellis, about the background inquiries on Anita and Weinraub, Ellis replied, "That wasn't done at our direction."

Not surprisingly, Ovitz had been subpoenaed to testify before the federal grand jury investigating Pellicano's activities.[219]

After the announcement of the indictments in the Pellicano case—and in perhaps the most remarkable admission I have ever seen from anyone in the publishing industry—our agent, Carmen La Via, replied to Gus just before our 5:00 P.M. deadline, saying: "There is no excuse for my lack of communication. I am preparing the list which has about 15-20 editors and you will have it tomorrow AM.

"Again, I apologize for my inexcusable lack of attention to you and Dan and the project."

Then, another agent in Carmen's office sent a second, more detailed response, explaining:

> Carmen does have certain communication deficiencies for which he usually compensates with a roguish charm. . . . I assumed you and Dan were being kept up to date with the submissions and rejections . . . we felt that we needed this to come back in the limelight with some important indictments e.g. Ovitz? Grey? etc. to make it fly and then we could go back to most of the places that turned us down. . . .
>
> We're still enthusiastic that there is [sic] legs to the [Pellicano] Brief.

In the end, Carmen failed to find a home for our book about Jules Nasso and Steven Seagal.

———

Between February 3-6, I sent the links to all of the key articles about the exploding Pellicano situation to Anita and Dave—seven in all. During that four-day period in which Anita Busch nearly became a household name among everyone in the entertainment industry, I did not receive a single reply either from her or from Dave.

At or about 4:00 P.M. on February 6, I called Dave at his office. During our conversation, Dave said Anita, based on all of my "hints," had asked him whether he knew about my book project with Nasso. Initially, he said, Anita was upset with his admission, even though he did not give her the details.

Dave continued to advise me "to surrender" to Anita and sign the separation agreement, insisting that, in the end, she would do the right thing and give me the book. I repeated that there was no way

I would give up my existing contract and place myself at Anita's mercy.

After my conversation with Dave, assuming that everything about my arrangement with Nasso and Dave's knowledge of it was now out in the open, I wrote a message to Anita, addressing Dave's confession to her:

> I spoke with Dave today who told me that he had cleared things up. Now that you know that I revealed everything in a July 24 email before I did anything on the Nasso book project—as per the instructions in your June 12, 2005 email—I am hoping that this issue is finally settled. No apology necessary.

What I did not realize at that moment was that Dave *had* confessed—but only sort of. He angrily replied to my message on February 7, saying: "I thought I made it clear to you today that I resent your attempt to cover your ass by trying to imply that I somehow approved of whatever it was you were doing with [Nasso]. As you know, nothing could be further from the truth."

Immediately, I replied:

> The issue is not what you did. You have been a loyal friend to both Anita and me in your heroic effort to protect Anita. And I have never, ever claimed to anyone that you approved of my role in the Nasso book project. You never did.
>
> The issue that Anita concocted on January 18 was that I had concealed my participation in the Nasso book from her and, thus, "betrayed" her. And, acting on that belief, she began to move legally against me—first by sending me that separation agreement drawn up by her attorney.
>
> Clearly, Anita was wrong. I never concealed this matter, and I didn't [betray] her.
>
> On June 12, 2005, in the wake of her unfair spring offensive against me, Anita instructed me, via email, to communicate with you if I had anything to say to her. On July 23, I called and told you that I had been approached about the Nasso project—even before I had my first conversation with Nasso. The following day, I memorialized my notification by sending you an email and giving you the details as I knew them. I left it to you as to whether or not to tell Anita. Knowing that she would be upset, you decided not to tell her. In fact, you were upset with me for giving you this information.

> Dave, if she had instructed me to use her sister as the intermediary, I would've told her about the Nasso project. Unfortunately, you were the one placed in the middle.
>
> Then, sometime during the past week, apparently after seeing the unfair grief I had been taking from Anita since January 18, you finally told her that I had notified you about the Nasso project last summer. As you know, I think that you took too long to tell her, but you were in a very difficult position.
>
> Once again, I have never told anyone that you approved of my role in the Nasso book project—only that I had notified you about it.

Neither Dave nor I copied our exchanges to Anita. However, that same day, Anita replied to my last email to her about my email exchange with Dave the previous July. Clearly, Dave *still* had not mentioned to her that I had put everything about the Nasso project in writing.

Anita wrote: "I'm very busy right now with things of a personal nature. I have no idea what you are talking about. [W]hat emails?"

Tired of all of this, I pried the door that Dave had opened with my next email to Anita, which I also copied to Dave, stating:

> Attached is the email you sent on June 12, 2005, culminating your unfair spring offensive against me [in which Anita said that she had nothing further to say to Dan and instructed him to communicate with her through Dave].
>
> With regard to my July 24 email about the proposed Nasso project, may I ask you to get it from Dave—since I originally sent it to him and the two of you are in regular contact. If Dave doesn't have it, I'll give it to you.
>
> To be clear, I felt that I had a responsibility to notify Dave about the Nasso project before I ever spoke to Nasso, especially since you had designated Dave as your representative in the attached email.
>
> Just to ensure that there is no misunderstanding, Dave never approved of my participation in the Nasso project. And I never asked for his approval. In fact, he didn't even want to hear anything about it. At all times, though, the most important consideration for Dave and me was to protect you, which we did in our own different ways. (My emphasis)

To my surprise, Dave was still refusing to accept any responsibility, writing on February 8:

Nice selective memory, Dan. You falsely claim that you left it up to me whether or not to tell Anita about what you were doing with Nasso. In fact, before you told me about it, you made me promise that I wouldn't tell anyone. I stupidly agreed. Believe me, if I hadn't made that promise, I would have told her immediately. Your attempt to cover your own ass by trying to put this on me is shocking.

And just so you'll know, in the future, all emails you send me will be sent, unread, to Anita.

I was incredulous over Dave's latest reply and decided that I had enough this. It was finally time for full disclosure. So, in my next email to both Anita and Dave on February 9, I wrote:

Dave: You are and always will be my brother. But you're wrong, and the attached July 24 email proves that you're wrong. I never extracted any kind of promise from you about this. Specifically, I wrote: "I leave it to you whether to tell Anita—who, as usual will place some nefarious spin on what's happening." Also, for the past three weeks, I have been protecting you. You haven't been protecting me. I begged you to tell Anita what you knew while she and her attorney were running roughshod over me, falsely accusing me of concealing my role in Nasso project and then trying to use this fabrication to force me to sign some bogus separation agreement. Through all of this, you remained silent, hanging me out to dry in the process. As much as I respect you, the simple fact is that you were a terrible intermediary.

Anita: You now have your June 12 email, instructing me to communicate with you through Dave, as well as my July 24 email to Dave, laying out the Nasso project before I ever spoke with Nasso. I followed your instructions and did nothing wrong. And Dave did nothing wrong, either. He was only trying to protect you—and, in an odd way, trying to protect me, too. By the way, I will never forgive you for causing this rift between Dave and me. Meantime, I await your next set of false charges against me. You made yourself look foolish on this one and caused a lot of damage in the process.

I hope you are safe and well. Both Dave and I have done everything possible to make sure that you stayed that way.

Perhaps we'll all see each other at John Connolly's book party. He's the big winner here.

Anita simply replied: "We must deal with later. My cat is dying."

And that was my last communication with Anita, directly or indirectly.

With regard to Dave, I knew that if this fight had been between me and anyone else in the world, he would have been on my side. But Dave, a very loyal friend, would never forget or ever be able to repay Anita for quitting her job as the executive editor of the *Hollywood Reporter* in support of him in 2002.

Just as their friendship had initially been my blessing, that same friendship had now become my curse.

PART FOUR:
Depression

32. *"I wouldn't do anything to hurt Anita"*

On February 11, 2006, the *New York Times* and the *Los Angeles Times* published major stories indicating that Anita's legal team had subpoenaed Michael Ovitz in her civil case against Pellicano. Both newspapers made public what Anita, Dave, and I had known for nearly three years: that Steven Seagal had been cleared by federal prosecutors for his alleged role in the June 20, 2002, threat against Anita who had joined the *Los Angeles Times* earlier that month. Prior to that, Anita had worked with Bernard Weinraub on their series about Ovitz's alleged financial improprieties. The series, published in the *New York Times*, ended on May 7, 2002.

This was an expansion of the information that the *New York Times* had buried in an article just four days earlier.

Really zeroing in on the big news, both newspapers reported that nine days after the Busch-Weinraub series on Ovitz concluded on May 16, one of Pellicano's LAPD sources had run the names of both Anita and Weinraub through a law-enforcement database. This was before Steven Seagal (or Jules Nasso) were on Anita's reporting plate at the *Los Angeles Times*.

The New York Times added: "Ms. Busch's lawyers stopped short of saying they believed that Mr. Ovitz had something to do with the threats against her. 'We view Mr. Ovitz as a person of interest, not yet as a defendant,'" according to Brian Kabateck, one of Anita's lawyers.[220]

Kabateck told the *Los Angeles Times*, "We feel very strongly that Mr. Pellicano did not threaten Anita for his own personal satisfaction. That it was done on behalf of somebody. . . . It is our view that this is an extremely serious situation and that it is not too much to ask Mr. Ovitz some questions. Maybe someone was trying to do this to please Mr. Ovitz. To curry favor with him. But we need to find out what happened and that is why we are continuing to ask questions."[221]

Soon after, the *New York Times* continued its big stories in this case with the most shocking to date. Reporters David M. Halbfinger and Allison Hope Weiner revealed:

> In April or May 2002, . . . Mr. Ovitz learned that a "group of people" were "coming after" him to attack his reputation, he told the F.B.I., and he hired Mr. Pellicano to investigate. . . .
>
> Mr. Ovitz told the F.B.I. that he met three or four times with Mr. Pellicano and spoke "multiple" times with him in June and July of 2002. Mr. Ovitz said he received an oral report about Mr. Weinraub, Ms. Busch and Mr. Geffen, but all Mr. Ovitz said about the report was that Mr. Pellicano called Ms. Busch "boring and not worth [Ovitz's] time." . . . Mr. Ovitz told the F.B.I., he wondered what Mr. Pellicano might say about him.
>
> Mr. Ovitz said he paid Mr. Pellicano $75,000 in cash, the last payment in late June or early July 2002.[222]

Also, on the afternoon of February 11, the former Mafia guy-turned-government-witness—whose wife Anita helped to save via her introduction to an anti-cancer program—called me to discuss the Pellicano indictments. During our conversation, I told him that my book project with Anita had ended badly.

Offering to help, the former mobster asked if I wanted him to speak to Anita in an effort to patch things up.

Imagining how Anita could use that against me—a major Mafia figure calling to speak with her on my behalf—I thanked him but asked him to resist the temptation to help me.

He laughed and said he understood.

Later that night, I received a message from Dave Robb, which he signed "Your brother," saying:

> My oldest friend died today. We had been best friends since high school. I went down to Torrance this afternoon to see his father and we had our own private memorial service.
>
> In my book's acknowledgment, I wrote, "To Tim Mounts, my oldest and wisest friend."
>
> Kelly is heart-broken. Tim had stayed with us many times when he came down from San Francisco. I've known for some time that he was dying. He was going to come see us in March, but I talked to him last week, and I knew then that he wouldn't be coming.
>
> We always [think] that we are going to see somebody at least one more time, but eventually, we are always wrong.
>
> I'm sorry for all the struggling you and I have been through lately. Just know that we are friends for life.

In my reply to Dave, which I again signed "Your brother by choice, not an accident of birth," I wrote:

> Wow, Dave. You actually put tears in my eyes with your message. While I was reading it to Mimi, I had to stop to collect myself.
>
> Hey, man, I couldn't agree more. We'll get through this—and probably laugh about it someday.
>
> Sorry about your buddy, Tim. I'm pretty sure that I met him—in fact, more than once. Cool guy—and lucky as hell to have you as a good friend for so long.
>
> Thanks again for your note. You have no idea how much it means to me. . . . On second thought, I think you do know.

———

On Friday, March 24, I received a call from Lloyd Grove, a reporter for the *New York Daily News*, whom I had met several years earlier while he was writing the "Reliable Source" column for the *Washington Post*. Somehow, Grove had learned about the dispute between Anita and me and called to ask about it.

I found myself defensive throughout the interview, wondering who the hell had placed me in this position. My top suspect was John Connolly who was still trying to sell his book.

I did not want to lie to Grove, but I did not want to tell him anything either.

On March 27, Grove, who protected the identity of his source, published the item in his column, writing:

> Life might soon get stickier for embattled Hollywood journalist and alleged Anthony Pellicano target Anita Busch. I hear she's been feuding with Washington writer Dan Moldea over a book project on which she initially collaborated, but now wants to kill.
>
> Busch is a potential witness in the wiretapping case against Pellicano and power players yet to be indicted. She's also suing the jailed private eye for "threats … on [her] life [that] traumatized her and brought her illustrious career to a halt."
>
> Those included the alleged illegal wiretapping of Busch's phone and—during her 2002 *L.A. Times* investigation of Steven Seagal and his possible links to a Mafia associate—her discovery of a dead fish with a rose in its mouth on her car, an apparent bullet hole in the windshield and a sign reading "Stop."
>
> I'm told Busch's legal team went ballistic when they saw Moldea's manuscript about her ordeal, warning it would damage her lawsuit, and Busch told Moldea she was pulling the plug. I hear Moldea is mad because he expects to share royalties. But he told me, "I wouldn't do anything to hurt Anita because of all she's been through, and I wouldn't do anything to hurt this federal investigation."[223]

On April 5, *L.A. Weekly* columnist Nikki Finke published a story in *Deadline Hollywood Daily*, confirming that Connolly, who would be publishing his second story about the Pellicano case in the June 2006 issue of *Vanity Fair*, had sold his book, *The Sin Eater*, to Atria Books, a fairly strong division of Simon & Schuster, a subsidiary of Viacom, which also owned Paramount Pictures, now run by Brad Grey, one of the top subjects in the Pellicano case.[224]

In his latest *Vanity Fair* piece, this one co-authored with Bryan Burrough—who, like Howard Blum, was a first-rate journalist—Connolly wrote:

> The one Ovitz "enemy" Pellicano is known to have wiretapped was Anita Busch, whose phone remained compromised up until the

month of the F.B.I. raids. However, there is no evidence that Ovitz
knew of the wiretap, nor that his interest in Busch had spurred it.
Prosecutors, however, are known to be examining whether Ovitz
was behind the intimidation of Busch. Initially, speculation had
centered on Steven Seagal, but the F.B.I. has all but cleared the actor
of involvement. At least two witnesses have been questioned by the
grand jury about Ovitz's links to the incident. . . Marshall Grossman,
Ovitz's lawyer, denies that Ovitz is being investigated and says he
had no connection with the crime, claiming, "At the time he allegedly
hired a third party to threaten Ms. Busch, Mr. Pellicano was not in
the employ of Michael Ovitz."[225]

After reading Connolly's second story in *Vanity Fair*, I knew that
there was no way that I was walking away from the messiest three
years of my personal and professional life without publishing my
own first-person account about the Pellicano scandal.

———

In the aftermath of the federal indictments, Chuck Philips of the
Los Angeles Times again interviewed Pellicano. And just as when he
spoke with him in 2003, Pellicano said that his clients had nothing to
fear, that he would never testify against them. Specifically, Philips
wrote:

> "My loyalty never dies," said Pellicano, 62. "You're not going
> to see me take the stand against the clients and employees and other
> people that are going to be testifying against me. I didn't rat them
> out. You understand? I am never going to besmirch a client or any
> other person that I gave my trust to or who gave their trust to me.
> I'm never going to do that. I am going to be a man until I fall—if, in
> fact, that happens."

With regard to the vandalizing of Anita's car, Pellicano once
again denied any role, saying:

> "Anybody knows that there is no way in the world that I am
> going to tell somebody to put a flower and a fish on somebody's car
> with a sign that says 'Stop.' C'mon," Pellicano said. You know the
> kind of guy I am. If I got a problem with you, I'm in your face."[226]

In the July 24, 2006, edition of the *New Yorker*, Ken Auletta published another remarkable story, managing to get Ovitz, among others, on the record. Auletta wrote:

> "I don't think anybody knew what this guy was doing, because this guy traded in information," Ovitz said of Pellicano, picking up a basketball and pacing slowly. "That's what he did. I used to watch *Perry Mason* reruns all the time. There was this guy who's a private detective, Paul [Drake], and he always came in at the last minute and slipped a note to Perry Mason in court at the most critical time. So now I say to myself, 'Let's see here, did Perry Mason ask Paul how he got that information?' Don't think so. 'Did Paul get it all legally?' Don't know. 'Was it just a blank slip of paper?' Probably. That's more than I ever got. . . ."
>
> Ovitz said that he couldn't speak for others, but that Pellicano "didn't produce anything for us to even ask about. The lawyers hired him. We got nothing, zippo."[227]

33. *"I wish that circumstances were different"*

On August 29, 2006, I sent Anthony Pellicano a letter, requesting an interview. I notified him that I was writing a book "in direct competition with John Connolly," whom I knew that Pellicano absolutely despised. More than anything else, I thought that simple fact would get me the meeting. In addition, I sent Pellicano a copy of my 1995 book about the murder of Senator Robert Kennedy in which I highlighted the sloppy investigative work performed by both the LAPD and the FBI, even though I still concluded that "Sirhan Sirhan did it, and he did it alone."

Specifically, I wrote:

> I am currently writing a book about the extraordinary controversy revolving around you. Needless to say, I am fascinated by the worldwide attention your case is receiving. Obviously, I cannot help but think how this situation has ravaged your family.
>
> Notably, I am in direct competition with John Connolly who is scheduled to publish his book in 2007. If you decide to speak with me, I will take a huge advantage and defeat him. If you decide to speak with him, he will take the advantage and defeat me.

I am hoping that you will speak with me—on your terms and at your convenience. Below is the address and telephone number for my home and office. Please feel free to call me collect anytime, day or night.

If you want me to come to California to meet you in person, I certainly will do so.

Also, I am an old friend of Jim Agnew, who told me to send you his best wishes. He added that—in his handful of dealings with you in Chicago—you always operated with honor and integrity.

Pellicano's response dated September 4—sent "from the joint"—was very cordial but ultimately dismissive. He told me:

I am not cooperating with the "cockroach" named John [Connolly], in any manner. He had written me, once, asking for an interview and I declined by not even answering his letter. I had heard that he was collaborating with Anita Busch, although that is hardly the reason for ignoring him. . . . I had also heard that **you** were collaborating with Ms. Busch. Although I had never met Ms. Busch, or had any contact with her whatsoever, she is certain, I am told, that I am her enemy. I am not. In any event, I am not inclined to get involved with anyone [who] has a relationship, or involved in any manner, with Ms. Busch. The [reasons] are simple: She is suing me, she is going to testify against me at trial, and apparently she has already testified, although I do not know to what, at a Grand Jury.

Consequently, it makes no sense whatsoever to participate with or otherwise work with you in any manner, having knowledge or the presumption, that you have or have had, a relationship or collaboration with Ms. Busch. If that were not the case, then I would be more inclined to communicate with you. [Pellicano's emphasis]

Giving him an overview of the gory details behind the split among Anita, John, and me, as well as my work on the Seagal-Nasso project with Gus Russo, I hoped to persuade Pellicano that I was an independent player. I wrote in my September 12 reply:

Just to answer your questions, Anita would not sign a collaboration contract with me until John Connolly became a part of our writing team and signed the 2003 contract, too. Connolly then betrayed both of us by accepting an assignment, without our knowledge, to write a piece about you for *Vanity Fair*—even though he was still under contract with us. (That story, his first of two about your case, appeared in the March 2004 edition of the magazine.) Needless to say, that caused major problems with Connolly, as well as the termination of our contract. Simultaneously, he promised that he was not going to write a competing book, but—as has been published in several newspapers—his book about you will be released by Atria Books, a subsidiary of Simon & Schuster, next year.

Indeed, Anita and I continued our project without Connolly. However, the *New York Daily News* accurately reported this past March 27 that she and I had a bitter falling out during the spring of 2005 after she gave the manuscript I had written to her attorneys in your civil suit. Persuaded that my work provided too much free discovery, Anita unilaterally decided to kill the entire project, which, in my opinion, violated our agreement. Because her best friend is like a brother to me, I did not take any action against her—although I continue to keep my options open. At that time, I had over two years on this project and refused to walk away empty-handed.

In the wake of Anita's bad decision, I received an introduction to Jules Nasso, who was a fairly dark character in our book, as well as a suspect as the person who ordered and paid for the vandalism of her car. However, Jules sat down with me and explained his side of the story in considerable detail, including his relationship and subsequent war with Steven Seagal, which cost him nearly a year in jail. Of course, I am convinced that Jules played no role in the threat against Anita, and that many of the allegations made against him by Seagal, who also wasn't involved in the Anita-car attack, were bogus.

Thus, I am hoping to vindicate Jules in my book, *which is actually a first-person account of my experiences during the federal investigation of you.*

Of course, Anita hit the roof in January/February of this year when I revealed in good faith that I had been dealing with Nasso. Anita and I have had no communication since around the time of your recent indictment, verbal or written. If I never speak to her again, it'll be too soon.

I can only imagine the ridiculous conspiracy theory [Anita will] concoct if and when she learns that I have corresponded with you. Yet, even though I am furious with Anita for the situation she put me in, I have not—and will not—do anything to jeopardize her safety or compromise her personal secrets.

Clearly, you are a stand-up guy, so you are hip to what I'm talking about. Obviously, you are protecting people, too—some of whom you probably can't stand. I can only imagine the pressure on you to flip. Consequently, you are probably being treated like an enemy combatant at Guantanamo.

Predictably, I was taken back when you wrote to me that Anita "is certain . . . that I am her enemy. I am not." That is the first time I have heard you or anyone else say anything like that. Is this a hint that you protected her from someone who wanted to do something far worse than a mere act of vandalism to her car? (My emphasis)

When Pellicano didn't respond to my second letter, our mutual friend, crime-researcher Jim Agnew of Chicago, offered to write to him, vouching for me and trying to get our connection back on track. In my subsequent letter to Agnew, I wrote:

Since 2003, I have known that Ovitz was behind the attack on the reporter. I know the whole story about how it was discovered. It's a major thread throughout my manuscript.

Between you and me, Pellicano has been protecting Ovitz from the outset. I know that as a fact. The question is whether Pellicano authorized the severity of the attack. In what he wrote to me in his reply to my first letter, he appears to insist that he did not.

Pellicano did answer Agnew's October 26 letter on November 1, saying:

As far as your friend Dan is concerned, I was flattered that he chose to write me and request an interview for his book. [H]owever I cannot reasonably entertain working with or being interviewed by a person who was working with an enemy to write a book about me and the ordeal. It just makes no sense whatsoever. He wrote two nice letters and I wrote him as nice a letter as possible and told him not to take my rejection personally, because it was not meant to be a personal decision. It just is not, in my opinion, a logical thing to do. I wish that he did not have a relationship with Busch or Connolly.

There are so many distorted, disinformative and otherwise erroroneous [sic] articles that have been written, and I have been told that there are at least four (4) books being pitched about me now, that I just do not care what is written. There is simply nothing that I can do about it in any event. Strange as it may seem, I led a very private life in California and tried as the best I could not to involve my family in any part of my business life, however as of late, I was unsuccessful. It took [its] toll and I am not happy about it.

In any event, I am staying strong, and will fight to the end. Come what may.

Despite two additional exchanges between Pellicano and me, I could not shake him of the notion that I was still in business with Anita and John. He concluded his letter of December 15 to me, saying:

> I wish that circumstances were different because I believe that we might have had a good working relationship. I do wish you the very best and will assist you to the extent that I can, should you proceed with your writings of my case or me. Somehow, I believe that you will be fair in your [assessments] and that would please me.

In my December 28 reply to Pellicano, I wrote:

> Of course, I accept your generous offer to "assist you to the extent that I can." That's just what I hoped you'd say. Once again, I will protect anything that you give me. . . .
>
> If you give me a written response, I will print this information as you have stated it. If you call me [my telephone number], I will tape record the conversation and memorialize your words. I will then send you a transcript, giving you the opportunity to amend or expand upon what you have said. In other words, I want you to use me to say whatever you want to say—in the manner you want to say it.
>
> I followed this process with Jules Nasso, who lauds my work. As I have told you, I am vindicating Jules from a series of false allegations that have haunted him for years.
>
> With your information, I can complete my own book project, which, as I told you, is a first-person account of my experiences during the federal investigation of you.
>
> The publication of this material will give you the opportunity to assess my work. When you have decided that you can trust me completely, then I hope that you will tell me your entire story, including the circumstances revolving around your legal problems.
>
> At that point and with your permission, I will either update my existing work or begin a new project with you.

With regard to Nasso and Seagal, Pellicano wrote to me on January 8, 2007, saying:

> I think that I'd better clear a few things up. I never had the pleasure of meeting Mr. Nasso.[228] After working a very short time for Seagal, I fired him. He and Michael Jackson were the only clients I ever did. I despised the man. He was, and remains, a

lying piece of shit . . . notwithstanding, a wife beater. Those are the kindest things that I could say about him. So to assume or allege that I would ever work for him to attempt to threaten a reporter is insane, at best. However that is what the FBI idiots thought and were told by an informant [Dan Patterson] and that is what they believed and used to get a search warrant to [invade] my offices. The rest is history and I am fighting them over this as we speak. . . .

I am confused. Are you writing a book about Jules Nasso or about me? Or both? If you are writing about Jules Nasso, then you certainly do not need my assistance. If [you] are writing about me and this case, then you will have to do the best you can. I cannot assist you in writing about my case, because it is still pending and I will go to trial, at least I hope that I will, in August of this year and need each and every moment to work on this matter. Even if I wanted to, I could not devote the time required, so you are on your own. Should you wish to fairly report on this case you will, if you do not, then you will not. That will be your decision. For whatever has and will be said about me, I am a man of honor and will remain so.

Again, I wish you the very best.

Speaking of Anita and John Connolly, Pellicano continued:

I find it incredible that Anita Busch would seek to write a book about me, and this case, while attempting to have me prosecuted and sued at the same time. Those will be interesting questions to ask her at the appropriate time.

John Connelly [sic] is a cockroach. You may care to research him, especially a *New Yorker* [sic] article that was written some time ago. He was never a detective for the NYPD, he was a patrolman. He purchased or otherwise obtained a gold shield, and for a while, before I exposed him, used it to gain access to information. Who is worse, he or I. In any event, he has caused me pain and grief by affecting my family. To assume that I would ever work with [him] and Ms. Busch is also insane, as I have said before. . . .

I have had many calls and other information passed on to me about Connelly's [sic] [attempts] at getting information to aid him in writing his proposed book. I cannot imagine it to be anything other than a regurgitation of what he, and others have already said. How boring. But, editors sometimes are swayed aren't they [?] He wrote me a letter asking for my participation, and it remains unanswered.

I have been told that he has had ghost writers assist him for his past articles. He is not a writer, so his product will undoubtedly

be a [collaboration] of some kind. We shall see. I obviously will
comment on it at the appropriate time. I will never waste my time
with a lawsuit, however. He will either write the truth or he will not,
so the content will reflect that fact when it comes to light.

However, Pellicano appeared to withdraw his previous offer to
assist me "to the extent that I can," unless he was simply posturing
for legal purposes. Specifically, he wrote:

For the record and for the legal purposes intended, please be
formally notified that I cannot assist you in your endeavors to write
about me and this case at this time. I cannot and will not provide
you with any information relative to this case while it is pending.
Your reporting of this matter is entirely your responsibility. I urge
you to be careful and fair in your reporting or authoring of anything
regarding me, or this case. I believe that you will.

You do have my permission to disclose to anyone you choose,
the fact that we are, and have been corresponding. Should that help
you, then please use that fact for purposes that you choose. I caution
you, however, that you should never give anyone the impression that
I am disclosing information about my pending case. You will find
yourself a witness and I am sure that you have better things to do,
and certainly better use of your time.

At the end of these exchanges, I found myself with a grudging
respect for Pellicano. No matter how you sliced it or diced it,
Pellicano, good or evil, appeared to be a stand-up guy.

On Sunday, April 1, 2007, I attended a book party for a
colleague at the home of Michael Nussbaum, a prominent attorney
in Washington. Also in attendance was Bob Woodward, the famed
reporter from the *Washington Post* with whom I had become
acquainted during my years as journalist. While we were talking, he
asked me what my latest book project was. When I replied that I was
working on the Pellicano wiretapping scandal, Woodard appeared
very interested and asked where the investigation was going.

"Michael Ovitz," I replied. "It appears that he might be the
real villain, at least as far as that part of the investigation revolving

around Anita Busch, the reporter from the *Los Angeles Times* whose car was vandalized."

When Woodward asked me what the principal evidence was against Ovitz, I recounted how Detective Mark Arneson had run Anita's name through the LAPD's computer on behalf of Pellicano on May 16, 2002—two weeks before Anita had joined that *Los Angeles Times* but just nine days after she had completed her series about Ovitz for the *New York Times*.

"Before we learned about that," I added, "the chief suspects were Steven Seagal and his producer, Jules Nasso. After receiving that information about the May 16th date, it was clear that Ovitz was working with Pellicano. There was no doubt in our minds."

Then I told Woodward that Anita and her attorneys had added Ovitz to her civil complaint against Pellicano, Proctor, the City of Los Angeles, and the phone company, among others, on November 6, 2006—after federal investigators revealed that Ovitz had paid Pellicano $75,000 to "investigate" Anita, along with several others.

Anita had amended her original complaint of May 2004. Her latest attorney, Ian Herzog, wrote that Ovitz was among those who were "directing, organizing, commanding, employing and/or hiring individuals to engage in the unlawful and tortuous conduct."[229]

In a comment to the *Los Angeles Times*, Ovitz's attorney, James Ellis, said, "My client had nothing to do with this. It's unfortunate that Ms. Busch has chosen to involve him in this matter."[230]

34. *"I will make a very big scene."*

On April 30, 2007, a Washington lawyer I knew introduced me to Deborah Jeane Palfrey, the so-called "D.C. Madam," who had recently been indicted on federal conspiracy charges, stemming from a prostitution ring that she had operated in the local metropolitan area from 1993 to 2006.

Smart, stylish, and a law-school dropout, Palfrey, who did have an undergraduate degree in criminal justice, had already become a sensation in the local media.

Following the introduction, Jeane and I hit it off, and she asked me to write her memoir. Although I was still raw and stinging from my horrible experience with Anita, I signed a collaboration contract with Jeane.

While we were putting together our book proposal, I discovered the telephone number of U.S. Senator David Vitter, a Republican from Louisiana, in Jeane's telephone records. I immediately called Jeane and asked her about him. She said that she never wanted to know her clients' real names, and that she had never heard of Vitter.

I then called porn king Larry Flynt. I was in the midst of an assignment as an investigative consultant for him, so I shared the Vitter story. Flynt and I concocted an elaborate scheme to release this information, deciding to leak it first to a reporter at *Time* magazine who presumably would then confront Senator Vitter. This was in lieu of forcing Flynt's staff to do it.

However, when the reporter called and asked for comment, Senator Vitter tried to pull an end-around, confessing instead to a reporter in his home state in an attempt to get ahead of the looming scandal. That move provoked the *Time* reporter to file his own story, explaining the specifics of what I had uncovered about Senator Vitter.

Although the subsequent scandal was huge, Jeane and I were unable to sell our book because, once again, Jeane truly did not know the real names of her clients in D.C. She had assumed that she would be safer not knowing them.

I immediately let Jeane out of our collaboration contract with no strings attached, and we remained friends, continuing to talk on the phone and to exchange emails. Jeane selected a staff reporter from *Vanity Fair* to replace me, but, in the end, she was also unable to sell Jeane's book project.[231]

———

In the midst of repeated delays for Pellicano's conspiracy trial, a breakthrough in the criminal case appeared to occur when Las Vegas software designer Daniel Nicherie, one of Pellicano's co-defendants, became the latest to plead guilty in the Pellicano case.[232]

Nicherie's brother, Abner, did not plead out and expected to stand trial with Pellicano. The Nicherie brothers were charged with participating in the conspiracy to wiretap Ami Shafrir, a Hollywood businessman.[233]

Another defendant in the Pellicano case was Terry Christensen, the attorney for billionaire businessman Kirk Kerkorian. Christensen faced charges that he had hired Pellicano to wiretap the telephone of Kerkorian's ex-wife, Lisa Bonder Kerkorian, in the midst of their paternity and child-support case.

Christensen and Pellicano would be tried in a separate trial that would follow the main event.[234]

Soon after, the *New York Times* obtained an earlier digitally taped conversation between Pellicano and Ovitz on April 11, 2002, which had been recorded in the midst of Anita's series about Ovitz's business operations in the *Times*. Appearing quite concerned, Ovitz said to Pellicano, "I need to see you. . . . I have a situation I need advice on. . . This is the single most complex situation imaginable."[235]

As expected, the trial judge in the civil cases, like Anita's, declared that they would not proceed until the criminal cases had concluded.[236]

On January 9, 2008, after another long hiatus, the trial judge in the Pellicano-conspiracy case, U.S. District Judge Dale S. Fischer, who denied all six of Pellicano's pre-trial legal maneuvers to have his case dismissed,[237] accepted the former PI's request, asking for permission to serve as his own attorney.

Speaking from the bench, Judge Fischer warned Pellicano: "If I were a defendant in this case, I would not consider for a moment representing myself. . . It is not a good idea. . . . If you mess up, you can't go to the court of appeals and say, 'I messed up.'"[238]

Pellicano insisted that he could not pay for the attorney who had been representing him, Steven Gruel of San Francisco, who, directly or indirectly through one of his associates, had repeatedly tried to persuade me to appear voluntarily as a witness for Pellicano to discuss my book project with Anita Busch and John Connolly.[239] Remarkably, Gruel never received any money for representing Pellicano.

On February 3, 2008, I sent Pellicano another letter, notifying him that I was going to attend his trial and saying:

> Of course, while I'm out there—my first trip to LA in nearly four years—I would like to pay my respects to you. Is there any way that I can see you during that week?
> Also, several Republican operatives have tried to make the case in the midst of the current Presidential campaign that you were hired by the Clintons for any number of purposes. May I ask: Were you ever employed by the Clintons or their attorneys for any reason? From what I understand, you were hired by CBS to analyze some tape recordings that involved the Clintons.
> Once again, I'm hoping to see you while I'm out there. I am willing to jump through whatever hoops are necessary to make that happen.

I ended my letter by giving him some good-natured ribbing, adding, "Good luck with your case—although I just can't believe that you made the decision to represent yourself." I knew that the veteran private investigator was thick-skinned, and could accept the comment.

In his reply, without addressing my questions about the Clintons, Pellicano appeared more interested in trying to get me to work for his defense, saying:

> I know that you wish to see me and would agree for you to do so, but there is no time to do that and this institution will not allow it to occur in any event. There have been so many that have tried, including "60" [M]inutes. I have, and will give some telephonic interviews.
> We had talked about your knowledge of Ms. [Busch] and the cockroach [aka John Connolly] before, but I never got the impression that you would willingly assist me with what you knew and went through with those two. If you are so inclined, at this point, to do so, I will arrange to have someone visit with you when you come to town. That would be very helpful to me.

Before concluding his letter, he defended his legal prowess, insisting: "As to my representing myself, there are reasons, and you may not be all that surprised after you see me in action."

Simply speaking, out of respect for my estranged brother, Dave Robb, I rejected each and every effort from Pellicano and his defense team to gain my cooperation at the trial.

———

At Thanksgiving 2007, I received a very simple email message from Dave, wishing me a happy holiday. This was the first time I had heard from him in over a year and a half—even though I had been slowly repaying the loan he made to me in 2005 during his lame attempt to hold the deal together between Anita and me, which he later sabotaged.

I sent him back a note, saying that we should both be looking for ways to get things back to normal.

In February, I sent Dave another check. I had now paid him back $5,500 of the $11,000 he'd loaned me while my deal with Anita was collapsing.

In response, Dave sent me a large box of California oranges.

After those exchanges, I sent him an email, notifying him that I was coming to Los Angeles for a few days to cover the Pellicano trial, and that I wanted to see him and his wife.

> I'm glad that you received my $2,500 check. I will be trying hard to pay off my debt to you in full within the next few months.
> Just so you know, I'm planning to come out there for a portion of the Pellicano trial. I can't imagine being in Los Angeles without seeing you. But, because so much is still unresolved, it might not be a good idea.
> Still, I'd really like to see you and Kelly.

As it turned out, the trial judge in the Pellicano case agreed to a brief postponement, causing me to reshuffle my plans.

About a week before the rescheduled trial began, I sent another email to several friends who were writers and law-enforcement officials in and around Los Angeles. Continuing a long-time tradition whenever I visited L.A., I invited them to meet me for dinner at Musso & Frank's in Hollywood after court adjourned on Tuesday, March 11.

Shortly after I sent out the invitation, Dave Robb shocked me with his response, saying: "I urge you not to come out here. If you do, I will come to Musso and Frank's and tell everyone there that you are stalking Anita. And I will make a very big scene."

Absolutely floored by Dave's reply, I wrote back, asking why he had waited so long to complain and saying:

> Inasmuch as I notified you by email on February 20 that I was going to attend the Pellicano trial, I have to assume that your threat is not serious. If you really had these concerns, you would have notified me two weeks ago. Also, I know that you would never flat-out threaten someone who has never been anything but a loyal friend to you, as I have always been.
>
> However, just to clear up any possible misunderstandings, I have not had <u>any</u> communications to or from Anita Busch since her last email to me on February 9, 2006. And those exchanges only resulted from her provably false charges against me regarding my meetings with Jules Nasso. (In addition, I have not been in Los Angeles since you and I attended that writers' conference in Manhattan Beach back in March 2004.)
>
> Trust me when I say that the only way I'd contact Anita would be through my attorney. And he would be furious with me if I did anything to the contrary.
>
> Dave, please assure me that you weren't serious with your message, in which you *falsely* accused me of stalking Anita. (My emphasis)

In his even more shocking reply, Dave repeated his charge that I was stalking Anita, writing:

> You are kidding yourself and everyone else if you think you are ever going to get a book published about the Pellicano case. You breached your contract with Anita Busch when you went behind her back and secretly met with and cut a deal with convicted organized crime figure Jules Nasso—a thug who was involved in the threat on Anita's life. No publisher in the world is going to publish a book about her, by you, if she is against it—and she is very much against it, and against you. She considers you a stalker, and so do I. You were asked to leave her alone, and then you were told to leave her alone, but you just won't stop. I knew this was something more than

a falling out over a book contract when you told me that you wanted
a "pound of flesh" from Anita. Those were your exact words—the
words of a stalker, and maybe worse.[240]

I will reimburse you for the cost of the airline ticket out here. I
won't even deduct it from the money you still owe me. I will send
you a check for it. Just send me a bill. I need your answer today. If
you insist on coming out here anyway, I will be sending this email
to everyone on your invitation list to Musso and Frank, and I will be
there too to straighten you out.

I'm sorry it has come to this, but you put your obsession with
getting revenge against Anita before our friendship a long time ago.

Joining the active Anita Busch-John Connolly smear campaign
against me, Dave then sent emails to several of our mutual friends
in Los Angeles, instructing them to end their friendships with me.
In addition, he sent his outrageous charge that I was "stalking"
Anita to a federal prosecutor, a mutual friend who shared Dave's
correspondence with me.

Along with the disappointment and hurt that I felt over
Dave's outburst, I also believed that, after such a long history of
honesty and integrity, he had become nothing more than Anita's
zombie-stooge.

In the aftermath of Dave's stunning lies, false accusations, and
even a physical threat, I immediately wrote a message to myself,
saying, "My 24-year friendship with Dave is now over."

In concluding this, I also decided to keep my plans and not
change anything.

"You once had a great friend named Dave Robb," someone I
trust told me. "He had a reputation for honesty and integrity and was
like a brother to you. Unfortunately, that Dave has gone away, and
all that is left is some dishonest impersonator who has flat-out lied
about and threatened you, even after you made your sincere attempts
to make peace with him."

Then, in the aftermath of his false charges and now a threat,
I decided to stop any future payments to Dave until I had begun
to recoup the thousands of dollars I had lost during my work with
Anita. I had already repaid $5,500 of the $11,000 debt—half of

what I once owed to Dave. He would now have to share the risk with me.

The next day, with no reply from me, Dave suddenly reversed course, writing, "I am now backing off" his threat to confront me at Musso's, adding that this situation was "tearing" his wife apart.

———

Near the eve of the upcoming trial, the publications that had covered the case closely, weighed in with their reporting:

Nikke Finke, *Deadline Hollywood*:

> After all this time—the years, the witnesses before the grand jury, the rumors, and the media coverage—I can tell you that the [129-page] trial memo filed last night by the U.S. Attorney's Office in the case of *United States v. Pellicano, et al* is *not* going to shake up Hollywood one iota. . . .
>
> Of course, the alleged activities negatively impacted all the victims' lives. But this trial memo is a long, *long* way from the bombshell that many thought would turn Hollywood inside out. Yes, Hollywood figures are mentioned in it prominently. But no specific charges among the 111 counts are leveled against any of them and, in some cases, they're victims. But perhaps more information will come out at trial since the government said it expects to call approximately 80 to 100 witnesses to testify before the jury.[241]

David M. Halbfinger, *New York Times*:

> A hedge fund manager, the billionaire founder of a buyout firm and the former wives of a television actor and a major real estate developer will be crucial witnesses at the racketeering trial of Anthony Pellicano, the Hollywood private eye, beginning next week.
>
> The four will testify that they paid Mr. Pellicano to wiretap their adversaries illegally and listened as he played back the results, prosecutors say. Former employees and suspected co-conspirators

will testify that he built a network of corrupt police officers and telephone-company workers to live up to his image as someone "who reliably obtained information that other investigators could not," according to a 129-page trial brief filed late Thursday.

The investigation captured Hollywood's imagination when Mr. Pellicano's office was raided in 2002 and his dossier on industry heavyweights was seized. But the case has fallen well short of earlier expectations. [242]

Greg Krikorian, *Los Angeles Times*:

Los Angeles police officer on Anthony Pellicano's payroll plumbed law enforcement databases for confidential information on two reporters after Hollywood super-agent Michael Ovitz told the private eye he believed the journalists had written negative stories about him, federal prosecutors alleged in court papers released on Friday.

The 129-page document, previewing prosecutors' strategy in next week's federal trial of Pellicano and four co-defendants, offers more detail than ever before about allegations that the onetime private investigator to the stars paid off cops, telephone company employees and others on behalf of his famous clients in Hollywood and Los Angeles' legal community.

The trial memorandum portrays Pellicano as the calculating ringleader of an enterprise that sought to dig up dirt for well-heeled clients facing divorce, civil lawsuits and even criminal charges including murder and multiple rapes.[243]

Janet Shprintz, *Variety*:

Once billed as the case that would bring down Hollywood kings and kingmakers including Brad Grey, Michael Ovitz and Bert Fields, the trial of private investigator Anthony Pellicano is scheduled to begin this week, albeit in a much diminished form.

The trial on federal wiretapping and racketeering charges now involves onetime P.I. to the stars Pellicano, who is representing himself, as well as four other defendants. . . . The [129-page] brief, a roadmap to the government's case, suggests Pellicano's actions in connection with Fields, Grey and Ovitz will play a substantial role at trial. Each has vociferously proclaimed his ignorance of Pellicano's tactics, and there is no indication that they or the dozens of other moguls and power brokers whose names littered the three-year investigation are in any legal danger.[244]

35. *"Anthony wants to give you the exclusive rights to his story"*

The long-awaited Anthony Pellicano conspiracy trial began on Wednesday, March 5, 2008, with U.S. District Judge Dale S. Fischer presiding. By the end of the day, the jury had been selected—eight men and four women, ethnically mixed. Opening arguments commenced the following morning.

I arrived in Los Angeles early on Saturday, March 8, and rented a car at LAX. I spent the weekend visiting friends, and then checked into a downtown hotel near the federal courthouse on Sunday night.

On Monday morning, the courtroom was dark, so I spent much of the day getting my press credentials in order, as well as introducing myself to people in and around the U.S. Attorney's office.

———

On Tuesday, I was the first spectator to walk into Courtroom 890. It was walnut-paneled with black-and-gray marble, a high-tech looking space with large flat-screen panels around the room, along with a large projection screen—with overhead lighting on an arched ceiling. Benches for spectators looked more like church pews, bolted to the floor which was covered with bluish-gray carpeting.

In front of the courtroom, Judge Fischer, an impressive-looking woman with short gray hair, sat in a large padded green swivel chair. Over her head on the marble wall was the seal of the United States of America. There was a large podium in front of the prosecution table, which was to my left as I faced the judge, and the defense benches were to my right.

The witness chair was to the judge's right, facing the jury box which contained twelve blue-padded chairs.

Even though I had press credentials, I chose to sit in the public-seating section on the last bench against the back wall which was made of material soft to the touch. A clock hung above my head.

The lead prosecutor, AUSA Dan Saunders, had curly chestnut-brown hair, and he was slightly balding. An Ivy Leaguer, he was well-dressed and sophisticated, a serious guy with excellent posture that occasionally made him seem almost stiff. Methodical in his presentation, Saunders had the difficult task of giving the jury information, based on documents, in mind-numbing detail.

Also in the courtroom sat the lead investigator on the case, FBI Special Agent Stan Ornellas, whom I had heard so much about from Anita. He was a powerful-looking bulldog of a man who resembled a Russian shot putter. His hands were as big as shovels. He had salt-and-pepper wavy hair. He had hard eyes but a lot of character in his face. Carrying a leather briefcase, he constantly darted in and out of the courtroom.

Anthony Pellicano appeared very thin, balding with gray hair combed straight back. He wore a prison-issued green windbreaker with a light-green T-shirt, baggy light-green pants, and white running shoes. I kept wondering why he hadn't demanded to wear a suit and tie, especially considering that he was representing himself. He also wore a gold wedding ring and glasses.

Pellicano looked old and even a little bent, a shell of what I expected to see. He appeared to have been completely defanged, sitting alone on a bench, a few yards away from his co-defendants.[245]

Every time he clumsily cross-examined a prosecution witness, I wanted to shout out from the back of the courtroom, "Hey, Anthony! Get a goddamn lawyer!"

Despite the bravado in his last letter to me, Pellicano's *pro se* defense was essentially no defense at all—even when he appeared to have important questions to ask or legitimate documents to enter into evidence. I simply could not understand why he was playing it this way.

By the end of my first day at the trial, I already felt that the evidence was so overwhelming that Pellicano was sure to be convicted. In my opinion, he had no chance of acquittal.

When I stepped onto the elevator on the morning of Wednesday, March 12, Dan Saunders was the only other person on board.

"How are you doing?" I rhetorically asked the AUSA after introducing myself and shaking his hand.

"Better yet," he replied, smiling, "how do *you* think I'm doing?"

I responded, "When you're up against a defendant who is representing himself and doing it so badly, you must be thinking, 'Minimal risk, maximum reward.' I mean, how can you lose?"

Saunders, who clearly did not recognize my name or connect me with Anita Busch, laughed, "It's not over 'til it's over."

During the morning break, with few people other than a handful of U.S. Marshals milling about, I noticed Pellicano, now dressed in a drab-green jumpsuit, talking to an attractive and well-dressed woman. After Pellicano turned and pointed to me, she walked to the back of the courtroom. Smiling, she introduced herself as Pellicano's investigator, Lynda Larsen, whom I remembered speaking with on the phone several months earlier while Pellicano's attorney, Steve Gruel, was trying to get me to testify as a defense witness against Anita Busch.[246]

Lynda asked if I was a journalist.

When I handed her my business card, she saw my name and replied, "Anthony thought that was you."

She returned to Pellicano, who then yelled out, "You're a lot better looking than I thought you'd be."

"I'm still going to Lourdes this summer to get my hair back," I replied.

Laughing, Pellicano and Larsen huddled again. She returned to me and said, "Let's get together after the hearing tomorrow and talk."

I nodded and said that I would like to do that.

For the short time I was at the trial, I made sure that I met most of the journalists who attended the daily hearings, as well as the defense counsels who were members of the trial's supporting cast. I shook hands with FBI Special Agent Ornellas, but I never told him my name.

The evidence of Pellicano's widespread wiretapping was even more overwhelming than I had thought the previous day. However, when Pellicano was first implicated in this matter in 2002, I really expected it to end with a cast that included Mafia guys and perhaps even a few dead bodies.

But nothing like that had ever happened. In fact, without the rough stuff, Pellicano appeared almost workmanlike in his determination to give his clients exactly what they needed.

Still, even though the *Los Angeles Times* was already describing the Pellicano trial as "yesterday's news,"[247] I started to sense that after I left Los Angeles in a few days, it would become the hottest ticket in town.

On Thursday morning, March 13, I ran into former LAPD detective Mark Arneson and his attorney, Chad Hummel, in the first-floor lobby at the courthouse. Both were tall, good-looking, well-dressed guys who appeared as characters right out of central casting—although Arneson seemed to be wearing a look of grave concern, perhaps even impending doom. When I asked the detective how it was going for him, he replied, "There are two sides to every story. I'm just going to tell the truth."

Later, during the afternoon break, Lynda Larsen, whom I had already come to like, asked me to meet her in front of the courthouse after the hearing.

Just as I had done for Jules Nasso, I took the opportunity to give Lynda a scapular for Pellicano which she walked over and gave to him, and then she promptly got into trouble with federal marshals for doing so. Apparently for security reasons, he was not permitted to keep my gift.

At the end of the day, Lynda and I met outside the courthouse on the sidewalk.

"Anthony wants to work with you," she said. "He likes you. Anthony wants to give you the exclusive rights to his story."

Seeing me laugh and shake my head, she asked, "What's so funny?"

"Lynda," I replied, "I've been sitting in the back of that courtroom. And I see what's going on. He's not even trying to win. He's decided to take the fall for everyone. . . . Hey! If I'm wrong and he wants to 'tell all,' I can get us a great deal in New York."

Without confirming or denying anything, Lynda just smiled knowingly. If I were to do a book with Pellicano, I would need Lynda. Instinctively, I fully recognized that she knew a lot. But, realistically, all I really wanted was an interview with Pellicano for my own book.

That night, I sent Lynda an email, saying: "Thank you again for making my day. Please put me to any test required, and then let's make this deal."

Referring to the scapular, Lynda wrote back:

> I'll talk to AP Monday in person at MDC [the federal prison],
> our usual visiting day because court is dark. This deal would be
> interesting to me, as well.
>
> I'll keep the [scapular] for AP, if you don't mind, for now. Later
> I can get it to him through his legal counselor at MDC so it won't get
> confiscated and thrown away.

On Sunday, March 16, I again wrote to Lynda—the day before
her meeting with Pellicano, saying in part:

> Once again, it was a pleasure to meet you in person and to
> connect with Anthony from across the courtroom. I apologize again
> for getting you into trouble because I wanted to give Anthony that
> scapular. Somehow, it just seemed the perfect gift for him at this
> particular time.
>
> With regard to our proposed arrangement, let me state, in
> writing, what is possible.
>
> Indeed, after watching Anthony in action, I now have the distinct
> impression that he is determined to take his secrets to the grave. He
> seems willing to sacrifice himself while simultaneously protecting
> his clients and fighting for his four co-defendants, whom he believes
> have been wrongly accused of RICO violations in what appears as
> a monumental overplaying of a potentially winning hand by the
> prosecution.
>
> To be sure, I just can't help but admire and respect Anthony as "a
> stand-up guy." But, of course, if I had my way, he would, of course,
> be telling all. I really hate to see Anthony take the fall for people like
> Michael Ovitz.
>
> In order for us to have any chance of receiving a legitimate book
> deal for Anthony's exclusive story, New York's publishers will insist
> that he "tell-all." If he does shock everyone and go that route, the
> advance could be huge. I have not consulted with an attorney, but I
> have been told that California's "Son of Sam Law" was struck down
> in 2002 by the state supreme court. That could leave the door open
> for Anthony's family to profit from the book. However, as in the O.J.
> Simpson case, Anthony's alleged victims could sue in civil court in
> an effort to recover damages should Anthony be convicted. . . .
>
> But, once again, if Anthony does not opt for the "tell-all"
> approach, our book will be a very difficult sale.

After discussing all of this with Pellicano, Lynda later wrote back
on April 7: *"AP called me today and asked if you could come this*

week to testify for him. He would like to give you exclusive rights to his autobiography—but can't tell-all, can tell some."

At that point, I knew that his proposed book project was dead. I wrote back to Lynda, saying:

> Although I'm still furious with Anita for her ham-fisted breach of our collaboration agreement, I have not retaliated against her or revealed her secrets. And my public testimony against her would be widely viewed as nothing more than an act of vengeance. Even though I have no trust or faith in her or her word, I grudgingly continue to be loyal to Anita and will protect her just as Anthony protects his clients, even those he doesn't particularly like.
>
> But you already knew that I was going to say that—didn't you?

36. *"There will never be a book"*

On March 24, 2008, four days after Brad Grey, the chairman of Paramount Pictures, denied during his sworn testimony any knowledge of Pellicano's illegal activities while he was working for Grey's management company,[248] the *New York Times* published a lengthy story about Anita Busch, which detailed the nightmare that she had endured since her car was vandalized in June 2002. Anita used this opportunity to throw roundhouse punches at the *Los Angeles Times*, her former employer. She specifically alleged "that the paper was too cozy" with Pellicano, a spiteful charge that Mrs. Nolte and I had earlier advised her to soft peddle.

The *Times* story also quoted Dave Robb, who claimed that Anita "suffered from a form of post-traumatic stress disorder."[249]

Because Dave had still not retracted his ludicrous charge that I had come to Los Angeles to stalk Anita, and because the Pellicano camp was still trying to get me to testify against her, I had decided to return to Washington and not stay for Anita's testimony, knowing that I had developed enough sources while at the trial to ensure that I would receive detailed accounts of the proceedings.

Also on March 24, David Poland of the *Movie City News* wrote a piece about Anita, saying, in part: "[T]here has never been a drama queen as dramatic as Anita. . . . The mockery she received from colleagues was natural payback for a career-long habit of acting out on others. . . . I hope she finds her next passion . . . and doesn't forget why so many people were so happy to see her run herself out of town."[250]

Meantime, information surfaced that the manager for computer security for Conde Nast publications which included *Vanity Fair*, was Wayne Reynolds, a former employee of Anthony Pellicano. During Pellicano's criminal trial, Reynolds was a witness for the prosecution. According to *Gawker*:

> The guy who runs tech security for Condé Nast has admitted lying to the FBI and lending his services to private detective Anthony Pellicano even though he knew Pellicano was tapping people's phones. He's also been accused, in the course of Pellicano's racketeering and wiretap trial, of leaking a pre-publication copy of *Vanity Fair* that Pellicano mysteriously obtained, and of bragging about bugging the office of his Condé Nast supervisor. So why does he still have a job?[251]

———

On the morning of April 9, Michael Ovitz took the witness stand. Marc Glaser of *Variety* wrote:

> Michael Ovitz said he turned to investigator Anthony Pellicano in an effort to avoid another ambush. . . .
> Ovitz was specifically frustrated by a series of negative articles about the company, penned by Anita Busch and Bernard Weinraub that appeared in the *New York Times* in 2002 and detailed the company's financial troubles and talent defections. One story described Ovitz as "having lost his powerful perch in Hollywood."
> The articles were "wildly embarrassing to myself and my family," Ovitz testified during his hour on the witness stand . . . . It was a rare moment in which he appeared uncomfortable in public.
> Ovitz said the articles were "fueled by rumor and innuendo," and he wanted desperately to find out where the reporters were obtaining their info. On top of that, AMG was facing a series of lawsuits that had to be dealt with before the company could be sold.[252]

Former *New York Times* reporter Allison Hope Weiner, now reporting for the *Huffington Post*, continued:

> As for Mr. Ovitz and Mr. Pellicano, they seemed to still have a mutual admiration society. Mr. Ovitz talked about how great Mr. Pellicano was, how helpful and how he paid him $75,000 in cash to get him information about these people who were saying and writing bad things about him and his company, AMG. . . . Mr. Ovitz also said that Mr. Pellicano needed the money to "run his business."
>
> And, on cross-examination, Mr. Ovitz took the opportunity to heap even more praise on the disgraced ex-private eye to the stars. "Mr. Pellicano always gave me good advice and when a lot of people were abandoning the ship, he didn't," recalled Mr. Ovitz.
>
> [T]he government clearly believes [based on Mr. Saunders re-direct of Mr. Ovitz] that he was behind the threats against Anita Busch.[253]

Here is how Ovitz responded to specific questions and allegations:

> **Q:** Did you have conversations with defendant Pellicano?
>
> **Ovitz:** Yes. . . .
>
> **Q:** Did you and defendant Pellicano discuss who was involved in this negative publicity?
>
> **Ovitz:** Yes.
>
> **Q:** Did that involve Anita Busch?
>
> **Ovitz:** Yes.
>
> **Q:** Did that also include Bernard Weinraub?
>
> **Ovitz:** Yes. Mr. Weinraub spent 20 years writing articles about me. . . .
>
> **Q:** What did you do with the information?
>
> **Ovitz:** It was information that was extremely helpful to me, but I couldn't speculate on what I would have done with it.
>
> **Q:** What were the benefits that you saw in this?

Ovitz: I would get information, and Pellicano would get money. I assumed he had information that would be helpful for me to get to the finish line of this deal. I wanted any kind of information. . . .

Q: Did he [Pellicano] give you embarrassing information about Anita Busch?

Ovitz: No. He was rather dismissive of her.

Q: Did he give you embarrassing information about Bernard Weinraub?

Ovitz: No.

Q: Did you ever hire Mr. Pellicano to put a fish on Anita Busch's car?

Ovitz: Absolutely not. . . . I assumed what he did was legal.[254]

After Ovitz completed his testimony and in perhaps the most dramatic moment of the trial, Anita took the witness stand.

The first report I read the following day appeared in the *New York Times*, which stated:

> A reporter who wrote damaging articles about Michael S. Ovitz, the onetime Hollywood power broker, broke down repeatedly in court on Wednesday as she testified about what she said were threats on her life orchestrated by the private eye Anthony Pellicano on Mr. Ovitz's behalf.
> The reporter, Anita M. Busch, said two men in a dark Mercedes nearly ran her down outside her own home in August 2002. "I remember thinking I was going to die," she said through tears. "I thought, 'This is how it ends.'"

Then, the *New York Times's* report continued:

> A lawyer for one of Mr. Pellicano's co-defendants pressed Ms. Busch about a memoir she said she had begun with two other writers, Dan Moldea and John Connolly. She said at first she had thought it could be a way "to survive financially." But she said she had concluded that she was being used and abandoned it. "There will never be a book," she said.[255]

When I read what Anita had claimed on the witness stand under oath, I was absolutely furious. I called one of my contacts from the trial in Los Angeles who sent me a copy of the entire transcript of Anita's testimony.

The following day, Connolly replied to Anita's charge that he and I had "used" her. He claimed to a blogger at the Pellicano trial that the reason for the breakup of our writing team was that Anita was upset because I "tried hitting on" her.[256]

Weary of these reckless and false statements from both Anita and Connolly, I responded to both of them on the blogger's site, providing an explanation of Connolly's betrayal of Anita and me, along with Anita's latest smear tactics against me.

Most notably, I scanned and posted the postcard that Anita had sent to me while she was on vacation seven months *after* the last time I had seen her in which she wrote:

> Dear Dan:
>
> Wish you were here!
>
> Love,
> Anita

In my reply to the blogger, I wrote: "Do you interpret her words as evidence that she was upset with me or that I had behaved inappropriately towards her? In fact, I was always a gentleman with her, as well as a loyal friend and colleague—just as I always was to Connolly until he double-crossed us. "[257]

Also, in an act of pure self-defense, I decided to create a webpage to address Anita's ongoing false statements about me, saying:

> Anita is not telling the truth about me and the fate of our book project. In the midst of her civil case against Anthony Pellicano and his co-defendants—for which she stands to make a tremendous amount of money—she decided, in writing, to sacrifice our book, which her attorneys supposedly feared would give too much "free information" to the defense. Then, when I complained, she launched a smear campaign against me, which continues to this day.[258]

In addition, along with the "wish you were here" postcard she sent me, I posted the following cards that I had also received from her.[259]

a. On her Christmas card in December 2003, Anita wrote:

> Dan—
>
> I'm blessed to have you in my life.
> Merry Christmas!
>
> Love,
> Anita

b. On a Valentine's Day card she sent to me in February 2004, Anita signed it, "Love, Anita."

c. On a birthday card to me in late-February, 2004, in which the printed inscription read . . . :

> "Happy birthday to a one-of-a-kind Brother" . . .

Anita added in a handwritten message:

> Dan—
>
> I know this won't arrive in time—but just wanted to say Happy Birthday!
> I'm glad I know you—I feel honored to know you.
> See you soon.
>
> Love,
> Anita

After I publicly released these exculpatory correspondences which Anita had apparently forgotten she had sent to me, the issue of my alleged bad behavior towards her, an unfair charge I deeply resented, suddenly ended. However, this experience put me on alert, recognizing Anita's ability and willingness to make false statements against me publicly.

— —

On April 16, Stan Ornellas, the now-retired FBI special agent who had directed the Pellicano case, testified at Pellicano's criminal trial, declaring during his sworn testimony that Michael Ovitz's decision to hire Pellicano had led to the vandalism of Anita's car.

In Allison Hope Weiner's blog, she reported that Ornellas—just as Anita, John Connolly, and I had—believed that Steven Seagal hired Pellicano to make the threat against Anita.[260] However, Weiner described the key moment when Ornellas changed his mind—when he learned that Detective Arneson had run computer checks on Anita and Bernie Weinraub, among others.

Weiner wrote in her story:

> "I received an audit of Mr. Arneson's run in May of 2002," said Agent Ornellas. The agent went on to tell the jury that the audit of Mr. Arneson's computer searches contained runs on Bernard Weinraub [and] Anita Busch. . . .
>
> "Mr. Weinraub and Ms. Busch had done a series of articles on Mr. Ovitz that same month," Mr. Ornellas said.[261]

It was that same information that convinced Anita, as well as Connolly and me, that Ovitz was involved with Pellicano, which she had learned from Tom Ballard, another FBI special agent, on June 12, 2003.

Ornellas also testified that he had questioned Ovitz who said that he had retained Pellicano "to gather information on individuals he thought were attacking him in the press."

Writing about the questioning of Ornellas by Chad Hummel, Detective Arneson's defense lawyer, Weiner continued:

> When Mr. Hummel again got up to question Mr. Ornellas on quadruple re-cross, he asked, "Is it possible that Mr. Ovitz had nothing to do with the threat against Ms. Busch?" "Yeah, it's possible," Mr. Ornellas answered skeptically, managing to sublimate an eye roll. And when Mr. [Assistant U.S. Attorney Kevin] Lally got up to do his quadruple re-direct, Mr. Lally asked the question that many of us have been wondering about since the start of this investigation, directly asking if Mr. Ornellas thought Mr. Ovitz was

responsible for the threat against Ms. Busch. "It was Mr. Ovitz," answered Mr. Ornellas without hesitation.

37. *"Linda wants to meet you"*

The only witness that Pellicano called to testify during his trial was an FBI audio technician who had already testified for the prosecution.[262] In fact, Pellicano did not even take the stand in his own defense, telling Judge Fischer: "I am not—Mister Pellicano is not going to discuss conversations with his clients. It's not going to happen. Ever. No matter what the consequence."[263]

Had I agreed to the numerous requests by Pellicano's defense team to appear at the trial, I would have been Pellicano's only new witness.

In his final argument to the jury, which completely validated my reasoning for refusing his offer to write his book, Pellicano, who referred to himself in the third person throughout the trial, described himself as a "lone ranger . . . [who] alone is responsible. That's the simple truth.

"He only allowed others to learn what he wanted them to. He alone made all the decisions, protected all of the secrets, protected all the clients."[264]

Predictably, on May 15, 2008, Pellicano and his four co-defendants, including former LAPD detective Mark Arneson, were all convicted by the federal jury.[265] Specifically, Pellicano was found guilty of 76 criminal charges against him.

Pellicano would be going deep into the federal-penitentiary system, knowing everything about the sins of his clients while protecting them and allowing them to move ahead with their privileged lives.

After the convictions, Anita released a statement, saying, in part:

> The full story of Pellicano's reach has yet to be told. To Pellicano and his wealthy clients, "winning" meant completely obliterating someone's life and livelihood. They saw the media as just another weapon in their arsenal and used and abused it to go after anyone in their crosshairs."

Reporter Steven Mikulan of the *LA Weekly* spoke with Elaine Jordison, a member of the Pellicano jury after the verdict.[266] Mikulan wrote:

> Many courtroom spectators had found Pellicano's cross-examination of Busch, who repeatedly broke down in tears, brutal and egregious — almost like the humiliation of a rape victim. Jordison didn't see it that way.
>
> "I didn't think he was bullying her," Jordison says, adding she wasn't moved by Busch's tears. Yet Jordison had deeper questions about Busch's behavior following the 2002 vandalism of her car. . . .
>
> Jordison says. "You'd think that as a reporter she'd have a little more backbone. But she was acting as though she was afraid to answer her front door."
>
> If anything, Jordison was far more sympathetic to the powerful subject of Busch and Weinraub's writing.
>
> "I kinda felt sorry for Michael Ovitz," Jordison says of the Hollywood mogul and co-founder of Creative Artists Agency. Journalists "Busch and Weinraub were trying to bring down his company."
>
> Jordison's stated belief that Busch and Weinraub were doing the very same thing that Michael Ovitz was doing — trying to get information — was revealing in this court narrative about those who view possession of other people's personal data as the key to success. Still, Jordison believes, Ovitz would have been better off ignoring what the two journalists were up to.
>
> "He should've left it alone," she says.

———

Shortly after Pellicano's conviction, I received a telephone call from a good friend, author Jim Bamford, who was at dinner with actress Linda Fiorentino, the star of such films as *Vision Quest, After Hours, The Last Seduction, Jade,* and *Men in Black.* Jim said that she wanted to meet with me and my former partner on the Jules Nasso book, Gus Russo.

A few weeks later, on August 19, Jim arranged for the four of us to have dinner at the Cosmos Club in Washington. As it turned out, Linda had a special relationship with Pellicano's ex-wife, Kat

Pellicano. Through that contact, she had also become close to Anthony Pellicano.

After dinner, Linda, Gus, and I went to Jim's townhouse in Georgetown. There, I met Linda's boyfriend, Mark Rossini, a well-known and respected FBI special agent in the New York field office. They were staying with Jim while in town.

The following morning, as planned the night before, I picked up Linda, and we had a five-hour breakfast during which she told me that Pellicano was again considering giving me the exclusive rights to his story. She laughed that she was there to vet me for the job while I was still only interested in simply getting an exclusive interview with him for my own book—regardless of "tell all or tell some."

The next day, Linda called and asked to meet with me again. At our lunch, she told me what she had not mentioned the day before, that Pellicano was still miffed that I had refused to testify against Anita at his trial.

I laughed, saying that Pellicano was a stand-up guy, and so am I. Later, I added in an email to Linda, "[H]ad I accepted the invitations from him, Steve Gruel, and/or Lynda Larsen to testify against Anita at the first trial, I would be dead now and forever in the journalism community."

Six weeks later, Linda's boyfriend, FBI Special Agent Mark Rossini, was charged with illegally using the bureau's computers to download a document which wound up with Pellicano's defense team. Soon after, Rossini was forced to resign from the FBI after a distinguished seventeen-year career. He pleaded guilty and was sentenced to a year's probation.[267]

Reporting on the Rossini case, Del Quentin Wilber of the *Washington Post* wrote:

> At the time he conducted those illegal searches, Rossini was dating the actress Linda Fiorentino, known for her role in *The Last Seduction*. Fiorentino had a previous relationship with Pellicano and wanted to help him, law enforcement officials have said.
> Assistant U.S. Attorney Tejpal S. Chawla wrote in court papers that in January 2007 Rossini gave a report about the Pellicano case to a person identified by Chawla in court records as "X." Law

enforcement sources have identified "X" as Fiorentino, and have said she gave the report to an attorney for Pellicano, who used the report to accuse prosecutors of withholding evidence from the defense team.[268]

In another story about this tragic episode, reporter Allan Lengel quoted me in his article about this sad case, saying:

> Dan Moldea, a noted author who has been working on a book for years on the Anthony Pellicano case, and has met Rossini and Fiorentino, [said]: "I don't know them well, but they're nice people. But I can tell you this about the Pellicano case, I can't think of anyone connected to this entire situation who has come out of this in one piece, not one person."[269]

The Pellicano case had turned poisonous for everybody who touched it.

38. *"I got a little careless, I regret that strongly"*

On August 29, 2008, a federal jury convicted Pellicano for a second time, along with his co-defendant, prominent Hollywood attorney Terry N. Christensen, a beneficiary of Pellicano's illegal-wiretapping operations.[270] Christensen—who had retained Pellicano who then wiretapped the phone of the ex-wife of his client, Kirk Kerkorian, during a child support legal battle—received a three-year prison sentence.[271]

At Pellicano's sentencing hearing, Anita spoke and suggested that the judge throw the book at the convicted private investigator, saying:

> I want to thank Judge Fischer for her patience and wisdom during this trial and thank you to the FBI and the U.S. Attorney's office.
>
> Mr. Pellicano, after you and your employers relentlessly attacked all of us and got caught after years of doing this to others, you and your lawyers just kept attacking. You attacked the FBI, the search warrant, a potential witness, the veracity of your victims, launched personal attacks on the lead FBI agent on the case and U.S. Attorney, went after the jury and then the verdict itself.

And you did most all of it through the *Los Angeles Times* where I unfortunately found out while working there that you had a trusted relationship with the lawyer advising me and one of the reporters that they had covering this criminal case.

In the sentencing memorandum you talk about how your life is ruined. Yes, well, YOU made that choice. None of your victims had a choice. You could have helped put these sociopaths with money behind bars, but to this day, you show contempt for this court and the law.

You have yet to take responsibility for your actions.

It was revealed only two weeks ago that an FBI agent named Mark Rossini pleaded guilty to illegally obtaining documents that were then used by your lawyer.

So every day you prove that you ran a criminal conspiracy and a criminal enterprise.

Your co-conspirator Mr. Kachikian aided and abetted you so that my computer was hacked into and 18 years of my musical compositions – which I considered my life's work – were destroyed.

When Mr. Turner and other co-conspirators at the phone company helped you tap my phones, you not only violated my privacy and that of my family and friends, but you violated the privacy of a journalist and her sources, undermining the very fundamentals of my profession. This attack was also on journalism and a newspaper's ability to gather the news.

By carrying out these crimes, you not only hurt me, you hurt my elderly parents, my brothers and sisters and my friends.

After these threats, I was afraid to come and go from my house. I was afraid to sit in my car for even a moment out in the street for fear that a car would speed up on me again, block me in and this time I would be killed. And that was a Catch-22 because I was also petrified to turn over the engine of my car for fear that it would blow up.

So, I would sit there and cry and pray and beg, "Please God, I want to live."

Or some days, after a night of nightmares, I would close my eyes and just scream really loud as I turned the key to the ignition. And when I didn't blow up, I'd wipe my eyes and go onto work at the *L.A. Times* and face the snickers from the disbelievers.

You and your employers not only used fear and intimidation, but you made sure people – your targets – were smeared in the press. And you and your clients used any means at your disposal to destroy people's employment. And you guys did it many times over many years. When it was my turn how very convenient it was for you that you already had long established relationships inside my employer.

The day after the first threat, the lawyer at the *L.A. Times*, Karlene Goller, wanted you on board to help because as she said, "He's done work for us in the past and he's done well by us." The editor told her no, but she did it anyway.

Without my knowledge or the knowledge of law enforcement, she had reporter Chuck Philips call you about my case. Philips had a longtime relationship with you as a news source and had worked for years alongside Karlene's husband.

I was new to the paper, but you weren't. And you used the relationships you had there against me. You made sure my newspaper didn't believe me so behind the scenes you could ruin my employment just like you and your clients did to other victims.

The day you were arrested, that's when the cover-up began at my newspaper. To this day their own reporters, editors and readers don't know the truth. And while you and your lawyers cried crocodile tears about media leaks, Philips – a reporter you helped for years – wrote story after story against the government's case. Information FED to him by your defense team. And because the men whose job it was to put an end to your criminal activity were now your targets – Dan Saunders and Stan Ornellas – your pal Philips wrote stories smearing their integrity.

And, of course, those stories were then approved by the same newspaper lawyer who looked to you for help. And this is just one example of how you and your clients used the media as a weapon.

Your convicted co-conspirator, Mr. Kachikian, even worked for the *L.A. Times*.

You reached inside the phone company, the LAPD, the Beverly Hills Police Department, the FBI ... and this city's largest newspaper.

So, I was on my own. And I was scared. I thought it was just a matter of time before I was going to be killed. I was scared to have any family or friends around me because I was afraid that they themselves might get hurt. And I struggled. I struggled hard to work as a journalist while battling constant fear ... Journalism was something I loved and what I lived for. But it became impossible for me to continue on as a journalist. My sources were afraid to talk to me on the phone. It wasn't long before everything was gone.

I no longer had my career. I no longer had my peace of mind. My income was dwindling. My life savings was disappearing. My health went downhill. I didn't even have my music. And I no longer had passion or faith in anything.

It was death by a thousand cuts ... and the cuts were deep and hard. I didn't deserve it.

I remember sitting alone one night, trying to think of something – anything – good that had come out of this. I realized that the only hope I had left was in a dogged, and thank God ethical, FBI agent named Stan Ornellas who I knew was out there every day working to try to put an end to this kind of domestic terrorism. Which is what it was.

I am thankful beyond words to these men and women who worked this case because they kept what happened to me from happening to anyone else.

Now, Mr. Pellicano, you have always spoken about a sense of honor. I understand. You know I know many of your former clients. Most of the ones I knew were never your friends and they were certainly never your family.

These people don't care about the kind of healthcare you get on the inside, the lousy razors that nick your face, the sandpaper for toilet paper, the mystery meat and candy bars from the vending machine.

They don't care that you won't be there to hold your own mother's hand when she gets sick or when she passes away.

Where is the honor in that?

You won't be there because of Michael Ovitz.

Your sense of honor is not wrong, Mr. Pellicano. It is misplaced.

To you and your wealthy clients, this was about winning – destroying our lives – at any cost. Well, look at the cost ... here in the courtroom today ... look into the faces of the ones you love.

You threw away your role as son to your mother and father to your children.

For money.

Sometimes money costs too much.

For what you have done to all of us and to your own flesh and blood, all I can say is that I fear for your soul when I think that God is just.

Thank you, your honor.[272]

Judge Fischer sentenced Pellicano to an additional fifteen years in prison.[273]

In its official response to Anita's serious allegations, the *Los Angeles Times* gingerly tried not to attack the victim while firmly insisting that she was not telling the truth:

As the *Times* has stated before, we take very seriously any threat made to our employees in the course of doing their jobs, and that

certainly included the threats to Ms. Busch. *The Times* cooperated
with law enforcement investigations in her case and provided
monetary and personal support — and protection — to Ms. Busch.

The paper has also made clear previously that neither the paper
nor its lawyers have ever hired Anthony Pellicano. Ms. Busch's
repeated suggestions that our lawyer said Pellicano had done work
for *The Times* is untrue. It's a matter of public record that Pellicano
has been an occasional source for journalists at the paper over the
years, both on the record and off. Journalists have many kinds of
sources when reporting their stories.

Ms. Busch went through a terrible experience as a result of
Pellicano's illegal activities, and her former *Times* colleagues
sympathize deeply with what she's suffered. We didn't include her
statements about *The Times* in this morning's story because they were
neither true nor new. All of us at *The Times* hope that the conclusion
of the trial will bring Ms. Busch peace of mind.[274]

During an interview with the Associated Press, Pellicano
expressed no remorse, telling a reporter, "I got a little careless, I
regret that strongly. Do I make apologizes? No, I'm responsible for
everything I've done."

Along with insisting that he played no role in the vandalism of
Anita's car in 2002 and that he would never violate the confidence of
his clients, Pellicano, with his usual flair, declared, "If there were a
way to help my family without breaking my own laws so to speak, I
would consider it. There would be a mass sale of books, there would
be eyebrows raised and some heads would roll, including some in
government."[275]

Unimpressed with everything that was happening or had
happened with the Pellicano case, the *Los Angeles Times* published
an OpEd piece, saying:

After years of breathless coverage in every newspaper and
magazine known to man, Anthony Pellicano was sentenced to 15 years
in prison on Monday for running an illegal wiretapping operation that
dug up dirt—or at least tried to unearth dirty laundry—on a host of
prominent Hollywood celebrities and industry insiders. A longtime
private investigator who engaged in everything from wiretapping
to computer fraud, Pellicano was supposed to bring down half of
Hollywood with him. But after years of titillating speculation, the

story was a bust. The news of Pellicano's conviction didn't make the front page of my paper, which put the story on the front of the California section, next to a winter storm story, while the *New York Times* buried its brief news account on Page 3 of its business section.[276]

With the federal prosecutions now complete, the fallout from the Pellicano caper continued as the civil cases which sprang from the criminal cases prepared for their own mini-dramas.

———

On June 17, 2009, I received an email from Dave Robb—the first since before the Pellicano trial when he falsely accused me of coming to Los Angeles to stalk Anita. In his message, he wrote: "I'm nearly broke. If you could repay what you owe, I'd appreciate it."

In response to Dave' brief note, I decided to get everything off my chest:

> First of all, I haven't made any money in several months and currently have my own serious financial problems—to which you contributed significantly.
>
> With your mind-numbing incompetence as the intermediary between Anita and me, you helped to cost me several years of valuable time and work, as well as a tremendous amount of money—a lot more than I owe you. The damage that you and Anita have done to me has been absolutely devastating—all because I had the audacity to defend myself after she unilaterally and illegally breached our signed contract. And then, going against the best interests of everyone involved, you allowed her to run roughshod over me.
>
> By becoming Anita's chief stooge while still under the guise of our neutral arbiter, you repeatedly excused her childish rants and remarkable dishonesty at my expense. The record clearly shows that I did everything I could to hold our doomed collaboration together after Anita suddenly decided, in writing, that our book project could jeopardize her civil case.
>
> Indeed, I never expected to be blindsided by people to whom I was always loyal and whom I considered to be my trusted friends. And I certainly never expected you—whom I considered "my brother"—to participate in Anita's shameless smear campaign against me. . . .

Then, after I started to repay my debt to you—in my naive hope that we could still make peace and remain friends—you sent me a reckless and malicious email on Tuesday, March 4, 2008. In this disgraceful message, you continued to flat-out lie about your prior knowledge of my communications with Jules Nasso, whom you wrongly insisted played a role "in the threat on Anita's life." In addition, you falsely and irresponsibly accused me of criminal behavior—with the ludicrous but defamatory claim that I was "stalking" Anita with the intention to harm her physically. Then, adding insult to injury, you threatened me in that same email—with your pledge to come to my March 11 dinner party at Musso & Frank's "to straighten" me out.

Further, you had the unmitigated gall to send this defamation to others, including but not limited to [a federal prosecutor who was a mutual friend].

All of your actions, along with Anita's blatant breach of contract, have been fully revealed and documented to my attorney. The only reason I have not yet moved forward with litigation is my blind loyalty to you—despite your complete and total treachery towards me. But I still reserve the right to exercise my legal options—or any other legitimate options to defend my position—when and if I choose to do so.

In short, you have twisted my noble efforts to make peace with you into nothing more than nefarious acts. You have interpreted my sheer restraint on many different levels as general weakness—instead of as my ongoing but inexplicable loyalty to you. . . . Dave, in my entire life, nobody has cut me as deeply as you have.

With regard to the money, my attorney believes that, legally, I owe you nothing—in light of all that you have cost me via your destructive role in this matter. However, I believe that, out of respect for our long and once-cherished friendship, I do have a moral obligation to repay that debt. And, in good faith, I have already repaid exactly half of what I once owed.

However, I am not inclined to pay anything more—even when I can afford to do so—until I receive a written retraction and apology for the false and malicious charges you leveled against me in your March 4, 2008, email, as well as a signed admission of the horrible job you did as the intermediary between Anita and me.

If you wish to discuss this or anything else, please have your attorney contact my attorney.

Your brother,
Dan

Shortly thereafter, Dave responded:

> Yes Dan, it's everyone else's fault that you are a coward and a traitor. I am sorry I ever met you. I hope you live a long life, sniveling and groveling all the way to the grave, and betraying each and every one of your friends.

To that, I came back with:

> You are completely delusional, Dave. You can't even see that I continue to be loyal to you.
>
> Show me how I have betrayed you or hurt you in any way—other than by refusing your unreasonable request to allow Anita to run over me. Meantime, she turned you into her personal zombie.
>
> You have absolutely no facts whatsoever to support your harsh assessment of me—not unlike the contents of your March 4, 2008, email, which has been and continues to be a total pack of lies you cannot support or defend. Once again, please retract and apologize for your false and defamatory charges in that email—so that we can move forward.
>
> Just so you know, I wish like hell that I could talk to you now about all that has happened since you allowed Anita to come between us.
>
> From my point of view, I will always treasure my friendship with you. My only regret is obvious.

In Dave's follow-up, he wrote:

> I tried to help you and you betrayed me. I asked you to stop and you wouldn't stop. I begged you to stop and you wouldn't stop. I offered you money to stop, and you said, "How much?" Now you are putting your lawyer on me. Good luck with that. You are a betrayer and a coward. I never want to see you or hear from you again. EVER. Able in the Bible had a brother too. Your phoney [sic] words mean nothing.

Seeing that Dave wasn't appreciating my attempt to make amends, I replied:

> Why are you being such a hard ass? I'm the injured party here, and I'm the one trying to make peace.

Also, how did I betray you? Anita was trying to cut my throat, and you were telling me to allow her to do it. Why would I agree to that?

Neither one of us was more important to her than her civil case and her dreams of a big payday. Allowing her case to take priority over our book, she saw that I was prepared to raise hell when she breached our book contract. And she was right.

That's when her smear campaign started against me. She put much of it in writing.

Regardless of anything you believe, you had absolutely no control over her. She rejected every one of your peace proposals, including my idea to bring you on as a third partner. Do you remember what she did? She wanted me to sign a document, voiding our existing contract. Then, she wanted to create a new contract with you—and then you would be permitted to have a completely separate contract with me.

She wanted a situation in which my name and her name would not appear in the same contract—thereby neutralizing any legal attack I might choose to mount against her in the wake of her breach.

And she knew that I would never take legal action against you if the book never materialized—which would probably be a requirement to any future settlement she might receive from the defendants in her civil case. Most likely, the defendants would require her to sign a non-disclosure agreement before giving her any large sums of money.

In your perpetual "let-Anita-have-everything-she-wants" thing, you advised me to allow her to void our existing contract. Had I done that, I would've forfeited all of my rights after years of work. Why would I do that?

My rejection of Anita's cynical plan wasn't a betrayal of you, Dave. Why did you take my dispute with her so personally?

And how can you possibly compare our situation to Cain and Abel? I never tried to harm you. I only rejected your advice to allow my business partner to cut me out of our existing business deal.

My problems with you began when you lied to Anita, saying that you had no prior knowledge of my communications with Jules Nasso. In fact, I put this information in writing and emailed it to you before my first conversation with him. Also, we talked about it several times on the phone.

And then you exacerbated everything with your March 4, 2008, email—in which you flat-out lied about and threatened me while I was in the midst of repaying my debt and making a sincere effort to make peace with you. In addition, you had the audacity to make your reckless and malicious charges public by forwarding that email to our mutual friends.

By becoming a willing participant in Anita's smear campaign against me, you lost my unconditional friendship.

However, I still believe that everything between us can be repaired. Once again, you must retract and apologize in writing for that email. That is the necessary first step.

Dave then ended this exchange, writing, "In the future, all of your emails will be deleted unread."

On June 17, 2009, four years to the day after their original indictment, Anthony Pellicano and Alexander Proctor pleaded not guilty to state charges that they had threatened Anita. The superior court case had earlier been delayed to make way for the federal criminal case.[277]

Four months later, on October 23, 2009, Pellicano and Proctor both changed their not guilty pleas to "no contest." Each was sentenced to three years in prison, which the superior court judge ruled would run concurrently with their federal sentences. Neither man would serve an extra day in custody.[278]

———

While the civil actions stemming from the Pellicano criminal cases were starting to gear up, reporter John Cook of the *New York Observer* published a story about John Connolly in which he cited an internal memo from the Church of Scientology that claimed Connolly was a "paid informant for the cult." Cook wrote:

John Connolly is a well-known, and well-liked, character in New York media circles. He's a former NYPD detective and stock broker who landed a third career as an investigative reporter for *Vanity Fair*, where he is a contributing editor, *Radar*, the *Daily Beast*, *Gawker*, and other outlets. Connolly is an investigator of the old school, employed more for his ability to run a license plate number than his facility with prose. In 1990, while freelancing for *Forbes*, he was accused by a federal judge of using his old NYPD badge to obtain sealed court documents. According to *USA Today*, his stint as a stockbroker ended in the 1980s with a $100,000 civil penalty and

lifetime ban from the Securities and Exchange Commission. He's a
mischievous tipster, an inveterate gossip, and an information broker
of the highest order. He speaks with a cartoonish New York accent
and knows literally everybody. And according to the two highest
ranking Scientology officials to ever leave the church, he's been a
paid informant for the cult for two decades.[279]

Cook said that he approached Connolly as a colleague and
asked him about this charge that Connolly claimed was "bullshit."
However, when Cook went to Connolly for comment on the record
for his story, Connolly was unavailable.

PART FIVE:
Acceptance

39. *"Subpoena or summons?"*

On April 29, 2011, a handful of bloggers reported that Anita had been deposed as she resumed her civil lawsuit against Anthony Pellicano and Michael Ovitz, as well as the City of Los Angeles and the local telephone company, among others.[280]

In an earlier court filing in December 2008, Eric George, Ovitz's lead attorney, stated in a fairly cold-blooded manner: "Plaintiff had full knowledge of all the risks, dangers and hazards [that came with being a journalist], if any, and nevertheless voluntarily and with full appreciation of the amount of risk involved, assumed the risk of loss to herself. . . . Plaintiff has been harmed, if at all, in whole or in part, by virtue of her own acts and omissions."[281]

Writing for Nikke Finke's *Deadline Hollywood*, Allison Hope Weiner reported:

> Although Busch refused to discuss Ovitz's defense or the details of her own complaint, she said in a statement to me that, "It's outrageous for Michael Ovitz or his attorneys to say that I assumed the risk when Ovitz hired a thug like Pellicano to go after me." She added that, "No one assumes the risk of criminal acts. This is not a third world country where reporters expect to be terrorized for reporting the news."
>
> Ovitz's lawyer Eric George responded to Busch's statement by telling me: "We sympathize with Ms. Busch, and the other victims of the criminal conduct which has resulted in several convictions to date. But for Ms. Busch to seek damages from Mr. Ovitz, who had

no involvement whatsoever in that conduct, is both regrettable and misdirected."[282]

The August 15, 2011, issue of *Newsweek* featured crazy-eyed, "Queen of Rage," GOP Presidential candidate Michelle Bachman on the cover. The issue also contained a story about Anthony Pellicano based on an interview that reporter Christine Pelisek had with him at his new home at Big Spring Federal Correctional Institution in Big Spring, Texas.

With Pellicano still embracing his "stand-up-guy" defense, Pelisek reported:

> The disgraced detective still insists that none of his clients knew anything about his wiretapping, in particular the high-powered lawyers, like [Bert] Fields, who employed him. "I didn't tell no one [sic] about the wiretapping," he says. "I didn't trust lawyers: they had an obligation to tell on me." Still, he adds knowingly, "You can turn a blind eye, but 99 percent of the lawyers out there don't care how the problem was solved." . . .
>
> Still, given the alternative of being a stool pigeon, Pellicano says he wouldn't have it any other way. "It was either I talked or go to jail and accept it like a man," he says.[283]

In addition, the magazine ran a sidebar on Anita, which concluded:

> If Busch wins money in any of her pending lawsuits, she says, she'll donate some of it to nonprofits that help crime victims, and might start an organization herself. "It's the Devil's money, so I'd like to do God's work with it."
>
> Most of all, Busch says, "I'd like it to come to an end. I'd like to start my life over."[284]

—————

As had happened during Pellicano's criminal trial, there were attempts to get me involved in Anita's civil case. Earlier, on March 31 and April 6, 2011, I had received telephone messages from Amanda Morgan, one of Ovitz's attorneys.

I simply ignored them, hoping to stay out of this legal battle, just as I had remained free of involvement in the criminal case. I was there simply as an observer.

At 9:02 P.M. on August 18, 2011, while working at the desk in my apartment, I heard someone knocking. As I opened the door, a well-dressed young man with a clipboard reached out and gently tapped the front of my shirt with a piece of paper.

Instinctively, I asked, "Subpoena or summons?"

"Subpoena," he replied. "You've just been served. . . . Could you sign this paper?"

He allowed me to glance at the subpoena.[285] As soon as I saw the case and the names of the attorneys who ordered the service at the bottom of the page, I nodded with resignation, saying out loud, "I was hoping that I could stay out of this. . . . Could you wait a minute, please? I need to call my lawyer."

After I called Roger Simmons, my long-time Maryland attorney and trusted friend, I accepted the subpoena but refused to sign the document on the process server's clipboard.

The subpoena required me to appear for deposition on September 14 at 8:00 A.M. at a legal-media facility in downtown Washington. Apparently, I would be answering questions from attorneys in both Washington and Los Angeles on closed-circuit television.

Later, after being contacted by Roger, Ovitz's lawyers responded with a gentle peace offering, suggesting that we had a degree of common cause and were in positions to help one another. They added that I might want to use this opportunity to "clear my name" or "set the record straight" in light of what Anita had said about me in her sworn depositions.

Apparently, she had claimed under oath that I was wholly dishonest and had committed criminal acts.

For their own purposes, Ovitz's attorneys seemed to want my help in authenticating certain documents and to verify Anita's handwritten notes.

To show good faith, they offered to send us copies of her depositions and any other materials that were not covered under a protective order issued by the trial judge. Indeed, we were even invited to become a party to and sign the protective order if we wanted to see everything.

If I signed the protective order, I would have some fairly restrictive burdens, duties, and obligations, which could ultimately jeopardize my ability to write this book. In the end, I refused to sign the protective order and agreed only to accept documents not covered under the judge's edict.

On August 25, Ovitz's attorneys officially withdrew their subpoena even before sending us the documents.

On August 31, I received copies of Anita's sworn depositions of April 14, July 21, and August 3, 2011, along with some attached exhibits. Even before reading anything, I was shocked to see that she had supplied the defense with a cache of our personal and private communications, as well as some of our work, including but not limited to draft book proposals and our last draft manuscript of May 11, 2005—the one she had approved and given to her attorneys.

Even though I recognized that she had been forced to release these documents under discovery, she had clearly done so without notifying me or my attorneys. To be sure, I still owned a forty-percent stake in this literary property—that was now on the public record.

Even more shocking after I began reading her sworn statements were her blatant false statements—and alleged perjury—*under oath*.

With Ovitz and even Pellicano virtually receiving passes from Anita's venom, I was clearly the heavy in her sworn depositions. Both Ovitz and Pellicano came across as Boy Scouts compared to me.

Anita's testimony against me was so unfair, especially with regard to the timing of certain events, that I started thinking that it was some sort of tactic. For reasons unknown, she appeared to be trying to place the responsibility for the contents of our entire manuscript on me, even though, under the terms of our collaboration contract, she had editorial control.

In addition, in order to cast aside any responsibility even for her personal notes or edits to our manuscript, she launched an all-out attack against me, blaming me for fabricating evidence and even forging documents attributed to her.

For instance, on June 12, 2003, Anita told me that she believed Ovitz was the person who had hired Pellicano to attack her. And there was a clear paper trail about this, even in Anita's own handwritten words. However, during her July 21, 2011, sworn deposition, the following exchange ensued about an October 2003 book proposal I had drafted for her approval:

> **Q:** At the time that you received this on October 11, 2003, was it your belief that Michael Ovitz had hired Pellicano to attack you?
>
> **Anita:** No.
>
> **Q:** Was it your belief—did you have reasonable suspicion at that point that it was Michael Ovitz that had hired Pellicano to attack you?
>
> **Anita:** Absolutely not.
>
> **Q:** Were you suggesting in this book that it was Michael Ovitz who had hired Pellicano to attack you?
>
> **Anita:** No.
>
> **Q:** Was Dan Moldea suggesting in his book that it was Michael Ovitz who had hired Pellicano to attack you?
>
> **Anita:** I think he wanted some high profile person to hang it on, but I don't know. We talked about many, many, many, many people.

Then, during her August 3, 2011, sworn deposition, the discussion about my work on the book continued as Anita escalated her attacks against me:

> **Q:** Would you have any reason to disbelieve Dan Moldea—if Dan Moldea said "I had been provided with personal notes from Anita Busch and I've accurately transcribed those notes."
>
> **Anita:** Yes.
>
> **Q:** Do you think he would lie about that?
>
> **Anita:** Yes.

Q: How come?

Anita: Because he made things up out of full cloth sometimes. And he was also—he just wasn't adhering to real basic Journalism 101 rules.[286]

Ovitz's attorney, Eric George, asked Anita for specific examples:

Q: Are you aware of any instance in which Dan Moldea had written something claiming that it was a transcription of your personal notes when, in fact, it wasn't?

Anita: There were numerous times where he said that he—there were numerous. It was a constant problem. There was [sic] constant inaccuracies.

Unable to get Anita to answer the direct question, George continued:

Q: Are you aware of any instance in which Dan wrote something that purported to be in your own words—

Anita: Yes.

Q: —from a diary or journal entry—

Anita: Yes.

Q: —and those words were inaccurate?

Anita: Yes.

Q: Which ones?

Anita: He did it all the time. I can't specify anything.

For the next twelve pages of Anita's sworn testimony, defense counsel George repeatedly asked her to cite a single instance in which I had fabricated any quote from any of her personal documents and then represented that quote as her own words in any of our work without her permission.

Anita could not cite a single occasion where I had done this.

In yet another instance, Anita was questioned about a portion of our manuscript in which we referred to an email exchange that she had with John Montorio, an editor at the *Los Angeles Times* on May 16, 2003:

> **Q:** You see there is a footnote that says, 'Email from Anita Busch to John Montorio"?
>
> **Anita:** Yeah, that is probably what [Moldea] did. I don't know.
>
> **Q:** Do you know if he accurately transcribed that e-mail?
>
> **Anita:** No, I have no idea.
>
> **Q:** Any reason to doubt it?
>
> **Anita:** Yes.
>
> **Q:** That e-mail?
>
> **Anita:** There is a reason to doubt everything he did.
>
> **Q:** Well, come on. Let's be fair to him.
>
> **Anita:** I am being fair.

After reading Anita's sworn depositions, I wrote a memo to myself, saying:

> My reaction is that I can defend everything. . . .
> No doubt, Anita has seen my webpage about her testimony at Pellicano's criminal trial—where I accused her of making "false statements," as well as running a "smear campaign" against me. She also knows that, sooner or later, we are going to consider a breach of contract legal attack against her. Consequently, she has decided to accuse me of being a liar [and] a fabricator. . . .
> Also, I can prove that Anita has flat-out lied about several key topics during her sworn testimony.

Anita had even denied ever using her code name for Ovitz—specifically "ED"—which was short for "evil doer" or "evil dude," even though there were already numerous examples on the record. She insisted that I had concocted this, as well.

In fact, Anita continually claimed that I had fabricated evidence and forged documents in my allegedly cynical and nefarious effort to focus the attention of our book on Michael Ovitz's role with Pellicano. In her latest version of events, she contended that this was why she had ended our partnership.[287]

The truth of the matter was that Anita had ended our partnership on May 25, 2005, when she unilaterally killed the book after her attorneys supposedly warned her that it would be giving too much "free information" to the defense in her civil case.

She put this in writing, although I was not sure whether she had disclosed that document to the defense during discovery. After reading her depositions, it appeared possible and even likely that she had been somewhat selective in what she had surrendered in discovery and what she had "lost."[288]

Regardless, there was not a single document in existence in which Anita complained that I—and I alone—was responsible for making Ovitz the villain of our book. That was a decision that she made—when she learned on June 12, 2003, from FBI Special Agent Tom Ballard that LAPD Detective Mark Arneson had run the background check on her on May 16, 2002, just nine days after she had completed her 2002 series of articles about Ovitz for the *New York Times*.

FBI Special Agent Stan Ornellas testified during Pellicano's criminal trial that his discovery of Arneson's May 16, 2002, background check on Anita had convinced him of Ovitz's involvement.

But, according to Anita's sworn testimony, she now claimed that she harbored no real suspicions about Ovitz prior to seeing his role with Pellicano featured in a *New York Times* stories in 2006. She insisted that I was alone in my supposed obsession to feature him in the book—against her wishes.

Soon after, a friend speculated that Anita's new tactic appeared to indicate that she had a potential problem with the statute of limitations in her civil case which was initially filed on May 28, 2004—without naming Ovitz. Her amended complaint against Ovitz—which was filed on November 6, 2006—might have been filed too late.

Consequently, when the documents she did reveal in discovery indicated her knowledge of Ovitz's alleged role as early as June 12, 2003—more than three years before she added him to her complaint and arguably long after the statute of limitations had expired—she seemingly decided to throw everything on me. By using me as her unwitting fall guy, she apparently hoped that she would get a quick but generous settlement from Ovitz, and that the record of the case would be sealed.

Thus, I would never know what she had said about me during her depositions, and I would never have the opportunity to defend myself against all of her false statements and diabolical machinations.

Then came a completely unexpected twist, which began when Ovitz's attorneys dropped a subpoena on me. Shortly thereafter, the enemy of my enemy became my friend.

———

A former counsel to the U.S. Senate Judiciary Committee, Eric George, was Ovitz's lead attorney. He was with the prominent Los Angeles law firm Browne George Ross, LLP. George said that he wanted to come to Washington, D.C., to meet. My attorney and I agreed to the meeting which was scheduled for September 14 at Morton's Steakhouse in Georgetown.

Five days before the meeting with George, I received a call from Debbie Wise, the wife of my attorney, Roger Simmons, saying that Roger had been rushed to a hospital in Hagerstown, Maryland, and had undergone emergency surgery. The immediate concern was that he was not going to survive. When I visited Roger three days later in the intensive-care unit and saw his grave condition, I feared the worst.

As Roger fought for his life, his young associate, Jodi Foss— whose uncle, Desmond Doss, a conscientious objector-turned-medic in World War II, won the Congressional Medal of Honor—accompanied me to Morton's to meet Eric George.

I was still in shock and even a little distracted due to my concern for Roger. I wanted him well and with me at this meeting. However, Jodi did an excellent job in Roger's absence.

Within seconds after shaking hands with Eric—who was impeccably dressed, cool, and even elegant—I asked, "At what point in her deposition did you say to yourself, Anita Busch is just flat-out lying?"

Eric smiled and said, "Pretty quickly."

I said that I was prepared to give them a fully documented sworn statement, addressing each and every charge that Anita had leveled against me. I told Eric, "If Anita gave up all of my materials without my permission, then I have no problem surrendering her documents, but only those documents that show that she lied about me."

In return, I wanted some sort of guarantee that I would be protected from any and all legal attacks that Anita and her zombie-stooges might mount against me. To my satisfaction, Eric proposed that he arrange to have his client, Michael Ovitz, indemnify me.

At that point, I asked, "Are you proposing that Ovitz and I sign an agreement?"

"I could draft some wording for your approval and then present it to Mike," Eric replied. "I'm sure that he would sign such an agreement."

A little stunned by the direction this conversation had taken, I said, "I want it understood that any sworn affidavit I execute, as well as any contract I might sign with Michael Ovitz, be transparent, and a matter of public record. I want nothing concealed."

"No problem," Eric declared. "Let me draw something up."

40. *"What I'm interested in now is fighting corruption"*

My arrangement with Michael Ovitz's attorneys had come about only because they had illuminated the depths of Anita's egregious smear campaign against me since 2005. In fact, before receiving the subpoena, I could not have imagined making such a deal, even though I would receive nothing more than legal fees and travel expenses.

But, clearly, Anita was now trying to destroy me, and she was unequivocally lying in her efforts to do so.

There was no way I could stay out of this. I had invested too much energy over too many years to simply "let it go."

Along with promising that I would always tell the truth in my sworn declaration—especially about what Anita and I thought about Ovitz—I specifically told Eric George that I could 1) provide additional notes given to me by Anita, stating that by June 12, 2003, she was convinced that Ovitz was the "only" person that could have been involved with Pellicano in the attack against her; 2) confirm that the challenged handwriting on the deposition exhibits was Anita's handwriting; and 3) produce "wet ink" documents that Anita had given to me in which she detailed her beliefs about Ovitz's involvement.

Mercifully, my attorney, Roger Simmons, had survived his near-death experience. But, because he was still recovering, Jodi Foss, Roger's young associate, continued to represent me.

In my sworn affidavit, which Jodi oversaw, I stated under oath:

> 1. I am over the age of 18 years old and competent to testify as to the matters contained herein based upon my personal knowledge.

> 2. I make this declaration under the penalty of perjury.

> 3. In May 2003, I began writing a nonfiction book with Anita Busch ("Ms. Busch") in the wake of the alleged attacks against her by Anthony Pellicano ("Mr. Pellicano"), hoping that we could get the book published, tell her important story, and make money on the back end.

> 4. Ms. Busch and I signed an Author Collaboration Agreement ("Collaboration Agreement") in January 2004. Although we would share the copyright and she would have editorial control, I would be the sole author. We gave the book the working title, *A Woman at Risk* (the "Book"). In addition, we originally agreed that we would split all advances and royalties 60-40 in her favor. I would work for free on this project and receive no money until we sold our Book project

to a publishing house. A true and accurate copy of this Collaboration Agreement is attached hereto as Exhibit A.

5. To assist in the composition of the draft proposals and draft manuscripts, Ms. Busch faxed and mailed to me no fewer than 170 single-spaced pages of detailed personal notes about how her life and career had been affected by the Pellicano investigation. These notes served as the foundation for our Book.

6. Between June 2004 and May 2005, I sent Ms. Busch four (4) clean and unmarked draft manuscripts, dated June [18], 2004, April 11, 2005, May 3, 2005, and May 10, 2005.

7. Ms. Busch provided handwritten edits for the first three (3) draft manuscripts, along with some typewritten material. However, she refused to approve the May 10, 2005, draft manuscript until I made a single change on page 230, which is the only difference between the May 10 and the final May 11, 2005, versions.

8. With my knowledge, Ms. Busch then submitted the approved 280-page May 11, 2005, draft manuscript, which consisted of chapters 1-31, to the attorneys for her civil suit, *Busch v. Pellicano, et al.* (Also, in my April 11, 2005, submission to Ms. Busch, I added a very rough first draft of chapters 32-42, which included pages 281 to 372.)

9. On May 25, 2005, Ms. Busch unilaterally halted our Book project because it supposedly conflicted with and jeopardized her civil lawsuit. She told me that her attorneys complained that our Book provided too much "free information" to the defense in her case.

10. I vigorously objected to her decision, provoking Ms. Busch to launch a smear campaign against me which continues to this day.

11. During her sworn testimony at Mr. Pellicano's criminal trial on April 9, 2008, Ms. Busch falsely claimed that she ended her collaboration with me because I had "used" her, a charge that was reported the following day in the *New York Times*.

12. On the same day as the *New York Times* article appeared, I responded to Ms. Busch's allegations on my personal website: http://www.moldea.com/Busch-response.html.

13. On August 18, 2011, I received a subpoena at my home from the lawyers for Michael Ovitz ("Mr. Ovitz"), a defendant in Ms. Busch's civil case. I immediately called my attorney, Roger C. Simmons, and asked him to fight it. He and his associate, Jodi Lynn Foss, quickly notified Mr. Ovitz's lawyers that we were willing to go to court to quash the subpoena.

14. In the days that followed, the subpoena was withdrawn. However, Mr. Ovitz's attorneys sent us several non-privileged documents from the case. We refused to sign a required protective order for additional privileged materials. The non-privileged documents we did receive included Ms. Busch's sworn depositions of April 14, July 21, and August 3, 2011.

15. I was shocked to see that Ms. Busch had provided my personal and private communications—as well as our draft proposals and the last draft manuscript of May 11, 2005—to the defense in her case without notifying me or my attorneys, even though I continue to own at least a forty-percent stake in this literary property.

16. Then, after reading Ms. Busch's sworn testimony—which was replete with false statements about me—I decided that I had no choice but to defend myself and to respond to her allegations, point by point. I do so in this Declaration.

I signed and executed my sworn declaration *at my attorneys' office, which was located in the state of Maryland on November 9, 2011—"under the penalty of perjury."*[289]

Among other things, I specifically showed Anita's repeated false statements under oath about her supposed refusal to believe that Ovitz was involved with Pellicano.

For instance, during her July 21, 2011, sworn deposition, Anita was questioned about the handwritten notes on a specific page in our manuscript and asked whether she had inserted the handwritten word "only" into the fourth paragraph of the text on that page.

Before the changes, the relevant typed text stated:

> Instead, she suddenly realizes that the person who hired
> Pellicano to attack her is the target of her series of articles for the
> *New York Times*, which ended on May 7, 2002, just nine days before
> [LAPD Detective Mark] Arneson submitted his report about Anita to
> Pellicano.

However, after Anita's handwritten edits for this paragraph, the text read (with her handwritten edits bracketed in bold lettering):

> Instead, she suddenly realizes that the [**only**] person who [**could have**] hired Pellicano to attack her is the [**subject**] of her series of articles for the *New York Times*, which ended on May 7, 2002, just nine days before Arneson submitted his report about Anita to Pellicano. (Emphasis added.)

Confronted with these specific changes by Eric George, Anita declared, even in view of what appeared to be her own edits, "Yeah, it's not accurate."[290]

When George asked why, Anita replied, "Because there was [sic] so many people that it could have been. I didn't know who it was."

George continued, "So when you made the change and you put 'could have,' which you said are your words, why did you do that?"

> **Anita:** Well, a lot of stuff was inaccurate. And quite frankly, there was stuff that I wouldn't even look at that he did that was completely fabricated and inaccurate.
>
> **Q:** You wrote the words "could have," correct?
>
> **Anita:** Yeah, he could have. 100 people could have at that point.
>
> **Q:** Why did you write "could have"?
>
> **Anita:** Because anybody could have at that point.
>
> **Q:** But you didn't write the word "only"?
>
> **Anita:** It doesn't look like my writing, no.
>
> **Q:** Is it possible it was you?
>
> **Anita:** No.
>
> **Q:** So—
>
> **Anita:** Because that's not what I thought.

Q: So it is your sworn testimony today you did not write the word "only"?

Anita: Yeah. It's not what I thought.

Q: Just focus on my question.

Anita: No, it doesn't look like my handwriting. And I wouldn't have thought that. I wouldn't have put that in there.

Q: Okay. So in other words, you did not write the word "only," that is not your handwriting?

Anita: No. I mean, I wouldn't have done it.

Q: Do you know whose handwriting it is?

Anita: It's probably Dan's.

Under intense questioning and in the midst of her persistent denials, Anita also tried to cast suspicion for this one-word change on her sister and even on Dave Robb. She also left open the possibility that the change had been made by John Connolly whom she said "was the co-writer of the book," even though he had been long gone from our team.

Anita simply refused to admit that she had handwritten the word "only."

Significantly, an admission that she had done this—which would indicate that she had realized that Ovitz was working with Pellicano against her as early as June 12, 2003—could have prompted the dismissal of her entire lawsuit and even invited the filing of sanctions against her and her attorneys for knowing that their case fell outside the statute of limitations.

Based on my personal and extensive knowledge of Anita's handwriting, there was no doubt in my mind that all of the handwritten edits that appeared—including the word "only"—were made by Anita and Anita alone. And there was actual proof that she had not been truthful about this.

While preparing my sworn affidavit, I located a subsequent incarnation of our draft book proposal with her additional handwritten notes on this particular section of the text.[291]

The original text now stated:

> Instead, she suddenly realizes that the **only** person who hired Pellicano to attack her was the **subject** of her series of articles for the *New York Times*. . . . (Emphasis added.)

The words "only" and "subject" had now been typed into the draft proposal—just as Anita had directed earlier.

But another key change made by Anita also made it clear that this newer proposal was written *after* the undated draft proposal with the challenged wording.

> * In this updated proposal, Anita re-added the handwritten words "could have," in the sentence which now read as corrected, "Instead, she suddenly realizes that the only person who **could have** hired Pellicano to attack her was the subject of her series of articles for the *New York Times*." (Emphasis added.)

> * In another handwritten note next to "could have," Ms. Busch wrote, "**already corrected this once before**." (Emphasis added.)

In what was Anita's attempt to scold me for not making a change in the manuscript, she wrote "already corrected this once before," which, years later, would serve as nothing less than an admission that she had made all of the corrections in that section.

In addition, continuing to explain her belief that "only" Ovitz could have been the person who hired Pellicano to investigate her, Anita had sent me her handwritten edits to the April 11, 2005, draft manuscript.

In the midst of a discussion in that manuscript about her June 12, 2003, conversation with FBI Special Agent Tom Ballard, Anita made the following handwritten addition:

> It could **only** have been Michael Ovitz. He would have been the **only** one interested in me at that time. . . .
> "Michael Ovitz," she hangs her head. "Michael Ovitz. I can't believe this."

> . . . . Anita now thinks it was Nasso & Ovitz together with
> Pellicano & his crew who did this to her. . . . .
> Anita hopes if Ovitz is guilty as she believes, then he will
> dangling [sic] from the same hook one day.[292] (Emphasis added.)

———

After the latest judge in the civil case recused himself, a long delay followed—and all proceedings were stayed—until a new judge could be found.

Meantime, Steve Gruel, Pellicano's rebooted attorney, filed papers with the court, requesting a bail hearing for the imprisoned former private investigator while his appeal was being heard by the U.S. Ninth Circuit Court of Appeals. Gruel expressed high confidence and predicted that Pellicano's 2008 conviction would be reversed. [293]

During the interim, an interview with Anita Busch appeared in the *Hollywood Reporter* on June 20, 2012, the tenth anniversary of the vandalism to her car. When asked whether she had found "a new career," Anita, who carefully took the time to accuse the Los Angeles District Attorney's Office of corruption in her case, replied, "What I'm interested in now is fighting corruption, exposing corruption, helping others who were victimized by the corruption. That's what drives me right now."[294]

After reading that, I made a note to myself with a link to the story, asking, "I wonder if that includes fighting those who commit perjury while fighting corruption?"

My writing coach, Mrs. Nancy Nolte, had been absolutely right. Depending on the circumstances, Anita used two basic personas in order to get what she wanted: 1) the crusading journalist who claimed the ethical and moral high ground against every other reporter; or, if that didn't work, 2) the hapless victim who demanded automatic respect and sympathy from anyone and everyone because of what she had been through.

———

On July 20, Anita once again emerged in the national press, speaking on behalf of the family of 23-year-old Micayla Medek, who was among those shot and killed by a gunman who opened fire in a crowded theater in Aurora, Colorado. As it turned out, Anita was a cousin of the father of the young victim.[295]

Quoted by the Associated Press, Anita said, "I hope this evil act . . . doesn't shake people's faith in God."[296]

In a subsequent AP story, Anita was described as "a spokeswoman" for some of the families of the twelve people who were killed during the massacre.[297]

Seeing Anita now actively promoting an anti-crime, anti-corruption, and God-driven agenda, I awaited news of her fourth deposition in her civil case, featuring the documents I had attached to my sworn declaration which had still not been made public.

Clearly, Ovitz's attorneys, who were keeping secret my cooperation with their defense, planned to ambush her with this new information.

Around the same time, at Pellicano's bail hearing in August, Anita spoke against Pellicano's bid for bail. *TheWrap* blog reported:

> Following an emotional appeal by frail, frightened-looking former *Los Angeles Times* writer Anita Busch, U.S. District Court Judge Dale S. Fischer Monday denied bail to Anthony Pellicano, once Hollywood's flamboyant gumshoe to the stars. . . .
>
> In her testimony, Busch—who also has written for *Variety* and the *Hollywood Reporter*—limped, and she had a wheelchair with her, which she did not use to enter the courtroom.
>
> She seemed scared of Pellicano and by the thought of his being released.
>
> "He is a domestic terrorist," she told the court. She questioned whether he had sufficient funds to pursue a vendetta against her and other victims. Turning to Steven F. Gruel, Pellicano's San Francisco-based attorney, she asked: "Who is paying Mr. Gruel? My life has been hell, and other victims have suffered."
>
> Gruel snapped back: "I've not gotten one penny."[298]

———

On Monday, August 20, 2012, at Anita's fourth deposition to deal with her statute of limitations problems, Ovitz's attorneys confronted her with additional evidence they had learned from me.

Seemingly without realizing that these new documents on the table had come from me, Anita continued to use me as her fall guy. She insisted that she did not believe that Ovitz was working with Pellicano in 2003, and that everything suggesting a Pellicano-Ovitz connection to the attacks on her in our draft manuscripts and book proposals was nothing more than my personal concoction which, she said, she had opposed.

As Eric George bombarded her with communications that she and I had exchanged, including time-stamped emails, she repeatedly denied writing them or could not recall ever having seeing them.

At some point during her deposition, apparently realizing that these documents could have only come from me, Anita returned to her default tactic of accusing me of dishonesty, using her usual venomous language.

Specifically, in lieu of denying the authenticity of each of these documents, she simply said with clear exasperation, "I think these are fabricated documents." Though she had no evidence to support that comment, Anita would continue that duplicitous theme for the remainder of her testimony.

In one exchange with Eric George—with her attorney, Ian Herzog, occasionally objecting—Anita, once again, was challenged to cite any document I had ever fabricated and, once again, she failed to come up with anything. With nothing else to use but her bold mendacity, she claimed that I had fabricated a conversation between Pellicano and Proctor, the same one I had recreated in a very rough early draft of our manuscript—that was based on the facts that Proctor had cited in his secretly recorded conversation with Dan Patterson in 2002.

Of course, she did not mention that, in the end, I had deleted the passage before she voiced any complaint.

Q: Do you have any specifics that you can tell me about where Dan Moldea fabricated something?

Anita: Many. He fabricated all the time. He fabricated quotes. He fabricated—yes, I can.

Q: Did he ever fabricate an e-mail, to the best of your knowledge, apart from the ones you just indicated?

Anita: I think once a fabricator, always a fabricator. He would fabricate anything.

Q: Can you identify a single e-mail, other than the ones we just talked about, that you believe were fabricated by Dan Moldea?

Anita: I can give you a pile of things he fabricated.

Q: Anything you can recollect as you're sitting here right now?

Anita: Yes.

Q: Any e-mails?

Anita: He fabricated --

Q: Just e-mails.

Anita: Yes.

Q: Okay. Go ahead.

Anita: He sent me an e-mail that had an entire conversation between Alexander Proctor and Anthony Pellicano back and forth with quotes all the way down. I was like, "Where did you get this? Where—did you interview these people?" He said, "No." He gave me—it was page after page of a conversation that he made up, fabricated, all the way down.

Q: Did he ever fabricate, in your experience, an e-mail where he created an e-mail purporting to be from him to you when, in fact, he never did send you such an e-mail?

Mr. Herzog: How would she know that? Go ahead and answer that question.

Anita: Yeah, I don't know. I mean --

Mr. George: You don't know –

Anita: But I wouldn't put anything past him, would tell you that.

Q: Did he ever fabricate, to your knowledge, an e-mail purporting to be from you to him, even though you, in fact, never sent that e-mail to him?

Mr. Herzog: Again, how would she know? Foundation.

Anita: I don't know.

Mr. George: You don't know.

Anita: I don't know, but he is capable of it.[299]

In addition, when Anita was asked about an incident—that, unknown to Ovitz's attorneys, involved her former live-in lover whom she called, "The Car Guy"—she claimed under oath that she did not even know his name and described him as "a friend of a friend" who had an "association with the Mafia."

The exchange where Anita, without hesitation or reservation, brazenly lied again, went as follows:

Q: After that general threat that the FBI warned you about in December of 2002, have you received any other threats?

Anita: January of 2003 something happened. I don't want to talk about any other stuff.

Q: Unfortunately we do need to know what happened in January of 2003.

Anita: I was at a hotel and somebody came outside the hotel room -- by the way, the night that I left and went to a hotel room, somebody came to the door there and was trying to get in the hotel room.

Q: You're referring to in June of 2002, correct?

Anita: Yeah, it was June 20th. And that night -- the night of -- I don't remember what night it was, but the paper set me up in a hotel. And that night somebody came to the door and tried to get into the hotel room and jiggled the handle and then called me on the phone. And I was like freaking out because nobody was supposed to know that I was there.

Q: What was the incident that occurred in January of 2003?

Anita: I had somebody just tell me that, you know, to be careful, that somebody wanted to know who I was talking to in Hollywood and just to be careful. And you know –

Q: Who gave you this warning?

Anita: Some guy that I used to know who was worried about my safety.

Q: What is his name?

Anita: I don't know his real name. He was a source. He was -- it was just some guy I knew.

Q: Was he a journalistic source or a friend?

Anita: He was just a -- he was a friend of a friend.

Q: And what was his -- you knew him by a pseudonym?

Anita: Just association with the Mafia.

Q: What was his nickname or –

Anita: He was something like -- I don't even remember. It was some weird nickname.

Q: Did he call you?

Anita: I was called and told that.

Q: And he was the one who called you, correct?

Anita: Uh-huh. Called from a pay phone.

Q: And do you recognize his voice when he called you?

Anita: Yeah.

Q: Is it that you don't know his name or you just don't want to reveal his name?

Anita: I don't know -- I don't want to reveal his name and I'm not sure of his full name.

Q: And then what happened after that?

Anita: It started to dissipate slowly.

Q: You indicated that after you got that warning, you received a threat. What was the threat?

Anita: No, I was just told if -- if I found myself on my knees with a gun in my mouth or a gun at the back of my head, that I needed to tell everything that I knew.[300]

Q: That's what the person on the phone told you?

Anita: Uh-huh.

Q: Yes?

Anita: Yes.

Q: Was he the one making the threat or –

Anita: No.

Q: -- was he warning you?

Anita: He was warning me.

Q: And who did he warn you was going to be putting a gun to your head?

Anita: No, it might have just been intimidation from -- might have just been intimidation.

Also during her deposition, she explained what she had been doing since leaving journalism in 2004. She disclosed that she had written a "spiritual memoir," along with three or four screenplays. In addition, she had worked as a consultant to Dick Wolf Productions and had some marketing assignments, including her work as a promoter for an unnamed Swedish pianist. Also, without citing specifics, she said that she had "done some research and investigation for people." However, she had not published any articles since leaving the *Los Angeles Times* in May 2004.

With regard to her health problems, Anita explained that she had torn a ligament while exercising in 2011. She believed that her injury was exacerbated by an "entrapped nerve" which she suffered during a subsequent physical-therapy session.

She also insisted that the stress from the Pellicano case had caused her general health problems, including problems with her immune system which "is no damn good anymore." Further, she described her history with her mental-health counselor.

With regard to her personal earnings, she said that she was currently on disability, adding that she made $67,451 in 2007, $66,404 in 2008, and $51,678 in 2009.

Before Ovitz's attorneys had the opportunity to disclose for the record that I had supplied the new documents and had even executed a sworn affidavit, Anita and her attorneys decided to end the deposition, claiming that the defense attorneys' questioning had exceeded the agreed upon time limit.

Although she clearly recognized that I had given Ovitz's attorneys some documents, Anita still did not know that I had executed a sworn statement on behalf of Michael Ovitz.

41. *"A defect of the Moldea declaration"*

On October 31, 2012, the Ovitz legal team filed its motion for summary judgment and later a motion for sanctions against Anita and her attorneys. In their motion to dismiss, Ovitz's attorneys accurately declared, "Busch concluded, on June 12, 2003, almost one full year before she filed her original complaint in this action, that it could have been Ovitz, and only Ovitz, who had hired Pellicano to attack her."

They also alleged in their motion for sanctions that the naming of Ovitz in the amended complaint in November 2006 was "fraudulently based on the false representation that Busch was unaware of her alleged claims against Ovitz when she filed her original, May [28], 2004 complaint. In fact, by her own admissions, Busch had concluded eleven months prior (on June 12, 2003) that Ovitz must have been behind Anthony Pellicano's 2002 attacks on her. Busch's and her counsel's conduct in misleading the Court to avoid summary dismissal of stale claims warrants the imposition of terminating sanctions against Busch and monetary sanctions against Busch and her counsel, the Law Offices of Ian Herzog."

By their demand for sanctions, Ovitz's attorneys were now aggressively pushing back. Sanctions, if granted by the court, can seriously damage a lawyer's career.

My sworn declaration, which I placed as a link on my website, was the centerpiece of both motions. I called the new webpage, *"How I got dragged into Busch v. Ovitz, Pellicano et al."*

In its press release after the filing, Ovitz's attorneys used a statement I had given them:

> I did everything I could to stay out of the Busch-Ovitz civil case. But, after receiving a subpoena from Michael Ovitz's attorneys and then reading Anita's sworn depositions, I could no longer remain silent. My affidavit in this matter is my self-defense against a woman who has cost me an enormous amount of time, money, and even personal friendships. She must be held to account for her actions.

———

On December 6, 72-year old Mickey Freiberg, Anita's friend and the agent who had caused so much ill-will between Anita and me, died of brain cancer. In a statement she made in the public comments section of the *Deadline Hollywood* website, she spoke as much about herself as she did Freiberg:

> After I testified in two federal trials, he told me, "You're the toughest woman I've ever known." . . . .
> Our last conversation was about death and the meaning of life. And how he knew he was going to go. And his horse spirit. And I told him that death was not the end and he would find that out and I told him what would happen to him. He asked how I knew. So I told him. He said, "You should write that up and then give it to me. I think I could sell that." I had to smile.[301]

After reading Anita's epitaph to Freiberg, I wondered whether she had ever told her beloved friend that she had secretly tape recorded a conversation with him in October 2003 about Michael Ovitz.

—•—

On January 8, 2013, John Connolly executed an affidavit on behalf of Anita, claiming under oath that the Ovitz-had-done-it theory was mine and mine alone—and not shared by either him or Anita.

Specifically, Connolly wrote:

> During the time we were working on the book, the three of us never reached agreement on who was behind Anthony Pellicano's actions against Anita. While Dan Moldea argued that it was Michael Ovitz, Anita remained convinced that it was Jules Nasso or someone associated with organized crime. She became even more adamant that it was Nasso after January 2004 when the U.S. Attorney released a document with a copy of a file seized from Pellicano's office which had Steven Seagal's name on the cover but with the client and attorney names redacted.

Of course, Connolly's statement was false. He flat out lied.

All three of us agreed that Michael Ovitz was "behind Anthony Pellicano's actions against Anita." Anita and I told him that secret on the night we invited him to join our writing team in October 2003.

In fact, everything was in writing, especially the circumstances revolving around Connolly's betrayal of Anita and me in December 2003 when we discovered his deal with *Vanity Fair* while he was under contract with us. In the end, he used his story in *Vanity Fair* to introduce Ovitz into the Pellicano scandal.

Two days after Connolly's affidavit, Dave Robb executed his sworn declaration, claiming that I had never notified him about my conversations with Jules Nasso.

Specifically, "my brother," Dave, stated under oath:

> When Anita learned [in January 2006] that Dan Moldea had been in contact with Jules Nasso about writing a book with Nasso, she was outraged and distraught. I was also astonished when I learned of this and confronted Moldea. He responded with an e-mail claiming that he had told me about his discussions with Nasso and left it up to me whether or not to tell Anita. This was blatantly false: he had asked me not to tell anyone what he was working on before revealing that he was working with Nasso. I was shocked that he was dealing with Nasso when Anita had so often expressed her fear of him. I sent Moldea an e-mail, a draft of which appears as Exhibit I hereto, recounting that he had fabricated the entire account of how he had revealed his Nasso contacts to me, and that he had betrayed Anita.[302]

This was false, as well—an account that conflicted with a bizarre exhibit, attached to his sworn declaration. This profanity-laced attachment was supposedly a "draft" of an undated email he claimed to have sent to me, noting that "a few days" after July 23, 2005, I had told him that I was "doing something with Nassau [sic]."

There was no actual email, only this supposed draft, which read:

> Dan lies:
>
> You are so full of shit I hardly know you anymore.
> You write: "On July 23, I called and told you that I had been approached about the Nasso project—even before I had my first conversation with Nasso. The following day, I memorialized my notification by sending you an email and giving you the details as I knew them. I left it to you as to whether or not to tell Anita."
> This is not the way it happened at all. . . . [You] started telling me that you were doing something with Nassau [sic]. I was shocked

and I immediately told you: "I don't want to hear about this!" Those were my exact words.

When you sent me an email "memorializing" your betrayal, I did not read it.

Now for you to say that it was up to me to tell Anita of your betrayal is a total lie.

Before you told me what you were doing, you told me not to tell anyone.

Clearly, you were scheming to fuck over Anita and me at that time.

You are living in a fantasy world and I am amazed that you are trying to put this on me.

This is what happened, and it makes me sick that I have to spend another two minutes of my life dealing with your fuck up.[303]

In addition, Dave's exhibit also stated that I had sent him the email with the details of my proposed plan to speak with Nasso, saying, "When you sent me an email 'memorializing' your betrayal, I did not read it."

Indeed, I did tell Dave about my proposed association with Nasso on July 23, 2005—and sent him a follow-up email the following day as he stated in his exhibit, not in January 2006, as he suggested in his sworn statement that accompanied this exhibit.

Essentially contradicting his own affidavit, Dave's exhibit confirmed that I had told him about the Nasso project in advance and that I had sent him an email with the details, an email he now claimed he did not read.

In the time-stamped July 24, 2005, email I had sent to Dave, I wrote: *"I gave you this information in confidence. I leave it to you whether to tell Anita—who, as usual will place some nefarious spin on what's happening."*

Once again, the reason I had given Dave this heads up was because of Anita's June 12, 2005, written demand: *"Anything more you have to say, you can speak to Dave and he can relay. I really have nothing more to say to you."*

Shortly after the release of these two sworn statements, I placed my responses to Dave and Connolly's versions on my webpage about this case, citing specific documents which proved they were not truthful.

And, of course, Anita claimed in her own sworn declaration of January 10, 2013, that the Ovitz-Pellicano conspiracy theory was mine and mine alone.

Specifically, she wrote:

> Defendant attempts to prove that I believed the [sic] Ovitz was the responsible party even before disclosure of April 2006 that he had hired Pellicano in 2002. This is largely based on the manuscript drafted by Dan Moldea. Moldea ignored facts which undermine his theory that Ovitz was responsible. The person responsible for Pellicano's threats against me was the subject of constant disagreement between [sic] myself, Dan Moldea, and John Connolly. I was convinced that Jules Nasso or someone connected with organized crime was responsible.

The simple fact is that the written record showed no such disagreement. Anita, Connolly, and I were on the same page about this matter that reached its climax when Connolly, after he betrayed Anita and me, featured Ovitz in his *Vanity Fair* story.

Furthermore, even if Anita was telling the truth that the Ovitz theory was mine and mine alone, she would also be admitting that I was right and she was wrong about Nasso.

After all, who did she end up suing? . . . Michael Ovitz.

The other major charge against me in Anita's sworn statement was that her discovery in January 2006 of my association with Nasso was the reason that our collaboration "broke down."

Specifically, she wrote:

> Apart from inaccuracies in Moldea's work [about Ovitz's alleged involvement with Pellicano], my relationship with him ultimately broke down in large part because I learned that he had met without my knowledge with Jules Nasso on a book proposal, knowing that I was terrified of Nasso because he or some other crime figures were likely behind Pellicano's attacks on me.

The fact that she had first learned about my association with Nasso in January 2006 is true. But I never concealed anything from her. Once again, as she had directed in June 2005, I went through Dave to tell her about Nasso, but Dave refused to tell her.[304]

Significantly, Anita's latest fabricated scenario that she had ended her partnership with me because of her discovery that I had betrayed her by dealing with Nasso was a new invention. She had never made any such claim during her sworn testimony at Anthony Pellicano's federal conspiracy trial where she testified under oath that she had stopped the book because she felt "used" by Connolly and me. Nor had she bothered to bring this up during any of her four depositions under oath in her civil case. In the midst of those venues where our book project was discussed at length, she provided other conflicting and equally false explanations.

———

On January 11, 2012, Anita's attorneys filed their responses to Ovitz's motions, falsely claiming, once again, that she never believed that Ovitz had been involved in the attacks against her as early as June 12, 2003, and that my association with Jules Nasso constituted a complete betrayal.

On January 14, my attorney was notified that Anita's lawyers had objected to the formatting of my affidavit because it had been executed in Maryland, not California.

Clearly, after having possession of my declaration for over a year, Ovitz's high-powered attorneys had not noticed this problem.

On January 16, Ovitz's attorneys asked me, via my attorney in Maryland, to sign a revised sworn declaration that was formatted in accordance with California law. That same day, my attorney emailed the re-formatted and re-executed affidavit to Ovitz's attorneys who then filed it with the court the following day.

Five days later, Anita's attorneys objected to my reformatted sworn declaration.

On January 24, the *Hollywood Reporter* published a summary of *Busch v. Ovitz*, saying:

> The initial suspicion of what triggered the dead fish and white [sic] rose centered on actor Steven Seagal and his former producing partner Jules Nasso, perhaps with mob assistance. At the time, Busch was preparing a big profile on them. . . .
>
> Along the way, Busch began to suspect Michael Ovitz, the former president of Disney who co-founded CAA, whom she also had been writing about extensively in 2002. It's hotly debated in court when and how Busch made that connection. . . . That year, she jotted down in notes, "Dear God...it could have only been one person...only one person makes sense and that is Michael Ovitz."
>
> But Busch says she only really connected the dots about "Ovitz's liability" in 2006 when *The New York Times* reported, based on FBI summaries, that Ovitz acknowledged hiring Pellicano a few months before the white [sic] rose incident.[305]

———

On January 25, Los Angeles Superior Court Judge Elihu M. Berle issued his ruling, throwing out my sworn declaration because I had executed it in the State of Maryland and not in the State of California. And, because Ovitz's attorneys' two motions were primarily based on my sworn affidavit, the judge threw out the two motions, as well.

In his opinion, Judge Berle, a 1969 Columbia University Law School graduate and a long-time Century City attorney who had been appointed to the bench in 1996 by then-Republican Governor Pete Wilson, wrote:

> Before going to some of the substantive issues, let me address some of the evidentiary objections. In support of the motion, defendant Ovitz filed a declaration of Dan Moldea. Plaintiff has objected to the declaration because it was not properly signed under penalty of perjury under the laws of the State of California as required under C.C.P. Section 2015.5.
>
> The Court sustains the objection to the Moldea declaration. And therefore, the declaration is not admissible evidence and cannot

support Ovitz's motion, citing *Ibarbia versus Regents of California*, 1987, 191 CAL APP. 3D, 1318.

In an attempt to remedy a defect of the Moldea declaration, Ovitz submitted a reformatted declaration of Dan Moldea. However, the Court will not consider this declaration for analysis whether Mr. Ovitz has met his initial burden to offer admissible evidence offered as this reformatted declaration was not submitted until the reply. A motion for summary judgment must be decided on admissible evidence. . . .

The Court previously notes that, even if the Court were to consider the reformatted declaration of Moldea, such declaration would not affect the finding that plaintiff has offered sufficient evidence raising triable issues of material fact. Plaintiff raised triable issues notwithstanding any contrary declarations made by Moldea. And so the Court is going to deny the motion for summary judgment or summary adjudication filed by defendant Ovitz.

Due to a technicality, it was a stunning victory for Anita. All the evidence of her false statements and alleged perjury was not even considered by the trial judge. Further, the judge did not seem to accept the fact that after June 12, 2003, there was no doubt in Anita's mind that Ovitz was at the core of the Pellicano investigation against her. The only questions revolved around whether he had confederates or whether he knew about the attacks in advance.

In a story about the ruling by the *Hollywood Reporter*, journalist Eriq Gardner wrote:

In deciding whether to allow the case to move forward, Judge Elihu Berle put the "pivotal question" this way: "Did [Busch] know actual facts to cause a reasonable person to believe liability is probable against Ovitz as opposed to mere suspicion that Ovitz was responsible for the alleged wrongful acts?"

The judge turned his attention to June 12, 2003, when an FBI agent allegedly told Busch that her name, as well as *NYT* colleague Bernard Weinraub, had previously been run through an LAPD database. Because the database search allegedly happened before she began working on a story about Seagal-Nasso and happened shortly after the two reporters had completed articles on Ovitz for the *NYT*, Ovitz asserted that on the date of the FBI interview, she believed that Ovitz had hired Pellicano.

But Busch denied being told her name was run in a LAPD database search.

"The evidence provided by Ovitz shows at most that [Busch] suspected that Ovitz was involved in the wrongdoing," Berle wrote. "Ovitz has failed to offer any actual facts that [Busch] knew that would possibly implicate Ovitz in the alleged wrongdoing other than the timing of the search of [Busch's] name."[306]

42. *"The Book Project from Hell"*

In early July 2013, one of Ovitz's attorneys told me that Judge Berle had ruled that Anita's case would be bifurcated—with an initial bench trial to determine the question of statute of limitations. If Anita survived that test, a second trial litigating the liability issues would follow about a year or so later.

At a bench trial, the judge decides. The second trial would be in front of a jury.

The procedural case would be heard during the week of September 23 in Los Angeles.

As I understood the law, most states apply an "objective" standard in measuring statute of limitations issues. For instance, would a reasonable person have known or reasonably believed that Michael Ovitz was the culprit before the statute of limitations ran? Did Anita have indications whereby she should have investigated sooner?

However, in *Busch v. Ovitz* which would be heard in a California superior court, Judge Berle would apply a "subjective" rather than an "objective" standard. In other words, if Anita did not personally believe that Ovitz was responsible during the statute of limitations period, that would be sufficient for her to survive this court test—even though a reasonable person, especially a journalist, would have recognized Ovitz's probable involvement much earlier.

The judge had created a battleground to determine whether Anita had actual knowledge of Ovitz's involvement before the statute of limitations barred her from filing suit and not whether she was reasonable in her responses to obvious indications of Ovitz's involvement.

Anita's entire case appeared to hinge on her ability to make me the fall guy—that I was alone in concocting the Ovitz-was-involved-with-Pellicano scenario and that any evidence to the contrary was fabricated—or criminally forged—by me.

Ovitz's attorneys said that they planned to call me as their key witness at the procedural trial, as we had stipulated in our contract. However, when we signed that agreement, we never thought that Anita would get past Ovitz's motion to dismiss because of all of her false statements under oath. We also never thought that my sworn declaration would be thrown out because it had been executed in the wrong state.

———

Most nonfiction authors receive an advance for their book projects on the basis of proposals given to their literary agents who then pitch them to the various publishing houses where a particular book or subject will fit with a publisher's list. After making their publishing deals through their agents—who then receive money from the publishers, take their fifteen-percent commissions, and then remit the balance to their clients—authors write a series of draft manuscripts until they are satisfied with a final version which they submit to their editors, who then begin the process of conceptual editing, line editing, fact-checking, and vetting.

In the end, their books are released, and the authors are reviewed and/or judged on the basis of his or her finished products. Books then succeed or fail based on the response of a reading public to the efforts of a publisher in promoting and publicizing them.

With my first seven non-fiction books, I had received advances for each to finish my research, interviewing, and writing. I had rarely, except with my first book, spent time and money developing a book project purely "on spec" as I had with Anita.

In the case of *Woman at Risk*, before receiving a publishing deal and at my own personal expense, I wrote a series of draft manuscripts about a still-unfolding story on behalf of a friend who was in trouble. After two years of work, she determined that she could make more money from her civil lawsuit than from our book, so she unilaterally terminated the book—using any excuse she could conjure up against me to justify this flagrant breach of our collaboration contract.

When I protested, she launched a smear campaign against me, giving false testimony under oath during Pellicano's criminal case about the reason she had ended the book project. She then augmented those untruths during her subsequent affidavits and depositions in her civil case.

Now, as the civil case headed for trial, Anita and her attorneys would attempt to have me judged by the earliest versions of both my draft manuscripts and book proposals—clearly works in progress— and then harshly condemn me for any mistakes that were made, even though most if not all of those mistakes were corrected in subsequent drafts.

To my knowledge, no author has ever been judged by such a standard in this kind of environment.

Despite her protests, Anita, who had absolute editorial control, had approved of the first 280 pages of the May 11, 2005, manuscript, which she then gave to her attorneys. She refused to give it to them until I made *every* change she wanted.

With regard to the issues during the upcoming trial, I would testify on Ovitz's behalf that Ovitz was, indeed, behind Pellicano's handiwork against Anita, who had known this since June 12, 2003, long before she added him as a defendant in her lawsuit.

The plan was that Ovitz's attorneys would use my timeline and supporting documentation to show that she had waited too long to sue him.

Simultaneously, we knew that Anita would accuse me in open court of forging documents, a major felony, during my supposedly fraudulent but inexplicable efforts to show that the person behind the attacks was Ovitz for use in our manuscript. And she would receive the support of both John Connolly and Dave Robb in their false and misleading sworn statements that I was the only member of our team who believed that Ovitz had been working with Pellicano.

And all of these ferocious charges and condemnations would be leveled against me in the midst of Anita's trial against . . . Michael Ovitz.

Knowing that I was Ovitz's key witness—and that I would be testifying that Ovitz was directly or indirectly involved in the attacks against Anita—my own unspoken fear was that the Ovitz attorneys would devise a scenario in which Anita and I would kill each other off at the trial so that neither one of us would have the standing to accuse Ovitz of being a villain.

We were beyond the looking glass with this situation.

———

During the interim before the trial commenced, three of the civil cases revolving around the Pellicano caper were decided:

* On October 19, 2012, a jury reached a verdict against Jacqueline Colburn who used Pellicano to wiretap the telephone conversations of her estranged husband, construction tycoon Richard D. Colburn of Beverly Hills. (He had died before the trial in the midst of their divorce proceedings which began in 1999.)
The jury awarded Richard Colburn's three children from a previous marriage and one of his former employees $3.9 million in damages.[307]

* Two months later, in mid-December, a lawsuit that Hungarian model Monika Zsibrita had filed against comedian Chris Rock was settled. Zsibrita had sued Rock, alleging that he retained Pellicano to investigate her after she claimed that Rock was the father of her daughter. Rock denied paternity and allegedly retaliated against the woman via Pellicano. The terms of the agreement were sealed.[308]

* On December 21, Judge Elihu Berle dismissed Bo Zenga's civil case against Brad Grey, still the president of Paramount, because the statute of limitations had expired before Zenga filed his litigation against him.
According to reporter Eriq Gardner of the *Hollywood Reporter*:

Unfortunately for Zenga, he waited until May 2006 to assert wiretapping allegations. . . . That created statute-of-limitations problems, meaning his claims were brought too late. Zenga had many tip-offs to what was happening. . . .

Grey, who has always denied knowledge of Pellicano wiretapping, was fortunate his adversary didn't follow up sooner on his suspicions. . .

The delay didn't serve him well. At a hearing in December, defense attorney Brian Sun said the facts of the case were "pretty much not in dispute" but that Zenga should have filed his claims quicker.

The judge accepted that reasoning, ruling that because he had a suspicion, Zenga had a duty to conduct a reasonable investigation. But Zenga waited, and thus his claims were barred by the statute of limitations.[309]

If that was the threshold for Judge Berle—"a suspicion" that would provoke a "reasonable investigation"—then Anita's case against Ovitz was not going to go any further. It would be over.

Seemingly confirming this on March 18, 2013, Judge Berle ruled against the plaintiff in *Sapir v. Cruise*, et al., citing problems with the statute of limitations. World-famous actor Tom Cruise and his world-famous attorney, Bert Fields, would not have to stand trial because of their association with Pellicano who had allegedly wiretapped on their behalf.

Reporting on the decision, the *Examiner* stated:

Judge Elihu Berle decided in favor of Cruise's motion for a summary judgment against former *Bold* magazine editor Michael Davis Sapir, who had filed the now-dismissed lawsuit back in 2009, claiming that the celebrity and his attorney had hired high-profile Hollywood detective Anthony Pellicano to investigate him.
. . .

In the recent ruling, Judge Berle determined that the statute of limitations prohibited Sapir's suit from proceeding, noting that in 2003 Sapir had been exposed to news reports about Pellicano that alerted the editor, and because the news reports should have raised reasonable suspicions, Sapir had a duty to investigate further.[310]

In its own report, the *Hollywood Reporter* added:

Cruise joins Brad Grey as escaping Pellicano-related lawsuits thanks to the claims being time-barred. Many other lawsuits proceed, including one against Michael Ovitz for allegedly hiring Pellicano to intimidate Anita Busch. Recently, the same judge ruled that Ovitz has failed to show that he's entitled to summary judgment on statute of limitation grounds.[311]

On that same day, the *Hollywood Reporter* also noted in a separate story that during a hearing on March 18 about Anita's civil case:

> [I]t appears that Pellicano's time to speak is coming. Among the other outcomes from Monday's hearing, Anita Busch's attorney is being given the opportunity to depose Pellicano separately from everyone else.
> That case could be headed toward a big Hollywood courtroom showdown.[312]

On September 5, the print edition of my memoir, *Confessions of a Guerrilla Writer: Adventures in the Jungles of Crime, Politics, and Journalism*, was released. The only reference to the Pellicano case was in an endnote that stated:

> In May 2003, I became involved in another doomed book project, revolving around the federal investigations and criminal indictments of Los Angeles private detective Anthony Pellicano, the so-called "Sleuth to the Stars." Directly or indirectly, usually working through a group of prominent Los Angeles attorneys, Pellicano had represented a wide variety of Hollywood celebrities, including actresses Roseanne Barr, Farrah Fawcett, and Elizabeth Taylor; actors Kevin Costner, Tom Cruise, and James Woods; corporate executives Brad Grey, Kirk Kerkorian, Michael Nathanson, Michael Ovitz, and Don Simpson, as well as Michael Jackson, George Harrison of The Beatles, and television personality Jerry Springer, among many others.
> My two years of free work on this matter served as a testament to the old adage, "No good deed goes unpunished." In fact, the fallout from this period continues to this day—even after Pellicano's conviction in 2008 for conspiracy and racketeering. I have described this situation to colleagues as "The Book Project from Hell," which, among other major consequences, led to the destruction of my long friendship with my "brother," Dave Robb. As of this writing, we haven't spoken in over seven years.
> Trusted friends have admonished me not to discuss this very complicated case in this work, preferring that I tell that story—if I must—in a subsequent stand-alone book.

Three months earlier, in June 2013, the *Guardian* newspaper in Great Britain identified Edward Snowden, a twenty-nine-year old contractor for the National Security Agency and the CIA, as the source of information that the NSA was collecting the telephone records of millions of Americans.

In the aftermath of the September 11, 2001, attacks on America, the world had entered a new age where privacy was no longer ensured and nearly everything said or written on either a telephone or a computer was being recorded and archived.

43. *"I didn't tape record my conversation with Mickey"*

Accused by Anita of unilaterally focusing the attention of our doomed book project on Michael Ovitz—with neither her approval nor blessing—I provided Ovitz's attorneys with copies of her numerous typed and handwritten notes, which clearly demonstrated both her approval and blessing beyond what I had already submitted with my sworn declaration. Notably, I only gave Ovitz's attorneys a small portion of the 170-plus pages of personal notes that Anita had sent to me—upon which the drafts of our manuscript were based.

On Saturday, September 21, 2013, my attorney, Roger Simmons, and I flew to Los Angeles for the trial, now scheduled to begin on Tuesday. On Sunday and Monday, we met with Ovitz's attorneys at the law offices of Browne George Ross in the Fox Plaza building in Century City, perhaps better known as the fictitious Nakatomi Tower from the first *Die Hard* movie. The director of that motion picture had already been convicted and sentenced for his role in the Pellicano scandal.

This was the second time I had met the articulate and sophisticated Eric George who remained the lead attorney in the case. During a routine prep session, I learned that my direct examination would be conducted by Jonathan L. Gottfried, a young and talented attorney who had received his undergraduate degree from Yale and his law degree from Harvard. He was assisted by

Abigail Page, another outstanding young attorney, who seemed to know the case as well as anyone.

Just to be clear, I received no money from Ovitz, other than my legal fees and travel expenses, for my participation at this trial.

My principal goal was to stop the smear campaign against me that had been waged by Anita Busch, Dave Robb, and John Connolly since 2005. But, in order to do that, I needed a decision from the trial judge which would expose Anita and the false statements she had made under oath during this litigation, especially those about me. With Anita's dishonesty publicly documented, I believed that the smear campaign, which had taken a tremendous toll on me, would finally come to an end.

The trial of *Busch v. Ovitz* began on September 24, 2013, at 10:00 A.M. in room 323 on the fourteenth floor of the Los Angeles Superior Courthouse in Koreatown. Ovitz's attorneys—representing the defendant who challenged the statute of limitations, the sole issue of this portion of the bifurcated case—opened first.

Anita and Michael Ovitz sat in the courtroom at their respective attorneys' tables.

I did not attend this initial hearing, because Judge Berle did not want potential witnesses altering their sworn statements based on the testimonies of others. Nevertheless, owing to the technology of today's modern world, I received regular updates about what was happening by cell phone and email.

Eric George gave his opening argument first, a very legalistic summary of Anita's burden of proof, saying in part:

> To hang these issues on the broadest possible skeleton, we know, Your Honor, that the initial Complaint by Ms. Busch was filed May 28, 2004. We know that Ms. Busch substituted Mr. Ovitz in as defendant doe for the very first time on November 6, 2006. So, of course, without the benefit of relation-back Ms. Busch's claims are time barred.
>
> One of the reasons why we submitted the trial brief, Your Honor, is to talk about the legal standards, and I'm not going to belabor them, but either of two standards would defeat relation-back, Ms. Busch.

No. 1, if Ms. Busch knew facts at the time she filed her original
Complaint, they would have caused a reasonable person to believe
that Ovitz's liability was probable. And the other means by which
she will not get the benefit of a relation-back is if her doe allegations
were a sham pleading on the ground that she actually did believe that
Ovitz's liability was probable when she filed her action on May 28,
2004.

Opposing counsel attempts to argue that evidence of her so-
called subjective beliefs is not relevant. Your Honor, it's not only
relevant, it's highly probative. No. 1, it's highly probative as to the
sham pleading issue.

No. 2, it's very relevant because it sheds light on what a
reasonable person would have believed if Ms. Busch believed
something at the time hence a reasonable person might have
believed it. Our trial brief also addresses that the burden of proof
on relation-back must rest with the plaintiff inasmuch as this
is an affirmative allegation that needs to be made as part of her
Complaint.

In his opening argument, Anita's attorney, 71-year old
Ian Herzog, a folksy and avuncular man with a good sense
of courtroom humor, went for my throat, portraying me as a
desperado, the person who insisted that Ovitz had been working
with Pellicano. Still, because everyone in the courtroom now knew
that Ovitz had been working with Pellicano, I didn't know how
Herzog kept a straight face while making this accusation against
me.

Herzog, speaking about my role as Anita's co-author, said in part:

There was this book that was being written by Anita with Mr.
Moldea. And the evidence in the case is going to be that there was a
lot of speculation, especially by Mr. Moldea, as to who was behind
Pellicano. Mr. Moldea was advocating for Ovitz as the Court will
recall in the summary motions.

Anita Busch said that's speculation, there's no facts to indicate
that.

And you have to understand Moldea's motivation, and he's
going to be here to testify. Moldea had no facts. He's speculating.
He didn't investigate. He too had to rely on the authorities. He
had nothing. He wanted—I think the evidence is going to show
that he wanted it to be Ovitz because that could really make the
book. Without having somebody as high profile and as significant

and as—at the level that Mr. Ovitz was and the controversy
surrounding a person like Ovitz who had his detractors and
his advocates, people loved him, people hate—high people in
Hollywood, the heads of the studios had relationships with Ovitz
that had issues with Ovitz.

So without having someone as high profile as Ovitz, as the
person who was behind Pellicano, it would have been old news. . . .

Moldea, this author of this book which, as you know from
the summary judgment, the defense relies a great deal about his
speculation and his conjecture as to whether it was Ovitz or not. He
certainly advocated for that. Anita did not. The other people who
were involved with the book didn't think there was any evidence to
indicate that it was Ovitz.

In this context, Herzog did not mention John Connolly who
implicated Ovitz in his two *Vanity Fair* articles.

Along with Anita and me, a handwriting expert was slated as the
Ovitz legal team's only other witness. I had been asked to submit
a sample of my handwriting for analysis—in the midst of Anita's
repeated claims that I had forged documents which, the defense
insisted, provided evidence of her first knowledge of Ovitz's alleged
role with Pellicano no later than June 12, 2003, which was outside
the statute of limitations.

I was already describing this day as the "demarcation date" in
this case.

After June 12, 2003—when Anita learned from FBI Special
Agent Tom Ballard that LAPD Detective Mark Arneson had
run a police-computer check on her for Pellicano on May 16,
2002—Anita had placed Ovitz at the center of the conspiracy
against her.

But Anita still had a huge problem. During her trial testimony
under oath, she would have to navigate through her numerous false
statements in the midst of four depositions under oath *before* she
knew that I was cooperating with Ovitz's attorneys. Also, she would
likely have to address the contents of documents she had given to
me but that she had failed to produce, for whatever reason, to the
defense during discovery.

To combat this, she and her legal team needed to discredit
me and portray Anita's role in the book project as distant and

uninvolved while downplaying the simple fact that she unfailingly and aggressively exercised the editorial control she was guaranteed in our contract. Already, they had taken two attempts I had made to create some immediacy in the narrative from a very rough draft of the manuscript—a recreated conversation and a scene of Anita swimming at the YMCA, both of which I had taken out before Anita ever made an issue out of them—and then depicted them as acts of corruption by an unethical journalist.

Consequently, when she was confronted with damning documents, indicating that she had filed her lawsuit against Ovitz outside the statute of limitations, she would predictably accuse me of fabricating or even forging these documents.

If cornered by a problem in a document that only she could have written, Anita would slough off any problems by claiming that they were simple mistakes, typos, or oversights.

———

Indeed, contradicting her previous statements from the depositions, Anita, Ovitz's first witness, now admitted that she held the following belief after her now-famous conversation with FBI Special Agent Tom Ballard on June 12, 2003: "That was before the Seagal stories. That was before I even joined the *L.A. Times*. Dear God . . . it could have **only** been one person . . . **only** one person makes sense and that is Michael Ovitz." (Emphasis added.)

However, she qualified her admission, saying, "That was my first impression. Yes"

Yet, even after admitting this, Anita adamantly continued to deny having made the handwritten edits for the following paragraph. (Her handwritten edits are bracketed in bold lettering— where she essentially said the same thing as what appeared in her notes about her conversation with Tom Ballard of the FBI):

> Instead, she suddenly realizes that the [**only**] person who [**could have**] hired Pellicano to attack her is the [**subject**] of her series

of articles for the *New York Times*, which ended on May 7, 2002, just nine days before Arneson submitted his report about Anita to Pellicano.

In addition, she also used the "first impression" dodge with another controversial portion of the notes of her conversation with FBI Special Agent Ballard with regard to the section in which she wrote:

> Ballard then asks me if I know some names. I don't know any of them. He asks the name of my writing partner at NYT. It's Weinraub. He said can you spell that? I do. He says, "that's a positive ID." I'm shell shocked at this moment. I say nothing. I pull off the road. I just sit there. **If Bernie Weinraub is on that list, which it appears that he is, then it is definitely Ovitz.** (Emphasis added)

———

With regard to John Connolly's betrayal of Anita and me over his secret deal with *Vanity Fair* in 2003, Anita, who had discovered his duplicity and was even angrier about it than I, portrayed herself, not just sitting in what we called "The Garden," but, as an actual passive bystander to the bitter dispute we had with Connolly:

> **Q:** [I]t's true, is it not, that you learned before March 1, 2004, that John Connolly was involved in drafting this story; is that correct?
>
> **Anita:** Yes.
>
> **Q:** And is it fair to say that as a result of that knowledge you no longer wanted to work with John Connolly in your manuscript that you were also working on with Dan Moldea? Do I have that right?
>
> **Anita:** Not exactly.

Q: What happened?

Anita: Dan was upset that John was writing the article and said that it would hurt the book. And he considered it a betrayal and so did I because I didn't have any experience writing books. I didn't know what it meant really.

Q: And was it as a result of that that you and Dan Moldea elected to stop working with John Connolly in connection with your book?

Anita: Yes, it regarded this article.

Q: As a betrayal?

Anita: Yeah. Dan explained it to me that way.

————

In another passage of the manuscript in which Anita had falsely accused me of fabrications, I had written:

Instead, she suddenly realizes that the only person who hired Pellicano to attack her was the subject of her series of articles for the *New York Times*, which ended on May 7, 2002, just nine days before Arneson submitted his report about Anita to Pellicano.

The man who threatened her must be [***Mister X], and she identifies him to the FBI..[313]

After repeatedly denying during her sworn depositions that she knew that "Mister X" was a direct reference to Ovitz, she finally admitted during her trial testimony that she did know.[314] Her caveat in this situation was that she was only going along with what I wanted to do.

Q: [W]here it says Chapter 36, there's a sentence that says, "The man who threatened her must be ..." Do you see that?

Anita: Uh-huh.

Q: And in the brackets it says "Mr. X and she identifies him to the FBI."

Anita: I didn't identify anybody to the FBI. That's a mistake.

Q: That's inaccurate?

Anita: Yeah, that's not accurate. What was the other thing you were asking me about?

Q: That's it. If this was inaccurate why didn't you make any edit to it?

Anita: I probably just read over it or something. But I didn't identify anybody to the FBI as behind the threats. I didn't know who was behind the threats. I mean Dan wanted to go with Ovitz and so I said, well, if it's going to be -- if you're going to go that route with Ovitz, it's got to be Jules or Steven, it can't be Ovitz. Didn't make sense. At that point.

Q: It was your practice generally to make sure that edits were made so that accuracy would be insured in this manuscript; correct?

Anita: Right. But Dan said we'd go over it many times so if I missed something not to worry about it. . . .

Q: Again, let's take a look at that same sentence. You didn't make any edit to it this time either, right, "The man who threatened him must be Mr. X and she identifies him to the FBI."

Anita: Yeah, but I -- I didn't do that. It's just an oversight.

Q: So you made the same oversight twice?

Anita: Yeah, I could have. I mean, you know, I just -- I didn't -- I didn't have -- I wasn't investigating that so I didn't know who it was so I couldn't have done that. I didn't identify anyone to the FBI. I didn't know who it was. . . .

Q: And you wrote this language on the left, "Why is Mr. X when you just identify him to the world here."

Anita: Yes.

344 Hollywood Confidential

Q: Mr. X was Michael Ovitz; right?

Anita: That's what Dan thought, yeah.

Q: What did you think at this time? You understood at this time when you wrote Mr. X that was Ovitz; right?

Anita: Dan wanted to go this route. So I allowed him to go that route, but there was so much information that I found out that pointed in all different directions actually. Especially to Jules.

Q: Let me just ask this as simply as I can. On or about February 15, 2005, when you wrote "Mr. X," did you understand Mr. X to correspond to Michael Ovitz?

Anita: Yes, I did. But law enforcement hadn't identified anybody at that point. So ...

Q: And indeed throughout the whole book collaboration process, every time you referenced Mr. X, you meant for that to mean Mr. Ovitz when you were communicating that to Dan Moldea; correct?

Anita: Dan put in Mr. X. My feeling was I didn't want to falsely identify -- falsely accuse anyone at all. I just didn't want anybody to be falsely accused because it was a serious crime.

———

Anita had repeatedly and categorically denied during her sworn depositions ever using "Ed" as a code name to identify Ovitz, even falsely claiming that I had forged some of those documents in which "Ed" appeared. But, during her trial testimony, she relented after finding herself trapped when confronted with documents only she could have written and in which she referred to Ovitz as "Ed." However, she cleverly qualified her use of that code name, saying that she did so on a case-by-case basis.[315]

Eric George did manage to back her down on at least one important document where "Ed" was used that she claimed that I had forged. Eric began his line of questioning by reading from Anita's earlier sworn deposition.

BY Mr. George [reading from Busch's earlier deposition]:

> **Q**: Did you write the next sentence: . . .'How can you forget Nasso's comments about what a stand-up guy Ed was in the *Vanity Fair* piece immediately after I was threatened?'
>
> **Q**: Did you write that to [Moldea]?
>
> **Anita**: No.
>
> **Q**: That's not your sentence?
>
> **Anita**: I think these are fabricated documents."

[Eric George stops reading from her deposition and continues with his questioning]

Q: That was your sworn testimony in deposition; correct?

Anita: Uh-huh. Yes.

Q: In fact, Ed, in the context of this document necessarily refers to Michael Ovitz. Would you agree?

Anita: Let me go back and look at it. This e-mail was about Jules trying to get to me, I believe.

Q: Well, let me focus you on the paragraph that's --

Anita: But some of it doesn't look like anything I remember or even thought so ...

Q: Let me focus you on 1, 2, 3, 4 paragraphs down, the second sentence. "How can you forget Nasso's comments about what a stand-up guy Ed was in the *Vanity Fair* piece?" Do you know of any person other than Michael Ovitz --

Anita: No, that was reference to Ovitz in that. In that particular use of it.

Q: So, Ms. Busch, if you wrote this e-mail, then, you referenced Ed as Michael Ovitz on January 19, 2006; correct?

Anita: Yes, at that point. Yeah. When I was speaking to Dan, but this other -- yeah, okay.

Q: And, indeed, this is a document that was produced by you in this litigation; correct? Look at the very bottom.

Anita: Okay. Then it's okay.

Q: This is not a fabricated document; correct?

Anita: No, probably not then.

Interrupting Anita's testimony because of a scheduling conflict, Ovitz's attorneys called handwriting analyst, Erich Speckin of the Michigan-based Speckin Forensic Laboratories, to the stand. He testified that, in his professional opinion, the disputed handwritten examples on the challenged documents were likely written by Anita Busch.

Significantly, with my handwriting sample in his possession, he did not indicate that any of the disputed documents had been written—or forged—by me.[316]

After all of the charges made against me for fabricating and forging documents, when Judge Berle asked Anita's attorney if he had any questions on cross-examination for the handwriting analyst, Herzog replied, "Would you be disappointed if I didn't ask you any?"

During a recess while I was in the lobby of the courthouse, I received permission to view the courtroom just for personal orientation purposes. I wanted to see where I would be sitting and how to get there.

In my notes, after seeing Anita for the first time since March 2004, I wrote:

> When I walked into the courtroom to see the layout, I saw Anita up front. She looked worn and haggard. I saw her again a few minutes later when she left the courtroom with her attorneys and headed for the elevators. She was limping noticeably. When she saw me, she stepped out of my sight until the elevator arrived. Then she limped in quickly.

After Anita resumed her testimony in the afternoon and I went back to my hotel, I soon received a notification to return to the courthouse. But, after I arrived, I was told that my testimony had been postponed by yet another series of Anita's on-the-stand emotional breakdowns.[317] In the midst of this, I felt like a placekicker who had split the uprights with a winning field goal—only to be told that the opposing head coach had called time out just before the ball was snapped, forcing the kicker to do it again.

Anita and her attorneys were apparently trying to freeze me.

During the final moments of Anita's testimony, Eric George asked her about a very detailed transcript she had prepared of her October 17, 2003, telephone conversation with her friend, Mickey Freiberg, the literary agent, about Michael Ovitz and his possible role in the attack against her.

> **Q:** Ms. Busch, you met in January of 2003 with a man named Mickey Freiberg; correct?
>
> **Anita:** Yes.
>
> **Q:** And Mickey Freiberg asked you at that point in time if Bert Fields or Michael Ovitz was involved in Pellicano's June, 2002, attack on you; correct?
>
> **Anita:** Yes.
>
> **Q:** And then you went ahead and you called Mickey Freiberg much later, in fact, on October 17, 2003, you called him; right?
>
> **Anita:** Yes.

Q: And you tape-recorded this conversation that you had with Mr. Freiberg; correct?

Anita: No.

Q: You did not tape-record this conversation?

Anita: No.

Q: Is this a transcription of that conversation?

Anita: It's what I did in notes and then I put it in the computer.

Q: It's your sworn testimony today that you did not tape-record your conversation with Mickey Freiberg?

Anita: No. I didn't tape-record my conversation with Mickey. I wrote it down, and I would put it—the way I worked I would write stuff down and then I would type it into the computer.

Q: And tell us your understanding of who Mickey Freiberg is.

Anita: Mickey Freiberg was—he's deceased.

Q: And what did he do for a living?

Anita: He was a literary agent.

Q: Did you ever tell Dan Moldea that you had recorded this conversation without Mickey Freiberg's knowledge?

Anita: I don't—no, he asked me—I don't remember. I don't remember, but I wouldn't have done that, and I don't have any tapes of Mickey Freiberg.

Eric George ended her testimony with that line of questioning, essentially suggesting that she had illegally taped this telephone call with her great friend and agent, Mickey Freiberg—a violation of law in California.[318]

It also was an act of hypocrisy on her part in view of all the hell that had been raised since Pellicano had illegally wiretapped her.

Blindsided, Anita's attorney, Ian Herzog, did not cross-examine his client about this matter.

44. *"ED was Ms. Busch's code name for Michael Ovitz"*

Michael Ovitz left the courtroom after Anita's morning testimony and did not return for the remainder of the trial. When I heard about this, I wondered how the judge would react to his decision to leave.

In the end, I never met Ovitz. I never even saw him.

When my attorney, Roger Simmons, summoned me to the courtroom, I felt nothing but confidence. I believed that I knew the facts of this case better than anyone in earshot. And, when I took the witness chair, I was determined to defend my name and reputation against the onslaught of false statements that had been made about me by Anita Busch during her eight-year smear campaign against me.

Throughout my testimony, Anita, who apparently could not face me, refused to sit at the plaintiff's table in front of the witness stand in the open courtroom, choosing instead to hide in a far corner of the courtroom and using a spectator to block her view of me and my view of her. But she could see the judge, and the judge could see her.

It was another interesting tactic inasmuch as Anita, playing her now-familiar role as the hapless victim, was trying to portray me as the heavy, and not only because I was in league with Ovitz. In fact, I had had a reporter-source relationship with Jules Nasso, a man she supposedly "was deathly afraid of," even though she had known for years that Nasso had nothing to do with any of the attacks against her or her car.

After I was sworn in and gave my name, Jonathan Gottfried, Eric George's young associate, immediately asked me about Anita's sworn testimony with regard to her allegedly illegal wiretapped conversation with Mickey Freiberg.

> **Q:** Mr. Moldea, can you just take a moment to familiarize yourself with this document.

> **Moldea:** I'm familiar with this document.
>
> **Q:** How are you familiar with this document?
>
> **Moldea:** This is a secretly tape-recorded conversation that Anita Busch gave me with her close friend Mickey Freiberg who wound up being our agent.
>
> **Mr. Herzog**: Move to strike. Speculation.
>
> **BY Mr. Gottfried:**
>
> **Q:** How do you know it was a secretly recorded conversation?
>
> **Moldea:** Because she told me it was.
>
> **Q:** Approximately when did you receive this document?
>
> **Moldea:** I received it in or about December of 2003.
>
> **Q:** Did you type up these notes?
>
> **Moldea:** No, sir.
>
> **Q:** Are you aware of who typed up these notes?
>
> **Moldea:** Well, it says, "Mickey Freiberg calls. I pick up the phone." So I'm -- it's Ms. Busch.
>
> **Q:** All right. Thank you. And who sent this to you?
>
> **Moldea:** Ms. Busch.[319]

Among the documents Ovitz's attorneys wanted me to authenticate were those in which Anita referred to "Ed," her code name for Ovitz. During her sworn depositions, she repeatedly denied that "Ed" was our reference to him. But during her earlier trial testimony she had suddenly conceded that "Ed" was Ovitz, but only on an occasional case-by-case basis.

> **Q:** And you received these notes from whom?

Moldea: Ms. Busch.

Q: Did you alter the typewritten words on this page in any way?

Moldea: No.

Q: If you please look at the middle of the first page beginning July 27th.

Moldea: Yes, sir.

Q: It states, "I call Ed back. He tells me Ed hired Pellicano three years ago." Do you see that?

Moldea: Yes.

Q: Whom does Ed refer to?

Moldea: Ed is Ms. Busch's code name for Michael Ovitz.

Q: Does Ed stand for something?

Moldea: It stands for evil doer or evil dude.

Q: When did Ms. Busch begin using the term "Ed" with you?

Moldea: I don't recall an exact day. It would certainly have been -- certainly in 2003.

Q: Did you ever understand Ed to refer to anyone besides Mr. Ovitz?

Moldea: No. Ed was always Mr. Ovitz.

Q: To be clear, when Ms. Busch used the term "Ed," did you ever understand Ed to refer to anyone besides Mr. Ovitz?

Moldea: No. Ed was -- Ed was Mr. Ovitz and no one else.

Q: During the two years, approximately two years that you worked with Ms. Busch, did she continue to use the term "Ed"?

Moldea: Yes.

Q: Did Ms. Busch provide any instructions to you regarding your use of the word "Ed"?

Moldea: Shortly after our conversation – our partnership with John Connolly ended -- she sent me an e-mail saying, "Don't use Ed's name any more in e-mails."

Q: Please look at the middle of the second page beginning, "Ed brought Seagal into Warner Brothers." Do you see that?

Moldea: Yes.

Q: And, again, whom did you understand Ed to refer to?

Moldea: Ed was Ms. Busch's code name for Michael Ovitz.

Throughout the pre-trial process and especially during the hearing about the statute of limitations issue, Anita's attorney, Ian Herzog, relentlessly attempted to distract the court's attention from Anita's belief that Ovitz and Pellicano were working together. Consequently, by using a vague timeline, he shrewdly emphasized specific events which demonstrated that Steven Seagal and/or Jules Nasso were the key suspects in the attacks against Anita.

In reality, all of that was made moot after June 12, 2003, when Anita received the news from FBI Special Agent Tom Ballard that Detective Mark Arneson had run the background check on her on May 16, 2002—two weeks before Seagal and Nasso even came to her attention but just nine days after she finished her series in the *New York Times* about Ovitz.

Providing this information to the Ovitz legal team was probably my most important contribution, because I gave them a solid date and a considerable amount of evidence to support the fact that Anita's views about the case radically changed on that day—"the demarcation date" of this case.

Even FBI man Stan Ornellas had become convinced that Ovitz was involved because of this evidence.

With regard to finding just who had hired Pellicano to investigate Anita, everything that happened prior to that date was essentially irrelevant. Neither Seagal nor Nasso were involved in any attack against Anita, although Anita had continued to harbor thoughts that Nasso might somehow have been Ovitz's co-conspirator.

Jonathan Gottfried questioned me about this:

> **Q:** And specifically, if you can recall, what did Ms. Busch tell you during that conversation of June 12, 2003, about Mr. Ovitz?

> **Moldea:** She was stunned and shocked and because, as I say, this is a demarcation date because before June 12, 2003, this case was looking like the scenario was something completely different, like it was a mob thing. But then after June 12th it sort of became a Hollywood thing.

> **Q:** So, again, focusing on this June 12, 2003, conversation was there anything else that Ms. Busch told you specifically about Mr. Ovitz?

> **Moldea:** That she was stunned that he would be involved in something like that. But it could only be Michael Ovitz. I mean the May 16th -- the May 16th running of the computer program by Mr. Arneson -- this was over two weeks before she joined the *L.A. Times* and before Jules Nasso and Steven Seagal even came on to [her] radar screen, but it was only nine days after her series with Mr. Weinraub on -- with Mr. Weinraub completed on Mr. Ovitz.

> **Q:** Where did you get that information from regarding the timing?

> **Moldea:** The May 16th?

> **Q:** Yes, the fact that the May 16 fell between certain articles that she wrote?

> **Moldea:** Well, it was -- it was -- it was -- it was known -- it was from Ms. Busch. Ms. Busch gave me that information.

Continuing with that theme, Gottfried continued:

> **Q:** During your collaboration with Ms. Busch did she ever tell you that she understood someone other than Mr. Ovitz was responsible for the incidents against her?

Moldea: She believed that Jules Nasso was possibly involved. She believed that it was still possible that Steven Seagal was involved. There were other characters who we discussed at length of their possible involvement, but Mr. Ovitz was always at the epicenter of the scenario. Whatever scenario was under discussion.

Q: And you had previously referred to June 12 as the demarcation day?

Moldea: That was the demarcation day, yes, sir.

Q: What did you mean by that?

Moldea: I meant all bets were off after June 12th, 2003. Prior to June 12, 2003, it looked like Steven Seagal, Jules Nasso, and some Mafia guys back East were possibly behind this threat to Ms. Busch. After June 12, 2003, it became Ovitz, and Ovitz was at the center of every scenario.

Q: And also to be clear when you say "it looked like," what are you basing this information on?

Moldea: On the running of the May 16th NCIC file I guess at the L.A.P.D. by Mark Arneson which was two weeks before Ms. Busch joined the *L.A. Times*, two weeks before Jules Nasso and Steven Seagal were on her radar screen, nine days after she completed her seven-part series with Mr. Weinraub for the *New York Times* on Mr. Ovitz. As soon as she said May 16, my reaction was Ovitz.

Also, I was asked how my partnership with Anita collapsed. I identified her email to me of May 25, 2005, in which she unilaterally stopped our book project because it would be giving too much "free information" to the defense in her civil case. I also identified her June 12, 2005, email in which she refused to speak with me any more—because I had the audacity to complain about her decision after I had worked for two long years on this project for free.

She told me: *"Anything more you have to say, you can speak to Dave and he can relay. I really have nothing more to say to you."*

Fulfilling that obligation when I was given the opportunity to work with Jules Nasso, I was questioned about my July 24, 2005, email to Dave Robb, informing him about my opportunity to work with Nasso.

> **Q:** Did you recognize this document?
>
> **Moldea:** Yes, I do.
>
> **Q:** How do you recognize it?
>
> **Moldea:** This is the e-mail I sent to Dave Robb on July 24th, 2005. [O]n background, Anita Busch, after she said that this book was interfering with her -- with her lawsuit and that we were giving too much free information to the defense in her case. I argued for a month. She -- on June 12th, 2005, she said, you're getting -- essentially she said, you're getting ready to do a legal attack on me. I have nothing further to say to you. If you have anything to say to me, go through Dave Robb. I had the opportunity to meet Jules Nasso. An author friend of mine came to me and said, "You'd be interested in this." And I said, "What an opportunity to go talk to this guy and find out what he knew." So before I said word one to Jules Nasso, I went, as Ms. Busch had instructed, to Dave Robb and I sent -- I read this to him over the phone on July 23rd, 2005. I then sent him the e-mail on July 24th, 2005, and this was -- I was doing exactly what Ms. Busch told me. I had -- this is exactly as I had written it. This -- I was doing exactly what Anita told me to do. "Go through Dave to get to me."
>
> **Q:** If I can direct your attention to the second page, the second to the last full paragraph. Did you write, "I leave it to you whether to tell Anita"?
>
> **Moldea:** Yes.

On cross-examination, Ian Herzog latched onto this theme in his questioning, dealing with an email Dave had sent to me—in which he claimed that I had never left it to him to tell Anita.

> **Q:** This is an e-mail from Dave Robb to you; right?
>
> **Moldea:** Sadly, yes. This is an e-mail from Dave Robb to me, yes.

Q: Where he's upset with you because you put him in an awkward position with regard to Anita Busch and Nasso; right?

Moldea: Yes, with an explanation.

Q: Okay. And Dave Robb had told you that – had said that you had asked him to be quiet about Nasso, about your dealings with Nasso, keep it a secret from Anita Busch; yes?

Moldea: That's a lie.

Q: But he said that, didn't he?

Moldea: Yes, he said that, and it's a lie.

Q: Okay. And you saw -- I'd like to have marked for identification 146, please -- 147.

(Marked for identification Exhibit No. 147.)

BY Mr. Herzog:

Q: Do you recognize 147, please.

Moldea: Yes, sir. This is Dave Robb's sworn statement as part of the motion for summary judgment package, yes.

Q: And it has -- an Exhibit A attached to it; right? Where he --

Moldea: Yes, it has an exhibit which completely contradicts what he says in his statement, yes. Yes.

Q: I'm not -- I'm trying real hard not to --

Moldea: I'm sorry. I'm trying real hard too, sir.

Q: And so you take issue with what he said under oath in this case?

Moldea: Completely.

Q: And everything he says, you say here or everything he says here you say is false?

Mr. Gottfried: Objection, Your Honor.

THE COURT: Objection sustained. The way the question is framed.

BY Mr. Herzog:

Q: Everything he said here is false.

THE COURT: Please rephrase it.

BY Mr. Herzog:

Q: Everything he said here is false.

Moldea: Everything -- I don't know what everything is. As you pointed out earlier I had done a response to John Connolly on my web page. I also had a response to Dave Robb. I stand by what I said in my response to Dave Robb.

Q: So if I understand it from your web page, you say Anita's not telling the truth, John Connolly's not telling the truth, and Mr. Robb is not telling the truth.

Moldea: Yes, sir.

Q: Okay.

Moldea: May I respond to that?

THE COURT: No. If other counsel want to ask you more questions, they can do so. Next question.

Predictably, Herzog also pressed me on the issue of my association with Jules Nasso and Anita's supposed view of him.

Q: Okay. And you understood that she was – I think we established this before, and I want to change the subject slightly, you understood that Anita Busch was deathly afraid -- or she says she was deathly afraid of Nasso; that's what she said?

Moldea: I think that's an exaggeration, sir. John Connolly was dealing with --

Q: Yes or no, sir. I'm trying to refrain from arguing with you.

Moldea: I am too.

Q: Thank you, sir.

Moldea: Yes, with an explanation.

THE COURT: You can explain your answer.

Moldea: Pardon me?

THE COURT: You can explain your answer.

Moldea: Thank you. John Connolly was dealing with Jules Nasso, and she communicated that to me in an e-mail I think it was October 30th, 2003. She said she had known about it over a year. It was matter of fact. There was no "I'm deathly afraid of Jules Nasso." It only became deathly afraid of Jules Nasso when the situation came with Dave Robb and I, which there's a long explanation, a prelude to. To say that she was deathly afraid of Nasso in 2006 is an exaggeration, sir. Jules Nasso had nothing to do with the attack on her.

BY Mr. Herzog:

Q: Well, can you point to any writing or any e-mail where Anita ever said Nasso had nothing to do with the attack on her?

Moldea: Not in -- my last communication with her was on February 9, 2006. That was the last communication of any kind I had with her and it was an e-mail. No. She never admitted it at that point, but for some reason -- I'm trying to think -- she has admitted it in her sworn deposition. She admitted it in her sworn deposition that Jules Nasso was not involved in the attack on her. Please check.

Q: I will.

Moldea: So will I.

In fact, I was right that Anita had said that she recognized that Nasso had no role in the attack against her, but I was wrong about where she said it.

She had told this to me in a January 19, 2006, email in which she wrote:

> While I BELIEVE that Jules Nasso did not have anything to do with the threat on my life, I also have evidence that he has not told the truth on important matters, matters of which you are unaware. (Emphasis Anita's)

Still on cross examination, in a further effort to discredit my version of events and motives, Ian Herzog questioned me about my relationship with Pellicano.

> **Q:** You also tried to – in addition to trying to do a book deal with Nasso where you were going -- you were trying to do a book deal with Nasso where you were going to exculpate him; yes?
>
> **Moldea:** I'm sorry. Trying to clear him?
>
> **Q:** Yes.
>
> **Moldea:** Yes, sir.
>
> **Q:** And you were going to try to -- also at the same time you were communicating with Mr. Pellicano, were you not?
>
> **Moldea:** I was trying to get an interview with Pellicano, yeah.
>
> **Q:** And you were trying to get him interested in doing a book deal with you too, weren't you?
>
> **Moldea:** No. He came to me and offered me the exclusive rights to his book. Through his investigator.
>
> **Q:** Who's the investigator?
>
> **Moldea:** Lynda Larsen.
>
> **Q:** And did Lynda Larsen have a copy of Anita's book?

Moldea: Of course not, no. Never. . . .

Q: On page 2 you put in here in the middle to Mr. Pellicano the person who you believed was responsible for trying to roust Pellicano -- roust Anita amongst others that telling Mr. Pellicano you're obviously a stand-up guy.

Moldea: This is the paragraph where I say I would never do anything to jeopardize her safety or compromise her personal secrets. Yes, I see that.

Q: It says, "You are obviously a stand-up guy."

Moldea: That's the paragraph after that, yes, sir.

Q: And you say down there, "Either way if we do work something out now or down the road, I shall protect you and your information"; yes?

Moldea: He was a source.

Q: And you wanted his -- you wanted to do a book with him to make him -- no?

Moldea: Not at this point. This is not when that happened.

Q: But you did want to do a book with him?

Moldea: No. That wasn't even on the radar screen at that point.

Q: Eventually you wanted to do a book with him? Yes?

Moldea: I was offered. I did not approach. I was offered. And I said no. You know I -- he wasn't telling the truth.

Q: You said, "Either way, if we do work something out down the road I shall protect you." All right. "Work something out." That had to do with a book; yes?

Moldea: I was writing my own book, sir, and I wanted him as a source for that. I was writing my own book.

Q: You were going to write your own book on what a stand-up guy he was; right?

Moldea: You know, in a weird way he was a stand-up guy, yes. But at the same time I was protecting Ms. Busch's interests. I never betrayed her.

—•—

After the conclusion of my testimony, Ovitz's attorneys took Roger Simmons and me to lunch at the famous Pacific Dining Car Restaurant on West Sixth Street in downtown Los Angeles. Shortly thereafter, Roger and I left Los Angeles and returned to Washington. As an indication of how pleased Ovitz's attorneys were with my testimony, they changed our tickets from coach to first class.

45. *"Turns out, fortuitously, [Dan] was right?"*

On October 2, 2013, Anita's attorneys opened their portion of the procedural trial by calling Lou Tedesco, a long-time friend and confidante of Anita's, as their first witness. FBI Special Agent Stan Ornellas was originally expected to testify for Anita, but, for reasons unknown, he was dropped from the witness list.[320]

I had briefly met Lou during one of my work visits to Anita. He was a pleasant man who appeared to be devoted to her. While staying with Anita from February 2003 to November 2004 on a roommate basis, he slept on a bed in her office.

Other than testifying that Anita once had a bodyguard and a remote car starter, he really did not appear to know anything relevant to the issues revolving around the statute of limitations in this case.

—•—

Although I was not present for Dave Robb's testimony, my subsequent reading of his statements under oath was absolutely gut-wrenching.[321] For instance, Dave completely denied that he had ever seen Anita's June 12, 2005, email to me which insisted that if I had anything to say to her that I now had to go through him.

According to Dave, the Ovitz scenario was my concoction— mine and mine alone, which was completely untrue. He also lied about the construction of our book, claiming that Anita, tired of arguing, simply yielded all decisions to me. In fact, he was the one who instructed me to become Anita's "stenographer," adding "just shut the fuck up and do what she wants!"

In one exchange with Anita's attorney:

> **Q:** Did Dan Moldea explain to you why he wanted it to be Mike Ovitz?
>
> **Robb:** Yes.
>
> **Q:** What was that?
>
> **Robb:** That Mike Ovitz would sell the book and all these other people wouldn't sell the book. He needed a big villain and Mike Ovitz -- there was a time when every poll that was taken among journalists in Hollywood, every magazine would come out with Hollywood's ten most powerful men or women. Mike Ovitz was No. 1 on every list for years -- for ten years in a row he was the most powerful man in Hollywood. He was the big game. Dan was a big game hunter. He went after Jimmy Hoffa. He went after the Kennedy assassination. He -- he liked the big stuff, and Mike Ovitz was the big stuff. Nobody ever heard of Jules Nasso.[322] Steven Seagal was a has-been. . . .
>
> **Q:** What influence, if any, did that have as to Anita's objections, if any, with regard to Dan Moldea focusing on Michael Ovitz?
>
> **Robb:** Well, she -- Dan is a very larger-than-life person. He is very dynamic and a bit of a bully, and she let him, basically after fighting with him and she -- for years believed it was Seagal and then Jules Nasso and through them the Gambinos, organized crime families, Bonannos was the other crime family back East. She just finally got tired of fighting with him and let him write the book as he wanted because it was all going to be -- it was all going to be moot once the indictments came out.

They would be revealed who was behind this threat, and then they would refocus the book after they knew who it was. . . .

Q: [D]id you discuss with Moldea the findings and whether or not that altered his view about how the book should be -- his view of his theory of the book?

Robb: Yes. He told me words to the effect that you'll see, it's Ovitz. Ovitz was behind this from the May 16 thing. He was -- it was like a dog with a bone and that's how he approached everything, whether he was right or wrong. And in this case it turned out he happened to be right, but it sure didn't look like it. And we didn't know. Anita didn't know. I didn't know. Anita and I both thought the evidence was pointing elsewhere.

Q: You're saying in retrospect?

Robb: Yes.

Q: What we know now --

Robb: Yeah. Yeah.

Q: Turns out fortuitously he was right?

Robb: Yeah.

With regard to my alleged betrayal of Anita by working with Jules Nasso, Dave corroborated Anita's version of events— by refusing to admit that I had told him about my prospective arrangement with Nasso even before my first conversation with him and that I put it in writing in my July 24, 2005, email to him.

Q: For how long a period of time had Dan Moldea -- for how long a period of time did you find out Dan Moldea had been meeting with Jules Nasso?

Robb: Oh, for some months before I found out about it. Some months.

Q: By some months --

Robb: Six or seven months.

On cross-examination by Eric George, Dave was questioned about his determination to paint me as a conspiracy theorist, which then backfired on him after he was confronted with a quote from his own 2004 book about Hollywood and the Pentagon[323].

> **Q:** Is there any book or publication by Dan Moldea that you believe promotes a conspiracy theory that's not founded by fact?

> **Robb:** I think there are elements of *Interference* that -- I mean of Reagan – *Ronald Reagan, MCA and the Mob* that stretched my credibility.[324]

> **Q:** And that book was published before 2004; correct?

> **Robb:** Yes.

> **Q:** And yet in 2004 you called Dan Moldea in writing, quote, "the best investigative journalist in America"; correct?

> **Robb:** Yes.

> **Q:** Because you believed that?

> **Robb:** I did. He was a hero of mine. I admired him greatly.

> **Q:** And you understand you were a hero of his too?

> **Robb:** Yes.

> **Q:** And when this Nasso thing came about, all ties and friendship were broken between you and he; right?

> **Robb:** Yes.

In a complete and total misrepresentation of how he learned about my possible deal with Nasso—before I ever even spoke with Jules—Dave's account not only conflicted with the time-stamped email I had sent him, but it also ran afoul of his own sworn declaration about the timing of this discovery. Dave testified under oath in open court:

The book was on hold and then I called Dan one day and said, "Dan, how are you doing? What are you up to?" And he said, "I'm fine, but I can't tell you what I'm up to." I said, "Oh, that's weird. Okay."

So I called him back a few days later and said—just to chat—"Hey, Dan, how are you doing? What are you up to?" He said, "Well, I'll tell you what, I can't tell anybody." I said, "All right." I figured he got some new book project, some—you know, some investigation he's working on. He did some investigating.

So he told me that he's been dealing with Jules Nasso on a book project between the two of them. And I said, "What? You and Jules Nasso are talking about doing a book? This is the guy that Anita and I both think was behind the threat on her life. And ruined her life. You've now gone over to the other side? What is this?"

And I said—I was just dumbfounded. It was like such a betrayal. I just couldn't believe it. And that's—there were a few conversations after that, and then I wrote him an e-mail saying, "I just can't believe who you are and what you've become."

Dave continued: "I had been friends with Dan for—since 1984 and now—I mean best friends with Dan. And now because of this, because of what I considered this terrible betrayal, our friendship was over because of this."

Frankly, I became very upset when I read this transcript. I could not believe that a man whom I considered to be "like a brother" to me could just flat out lie the way he did—under oath in a court of law.

What was my betrayal? How did I betray Dave—or even Anita for that matter?

Of course, Dave continued to make false statements about whether or not he received my time-stamped July 24, 2005, email in which I told him that I had the opportunity to make a deal with Jules Nasso *before* I ever spoke with Nasso.

> **Q:** This was an e-mail from Dan Moldea to you, sir, sent on or about July 24, 2005; correct?

> **Robb:** Appears to be.

Q: And its subject line is "the Nasso opportunity." Right?

Robb: That's what it says.

Q: Did you read this or is this the one where in another exhibit you said, "When you sent me an e-mail memorializing your betrayal, I did not read it." Did you read this?

Robb: I'm not sure.

Q: Well, let me focus you on the second to the last paragraph. It's on page 2. Mr. Moldea writes to you, "I gave you this information in confidence. I leave it to you whether to tell Anita who as usual will place some nefarious spin on what's happening." Did you read that on or about July 24, 2005?

Robb: I don't recall. If it's true -- I mean if he wrote this, then what he wrote is a lie. Because he didn't leave it to me to tell her.

Q: Sir, you received this e-mail on July 24, 2005; correct?

Robb: I don't know if that's correct.

Q: And if you did receive it, then you received the information that says, "I leave it to you whether to tell Anita"; correct?

Robb: If I did receive it and those—that was written in it, I don't know if I read it. As you know I stopped reading his e-mails. I don't know the dates.

Q: Okay.

Robb: But if you're saying that's what he's saying, I'm saying it's not true what he's saying. He didn't leave it to me to tell Anita. He told me not to tell anyone.

Also, amazingly enough while being questioned by Anita's own attorney, Dave corroborated one of the major points in my sworn testimony that Anita had actively denied in her previous statements under oath.

Q: And how would Anita from time to time denominate Mr. Ovitz in some of her editorial corrections? Some of her edits?

Robb: I think she used the term ED.

Q: Okay. Now, was it discussed as to why he would use Mr. X for Ovitz or she would use ED for Mr. Ovitz versus his name?

Robb: Yes.

Q: What?

Robb: Well, they didn't know it was really him so they had to be careful if somehow their notes fell into the wrong hands that they would be accusing somebody who -- they were just being very circumspect about who they were going to be accusing.

Near the end of his testimony, Dave had the following exchange with Ian Herzog about the number of emails he exchanged about "this matter":

Q: On e-mails, how many e-mails do you think you exchanged over time with regard to this matter?

Robb: Maybe 30 or 40.

Q: Have you researched any of them?

Robb: I don't have any of them left. My computer ate them or something. After so many years it doesn't save the sent or the -- or the received. They just fall off.

By his own admission, Dave lost every email he had in his computer that was relevant to the Pellicano caper. At the same time, I had kept and backed up nearly everything—every email, every book proposal, every draft manuscript. Asking the court to believe him over me, Dave could not produce anything other than a supposed "draft" of an email that I had never received.

46. *"Jules Nasso, who I was deathly afraid of"*

After Dave Robb's appearance, Anita returned to the witness stand, questioned on direct by her own attorney, Ian Herzog.

Early into her testimony—in an effort to nullify the monumental significance of the May 16, 2002, date and its proximity to the completion of her series of articles about Michael Ovitz for the *New York Times*—Anita performed an about face with a completely new strategy in her attempt to manipulate the timeline established by the documents I had given to Ovitz's attorneys.

She now claimed that she had been "collecting string" on Seagal and Nasso—*before* she joined the *Los Angeles Times* on June 3, 2002, and *before* Jules Nasso's indictment the following day.

Specifically, she claimed that her key source was a man named Phil Goldfine who—suddenly, in the midst of this trial—had become the key figure in Anita's attempt to mitigate the timing issue of what she knew and when she knew about Ovitz.

> **Q:** Okay. And with regard to that one, did you communicate with anybody that was associated with Seagal, Nasso, organized crime to—that would give them information that you were making inquiry along these lines?
>
> **Anita:** Yes.
>
> **Q:** And who was that?
>
> **Anita:** Phil Goldfine who was the president of production at Steven Seagal's Steamroller Productions.
>
> **Q:** And what kind of questions were you asking him?
>
> **Anita:** What he knew about the lawsuit [*Nasso v. Seagal*], what the dispute was about, maybe some people I could talk to on it.

According to Anita's new version of events, Goldfine became an issue in the notes Anita had given me with regard to her July 2003 conversations with FBI Special Agent Stan Ornellas.

Questioned about this matter by her own attorney, Anita claimed under oath that the information Goldfine, whom she had identified in court as her "confidential source," had provided her with "the ground work that I laid to be able to get the story" about Seagal and Nasso.

> **Q:** And what was the information that you wanted to tell the FBI about Goldfine?
>
> **Anita:** That I had been talking to Phil Goldfine and Steven Seagal's company for months.
>
> **Q:** About?
>
> **Anita:** Two issues. Two issues. One was a business plan that he was helping me crunch numbers on. He was very good with financials and the other one was that he was guiding me to—we had been talking about the lawsuit, and he had been guiding me to other people to talk to on the Seagal-Nasso.
>
> **Q:** Sources for your articles?
>
> **Anita:** Yes.
>
> **Q:** Okay. *And did you use some of the information that Mr. Goldfine gave to you before May 16 in order to go to sources that ultimately wound up in these articles that you wrote in June of 2002?*
>
> **Anita:** *It's the ground work that I laid to be able to get the story.*
>
> **Q:** *Okay. Then with regard to here -- and this -- so we'll be oriented. This is something that is in the notes that you gave to Mr. Moldea; right?*
>
> **Anita:** *Yes.* (Emphasis added)

Also during this line of questioning, Anita created a little drama about her decision to "confess" her association with Goldfine, as if it actually had some real importance. Her attorney read from her notes of June 12, 2003, stating:

> On the way home, I call Tom Ballard and confess about my relationship with a person close to Seagal—Seagal, namely Phil. I tell him"—okay. . .

By stopping his recitation of her notes at that point, Herzog did not read what she said next, which had everything to do with Ovitz and nothing to do with Seagal:

> . . . . I also tell him that I agreed to join the L.A. Times on May 20. The series of articles I did with the NY Times ended in May.

Because I was busy in Washington for the remainder of the trial after my testimony, I did not really understand the significance of her sworn testimony. But after the completion of the case, I went through Anita's notes to me concerning Phil Goldfine.

In fact, she wrote in her personal notes: "I did not use Phil as a source because of where he worked," specifically at Seagal's production company.

According to Anita's notes to me in 2003 about her communication with Goldfine, three days after the vandalism of her car:

> I had a meeting on Sunday [June 23, 2002] in the morning at a friend's house about my business plan. I couldn't cancel it under any condition. Another person was supposed to meet us, Phil. He is the president of Seagal's company. When I made the other calls to sources, I called a mutual friend and asked him to tell Phil not to come. I told him that something happened and he cannot come. I told him not to call me and we couldn't talk for a long while. **I did not use Phil as a source because of where he worked. (I think he answered like two questions and then I told him that I didn't want to abuse our friendship by using him as a source. He appreciated it.)** He hates Seagal and has been looking for a job for the past two years. He is one of my best friends out here. I've known him for about 10 years. He is one of the most honest people I've ever known and very discreet. He had been helping me on my financials for my business plan and continues to help me put stuff together.[325] (Emphasis added)

Anita referred to Goldfine again in an entry for June 12, 2003, the demarcation date when FBI Special Agent Ballard told her that LAPD Detective Arneson had run her background check on May 16, 2002. According to Anita's notes:

> I then drive to Phil's office, Steven Seagal's Steamroller Prods. I tell them my fake code name and get inside the gate. I walk into his

office. Some assistant comes out. I tell him my fake name. He goes back to get Phil. While I wait, I am surrounded by movie posters of Steven Seagal. I just laugh to myself, thinking no one on earth would even believe how bizarre this all is.

Phil comes out and I hand him my bio. He is trying to get money together for the business plan for me and thinks he finally has an investor.

We walk [out of the building] and the first thing he says is "am I in any physical danger? [sic] "no, you're fine, but I need to tell the FBI that I know you and that we were working on the business plan in May." "Why? [sic] He asks. I tell him that something has come up and I just have to tell them. We walk into a restaurant [on the lot] and sit down. I said you might get a call from the FBI guys. He said that's fine. He said nothing has anything to do with me. I tell him I know that. **I tell him that I have to tell the FBI the truth and tell them that we are friends. I told him I feel comfortable telling him his name because he was not a source of mine on the Seagal stories. He says, "I know I wasn't." . . . I said, Phil, you had nothing to do with anything. Nothing. And everything I was looking at happened many years ago. You were not involved.** You have nothing to worry about. He agrees and feels fine. (Emphasis added)

Shortly after her conversation with Goldfine on June 12, 2003, she called Special Agent Tom Ballard. According to her notes, she told the FBI agent:

I was working on a business plan with Phil Goldfine who is the president of Steven Seagal's company. I said he is a close friend. **I tell Tom that he was not a source on the stories, but he was helping me on putting together the financials on my business plan.** I said that he does that for a lot of companies. So that's what was going on at the time. (Emphasis added)

In other words, in her sworn trial testimony, Anita claimed that she had been talking to Goldfine who she suddenly insisted was her main source about Seagal and Nasso. She added that he had been providing information about them to her long before May 16, 2002, and long before Seagal and Nasso became public property after Nasso's indictment on June 4, 2002. According to Anita, the information provided her with the "ground work" she needed to do her reporting on Seagal and Nasso.

And she claimed that she supposedly told me this in the 170-plus pages of notes she sent to me.

Yet, according to her actual notes, she specifically wrote that she *never* used Goldfine as a source—before or after Nasso's indictment.

Consequently, Anita either misled the court under oath with her cock-and-bull story about Phil Goldfine being her key source on Seagal and Nasso, or she made a false statement to FBI Special Agent Tom Ballard on June 12, 2003, saying that Goldfine was never a source.

Because I did not give Ovitz's attorneys the portion of Anita's personal notes in which she discussed Phil Goldfine—he had never been mentioned in this context before—the lawyers never picked up on any of this and, thus, never challenged the contradictions in her statements.

While discussing my purported obsession with making Ovitz the villain of our book, Anita reverted to her "babe in the woods" routine and had the following exchange with her attorney:

> **Q:** Okay. Now, at times did you succumb to Moldea's notion that it was Ovitz?
>
> **Anita:** Sometimes.
>
> **Q:** And then what would happen?
>
> **Anita:** Then I'd find out that Jules was close, close, close, close friends with Pellicano[326] and ...
>
> **Q:** Would you vacillate back and forth?
>
> **Anita:** Yes.
>
> **Q:** Why?
>
> **Anita:** Because I was scared.
>
> **Q:** Scared of what?
>
> **Anita:** Getting killed by the mob.

Q: So did you feel it was safer to say it was Ovitz than to say it was the mob? Pardon?

Anita: I didn't know what to do. I was being led around by my nose. I was so scared. Honestly I didn't know what was going on. I didn't want to get killed. I was just trying not to get killed.

Q: So if you felt that if it was Ovitz you were safer than if it turned out to be Nasso?

Mr. George: Objection. I'd ask that counsel not lead the witness.

THE COURT: Objection sustained. Please rephrase your question.

BY Mr. Herzog:

Q: Why did you vacillate as between Ovitz and Nasso?

Anita: There was so much information pointing to the mob and to Nasso. There was just so much.

Q: And did Mr. Moldea ask you to -- when you were writing the book and editing it -- to come up with any speculation you could with regard to Ovitz?

Anita: It was all speculation. We didn't know. We didn't know until the government told us what was going on. Until they filed. And they filed -- when they filed that thing, it says guys back East again. Then I was, like, God Almighty.

Q: But with regard to writing the book, what was your understanding as to what your role was in helping Moldea developing the theme that it was Ovitz?

Anita: I -- I did what he asked me to do. I did what Dave asked me to do.

Even though Anita and I, along with John Connolly, were always on the same page that Ovitz was at the hub of this situation, the venom spewed at me for supposedly being the only one to promote this conspiracy theory was preposterous. No matter how anyone cut it, this case was *Busch v. Ovitz*, not Busch v. Nasso or Busch v. Seagal—both of whom have essentially been cleared of any role in any attack on her and her car.

When the subject came around to the dissolution of our book project, Anita refused to admit that she even wrote the key May 25, 2005, email to me in which she declared that she was stopping our book project because it would be giving to much "free information" to the defense. Instead, she suggested that I had altered this document to make it appear as though she had.

> **Q:** Ms. Busch, this is a true and correct copy of an e-mail you sent to Dan Moldea May 25, 2005; correct?
>
> **Anita:** I don't know that it is actually. Look at the bottom. It's different from every other e-mail.
>
> **Q:** Well, let me ask you a simple question. Did you write this?
>
> **Anita:** I don't remember writing this. And I'm not sure that it's—I don't know what this is. The bottom is totally different and has a two on the bottom.
>
> **Q:** With the exception of the No. 2 and just focusing on the content of the e-mail, did you write and send this e-mail to Dan Moldea?
>
> **Anita:** I don't remember writing this actually.
>
> **Q:** It does state, does it not, "The attorney's main concern as I told you before is why give out free information that can have holes poked into it. Those things I told you were some of the top concerns of what would need to change and why it would be hurtful to me and my case."
>
> **Anita:** Why is the—why is the—hold on a second. Why is this in a totally different type face than everything else?
>
> **Q:** Ms. Busch, if you'll just please give me the courtesy of finishing this.
>
> **Anita:** Some things don't look right. . . .

Q: I don't want to put words in your mouth, but to the best of your recollection, is it possible you wrote this? Possible you didn't? You just don't remember or are you denying you wrote this?

Anita: I think it's questionable because the type face is different. The bottom is different. I'm just telling you. . . .

Q: Apart from being questionable just looking at the content.

Anita: The content was—the book was going to go out and would be out in discovery anyway, so . . .

Q: I just want to focus you on my question. Looking at the content, is your testimony it's possible you wrote it, possible you didn't?

Anita: I don't remember writing this at all. That's my answer.

When she was asked her why our partnership did break up, Anita continued to mislead.

Q: In that regard, the next question then would be is -- with regard to your relationship with Moldea, Dan Moldea, what caused it to break up.

Anita: I found out that he had tried to get into business with Jules Nasso, who I was deathly afraid of.

Anita was shown an email she had sent me on January 19, 2006, in which she wrote:

While I BELIEVE that Jules Nasso did not have anything to do with the threat on my life, I also have evidence that he has not told the truth on important matters, matters of which you are unaware. (Emphasis Anita's)

Responding to this smoking gun—her own message where she revealed that she did not believe that Nasso was involved—Anita replied under oath that it was simply a typo, saying: "I meant to say 'while *you* believe. . . . It was just a mistake.'"

She claimed that she sent me a follow-up email to correct this, which she did not produce.

Once again, Ovitz's attorneys chose not to press her on this important inconsistency which would have annihilated a basic pillar of her case: that she "was deathly afraid of" Nasso.

———

Remarkably, under questioning from her own attorney and after her repeated earlier denials, Anita again admitted that she had used the code name, "Ed," to identify Ovitz:

> **Q:** And with regard to the mechanics of writing the book, I see in the book that there are references to X or --
>
> **Anita:** Evil doers.
>
> **Q:** ED being references to Ovitz.
>
> **Anita:** Uh-huh.
>
> **Q:** Yes?
>
> **Anita:** Yes.
>
> **Q:** Okay. Why use that code X or ED for Michael Ovitz in the book?
>
> **Anita:** Well, we didn't know who it was. We didn't want to falsely accuse anybody. If that got out anywhere. I mean it's just -- you don't do that to people.[327]

———

The trial ended on October 22, 2013. The wait for the judge's decision began. In one of his final statements from the bench, Judge Berle summed up this procedural case about the statute of limitations, stating: "The question is what Ms. Busch knew and when she knew it."

In the aftermath of closing arguments, I made the following addition to my website:

> After the judge renders his decision, I am willing to submit my sworn testimony to the Los Angeles District Attorney's Office and pledge my full cooperation—as well as full disclosure—to any subsequent investigation as to who testified honestly under oath and who did not during the trial.
>
> I challenge Anita Busch and Dave Robb—who have repeatedly made provably false statements about me, even under oath—to make that same offer.

47. *"Anita is a force of nature"*

In mid-November 2013, *Deadline Hollywood* announced that it had hired the former executive editor of the *Hollywood Reporter*, Anita Busch, as its new film editor. She was expected to begin reporting on box-office statistics and newly released films for the popular entertainment site, which had been founded and operated by the recently and unceremoniously ousted Nikki Finke, a long-time rival of Anita.[328]

The announcement was made by *Deadline Hollywood* co-editors Nellie Andreeva and Mike Fleming. Their story stated:

> "We thought Anita had put the entertainment business in her rearview mirror, but we jumped at the chance when we discovered that she wanted to return to journalism," said Andreeva and Fleming. " . . . To say she is one of the most aggressive, resourceful and thoughtful journalists we've seen in our time covering Hollywood is underselling her. Anita is a force of nature." . . .
>
> Said Busch, "I look forward to working with the staff at *Deadline*, especially Mike and Nellie who are great people and top-notch reporters . . . I've always known that journalism is what I was born to do, and can't wait to return to the work that I love."[329]

Soon after, Dave Robb began reporting for *Deadline Hollywood*, too.[330]

After the *Busch v. Ovitz* attorneys' exchanges of and responses
to each other's post-trial briefs and their subsequent oral arguments
on January 9, 2014, Judge Berle began his final deliberations.
Notably—even after the handwriting expert's unchallenged
testimony during the trial, which vindicated me in the aftermath of
false charges that I had forged documents—Anita's attorneys' written
submissions to the court continued to accuse me of manufacturing
facts and fabricating evidence.

Meantime, while waiting for the judge's ruling, I came across a
website for attorneys to evaluate the judges before whom they appear.[331]

In one review, a Los Angeles attorney wrote:

> Judge Berle is an old school judge. And when I say that it means that
> a person that cares about your sincerity. Never lie to a judge. But never
> lie to this one. He cares about doing the right thing. But will absolutely
> not care about you if you [misstate] the evidence or any facts. . . .
> And that's the way it should be. I just do not like judges that
> have a predisposition. All I want is an even handed judge.

In a second review, another civil attorney said:

> I get a good vibe from this judge - I think he deep down really
> cares about justice and wants to right the wrongs of the past, even
> when those involve the dishonesty or mistake of other judges in his
> jurisdiction - he wants the person who was wronged by a bad or false
> [judgment], to be made right and restore their property and dignity.
> This is a judge who is not afraid to really be about truth and justice.

Judge Berle's integrity aside, throughout her appearances
on the witness stand, Anita Busch had given Oscar-winning
performances—Scarlett O'Hara meets *Goodfellas*—while managing
to out-minutia Ovitz's attorneys. Although they knew the law very
well, they were no match for Anita's flexible version of the facts and
her remarkable ability to muddy the precise timing of key events.

The main question was whether Judge Berle could see through
Anita's act.

My prediction? Anita, a legitimate victim, had gone to Judge
Berle, asking for justice. After he agreed to hear her case, she repaid
him by repeatedly making false statements under oath. I couldn't
believe that the judge would reward her bad behavior.

I was wrong.

On April 3, Judge Berle rendered his decision, going right down the line with Anita and her attorneys and accepting their provably false facts and skewed timeline. Inexplicably, the judge further rewarded Anita by describing her as "a highly credible witness."

Supporting his opinion, Judge Berle wrote: "Plaintiff's handwritten manuscript edits for a potential book depicting June 2003 events . . . include the statement: 'It could only have been Michael Ovitz. He would have been the only one interested in me at the time."

But the judge was mistaken. Anita never testified to this. In fact, she specifically said that she did not remember making these handwritten edits, "because that's not what I thought at the time."

Judge Berle then proceeded to dismiss all of the other real evidence about Anita's firm belief that Ovitz was working with Pellicano between her game-changing conversation with FBI Special Agent Tom Ballard on June 12, 2003, and the filing of her lawsuit on May 28, 2004. In particular, he ignored Anita's own written recitation of her contacts with FBI Special Agent Stan Ornellas about Ovitz that had helped form her unshakeable belief that Ovitz had been working with Pellicano.

Then, along with dismissing all of that evidence and testimony, Judge Berle completely bought into Anita's conflicting story about Phil Goldfine, saying:

> 13. Plaintiff was trying to put together a "string" on a story that had to do with Nasso, Seagal, organized crime and Hollywood, after the filing of the lawsuit between Nasso and Seagal in early 2002.
> 14. Plaintiff was communicating with Phil Goldfine, president of Seagal's production company, for months before May 16, 2002, "and very specifically about Seagal-Nasso in the weeks prior to that date.

This statement by the judge begs the question as to whether Anita had lied to the FBI or whether she lied to the court about the role of Phil Goldfine.

In addition, Judge Berle quoted and appeared to embrace Busch's testimony when she was asked, "Now, at times did you succumb to Moldea's notion that it was Ovitz?"

"Sometimes," she replied.

"And then what would happen?"

"Then I'd find out that Jules was close, close, close, close friends with Pellicano. . . ."

In fact, Nasso was never a friend of Pellicano, "close" or otherwise. He barely knew the man. And yet Judge Berle featured this false statement in his ruling and embraced it as The Truth.

Further, the judge wrongly claimed that Ovitz's theory was based on nothing more than the timing of Anita's stories in the *New York Times*.

> 65. Ovitz contends, in essence, that because Plaintiff wrote allegedly negative articles about him which were published in the *New York Times* during March-May 2002, Plaintiff had sufficient knowledge at the time she filed her Complaint in May 2004, that Ovitz was probably liable for hiring Pellicano to wiretap her telephone and engage in other nefarious conduct in the summer of 2002.
>
> 66. Ovitz's arguments focus on Plaintiff's suspicions. [California law], however, does not require a plaintiff to specifically name [sic] an individual as a defendant where suspicions do not rise to the level of "actual knowledge."

While reading the opinion and seeing how Judge Berle had cherry-picked his evidence to support it—and had done such a poor job in the process—I felt that, more than anything else, he was simply determined to hammer square pegs into round holes in order to punish Michael Ovitz.

Although Judge Berle would preside at the upcoming liability trial, the final decision in that case would be made by a jury.

Writing of the judge's decision, Anita's new employer, *Deadline Hollywood*, played it straight with a dispassionate news story—using no comment from Anita—saying:

> In response to Ovitz's claim that Busch wasn't in fact unaware of the true identity of "Doe," Judge Berle called her "a highly credible witness." Busch's longtime attorney Ian Herzog called the decision "a great win for Anita. She has been through a terrible ordeal, to have her life threatened the way it was, and all of the bad things that happened after, which led her to find out the true evildoer here was

Michael Ovitz. Now we have the chance to prove he was the true enabler behind Pellicano."

Speaking on behalf of Ovitz, Eric George told *Deadline Hollywood*:

> Today's ruling dealt solely with the timeliness of Anita Busch's claims," George told *Deadline*. "Michael Ovitz provided no testimony in the course of this proceeding. When there is a trial on the merits, we will prove that Michael never did – and under no conceivable circumstances ever would – countenance any attack on any other person."[332]

———

On Tuesday, February 3, 2015, at the federal prison in Big Springs, Texas, Eric George and Evan Marshall, on behalf of Michael Ovitz and Anita Busch, respectively—along with several other attorneys involved in the civil case—deposed Anthony Pellicano.

Actually, it was not really a formal deposition. As arranged beforehand, because the Ninth Circuit was still considering his appeal, Pellicano agreed to answer questions but not under oath. Still, the questioning would provide some extremely interesting moments.

Pellicano said that in or about April 2002 he received a call from Michael Ovitz who expressed concern with what he described as "the Pink Mafia," also known as "the Gay Mafia" in Hollywood, adding that it was "the single most complex situation imaginable." Pellicano specifically said that Ovitz was "ranting and raving" during their telephone conversation.

Ovitz gave Pellicano a list of about forty names, two of whom were Anita Busch and Bernard Weinraub. Ovitz alleged that the people on this list "were out to get him."

Pellicano told Eric George:

> Well, you have to understand I wasn't really all that interested at the time, to be honest with you. [Ovitz] was going on and on, and I told him, "Why is it bothering you?"

> We had a long, personal conversation about why this is getting to
> him. He went on about his family being affected and all that, and I said,
> "Well, look, I will look into it. I will see if this so-called conspiracy"—
> he rattled off names, a bunch of names, at least 40 names, and as Mr.
> Marshall mentioned, one of my friends—my best friends in the world and
> other clients of mine, to be honest with you. So I told him I would look
> into it.

Pellicano recalled that Ovitz gave him $80,000 with the
understanding that he would give him another $20,000 for what was
a $100,000 project, specifically "to look into this Pink Mafia thing
for him."

Pellicano admitted that Anita had been on his radar screen
twice before his 2002 conversation with Ovitz. The first was his
investigation of her while she was with the *Hollywood Reporter*.
The second, Pellicano believed but was not sure, was merely
a "query" about her after she left the *Hollywood Reporter* and
while she was freelancing for several publications, including
Premier.

When Anita's attorney, Evan Marshall, asked for specifics,
Pellicano snapped, "I am not going to tell you." However, he
conceded that he had been retained for "three or four" other matters
by the law firm, Gorry Meyer & Rudd, which then represented
Ovitz, among other clients, including Steven Seagal many years
earlier.[333]

Pellicano insisted that Ovitz *never* hired him to investigate
either Anita or her one-time partner at the *New York Times*, Bernie
Weinraub. According to Pellicano, he only opened files on them, just
as he did with many of the forty or so subjects on Ovitz's enemies
list.

Pellicano said that he believed that Alexander Proctor had
vandalized Anita's car in June 2002, but only because Proctor had
admitted it during his tape-recorded conversation with FBI informant
Dan Patterson, whom Pellicano alleged had called and asked for
$30,000 in return for his silence. Pellicano testified that he told
Patterson, "If you have evidence that I committed a crime, you

should call the FBI." Pellicano said that he even gave Patterson the FBI's phone number.

Although Pellicano acknowledged that Proctor had also claimed on tape to have performed this task on his behalf, Pellicano insisted that he played no role in this matter.

When Marshall asked Pellicano why Proctor would have vandalized Anita's car without authorization, the former private investigator speculated that Proctor was trying "to impress me."

Consistent with his previous statements to several reporters, including me, Pellicano declared: "[T]hat's the craziest thing in the world. I have been in business for 40 years and in Los Angeles since 1982. Anybody who knows me knows that that [sic] is the stupidest thing that I have ever heard in my life and has—there is no justification for it at all, to vandalize a car and put a rose on it. It makes no sense to me. . . . What does a fish in a pan and the word 'Stop' and a hole in the windshield? What does that do? I mean, why would somebody want to do that?"

Pellicano added that he never had any conversations with Proctor about the vandalism and never gave him any money for doing it. However, Pellicano admitted that he had mentioned to Proctor many years earlier that he had represented Steven Seagal, a name that Proctor also brought up during his recorded conversation with Patterson. It was that statement that placed Seagal at center stage of this investigation—even though Seagal, despite his many faults, was an innocent man, wrongly accused with regard to the Busch case.

Although he admitted to instructing one of his associates, Denise Ward, a former LAPD officer, to go to Anita's home and photograph the area, including her car, Pellicano denied ever ordering Ward to perform any actual surveillance on her.

Pellicano openly acknowledged and even boasted of wiretapping numerous telephones, but he denied ever asking a Pacific Bell employee to place a surveillance device on any target's phone. And he specifically denied ever intercepting Anita's calls.

Pellicano said that he could not recall whether or not he had ever asked Mark Arneson to run the May 16, 2002, police computer check on Anita. Notably, Pellicano, in advance, had refused to testify about his co-defendants, like Arneson. However, he did admit that between 1999 and 2002, he paid Arneson a minimum of $2,500 a month for one-hundred hours of work at $25 an hour. Also, Arneson was on call, available for additional assignments from which he could make even more money.

In the midst of his deposition, Pellicano lamented, "I am the only private investigator in history that got charged with RICO for getting driver's license information."

Further, although he admitted to being acquainted with *Los Angeles Times* reporter Jim Newton, he denied knowing Newton's wife, Karlene Goller, the newspaper's legal counsel, whom Anita had placed at the hub of one of her conspiracy theories. "I don't know who she is," Pellicano said, adding that he had never spoken to Newton about Anita. However, Pellicano did admit discussing Anita after the vandalism to her car with Chuck Phillips, another *Times* reporter—although he could not recall specifically what they discussed.

Pellicano insisted that the only reason why he pleaded "no contest" to threatening Anita in the superior court case was because he was in the midst of treatment for a "brain disorder" which severely affected his eyesight. In lieu of remaining in the county jail for the duration of a 120-day delay in his trial during which time he would receive inferior care, Pellicano opted to plead "no contest," so that he could be sent to a hospital in Arizona for treatment.

Further, Pellicano scoffed at any suggestion that Ovitz was guilty of any wrongdoing in this matter. Eric George drove this point home during his line of questioning:

> **Q.** Did Michael Ovitz ever, ever at any point in time ask you to threaten or scare anyone?
>
> **Pellicano:** No.

Q. Did he ever ask you at any point in time to tell anybody to stop doing anything?

Pellicano: Stop doing what?

Q. Reporting on him.

Pellicano: Never asked me to tell anybody to stop reporting on him. He wanted to stop the conspiracy, yeah.

Q. Did he ever ask you to do anything for any conspiracy to be stopped?

Pellicano: Yeah. He wanted to know was there this conspiracy and put an end to it.

Q. Other than learning information from you, did he want you to actually do anything?

Pellicano: Well, when you say "do anything," you have got to be more specific.

Q. Okay. Fair enough. Did he want you to threaten somebody --

Pellicano: No.

Q. -- so that they would stop doing anything?

Pellicano: No.

Q. Did he want you to put any object on anybody's car?

Pellicano: No.

Q. Did he want you to specifically put somebody in fear for their own safety or the safety of their property?

Pellicano: Never.

Q. So is it fair to say that the scope of what Michael asked you to do -- what Michael Ovitz asked you to do for him was to look into certain facts and gather certain information?

Pellicano: Well, he never asked me to do any of that stuff. . . .

Q. To the best of your knowledge, did Michael Ovitz have any knowledge of any attack including any fish or rose being placed on Anita Busch's car before that attack occurred?

Pellicano: I don't know how he could have, because I didn't.

Q. To the best of your knowledge, did Michael Ovitz play any role in any attack including placing a fish or rose or the word "Stop" on Anita Busch's car?

Pellicano: Never.

Q. Did you ever provide any information on Anita Busch to Michael Ovitz?

Pellicano: I didn't provide him with any information about any of those people.

Q. Now, as you testified, it is correct, is it not, that you did no surveillance on Anita Busch yourself; is that correct? You never did any surveillance --

Pellicano: No.

Q. -- on Anita Busch?

Pellicano: Myself, no.

Q. And you never had your office do any surveillance on Anita Busch yourself as distinguished from taking a picture of her home; is that correct?

Pellicano (as his own attorney): I've got to instruct not to answer that.

Q. Let me see if I can break this down so we don't get into any issue like that. Did you ever instruct anybody to go to the home of Anita Busch's parents?

Pellicano: Never.

Q. Did you ever instruct anybody to follow Anita Busch?

Pellicano: I might have.

Q. Do you recollect one way or the other?

Pellicano: I have to instruct not to answer.

Q. Did you ever learn -- did you ever instruct anybody to engage in any conversation with Anita Busch?

Pellicano: I don't think I understand the question. The question is: Did I ever ask anybody to have conversations with Anita Busch?

Q. Exactly.

Pellicano: Probably.

Q. Do you recollect anything specifically about that?

Pellicano: No.

Q. Did you ever instruct anybody or ask anybody to have any conversations with Anita Busch in which any threat was conveyed to Anita Busch?

Pellicano: Never.

Q. Did you or anybody on your behalf ever tamper in any way with Anita Busch's car?

Pellicano: No. . . .

Q. Did you ever cause Anita Busch's computer to be hacked or compromised in any way?

Pellicano: Never.

Q. It is correct, is it not, that Michael Ovitz never asked you to interfere with the publication or writing of any articles regarding him?

Pellicano: No. He asked me to look around and see if there were any.

Q. Is it also correct, though, that he never asked you to interfere with the publication or writing of them?

Pellicano: Never.

At the end of his deposition, Pellicano, who would lose the appeal to overturn his racketeering convictions in late-August 2015, said: "What I did was try and assist you guys with these cases. I am amazed you guys didn't come to me five or six years ago. It drives me crazy that nobody asked me questions until now."[334]

———

In mid-October 2015, I learned that the City of Los Angeles, atoning for former Detective Mark Arneson's illegal search of the LAPD's computer database for information about Anita, had reached a tentative settlement with her. Judge Berle approved the agreement on February 29, 2016.

During a case hearing on September 8, 2017, a settlement between the phone company and Anita was also reported.

The money Anita and her attorneys made from their settlements gave a badly needed war chest to the woman who has been running a twelve-year smear campaign against me, which included false charges that I had committed criminal acts. And, based on the gossip I was hearing from friends and sources in Los Angeles and New York, she was going to use a portion of whatever money she made from her litigation to seek revenge on me, because I had the audacity to defend myself against her cynical and dishonest attacks—with the help of Michael Ovitz's legal team.

In effect, just as during the earlier procedural case, I have taken sides in this conflict, leading to the upcoming liability trial.

Seeing that Anita, sooner or later, was going to step up her attacks against me, I called Eric George, still Ovitz's lead counsel, and gave him the details of Anita's conflicting story about Phil Goldfine at the earlier trial. I also explained to Eric how the information I had might annihilate a basic pillar of Judge Berle's decision, which gave this very dishonest woman a very big victory by allowing her case to proceed.

Eric appeared to be stunned by this news. And he was further taken aback when I explained to him that the book I was writing, disclosed during my trial testimony, was nearly finished.

While I had Eric on the phone, I took the opportunity to request an interview with Ovitz. Eric warned that Ovitz could not answer my questions until after he was deposed by Anita's attorneys, who finally questioned him under oath on April 14, 2016.

In the aftermath, I tried but failed to obtain a copy of his sworn deposition. However, I did ask Eric for answers to ten written questions. As of this writing, they still have not been answered— although I have been assured that, sooner or later, they will be.

My ten questions for Ovitz are:

1. Could you provide a description of your personal/professional relationship with Jules Nasso and when you last saw/spoke with him?

2. Could you provide a description of your personal/professional relationship with Anita Busch, including the circumstances of the infamous MSG incident in 1994?

3. How and when did you first learn about the June 2002 vandalism to Busch's car?

4. Upon learning about this incident, did you wonder whether it had anything to do with your arrangement with Anthony Pellicano in which Busch was one of forty or so people you had paid him to investigate?

5. Why did you feel it was necessary to authorize these investigations?

6. Did you ever ask Pellicano if he had anything to do with the alleged threats to Busch?

7. What were the circumstances of your first contact with law enforcement about the Busch matter, i.e. were you confronted about your arrangement with Pellicano or did you volunteer it?

8. Since Pellicano's arrest in November 2002, have you ever paid any money to him and/or any member of his family, directly or indirectly?

9. Have you ever paid any money to Alexander Proctor and/or any member of his family, directly or indirectly?

10. Pellicano's unsworn February 2015 testimony in deposition, if true, is not only exculpatory for you, it is also a complete vindication. Assuming that this is correct, how have you dealt with being wrongly accused all of these years?

On November 8, 2017, Judge Berle, ruling on a motion by Ovitz's attorneys, severed Pellicano from the upcoming liability trial, forcing Anita and her legal team to face Ovitz and Pellicano in separate trials.

The following day, because of alleged procedural errors by Anita's attorneys, past and present, Judge Berle dismissed the case against Alexander Proctor, who had been living quietly in Canada since his release from prison in October 2011.

Barring a settlement among the remaining litigants, the stage is now set for what could be a dramatic 2018 conclusion to this Hollywood melodrama—sixteen years after Alexander Proctor had allegedly vandalized Anita Busch's 1996 silver Audi, leaving a rose, a dead fish, and a sign that said, "STOP," on her windshield.

ENDNOTES

PROLOGUE

[1] Bernard Weinraub, *New York Times*, "Papers Battle to Control Hollywood's Buzz," May 3, 1999.

[2] No byline, Associated Press, "*Hollywood Reporter* writer quits after publisher kills story," April 27, 2001.

[3] Sharon Waxman, *Washington Post*, "Hollywood Editors Quit Over Publisher's Comments," May 1, 2001. The other editor at the *Hollywood Reporter* who resigned in protest was Beth Laski.

[4] Robert J. Dowling, *Hollywood Reporter*, "TradeViews," May 4, 2001.

[5] Charles Fleming, *Los Angeles Times*, "Hollywood: The Journalism of Adoration," May 20, 2001.

PART ONE

[6] The Busch-Weinraub seven-part series about Ovitz appeared as follows:

* Bernard Weinraub & Anita M. Busch, *New York Times*, "Audit Adds to Ovitz's Troubles in Hollywood," March 22, 2002.

* Bernard Weinraub & Anita M. Busch, *New York Times*, "Ovitz Film Unit Loses Partner, Putting Future In Some Doubt," March 23, 2002.

* Bernard Weinraub & Anita M. Busch, *New York Times*, "Hollywood Watches Ovitz Star In Tale of Thwarted Ambition," March 25, 2002.

* Anita M. Busch, *New York Times*, "Actor Defects From Ovitz, Another Setback for Troubled Agency," April 11, 2002.

* Bernard Weinraub & Anita M. Busch, *New York Times*, "Ovitz Is Said To Be Seeking Graceful Exit," April 24, 2002.

* Bernard Weinraub & Anita M. Busch, *New York Times*, "A Faded Hollywood Power Broker Relinquishes His Talent Business," May 6, 2002.

* Bernard Weinraub & Anita M. Busch, *New York Times*, "Talent Agents and Managers Look for Profits As Turf Shifts," May 7, 2002.

[7] James Bates, *Los Angeles Times*, "Lew R. Wasserman, 1913-2002: The Hollywood Mogul and Kingmaker Dies at 89," June 4, 2002.

[8] Perhaps the most notorious of those charged was Peter Gotti, the older brother of mobster John Gotti. The younger Gotti died of throat cancer while in federal prison hospital in Springfield, Missouri, on June 10, 2002, just six days after his brother's indictment.

[9] Anita M. Busch and Paul Lieberman, *Los Angeles Times*, "N.Y. Arrests Have Ties to Hollywood," June 5, 2002.

[10] Anita M. Busch, *Los Angeles Times*, "Claims Seagal Started FBI Probe Called 'Absurd,'" June 6, 2002.

[11] Paul Lieberman and Anita M. Busch, *Los Angeles Times*, "Mob Said to Have Threatened Actor," June 12, 2002.

[12] In author Cheri Seymour's 2010 book—*The Last Circle: Danny Casolaro's Investigation into The Octopus and the PROMIS Software Scandal* (TrineDay)— she wrote: "A source of information which Danny may have read, *Dark Victory: Ronald Reagan, MCA, and the Mob*, by Dan E. Moldea, could have been the inspiration behind Danny's identification of 'The Octopus,' and it would have corroborated some of Danny's findings in his own investigation. Dan Moldea called this unholy alliance 'The Octopus' in his 1986 book."

As part of his work, Casolaro was investigating a Department of Justice investigation of MCA, which I had detailed in a June 1988 article in *Regardie's*, "MCA Music & the Mafia: Did the Justice Department cut Reagan's Hollywood pals a break?" Also, this case was the subject of investigative journalist William Knoedelseder's excellent book, *Stiffed: A True Story of MCA, the Music Business, and the Mafia* (HarperCollins, 1993).

[13] John Connolly, *Spy*, "Man of Dishonor," August 1993.

[14] George Rush and Joanna Molloy (with Kasia Anderson and Dakota Smith), *New York Daily News*, "Daily Dish: Unsettling Reports," July 11, 2002.

[15] Jeffrey Wells, *Reel.com*, "Hollywood Confidential: Words and Consequences," July 12, 2002.

[16] No byline, *The Smoking Gun*, "The Man Who Bagged The Pelican," August 7, 2007.

[17] Paul Lieberman, *Los Angeles Times,* "When Life Imitates a B-Movie," July 12, 2002.

[18] Paul Lieberman, *Los Angeles Times*, "Alleged Extortion of Actor Detailed," July 17, 2002.

[19] In 2011, Ned Zeman published a memoir, *The Rules of the Tunnel: My Brief Period of Madness* (New York: Gotham Books), which chronicled "his attempts to control clinical depression through myriad doctors, hospitals, psychiatric meds and finally electroconvulsive therapy, all while juggling a high-profile career as an editor for *Vanity Fair*."

   In his deposition on February 3, 2015—during which he refused to be sworn—Pellicano insisted that the alleged attack against Zeman on Laurel Canyon never happened, adding, "the man has got some serious mental problems."

[20] Jim Romenesko, *Jim Romenesko's MediaNews*, "Most *Los Angeles Times* staffers believe Busch's mob threat claim is b.s.," August 29, 2002. Notably, the *Los Angeles Times* criticized Romenesko's harsh headline in an official statement, approved by newspaper counsel Karlene Goller: "Our reporter WAS threatened. After discussions with law enforcement, we took the measures recommended to ensure the safety of our reporter." (Emphasis by the *Los Angeles Times*)

[21] Rick Barrs, *New Times L.A.*, "The Finger: Busch League," August 29, 2002.

[22] Ralph Blumenthal, *New York Times*, "A Mob Case, and a Scene Straight Out of Hollywood," July 14, 2002.

[23] David Carr, *New York Times*, "Threat Is Reported in Blackmail Inquiry Prompted by Actor," September 4, 2002.

[24] No byline, Associated Press, "Seagal-Mafia Reporters Threatened," September 5, 2002.

[25] George Rush and Joanna Molloy, *New York Daily News*, "Daily Dish: Under siege," September 5, 2002.

[26] Ned Zeman, *Vanity Fair*, "Seagal Under Siege," October 2002. Also see: Ned Zeman, *Vanity Fair*, "Postscript," May 2007. In this story, Zeman recounted his 2002 story, as well as the alleged threat against him.

[27] John Brodie, *Variety*, "Above the Line," September 20-26, 1993.

[28] In February 2000, Connolly was among those who contributed $1,000 to help me renovate my personal website.

[29] Anita M. Busch, *Los Angeles Times*, "Ovitz Is Sued by Another Former Top Exec of AMG," October 8, 2002.

[30] Gina Keating, Reuters, "Man charged for threatening *L.A. Times* reporter," October 17, 2002.

[31] No byline, *New York Times*, "Detective Accused of Threatening Reporter," October 18, 2002.

[32] Anthony M. DeStefano, *Newsday*, "Lawyer: Feds Probe Seagal Role in Threats," November 5, 2002.

[33] Bill Hewitt, *People*, "Trouble Shooter," September 20, 1993.

[34] Bill Bastone, *TheSmokingGun.com*, "Actor Steven Seagal . . . ," November 22, 2002.

[35] Nikki Finke, *L.A. Weekly*, "The Pelican Briefs," November 13, 2003. Also see: Greg Krikorian and Chuck Philips, *Los Angeles Times*, "Pellicano defense focusing on FBI agent," December 17, 2007.

[36] Matt Lait and Scott Glover, *Los Angeles Times*, "Suspect Links Actor, Threat," November 22, 2002.

[37] No byline, Reuters (via the *New York Times*), "Seagal Linked to Threat to *L.A. Times* Reporter," November 22, 2002.

[38] Scott Glover and Matt Lait, *Los Angeles Times*, "Feds Charge Sleuth to the Stars," November 23, 2002.

[39] Jahoda died of liver disease on May 7, 2004.

[40] John Kass, *Chicago Tribune*, "Unearthing of Taylor's 3rd husband grave still a Chicago mystery," March 23, 2011.

[41] Bernard Weinraub, *New York Times*, "Talk of Wiretaps Rattles Hollywood," November 11, 2003.

[42] Debbe Jonak, *Daily Herald*, "Anthony Pellicano: Private Eye," April 29, 1978.

[43] Peter Wilkinson, *GQ*, "The Big Sleazy," January 1992.

[44] Rod Lurie, *Los Angeles Magazine*, "I Was on the *Enquirer's* 'Hit List,'" October 1990.

[45] John Brodie, *GQ*, "Watching the Detective," March 2003.

[46] John Connolly, *Los Angeles*, "The Pellicano Brief," February 1994.

[47] To all intents and purposes, Pellicano inherited that distinction from the former "Sleuth to the Stars," Fred Otash, a former LAPD officer who became a Los Angeles private investigator, working on cases involving Marilyn Monroe, Judy Garland, and Anita Ekberg, as well as Frank Sinatra, Errol Flynn, Vic Damone, and Frankie Avalon. He did investigations for *Confidential Magazine* and published a book, *Investigation Hollywood!*, in 1976.

Otash, who supposedly mentored Pellicano when he first arrived in L.A., died in 1992 at age 70.

[48] Prior to the Jackson case, Pellicano had worked on behalf of Michael Nathanson, the president of production for Columbia Pictures, who was linked to Heidi Fleiss, a Hollywood madam. (See: Nikke Finke, *DeadlineHollywoodDaily.com*, "Pellicano Trial: Now That's Humilitainment!" March 26, 2008.)

[49] Pellicano portrayed Fuhrman as an exhausted and depressed cop, who just wanted to write novels about police work. "He was upset with his job. He was upset with the LAPD. He was upset with his boss. He was upset with a lot of things," Pellicano said. (See: Michael Fleeman, Associated Press "Fuhrman burned-out cop trying to impress—P.I.," August 18, 1995. Also see: Lorraine Adams, *Washington Post*, "Past Paints Troubling Portrait of Simpson Case Detective," August 22, 1995.)

[50] Graham Brink, *St. Petersburg Times*, "Expert's past raises queries," December 7, 2000.

[51] Debbe Jonak, *The Daily Herald* (of suburban Chicago), "Anthony Pellicano: Private Eye," April 29, 1978.

[52] This was a reference to the August 16, 2002, incident with the dark-colored Mercedes in front of her home.

[53] George Rush and Joanna Molloy, *New York Daily News*, "Daily Dish: Betting the Farm," December 30, 2002.

[54] Sharon Waxman, *Washington Post*, "Better Than Fiction: Hollywood Hit Man," November 30, 2002.

[55] No byline, *Washington Post*, "Corrections," December 3, 2002.

[56] No byline, *New York Post*, "Lawyer: Nasso didn't make threats," December 10, 2002.

[57] Eugene Tong, Associated Press, "Hollywood private eye pleads innocent in explosives case," December 23, 2002.

[58] William Glaberson, *New York Times*, "Coming Soon to a Crowded Courtroom, Steven Seagal," February 9, 2003.

[59] Paul Lieberman, *Los Angeles Times*, "Seagal Testifies, Explains His Ties to Mob Family," February 12, 2003.

[60] William Glaberson, *New York Times*, "A Mob Plot Worthy of the Movies, but Seagal Says It Took Place in Real Life," February 12, 2003.

[61] No byline, *The Smoking Gun*, "The 'Lawman' and the Mobster," December 2, 2009.

[62] Letter from Roslynn R. Mauskopf to U.S. District Judge Frederic Block, February 7, 2003.

[63] No byline, Associated Press (appearing in the *New York Times*), "Steven Seagal Testifies at Mob Trial," February 11, 2003.

[64] Paul Lieberman, *Los Angeles Times*, "Seagal Testifies, Explains His Ties to Mob Family," February 12, 2003.

[65] On April 15, 2003, Peter Gotti was sentenced to nine years and four months in a federal prison.

[66] John Brodie, *GQ*, "Watching the Detective," March 2003.

[67] Cindy Adams, *New York Post*, "Celeb private eye fights public woe," March 3, 2003.

[68] For those interested in my role in the impeachment drama, including the Flynt Project, please see my 2013 memoir, *Confessions of a Guerrilla Writer*, Chapters 117 to 137. In the wake of the President's acquittal, I faced possible indictment after the Republican National Committee filed criminal charges against me with the Department of Justice for felony obstruction of Congress, jury tampering, and blackmail. In the end, I was not charged.

[69] *U.S. v. Anthony Pellicano*, 01-1278-DT, "Application for Review of Order Setting Conditions of Release/Detention, Pending Trial, and Order," February 27, 2003.

[70] David Rosenzweig, *Los Angeles Times*, "Pellicano Accused of Wiretapping," March 13, 2003.

[71] No byline, *Los Angeles Times*, "Dismissal Sought in Threat Case," March 1, 2003. The U.S. Supreme Court case was *Scheidler et al. v. National Organization for Woman, Inc. et al.* (01-1118) 267F.3d 687, reversed.

[72] Matt Lait, *Los Angeles Times*, "Suspect Charged in Threat on Reporter," March 18, 2003.

[73] U.S. government press release, "Remaining Three Suspects Arrested and Indicted For Involvement In Nationwide Fraud Scheme," January 8, 2002. The three suspects were Daniel C. Patterson, Alexander Drabkin, and Michael Itaev. They were accused of swindling "two Los Angeles area businesses out of a combined total of $574,490 in gold, platinum, and rhodium products and a New Jersey business out of another $494,467," according to the press statement.

[74] William Bastone, *TheSmokingGun.com*, April 4, 2003.

[75] On April 9, 2003, I found articles that had run in *The Record* on April 6 and 7, both written by reporters Randy Diamond and Jeff Pillets, who focused on the circumstances of the 63-year-old Prisco's August 2002 release from prison.

Diamond and Pillets reported that Seagal's visit to the prison to meet Prisco in 2001 was arranged by Prisco's relative, Bob DeBrino, an ex-New York police officer-turned-"Hollywood producer and agent." The journalists added: "DeBrino said Prisco, who authorities contend once controlled a gang in New Jersey from a Bronx social club, was a co-author of a screenplay behind bars, about aliens saving the Earth. The two have already discussed a project about an undercover officer who infiltrates organized crime. DeBrino said Prisco also could be a consultant on a film about friends from an urban neighborhood whose lives take divergent paths up the corporate ladder and down into the criminal underworld."

[76] Declaration of FBI Special Agent Stanley E. Ornellas, March 31, 2003. This document appeared in *United States of America v. Anthony Pellicano*, (U.S. District Court for the Central District of California, CR 02-1278-DT), "Government's Opposition to Defendant's Motion to Suppress Evidence, March 31, 2003.

[77] Luke Ford, lukeford.net, "Profile: Anita Busch," undated.

[78] Ford stated on his website that Connolly had written to him. Ford wrote: "Connolly writes 11/6/02: Luke Ford, I was unaware of your website until this afternoon. Someone directed me to the Anita Busch articles. I'm quite impressed by your work. Very well researched and documented. Continued success. I also agree with your suggestion that the threats to Busch and Zeman originated in the [Steven] Seagal camp. I can assure you that Anita Busch was not the first reporter/journalist to ever be threatened by the 'Seagal camp'. My sources tell me to expect more arrests and that one of them, not an actor, will be someone very well, known in Hollywood. Stay tuned."

[79] Luke Ford, lukeford.net, "Profile: John Connolly," undated.

[80] Ken Auletta, *New Yorker*, "Beauty and the Beast," December 16, 2002.

[81] Walter Kim, *Time*, "Shut up by Talk," June 12, 2000.

[82] In my opinion, editorial control meant that Busch had the final say about the contents of the final draft manuscript submitted to the publisher. Until then, I had the right to advocate my point of view about anything and everything, including those matters dealing with style, content, organization, and sourcing—even when she clearly disagreed.

[83] Affidavit of FBI Special Agent Stanley E. Ornellas, January 14, 2003, pp. 17-21. Busch had sent a memorandum about her problems with her phone to Stan Ornellas on December 9, 2002.

[84] Paul Pringle, *Los Angeles Times*, "Hollywood PI Vows to Fight," May 20, 2003.

[85] In 1996, the two lead LAPD detectives in the O.J. Simpson murder case selected me to write what became our 1997 best-selling book, *Evidence Dismissed: The Inside Story of the Police Investigation of O.J. Simpson*, a personal chronicle of their work. In fact, Jim Newton was the detectives' first choice. But, for personal reasons, Newton had to leave the partnership—but not before completing an excellent proposal about the book project. It was so well done that I called and asked Newton if the detectives and I could use it to help sell our book.

    With no hesitation, Newton gave us permission to use it for anything we wanted.

[86] Busch alleged that John Montorio and Karlene Goller "were telling me to, during the course of the Grand Jury, to lie to the Grand Jury. I didn't want to do that. I didn't feel it was right." (Deposition of Anita Busch, Volume IV, August 20, 2012, pp 509.21-510.6.)

[87] On or about May 16, 2008, Newton put his defense in writing in a letter to blogger and Los Angeles County Deputy District Attorney Patrick Frey of *Patterico's Pontifications*, saying:

> I'm not sure what I'm being accused of here. Did I, like dozens of people, receive a $5 clay paperweight from Pellicano some years ago? Yes. It was amusing and almost entirely without value. I lost it when I moved desks and haven't seen it since.
> I never had anything to do with the coverage of Anita's case — did not attend a single meeting about it, did not work on any stories relating to it. Nothing. By then I was covering City Hall, and there was no reason for me to be involved in it.

My use of Pellicano as a source dates back to the Michael Jackson years when I was responsible for our coverage of the LAPD, and yes, I interviewed him, along with other sources — reputable and otherwise — many times throughout those years (well before I was married to Karlene, incidentally). Neither I nor anyone else ever suggested hiring him or "bringing him on board." I interviewed him, checked the information he gave me, used it when it checked out, discarded it when it didn't. I once interviewed him at his office — the only time I ever met him in person — but I never "toured" it other than to look around before and after talking with him. I treated him very warily, in part because I was warned against trusting him by other sources, notably Johnnie Cochran and the lawyers in his firm.

I have never "protected" my wife from anything at the paper or otherwise. She doesn't need it.

If Anita or you or anyone has a challenge to anything I've written or done at the paper, I'm happy to address it. But this is a nonsense tissue of innuendo based on a paperweight.

[88] Richard Winton and Andrew Blankstein, *Los Angeles Times*, "Officer Allegedly Snooped in Database," June 4, 2003.

[89] In another set of typed notes—Busch had handwritten, "BOMBSHELL . . . DAN—HIGHLY CONFIDENTIAL - WILL NOT DISCUSS ON PHONE"—in which she gave me a separate chronicle of her June 12, 2003, conversations with FBI Special Agent Tom Ballard which contained some additional details:

> He asks me for my license plate number. I find it to be a really odd question, but give it to him. He asked me if Stan told me the date that the cop dug into my file. I said all I know is that it's before the June 20 incident occurred. He tells me it was May 16. [Anita added a handwritten note at the end of that typed sentence: "First Seagal story was June 5th, two days after I started under contract at the L.A. Times."]
>
> I am stunned but remember the questions from the Grand Jury about if there was anything I was working on in May. He asks me if there was anything I was working on or doing in May that might have prompted this. I said during that time, I had finished up Michael Ovitz stories at The New York Times and was negotiating to go to the Los Angeles Times. I told him I was still following the Michael Ovitz "saga."
>
> I said that was the only thing I was working on. I tell him that I hadn't yet agreed to the contract with the L.A. Times until May 20. I said there were stories I was following regarding Ovitz and at one point, I knew it would be for the L.A. Times. I think I might have emailed them to my editor before I signed the contract, I said. . . .

> He asked me what the name of the guy was at the New York Times
> that I was writing the stories with. I tell him Bernard Weinraub. He asks
> me to spell it. I do. He says, "that's a positive i.d." (Busch's emphasis)

[90] In my notes, I wrote: "In February 2003, Stan asked Anita whether she had anything about Ovitz." Busch gave me a handwritten letter, referring to her February 2003 meeting with Ornellas—four months *before* she received her call from FBI Special Agent Tom Ballard about Detective Arneson's May 16, 2002, database check on Busch who wrote to me:

> DAN—THIS CAN'T BE PART OF THE MANUSCRIPT BUT
> STAN & I SAT DOWN AT ONE POINT IN FEBRUARY. . . . I TOLD
> HIM EVERYTHING. . . .
> He asked me if I was investigating Ovitz. I said no. He asked
> why not. I said because sometimes you need to leave a person alone—
> besides I was supposed to be looking at the relationship between Jules
> & Steven.
> I gave him a list of names of possible people & their connections to
> Jules & Steven—I told him that Ovitz brought [Seagal] into Hollywood
> after he was mobbed up. (Busch's emphasis)

[91] Along with Ovitz, the other four founders of CAA were William Haber, Ron Meyer, Rowland Perkins, and Mike Rosenfeld.

[92] Johnnie L. Roberts, *Newsweek*, "King of the Deal: Michael Ovitz is after his biggest prize yet. How much is enough for 'the most powerful man in Hollywood?" June 12, 1995.

[93] Bryan Burrough, *Vanity Fair*, "Ovitz Agonistes," August 2002.

[94] Busch faxed to me a document about this matter on October 19, 2003. In that communication, she wrote in the third person:

> During the series, Ovitz personally flew into N.Y. & met with
> Times editors trying to get [crossed out word] Weinraub fired. It wasn't
> the 1st time he tried to get Weinraub fired.
> **In the end Ovitz blamed Busch & Weinraub for his demise.**
> **Ovitz later [word unknown] them as part of a gay mafia bent**
> **out to destroy him & drive him out of Hollywood.** (Emphasis added.)

[95] Cynthia Cotts, *Village Voice*, "Press Clips: The Media and the Moguls – *The Times'* Grudge Against Ovitz," August 14-20, 2002.

[96] Richard Johnson (with Kimberley Ryan), *New York Post*, "With less than love, from Mike," November 7, 1994.

[97] Richard Johnson, *New York Post*, "Page Six: L.A. Private Eye's No Canary," July 21, 2003.

[98] Paul Lieberman, *Los Angeles Times*, "Former Seagal Associate Plea-Bargains in Plot to Extort Actor," August 7, 2003.

[99] No byline, *Los Angeles Times*, "Threat Suspect Is Guilty in U.S. Case," September 30, 2003.

[100] No byline, Associated Press, "Trial opens for LA celebrity private investigator facing weapons charges," October 9, 2003.

[101] David Rosenzweig, *Los Angeles Times*, "FBI Agent Testifies in Hollywood Investigator's Trial," October 9, 2003.

[102] No byline, *The Smoking Gun*, "The Man Who Bagged The Pelican," August 7, 2007.

[103] Nikke Finke, *Deadline Hollywood Daily*, "Pellicano Prosecutor: Hollywood Wannabe," May 6, 2006. Also see: William S. Dobkin, *Great Neck Record*, "1979 South High Graduate In Hollywood Spotlight," June 8, 2006.

[104] Actually, after the alleged attempt to run her down in the street in front of her home in August 2002, Busch made no secret of her suspicion that Ornellas was leaking information about her to "the guys back east." Upon the arrest of Alexander Proctor, Busch reversed herself and apologized to Ornellas.

[105] Cindy Adams, *New York Post*, "Tough guy left holding the bag," October 15, 2003.

[106] More often than not, authors look for the most sympathetic ear and eye in an editor and an agent. That symbiosis can make a book more successful.

[107] Ken Auletta, *New Yorker*, "Hollywood Ending: Can a wiretap scandal bring down L.A.'s scariest lawyer?" July 24, 2006.

[108] Janet Shprintz, *Variety*, "FBI questions legal eagles in wiretap probe," November 5, 2003.

[109] No byline, *New York Times*, "F.B.I. Said to Query Celebrity Lawyers About Wiretaps," November 7, 2003.

[110] Nikki Finke, *L.A. Weekly*, "Deadline Hollywood: The Pelican Briefs," November 14-20, 2003.

[111] Mark Lewis, *Forbes*, "Tom Clancy: The Sum Of All Careers," June 27, 2002.

[112] Henry Weinstein, Greg Krikorian and James Bates, *Los Angeles Times*, "FBI Probe Shakes Up Hollywood's Top Lawyers," November 8, 2003.

[113] Bernard Weinraub, *New York Times*, "Talk of Wiretaps Rattles Hollywood," November 11, 2003.

[114] Dan E. Moldea, *Regardie's*, "MCA and the Mob: Did the Justice Department cut Reagan's Hollywood pals a break?" June 1988. The complete story of Rudnick's MCA investigation is contained in William Knoedelseder's excellent book, *Stiffed: A True Story of MCA, the Music Business, and the Mafia* (HarperCollins Publishers, 1993).

[115] Email from Dan Moldea to Anita Busch and John Connolly, November 12, 2003; 7:36 P.M.

[116] Wendy Thermos, *Los Angeles Times*, "Masry Is Cleared of Harassment," June 6, 2002.

[117] Scott Glover, Matt Lait and Richard Winton, *Los Angeles Times*, "Attorneys Heard Pellicano Tapes," November 14, 2003. The Jones case also provoked criticism from Los Angeles County District Attorney Steve Cooley, who chastised federal prosecutors for not cooperating with his office in the midst of his attempt to discover whether Pellicano had wiretapped the phones by local prosecutors, especially those involved in the Jones matter. Also see: Andrew Blankstein and Richard Winton, *Los Angeles Times*, "Cooley Demands Details on U.S. Wiretap Inquiry," December 11, 2003.

[118] Andrew Blankstein, *Los Angeles Times*, "Pellicano Is Wed on Verge of Prison," November 16, 2003.

[119] Laura M. Holson and Bernard Weinraub, *New York Times*, "Investigator to the Stars Is Hot Topic in Hollywood," November 17, 2003. Notably, Dimond had earlier told the *New York Post*, "I [was] positive my phones were tapped—I heard lots of clicking and cracking noises on the line and then my words started coming back to me through others. . . . I would call new sources and they would tell me, 'We understand you've heard X, Y, and Z' so I knew my phone had to be tapped." (See: Michael Starr, *New York Post*, "Jacko Anchor Bugged By P.I.," November 12, 2003.)

[120] Actually, Schwarzenegger had approached Pellicano, asking him to do opposition research on him—just to see what his political opponents could come up with if he ran for governor of California. Pellicano reportedly gave the assignment to Barresi. (See: Nikke Finke, *LA Weekly*, "Arnold, Pellicano and Politics," November 21-27, 2003.)

[121] Chuck Philips, *Los Angeles Times*, "Pellicano Taking His Secrets With Him to Federal Prison," November 17, 2003.

122 Roger Friedman, Fox News, "Jacko: Did Private Eye Tape Him?" February 27, 2004.

123 Matt Lait and Scott Glover, *Los Angeles Times*, "Pellicano Allegedly Linked to Threat," November 20, 2003.

124 David Rosenzweig, *Los Angeles Times*, "10-Year Sentence for Threat Suspect," January 13, 2004.

125 George Rush (Rush & Molloy), *New York Daily News*, "Daily Dish: Ovitz, for worse & worser," January 14, 2004. Connolly often leaked stories to Rush. He earlier admitted to me that he had given the first published story about the June 20, 2002, vandalism to Busch's car to Rush who published the news in his column a few weeks later on July 11.

126 Kat Pellicano's interest in writing a book about her ex-husband was the subject of Bernard Weinraub's December 26, 2003, article in the *New York Times*, "Ex-Wife of Investigator Involved in Wiretap Inquiry Wants to Talk to Publishers, Not F.B.I."

127 Daniel A. Saunders, Assistant U.S. Attorney, Los Angeles, "*United States of American v. Anthony Pellicano*, No. CR 02-1278 (A) – DT - Government's Position Re: Sentencing Factors and Response to Defendant's Position: Declaration of Daniel A. Saunders; Exhibits," January 23, 2004. pp. 4-8.

128 Bernard Weinraub, *New York Times*, "U.S. Offers Evidence Linking Hollywood Figure to Threat," January 23, 2004.

129 Saunders brief, pp. 18, 31.

PART TWO

130 David Rosenzweig, *Los Angeles Times*, "Pellicano Is Sentenced to 30 Months," January 24, 2004.

131 Howard Blum and John Connolly, *Vanity Fair*, "The Pellicano Brief," March 2004.

132 Rush & Molloy, *New York Daily News*, "Daily Dish: P.I. a Bill Collector?" February 1, 2004.

133 Scott Glover and Matt Lait, *Los Angeles Times*, "Pellicano Was Often a Key Prosecution Witness," February 1, 2004.

134 George Rush and Joanna Molloy, *New York Daily News*, "Daily Dish: Surveillance," February 9, 2004.

135 Drew Griffin, CBS 2 (Los Angeles), "The Real Source Part 2: Tabloids & Pellicano," February 12, 2004. Jim Mitteager died in 1997.

[136] Michael Weissenstein, Associated Press (via *Newsday*), "Producer sentenced in Seagal shakedown," February 17, 2004.

[137] Reginald Patrick, *Staten Island Advance*, "Film producer gets year and a day," February 18, 2004.

[138] Letter from Michael Eisner to Michael Ovitz, October 9, 1996.

[139] Michael Cieply and James Bates, *Los Angeles Times*, "As Spender, Ovitz Was $6-Million Man," February 28, 2004.

[140] Christopher Byron, *New York*, "Other People's Money: The Curious Saga of the Wall Street Broker Who Informed for the Government While His Clients' Funds Vanished," September 17, 1990.

In a February 26, 1994, article, "New Twist on an Old Rivalry," by Howard Kurtz in the *Washington Post*, Connolly, despite the evidence, described much of Bryon's story as "nonsense" and "absurd."

[141] Complaint, *Anita Busch vs. Anthony Pellicano, et al*; Superior Court of the State of California for the County of Los Angeles (Case No. BC316318), May 28, 2004.

[142] Caitlin Liu, *Los Angeles Times*, "Reporter in Seagal Stories Files Suit," June 2, 2004.

[143] *Bo Zenga v. City of Los Angeles, et al.* (Superior Court of the State of California, Country of Los Angeles, Central District, "Complaint.")

[144] *United States of America v. Julius Nasso, et al.* (United States District Court, Eastern District of New York, Cr No. 02-606 [FB]), "Memorandum of Law in Support of Julius Nasso's Motion to Compel the Government to File a Rule 35(b) Motion to Reduce His Sentence for Substantial Assistance," July 13, 2004.

Hantman was concerned with the situation revolving around the alleged friendship between Seagal and the former special agent in the charge of the Los Angeles field office, Robert Iden, who gave up that job in 2004 to head California's office of homeland security. The following July, Iden left to accept a job as the chief of security for the Walt Disney Company, worldwide.

[145] Op cit. Hantman quoted from: Daniel A. Saunders, Assistant U.S. Attorney, Los Angeles, "*United States of American v. Anthony Pellicano*, No. CR 02-1278 (A) – DT - Government's Position Re: Sentencing Factors and Response to Defendant's Position: Declaration of Daniel A. Saunders; Exhibits," January 23, 2004. pp. 4-8.

[146] In late June 2004, the documentary—*The Hunting of the President: The Ten-Year Campaign to Destroy Bill Clinton*—premiered in Washington, D.C. and opened at theatres around the country. I had a brief cameo in the film

which was written and directed by Harry Thomason and Nickolas Perry—and based on the bestselling book released by reporters Joe Conason and Gene Lyons in 2000. In 1998, I had published, *A Washington Tragedy: How the Death of Vincent Foster Ignited a Political Firestorm.*

In both my book and the film, I discussed the right-wing fabrications about the circumstances of the suicide of White House attorney Vincent Foster, whom some insisted had been murdered. In addition, I was critical of a stable of Washington journalists who had served as cheerleaders and stalking horses for Kenneth Starr's witchhunt against the President and the First Lady in return for alleged illegal leaks.

[147] Janet Shprintz, *Variety*, "Mike's Revenge," August 2, 2004.

[148] No byline, *New York Times*, "Ovitz Dropped From a Part of Disney Suit," September 11, 2004.

[149] Rachel Abramowitz, *Los Angeles Times*, "Judge Vacates Ovitz's Award," October 14, 2004. In 2006, Cathy Schulman and Paul Haggis won the Academy Award for "Best Picture" for their work on the film, *Crash*.

[150] Richard Verrier, *Los Angeles Times*, "Ovitz Details Pain of Split with Eisner in Emotional Testimony," October 28, 2004.

[151] Laura M. Holson, *New York Times*, "Eisner Says Ovitz Required Oversight Daily," November 17, 2004.

[152] Roger Friedman, Fox News, "Grand Jury Still Meeting in Pellicano Case," November 30, 2004.

[153] Claudia Eller and Sallie Hofmeister, *Los Angeles Times*, "Likely New Studio Chief Still Has a Lot to Learn," January 3, 2005.

[154] Brad Grey, the top executive of Brillstein-Grey Entertainment, was named chairman and chief executive officer of the Paramount Motion Picture Group on January 6, 2005. See: Bill Carter and Lorne Manly, *New York Times*, "Talent Manager Named Paramount Chief," January 7, 2005. Also see: Claudia Eller, *Los Angeles Times*, "Hollywood's Powerful Put Aside Theirs Feuds to Toast Their Newest Rival at Paramount," February 26, 2005.

[155] David Rosenzweig, *Los Angeles Times*, "Detective Seeks Nullification of His Conviction," January 12, 2005.

[156] Ebbins, an alumnus of the William Morris Agency, was the former road manager for several musicians, including Billy Eckstine, Vic Damone, and Count Basie. (See: No byline, *Los Angeles Times*, "Bernie Ebbins, 88; Road Manager for Billy Eckstine and Count Basie," January 11, 2005.)

[157] Earlier, Busch had told me, "I just can't sign the truth away for money. Doing so would go against everything I believe in."

[158] Dr. Nancy Nolte, who lives in Boulder, Colorado, had been a journalist and a book editor, as well as a college-level writing instructor before receiving her PhD. in European theatre.

[159] In the June 18, 1995, review of *The Killing of Robert F. Kennedy* in the *New York Times Book Review*, reviewer Gerald Posner threw a bouquet to Mrs. Nolte, saying: "Mr. Moldea dedicates the book to his writing coach, Nancy Nolte, and properly so, because this is the best written of his books, finished in a clear and easy style."

[160] Email from Dan Moldea to Anita Busch, April 15, 2005; 4:40 P.M.

[161] On his internet blog on March 23, 2005, Hollywood columnist James Bacon published a short piece about Busch's novel, saying, in part: "I recently read a most interesting book manuscript titled *Molly Keating*, the story of a farm girl who gets involved with the Chicago Mob in the Capone era. The story is by Anita Busch. . . . Molly runs away from farm life and eventually winds up as the girlfriend of Johnny Torrio, fictionalized as 'Sam Fazio,' but easily recognized as Torrio in the manuscript. Torrio was the gang boss who imported Capone from Brooklyn to Chicago."

[162] In the June 18, 2004, rough draft of the manuscript, I had opened the first chapter about Busch with her swimming at the YMCA on Santa Monica Blvd. This was based on information I had received from Busch that this was a routine activity she did—as evidenced by the fact that I had no idea that she was a swimmer, that she swam at the YMCA, and that the YMCA was located on Santa Monica Blvd. until she told me. During an early revision of the rough draft, I felt less and less comfortable with the passage because I could not prove that she had been swimming on that particular day. Consequently, I took the passage out on my own. It did not appear in the draft manuscript of April 11, 2005.

[163] In the June 18, 2004, rough draft of the manuscript, I had toyed with the idea of opening the book—either as a Preface or a first chapter—with a recreated conversation between Anthony Pellicano and Alexander Proctor, based on the actual tape-recorded conversation between Proctor and Dan Patterson during which Proctor detailed his conversations with Pellicano. I placed three asterisks (***) at the beginning of that section which symbolized a flag to me that something needed to be fact checked or revised. In this particular case, I was hoping that the January 2004 wiretap evidence released by the U.S. Attorney's Office in Los Angeles would corroborate what I had speculated. But, because federal prosecutors had extensively redacted these transcripts which I only read prior to preparing the April 11 draft manuscript, I fully recognized that I couldn't support the facts contained in this recreated conversation. At that point, on my own and with no prompting from Busch, I

unilaterally removed this section. It did not appear in the draft manuscript of April 11, 2005.

[164] Busch explained the Gambino-nurse-tattoo story as follows during a stay she had in the hospital on or about May 19, 2004:

> I was in the hospital. My body had given out. It had just given out. After two years of thinking every day you're going to get killed, something happens, and so my body gave out, and I ended up with a fever, 102.9 I think it was. I don't remember. It was a high fever, and I went to the doctor at 8:00 in the morning, and my fever was that high and he put me in the hospital and told me that this was all going to kill me. And I knew it was killing me. So I ended up in the hospital and the night nurse came in and she had "Gambino" tattooed on her arm. . . . I wanted to get out of there. I didn't know what I had done wrong, and I thought I was going to get killed so I just wanted to get out of there, and I called Lou and I said, "You got to get me out of here, you got to get me out, I'm going to get killed."

[165] "Additions, corrections, amplifications," Moldea's response to Busch's edits of the April 11, 2005, manuscript, May 2, 2005. Believing that I had lost the June 18, 2005, draft manuscript, Busch took the opportunity to charge that she had made corrections that I never added to the manuscript. However, when I found the June 18 draft—with her handwritten notes—it was clear that I had made every one of her changes. Consequently, I wrote Busch a defense in response to her charges against me—none of which were true:

> * Busch falsely accused me on thirteen separate occasions of not making corrections she instructed to make—when, in fact, she never made the corrections or she never notified me about these corrections.

> * Busch a falsely accused me twice of misspelling words that I spelled correctly.

> * Busch falsely accused me of plagiarism. The article she cited contained no such wording.

> * Busch falsely accused me of wrongly changing text which she, herself, had changed in the previous draft manuscript.

> * Busch falsely accused me of not making punctuation changes in previously-published articles, even though the punctuation was correct as I had cited it.

    * Busch falsely accused me of not making a change in which she wrote in her corrections to the June 18, 2004, draft manuscript that she needed more information in order to make the change.

    * Busch falsely accused me of having the 2-24-2003 emails between John Spano and her in my possession. However, our Catalogue of Documents proved that she never gave me those emails.

    * Busch falsely accused me of incorrectly citing a *Vanity Fair* story in which she was mentioned. In fact, my cite was correct.

[166] Nevada Gaming Commission and State Gaming Control Board Exclusion/ Ejection List. See: http://gaming.nv.gov/index.aspx?page=72. Anthony Spilotro was murdered in June 1986.

[167] The working title for Busch's book with her mobster lover, aka The Car Guy, was *Waiting for Fly Boy.*

Busch also told me that The Car Guy had introduced her to an old man she code named, "Dinosaur," whom she described to me as "a once-powerful, now-retired Mafia figure." We used this description in our May 11, 2005, manuscript, which Busch approved before sending it to her attorneys.

Busch added in her notes to me that during her famous June 12, 2003, conversation with FBI Special Agent Tom Ballard, "He asks me about a few restaurants. If I ever visited any particular restaurants. One haunts me. I think I have met with Dinosaur there. I feel like I got punched in the stomach. He says the Pizza Connection one [sic]. I say I can't say about that one, but I'm sure it is the one. He asks me about another. I said that the last time I was there was when Clint Eastwood, and his agent Lenny Hirshan and I celebrated our birthdays together there. I want to stay on that subject and not the other restaurant. UGH!"

In another version of that same story, Busch wrote: "Tom said that he had a question for me. Have I ever been in these restaurants . . . Matteo's. Enzo. Morton's. I tell him that I've been in Matteo's but not for years. The last time I was there was having dinner with Clint Eastwood. We have the same birthday. [Ballard] asked me how I knew Clint. I told him that I was friends with his agent.

"He asked me about Enzo. He said, you know the restaurant? He said the Pizza Connection. I said, uh, yeah I know about that and I'd rather not say."

Notably, in its February 28, 2008, memorandum to the court prior to the opening of the Pellicano criminal trial, federal prosecutors included a section, titled, "Arneson False Statement," which stated:

On July 9, 2003, Mark Arneson, who previously had resigned from the LAPD rather than participate in a compelled interview with Internal Affairs regarding his database inquiries, was interviewed at the United States Attorney's Office in the presence of his counsel. The interview was governed by a standard "proffer" agreement providing that Arneson's statements could not be used against him as long as he was completely truthful. He was not.

Specifically, when asked about his inquiries of law enforcement databases on the name "Anita Busch," Arneson affirmatively asserted that his inquiries on Busch were related to a legitimate gambling investigation he was working on in his capacity as a vice squad detective in the LAPD Pacific Division. Arneson stated that as part of that investigation he and other detectives conducted surveillances at previously identified gambling and organized crime hangouts, including Enzo's Pizzeria and Matteo's Restaurant. Arneson recalled seeing a woman he believed to have been Busch at Enzo's and Matteo's on repeated occasions, and said that he conducted inquiries on her in order to determine whether or not she was involved in gambling or other organized crime activities. Arneson further claimed that no surveillance reports were generated documenting his observations of Busch, and said that whatever documentation he received as a result of his inquiries would have been discarded when Busch was eliminated as a potential suspect in the investigation.

The evidence will show that this Arneson's story regarding Busch was a complete fabrication. For example, Busch will testify that she has never eaten at Enzo's Pizzeria, and did not eat at Matteo's Restaurant on or around May 16, 2002, the date that Arneson conducted his computer inquiries of Busch. . . .

[168] Allison Hope Weiner, *New York Times*, "Telling Hollywood It's Out of Order," May 15, 2005.

[169] *United States of America v. Anthony Pellicano* (United States Court of Appeals for the Ninth Circuit, Case no: 04-50043; D.C. No. CR-02-01278-DT) "Memorandum," January 9, 2005.

[170] No byline, *NewsMax.com*, "Court Unseals Clinton Sleuth's Secret Tapes," June 10, 2005.

In another story with no byline on June 25, 2005, "Hillary's Detective Charged with Intimidation," *NewsMax* added: "In 1992, the Clintons recruited Pellicano to contact some women on a list of 19 so-called 'bimbo eruptions' that had been leaked to the press. Some of the women later complained to then-Bush 41 campaign director Mary Matalin that they had been threatened."

Similar *NewsMax* stories included: No byline, *NewsMax*, "Pellicano Tapes Could Spell Trouble for Bill and Hillary," November 12, 2003; and No byline, *NewsMax*, "Hillary's Lawyer Denies Pellicano Link," November 23, 2003.

Actually, Pellicano had only made a $500 contribution to the Clinton campaign on December 11, 1991.

During a defamation case filed by Gennifer Flowers, Hillary Clinton responded to a set of interrogatories in which she was specifically asked whether Pellicano had ever worked for the Clinton campaign. In her official reply on November 5, 2003, Senator Clinton stated: "I am not and was not aware that in fact one Anthony J. Pellicano was retained or employed" by the Clinton campaign. (See *Flowers v. Carville, et al.*, U.S. District Court for the District of Nevada, Case No. cv-s-99-1629 PMP, "Defendant Hillary Rodham Clinton's Objections and Responses to Plaintiff's First Set of Interrogatories to Defendant Hillary Rodham Clinton," November 5, 2003, p. 15.)

[171] David Lauter, *Los Angeles Times*, "Expert Says Clinton Phone Tape Was 'Selectively Edited,'" January 30, 1992.

[172] Nikki Finke, *L.A. Weekly*, "Requiem for Anita Busch," June 23, 2005.

PART THREE

[173] Gus Russo, *Supermob: How Sidney Korshak and His Criminal Associates Became America's Hidden Power Brokers*," (New York: Bloomsbury, 2006).

[174] In August 1999, Wiatt became the president and CEO of the William Morris Agency.

[175] When I asked Nasso about his odd remark to Ned Zeman of *Vanity Fair* that his house was "Ovitzean," Jules replied that it was simply a tribute to Ovitz who had built a "Zen-like CAA building."

[176] For more information about Danny Provenzano, see: Bob Ingle and Sandy McClure, *The Soprano State: New Jersey's Culture of Corruption*, (New York: St. Martin's Press, 2008.) The authors wrote:

> Danny was sentenced to ten years in prison after pleading guilty in 2003 to racketeering. He was among eight named in a forty-one-count indictment charging beatings, kidnappings, and murder threats to extort $1.5 million from a dozen victims. . . . Prosecutors said they caught Provenzano on tape boasting of his Genovese crime family ties.

[177] Letter from Robert J. Hantman to Amrita Ashok, U.S. Probation Officer, "Re: Julius R. Nasso CR 02-606," January 30, 2004, p. 15.

[178] *Julius R. Nasso v. Loeb & Loeb*, "Verified Complaint," Supreme Court of the State of New York, County of Richmond (Index Number 010448/04), February 10, 2004, pp. 11-16. Also see: Federal Bureau of Investigation, FBI-302 reports, April 3, April 15, May 5, and May 10, 2002.

[179] United States Grand Jury, Eastern District of New York, "Witness: Steven Seagal," May 9, 2002, p. 7.

[180] *United States of America v. Julius Nasso, et al.* (United States District Court, Eastern District of New York, Cr No. 02-606 [FB]), "Memorandum of Law in Support of Julius Nasso's Motion to Compel the Government to File a Rule 35(b) Motion to Reduce His Sentence for Substantial Assistance," July 13, 2004, pages 8-9.

[181] Affidavit of William McMullan in support of Julius R. Nasso's Motion to Compel the Government to File a Rule 35(b) motion," July 12, 2004, paragraphs 42 and 44.

[182] According to the August 7, 2007, edition of *The Smoking Gun*:

> In interviews with the FBI, Patterson claimed not to recall asking Levin for any money, adding that he did not set out to do anything illegal with regard to the highly unorthodox call to the defense attorney, according to one FBI report. In a subsequent report, Patterson noted that he was "in trouble financially with his attorney" and may have mentioned an amount of money to Levin.
>
> When federal investigators first learned of the Levin contact, Patterson "admitted briefly discussing the investigation" with him, but stated "he did not receive any money." For this serious security breach, Patterson was "admonished for divulging information," though not benched from the Pellicano probe. . . .
>
> For law enforcement officials, Patterson's credibility is of little importance. His tapes are what matter. His unpaid bills, legal judgments, bankruptcy, shady investment schemes, and litigation history are meaningless.

On July 22, 2015, the attorneys in *Busch v. Pellicano, et al.*, deposed Patterson who repeated under oath his conversation with Levin, adding: "He didn't promise any money nor did I ask for money. . . . I just told Levin that I was having problems with paying my attorney. . . . And that could he help me with legal assistance not money. I told him that specifically. . . . It wasn't any kind of bribe or anything like that—or extortion."

[183] United States Court of Appeals for the Second Circuit, *United States v. Peter Gotti, et al.*, "Appeal from a judgment entered in the United States District Court for the Eastern District of New York (Block, J.), convicting defendants of violating and conspiring to violate the Racketeer Influenced and Corrupt Organizations Act ('RICO') . . . Affirmed in part; vacated and remanded in part," Decided: July 12, 2006.

[184] William Glaberson, *New York Times*, "A Movie Tough Guy Tells of a Shakedown That Wasn't Scripted," February 12, 2003.

[185] William McMullan, Interview with Mark Bermuda, September 17, 2002.

[186] William McMullan, Interview with Wade Sinclair, September 17, 2002.

[187] William McMullan, interview with Vincent Palumbo, September 25, 2002.

[188] *Julius R. Nasso, etc. v. Steven Seagal, et al*, (United States District Court, CV-03-0443), "Opinion," April 11, 2003.

[189] *United States of America v. Vincent Nasso, Julius Nasso*, (U.S. District Court, Eastern District of New York, CR-02-606), "Transcript of Criminal Cause for Pleading before the Honorable Viktor V. Pohorelsky," August 13, 2003, pp. 57, 59.

[190] *United States of America v. Vincent Nasso, Julius Nasso*, (U.S. District Court, Eastern District of New York, CR-02-606), "Judgment Including Sentence Under the Sentencing Reform Act," February 17, 2004.

[191] *United States of America v. Vincent Nasso, Julius Nasso*, (U.S. District Court, Eastern District of New York, CR-02-606), "Transcript of Criminal Cause for Sentencing before the Honorable Frederic Block," February 17, 2004, pp. 52.

[192] Op cit, p. 30.

[193] *United States of America v. Julius Nasso, et al.* (United States District Court, Eastern District of New York, Cr No. 02-606 [FB]), "Memorandum of Law in Support of Julius Nasso's Motion to Compel the Government to File a Rule 35(b) Motion to Reduce His Sentence for Substantial Assistance," July 13, 2004, page 17.

[194] Letter from Tony Garoppolo, Chief U.S. Probation Officer (via Michael J. Glatthaar, Deputy Chief U.S. Probation Officer) to Stephen White, New York, CCM Office, September 15, 2004. Specifically, Nasso was classified as CIM, Central Inmate Monitoring, the category given to the highest security risks.

[195] It was the famous surveillance bug in the dashboard of Avellino's Jaguar—placed on orders from Ronald Goldstock, the respected head of the New York

Organized Crime Task Force—that led to the 1985 landmark indictments of the heads of the top Mafia families in New York, along with their chief aides.

Anthony Salerno, the head of the Genovese crime family, as well as Anthony Corallo and Carmine Persico of the Lucchese and Colombo crime group, respectively—along with two underbosses—were convicted in the RICO conspiracy case. Each received a hundred years in prison and was fined $240,000 at their sentencing on January 13, 1987.

[196] In 2007, Rossi and Lowen Pharmacy became the targets of a federal narcotics investigation, culminating with the seizing of over $8 million of illegal steroids. Nasso was not implicated in any wrongdoing. On January 28, 2008, the 56-year-old Rossi was found dead in his office with gunshot wounds to his head and chest. After recovering the weapon and a farewell note at the scene, police officials concluded that Rossi had committed suicide. (See: Bruce Lambert, *New York Times*, "Co-Owner of Pharmacy Is Fatally Shot," January 29, 2008.)

[197] Julius R. Nasso (movant), "Motion," *United States of America v. Julius R. Nasso*, February 15, 2005.

[198] No byline, *New York Daily News*, "Producer's sequel to prison saga," August 25, 2005.

[199] Campbell Robertson, *New York Times*, "A Producer Is Back on Location and Ready to Celebrate," August 29, 2005.

[200] David M. Halbfinger and Allison Hope Weiner, *New York Times*, "Hollywood Waits to See Wiretapping Indictment," October 19, 2005.

[201] Rush & Molloy, *New York Daily News*, "Side Dish," October 19, 2005.

[202] Richard Johnson with Paula Froelich and Chris Wilson, *New York Post*, "Page Six: Hollywood Sweats P.I. Case," October 23, 2005.

[203] Transcript, *CNN Nancy Grace*, "Michael Jackson's PI Behind Bars," October 27, 2005.

[204] No byline, *Radar Online*, "CBS Whacks Pellicano Expose," November 17, 2005.

[205] No byline, *Radar Online*, "Perp Walk for Pellicano Pals," November 22, 2005.

[206] Laura Sydell, National Public Radio, "All Things Considered: Inside the Pellicano Files," November 23, 2005.

[207] Cindy Adams, *New York Post*, "Letters from pen to some pen pals," December 20, 2005.

[208] Press release, U.S. Department of Justice, Debra Wong Yang, United States Attorney, Central District of California, "Two Plead Guilty to Felony Charges Related to Investigations Conducted by Anthony Pellicano," January 10, 2006.

Another person charged who later pleaded guilty was George Kalta, a businessman in Valencia, California. After he was charged by a woman with sexual assault, he paid Pellicano $75,000 in 2001-2002 to wiretap her phone. (See: Greg Krikorian, *Los Angeles Times*, "Another Case Is Linked to Pellicano," February 18, 2006.)

[209] Greg Krikorian, *Los Angeles Times*, "Pair Linked to Pellicano Enter Guilty Pleas," January 10, 2006.

[210] Suzanne Hansen, *You'll Never Nanny in This Town Again: The True Adventures of a Hollywood Nanny*, (Crown, 2005).

[211] Ned Zeman, *Vanity Fair*, "Seagal Under Siege," October 2002.

[212] I made repeated attempts to interview Steven Seagal. He did not respond to any of my requests.

[213] Greg Krikorian, Henry Weinstein, and Chuck Philips, *Los Angeles Times*, "Private Eye May Be Tried Again," February 3, 2006.

[214] Greg Krikorian, *Los Angeles Times*, "Music Figure Held in Pellicano Case," February 5, 2006.

[215] David M. Halbfinger and Allison Hope Weiner, *New York Times*, "New Wiretapping Charges Are Set in Hollywood Case," February 4, 2006.

[216] Press release, U.S. Department of Justice, Debra Wong Yang, United States Attorney, Central Division of California, "Anthony Pellicano, Two Others Named in Federal Racketeering Indictment," February 6, 2006. Others allegedly wiretapped by Pellicano included but were not limited to: Erin Finn, Ami Shafrir, Lisa Gores, Laura Buddine, Vincent "Bo" Zenga, Aaron Russo, Keith Carradine, Laura Moreno, Kissandra Cohen, Michael Rosen, and James Orr.

[217] David M. Halbfinger and Allison Hope Weiner, *New York Times*, "Detective's Employer Knew About His Sleuthing Device," February 12, 2006.

[218] David Halbfinger and Allison Hope Weiner, *New York Times*, "A Detective to the Stars Is Accused of Wiretaps," February 7, 2006. Also see: Greg Krikorian and Andrew Blankstein, *Los Angeles Times*, "Pellicano and 6 Others Are Indicted," February 7, 2006.

[219] David Halbfinger and Allison Hope Weiner, *New York Times*, "Broader Inquiry Examines Ovitz Ties to Detective," February 15, 2006.

PART FOUR

[220] David M. Halbfinger and Allison Hope Weiner, *New York Times*, "Reporter's Lawyers Subpoena Ovitz in Hollywood Suit," February 11, 2006.

Five months later, Weiner, who had earned her law degree twenty years earlier, created a stir for "allegedly misrepresenting herself in an effort to interview Anthony Pellicano," according to a July 6, 2006, article in the *Los Angeles Times* by Chuck Philips. "Weiner . . . got into the jail last month after presenting a State Bar of California card and asking to speak with the investigator." According to Philips, the "Metropolitan Detention Center in Los Angeles has barred [the] *New York Times* reporter from the facility."

[221] Greg Krikorian and Andrew Blankstein, *Los Angeles Times*, "Ex-Reporter's Lawyers Subpoena Ovitz in Lawsuit Against Pellicano," February 11, 2006.

[222] David M. Halbfinger and Allison Hope Weiner, *New York Times*, "F.B.I. Links Big Film Names to a Detective," April 14, 2006.

[223] Lloyd Grove, *New York Daily News*, "Static hits wiretap book plan," March 27, 2006.

[224] Nikki Finke, *Deadline Hollywood Daily*, "Updated: Pub Confirms Pellicano Bio Book," April 5, 2006. Judith Curr, the executive vice president and publisher of Atria, said of Connolly's book: "*The Sin Eater* will be to Hollywood what *All the President's Men* was to Washington." (See: Chuck Shelton and Kimberly Maul, *The Book Standard*, "Tinseltown Spy and Badass Go-To-Guy Anthony Pellicano to Get Expose Treatment," April 5, 2006.)

[225] Bryan Burrough and John Connolly, *Vanity Fair*, "Talk of the Town," June 2006. Three of those discussed in the story—Brad Grey, Brad Pitt, and Adam Sandler, along with a representative of the late Chris Farley— insisted that the descriptions of their roles with Pellicano were inaccurate. A spokesperson for Grey claimed that the story even contained "total fabrications."

An article in the April 27, 2006, edition of *Variety* by Gabriel Snyder, added: "Cindy Guagenti, who reps Pitt and Sandler, said in a statement, 'Brad Pitt, Adam Sandler and the late Chris Farley have never once engaged the services of Anthony Pellicano, either directly or through a representative.'"

[226] Chuck Philips, *Los Angeles Times*, "Pellicano Won't 'Rat Out' Clients," June 10, 2006.

[227] Ken Auletta, *New Yorker*, "Hollywood Ending: Can a wiretap scandal bring down L.A.'s scariest lawyer?" July 24, 2006.

[228] Nasso told Gus Russo and me during our interviews with him in August 2005 that he and Pellicano had met "a couple of times a long time ago," but that, in or about 1990, Steven Seagal instructed Nasso to stay away from Pellicano.

[229] Herzog's associate was attorney Evan Marshall.

[230] Andrew Blankstein and Greg Krikorian, *Los Angeles Times*, "Ovitz named in Pellicano case," November 9, 2006.

[231] After a week-long trial, Jeane Palfrey was convicted by a federal jury on April 15, 2008. The judge set a July date for sentencing. I had lunch with her twice during her trial, but did not see or talk to her again after her conviction. On May 1, Jeane hanged herself at her mother's home in Florida. She left two long handwritten suicide notes—one to her mother and the other to her sister. Police investigators confirmed that she had committed suicide.

[232] Greg Krikorian, *Los Angeles Times*, "Pellicano co-defendant pleads guilty to federal fraud and wiretapping charges," December 13, 2006. (Daniel Nicherie had pleaded guilty on December 12.)

John McTiernan—for whom Pellicano had investigated his estranged wife, Donna Dubrow—pleaded guilty in 2006 to lying to federal agents. However, he had his attorneys void the plea in 2009. In 2010, McTiernan pleaded guilty again to the same charge, along with one count of perjury for lying to a federal judge during his attempt to void his earlier plea. He was sentenced to a year in prison. (See: No byline, Associated Press via *New York Times*, "California: *Die Hard* Director Is Sentenced to Year in Prison," October 5, 2010.)

On August 3, 2009, Robert Pfeifer received a two-month sentence which he had already served, along with four months of home detention, 120 hours of community-service work, and a $5,000 fine.

On November 3, 2009, Joann Wiggan, a former phone company employee, was convicted for lying to FBI agents, as well as to the grand jury and during her testimony at her first trial in 2006. The judge sentenced her to 41 months in prison, along with a $7,500 fine and two years of supervision after her release.

On February 8, 2010, Sandra Carradine was sentenced to 400 hours of community service, along with two years' probation, and a fine of $10,000.

[233] Greg Krikorian, *Los Angeles Times*, "Pellicano co-defendant pleads guilty to felonies," December 13, 2006.

[234] David M. Halbfinger, *New York Times*, "Wiretap Case Split Into Two Trials," February 20, 2008.

[235] No byline, *New York Times*, "Excerpts and Audio: The Pellicano Case," May 20, 2007. The following day, the *Times* published a story by David M. Halbfinger and Allison Hope Weiner, "In Court Files, Hollywood's Mr. Fix-It at Work," saying: "Ovitz later told the F.B.I. that he asked Mr. Pellicano to learn what would be printed about him in the coming months and to uncover embarrassing information about his enemies that he could use against them, documents show. Mr. Ovitz's lawyer declined to comment for this article."

[236] No byline, Associate Press, "Judge: Civil wiretapping cases delayed until criminal trial ends," April 2, 2007.

[237] No byline, Associated Press in the *New York Times*, "Setback for the Defense in a Hollywood Wiretapping Case," January 1, 2008.

[238] Greg Krikorian, *Los Angeles Times*, "Judge says Pellicano can represent himself at trial," January 9, 2008.

[239] Gruel's investigator, Lynda Larsen, called to solicit my cooperation on July 7 and July 28, 2007. We had pleasant conversations, but I refused to cooperate on both occasions. I also spoke personally to Gruel, a former federal prosecutor, on July 17 and August 29, 2007. Also, on September 6, 2007, Gruel called and asked me if I had a copy of the FBI-302 report in which Steven Seagal discussed his falling out with Pellicano. Trying to show some good faith to the attorney for the man I still wanted to interview, I found and faxed this declassified document to him later that same day.

[240] For the record, I do not remember ever saying to Robb that I wanted a "pound of flesh" from Busch. If I actually did use that language—which is a common idiom taken from Shakespeare's *Merchant of Venice*—it was stated in anger and frustration to a person with whom I had been very frank during our twenty-year-plus friendship. I certainly never wished or plotted any physical harm to Busch. And it was and continues to be ludicrous to claim anything to the contrary.

[241] Nikki Finke, *Deadline Hollywood*, "What A Surprise! Hollywood Only A Bit Player In Feds' Memo For Pellicano Trial," February 29, 2008.

[242] David M. Halbfinger, *New York Times*, "Eclectic Mix to Testify at Hollywood Detective's Trial," March 1, 2008. After leaving the *New York Times*, Allison Hope Weiner, who had written numerous stories about the Pellicano case with Halbfinger, published a must-read, blow-by-blow daily blog during the trial for the *Huffington Post*.

[243] Greg Krikorian, *Los Angeles Times*, "New details offered in private eye's case," March 1, 2008.

[244] Janet Shprintz, *Variety*, "Pellicano trial to begin this week," March 2, 2008.

[245] Anthony Pellicano represented himself, pro se. Mark Arneson's attorney was Chad Hummel; Rayford Earl Turner had Mona Soo Hoo; Kevin Kachikian was represented by Adam Braun; and Abner Nicherie's lawyer was Lawrence Semenza.

[246] Lynda Larsen executed a damning sworn declaration against Dan Patterson on March 15, 2007.

[247] Rachel Abramowitz, *Los Angeles Times*, "Pellicano trial is 'yesterday's news,'" March 8, 2008.

[248] Greg Krikorian, *Los Angeles Times*, "Paramount's Grey says he knew of no illegal activity by Pellicano," March 20, 2008. Also see: David M. Halbfinger, *New York Times*, "Paramount's Grey Denies Knowing of Any Wiretapping," March 21, 2008.

[249] David M. Halbfinger, *New York Times*, "Journalist in Pellicano Case Will Get Her Day in Court," March 24, 2008. Busch had given me a document about the following categories of symptoms she admitted to suffering: Feeling overwhelmed, Lack of capacity for enjoyment, Mistrust, Changes from typical behavior, Hyperalert-hypervigilance to environment, Social withdrawal/silence, Suspiciousness, Change in values, Difficulty concentrating and deciding, Memory problems, Overly critical of self or others,. Overly sensitive, Preoccupation with the event, Repetitive-intrusive thoughts of the event, Shortened attention span, Fatigue, Grinding teeth, and Sleep disturbances and nightmares.

[250] David Poland, *Movie City News*, "The Sting of Irony," March 24, 2008.

[251] Ryan Tate, *Gawker*, "Condé Nast's Lying Tech Guy Questioned About Leaking, Spying," April 7, 2008. Also see: David Carr, *New York Times*, "*Vanity Fair* and the Private Eye," April 7, 2008.

[252] Marc Glaser, *Variety*, "Michael Ovitz Takes the Stand," April 9, 2008.

[253] Allison Hope Weiner, *Huffington Post*, "Pellicano Trial: Ovitz in the Spotlight and in the Clear and Anita Busch in Tears," April 9, 2008.

[254] Nikki Finke, *Deadline Hollywood*, "Ovitz Testifies Busch/Weinraub NYT Articles 'Wildly Embarrassing,'" April 9, 2008.

[255] David M. Halbfinger, *New York Times*, "At Trial, Hollywood Power Broker Says He Wanted Only Information," April 10, 2008. Also see: Anne Thompson, *Variety*, "Busch, Pellicano face off," April 9, 2008.

[256] John Nazarian, *Desperate Exes*, "Pellicano Trial: The Dead Fish," April 11, 2008.

[257] John Nazarian, *Desperate Exes*, "Pellicano Trial: Response from Dan Moldea to Busch and Connolly," April 12, 2008.

[258] See: http://www.moldea.com/Busch-response.html.

[259] See: http://www.moldea.com/Busch-cards.html.

[260] When it became clear that Seagal was innocent of any role in the attack against Anita Busch and Ned Zeman, among other false charges, he began demanding an apology from the FBI, claiming that these rumors had adversely affected his film career. In an interview with Chuck Philips of the *Los Angeles Times*, Seagal, then 56, said, "False FBI accusations fueled thousands of articles saying that I terrorize journalists and associate with the Mafia. . . . These kinds of inflammatory allegations scare studio heads and independent producers—and kill careers." (*Los Angeles Times*, "Action star Seagal wants FBI apology," August 17, 2007.)

[261] Allison Hope Weiner, *Huffington Post*, "Michael Ovitz Fingered Over Threats to Anita Busch," April 18, 2008. Also see: Nikke Finke, *Deadline Hollywood*, "Pellicano Trial Testimony: Ex-FBI Agent Believes Ovitz Behind Anita Busch Threat," April 18, 2008.

[262] David M. Halbfinger, *New York Times*, "Rising to His Defense, Pellicano Is Done Quickly," April 12, 2008.

[263] Carla Hall, *Los Angeles Times*, "Private eye Pellicano says he won't rat on his clients," April 24, 2008.

[264] David M. Halbfinger, *New York Times*, "Pellicano on Pellicano: He Was No Mastermind," May 1, 2008.

[265] Greg Risling, Associated Press, "Targets of Pellicano happy with verdict," May 15, 2008. Also see: David M. Halbfinger, *New York Times*, "Investigator to the Stars Is Convicted in Wiretaps," May 16, 2008; Carla Hall and Tami Abdollah, *Los Angeles Times*, "Private eye to the stars is guilty," May 16, 2008.

[266] Steven Mikulan, *LA Weekly*, "Pellicano Juror Reveals Inner Workings," May 16, 2008.

[267] Del Quentin Wilber, *Washington Post*, "Former FBI Agent Gets Probation in Hollywood Spy Case," May 14, 2009.

[268] Del Quentin Wilber, *Washington Post*, "Ex-FBI Agent Sentenced to Probation in Pellicano Case," May 15, 2009.

[269] Allan Lengel and Rachel Leven, *Tickle the Wire*, "The Raven Haired Actress and the Fall of a Dapper FBI Agent," September 14, 2009. An earlier story

was published by Jeff Stein on his *SpyTalk* blog for *Congressional Quarterly*, "Actress, FBI Agent, Wiretapper, Spies: A Washington Love Story," on December 3, 2008.

In the midst of all of this news, I received reports that Fiorentino was very upset with me over my cooperation with the article by Jeff Stein who is one of my closest friends. (Stein had known Fiorentino through Rossini long before I met her.) Since my comments to Stein were fairly benign, I never fully understood what the problem was. But then, on May 27, 2009, Fiorentino sent an email, inviting me to have breakfast with her while she was in Washington on business. During our meeting on May 28, she apologized for any misunderstanding. To this day, I still don't know what either the problem or the misunderstanding was.

[270] Victoria Kim, *Los Angeles Times*, "Attorney, Pellicano guilty of snooping," August 30, 2008. Also see: Brooks Barnes, *New York Times*, "Pellicano and a Top Lawyer Are Convicted," August 30, 2008.

[271] Dave Itzkoff, *New York Times*, "Hollywood Lawyer Sentenced in Wiretap Case," November 25, 2008.

[272] No byline, *Patterico's Pontifications*, "Pellicano Sentenced to 15 Years; Read Anita Busch's Sentencing Statement, Including Her Commentary on the *Los Angeles Times*," December 15, 2008.

[273] Shortly after Pellicano was sentenced, his co-defendants also received their punishment. LAPD Detective Mark Arneson and former phone company technician, Rayford Turner, were each sentenced to ten years in prison. Abner Nicherie received a twenty-one-month sentence. Also, Kevin Kachikian, the creator of Telesleuth, was sentenced to twenty-seven months in prison.

[274] No byline, Patterico's Pontifications, "*L.A. Times* Responds to Busch's Statement," December 16, 2008. Speaking on behalf of the *Los Angeles Times* was David Lauter, the newspaper's California Editor.

[275] No byline, Associated Press, "Pellicano: No apologies to those he spied on," December 16, 2008.

[276] Patrick Goldstein, *Los Angeles Times*, "The Big Picture: Anthony Pellicano case: A Hollywood bust," December 16, 2008.

[277] Victoria Kim, *Los Angeles Times*, "State trial against Pellicano, alleged accomplice set to start," June 17, 2009.

[278] No byline, Associated Press, "LA private eye pleads no contest in threat case," October 23, 2009. Also see: Robert Faturechi, *Los Angeles Times*, "Anthony Pellicano gets 3 years for threatening *L.A. Times*, reporter," October 24, 2009.

[279] John Cook, *New York Observer*, "Was a *Vanity Fair* Editor Secretly Working for the Church of Scientology?" March 1, 2011.

PART FIVE

[280] No byline, *TheWrap*, "Anita Busch Deposed as Lawsuits Against Michael Ovitz, Anthony Pellicano Revived," April 29, 2011.

[281] No byline, *TheWrap*, "Ovitz Rejects Anita Busch's Lawsuit, Says: She 'Knew the Risks,'" April 29, 2011.

With regard to Eric George's point about journalists and the expectation of blowback from their work: On June 12, 2014, Keith Olbermann of ESPN interviewed me about the re-release of my 1989 book, *Interference: How Organized Crime Influences Professional Football*. During our exchange, Olbermann noted how the NFL had struck back at me after I started my investigation of its connections with the Mafia. I replied: "I'm a big boy. I've taken on the Teamsters. I've taken on the Mafia. I've taken on MCA. I've taken on the LAPD. I've taken on the FBI. I know that when you start a fight with a major institution, that major institution is going to defend itself. And I expected the NFL to defend itself against me and to come at me. To me, I was fair game, and they were fair game. Just because you start a fight doesn't mean that you're the one who is going to end it."

[282] Allison Hope Weiner, *Deadline Hollywood*, "*Anita Busch Vs. Michael Ovitz*: Status Report," May 20, 2011.

[283] Christine Pelisek, *Newsweek* aka *The Daily Beast*, "Hollywood Hacker Breaks His Silence," August 15, 2011.

[284] Kate Aurthur, *Newsweek*, "Pellicano Target: 'I Was Scared Every Day,'" August 15, 2011.

[285] Subpoena, Superior Court of the District of Columbia, Civil Division, Case number 0006650-11, *Anita Busch v. Anthony Pellicano*, August 15, 2011.

[286] Busch made this same charge against former *New York Times* and *Washington Post* reporter Sharon Waxman: "I think she's even one of the worst journalists I've ever encountered. I've never seen anybody that ignores the basics of Journalism 101 as she does." (See: John Koblin, *New York Observer*, "Get Me Rewrite!" April 21, 2009.)

[287] During her previous sworn testimony at Pellicano's criminal trial, she told the prosecutor on re-direct that she had killed our book project because she felt "used" by John Connolly and me. In this context, she made no mention of Michael Ovitz, Jules Nasso, or my alleged fabrications in the manuscript.

[288] Busch had sent an email to me on March 19, 2004, saying: "[A]ll mail in my incoming saved mail file on my computer is gone. This happened once before with January 03 but I had it all printed out."

[289] *Declaration of Dan E. Moldea*, Superior Court of the State of California for the County of Los Angeles, "In Re Pellicano Cases: *Anita Busch v. Anthony Pellicano, et al.*," Case number BC316318, November 9, 2011. Also see: Common Interest Agreement, signed by Michael Ovitz on November 8, 2011, and Dan E. Moldea on November 9, 2011.

[290] Just to be clear, at all times—before, during, and after this draft manuscript—I understood that Ovitz was "the subject of [Ms. Busch's] series of articles for the *New York Times*."

[291] Busch faxed these handwritten edits to me on February 15, 2005. Her fax number was at the top of the page, along with her initials, "AB."

[292] Declaration of Dan E. Moldea, November 9, 2011, Exhibit C, pages 2-3. In this sworn statement, I documented additional false statements under oath that Busch had told about:

> * her use of "Ed," aka "Evil doer," as her code name for Ovitz— which she denied in spite of numerous communications in which she used this acronym.
>
> * her knowledge of my use of another reference for Ovitz, "Mister X," in one of our book proposals—whom she identified in a handwritten note,
>
> * my account of an alleged attempt by two men in a Mercedes to run her down on the street in front of her home—which I based on her own notes about the alleged incident,
>
> * my account of her appearance before a federal grand jury investigating the Pellicano case in May 2003—which I based on her word-for-word account contained in her personal notes,
>
> * my account of an email exchange she had with John Montorio, a top editor at the *Los Angeles Times*—which was an accurate recitation of the documents that she gave me,
>
> * my account of how, as Anita told me in a handwritten note: "Among all of the media people who have written about his demise, Ovitz singled out Bernie Weinraub and Anita for their *New York Times*

series, alleging that they were part of an organized conspiracy to get him."

       * and even the destinations of her summer vacation in 2004—which she had disputed under oath but that I accurately cited from her personal notes.

[293] Christine Pelisek, *The Daily Beast*, "Will Celebrity Snoop Anthony Pellicano Get Sprung?" June 21, 2012.

[294] Matthew Belloni, *Hollywood Reporter*, "Pellicano Victim Anita Busch Breaks Silence to Oppose Bail Request, Reveal New Questions in Wiretap Case (Exclusive)," June 20, 2012.

[295] Robin Abcarian, *Los Angeles Times*, "Colorado shooting: Micayla Medek, 23, was killed, relative says," July 20, 2012.

[296] No byline, Associated Press, "Mom of 6-year-old killed in Colorado movie theater massacre in critical condition," July 21, 2012.

[297] No byline, Associated Press "Families of Colo. theater shooting victims speak," August 28, 2012.

In an August 24, 2016, story for Reuters, "Colorado movie gunman is 'monster' destined for 'hell,' victim says," reporter Keith Coffman wrote:

> The Colorado movie massacre gunman is destined for the "darkest, most painful part of hell," a sobbing victim testified Monday at the start of a three-day hearing after which James Holmes will be formally sentenced to life without parole.
> "I will never forgive the monster that sits in this courtroom, smiling and laughing with his defense attorneys when the jury and your honor are out of the room," said Anita Busch, whose second cousin Micayla Medek was among the dozen people Holmes killed.
> She said there were no words to explain the agony and despair Holmes had put their families through.
> "[He] will reside in the deepest, darkest, most painful part of hell."

[298] Frank Swertlow, *TheWrap*, "Anthony Pellicano Denied Bail After Impassioned Anita Busch Plea," August 13, 2012.

[299] Among Busch's other false statements:

      * When Busch was asked under oath who "B. Ebbins" was, she described him as "somebody that Dan interviewed." In fact, Ebbins—from whose home Busch would fax me documents—described Ebbins

to me as her "grandfather and best friend." I didn't even know the man,
except through Busch and Dave Robb.

* Busch claimed that she never discussed a belief with Stan Ornellas that
Ovitz was behind the attacks, saying, "No. He just asked me a lot of
questions about a lot of different people." However, Busch had given
me several documents, including her notes of conversation she had with
Ornellas on July 23 and 28, 2003, about Ovitz in which she wrote:

> I call XX. [sic] **He tells me that "ed" hired Pellicano three years
> ago.** The person who tells me this asks why I am asking about it. I say
> for obvious reasons. He is stunned. He tells me that he used to use Gavin
> DeBecker. He might still use Gavin DeBecker. Now, I am stunned.
>
> He also tells me that **a good friend of his said "ed" told him** that he
> was going to get even with everyone someday—and he was going to do it
> one by one. (Emphasis added.)

Busch continued that, after her discussion with the FBI agent, she
said "a prayer," asking in part:

> "Please allow [the FBI] to get this monster, and if you won't allow it,
> **please cleanse his (ed's) blackened soul.**" (Emphasis added; Ms. Busch's
> parenthesis)

* Busch claimed under oath, "I never talked to Gavin de Becker," a
Los Angeles private investigator, but then later during her deposition,
she went into detail about a conversation she did have with de Becker,
adding that he had also sent her a book, *Fear Less*—"it actually helped
me," she said.

[300] In her four-page "confession" to me about "The Car Guy" in May 2003, Busch
recounted exactly the same story: "Later, [The Car Guy] told me he was going to
give me a bit of advice that might save my life someday. He said, if I ever found
myself in a position where I'm down on my knees with a gun to my head, don't be
brave. He said tell them what you know."

[301] Anita Busch, comment in response to "R.I.P. Mickey Freiberg," at *Deadline
Hollywood*, December 7, 2012, 4:58 P.M.

[302] Notably, in early 2012, Robb released his second book—*The Gumshoe and the
Shrink: Guenther Reinhardt, Dr. Arnold Hutschnecker, and the Secret History
of the 1960 Kennedy/Nixon Election*. Robb approached several authors, some of
whom were close friends of mine, to write favorable quotes about his work. Two
of them—Larry Leamer and Gus Russo—called and asked me how I wanted them
to handle his request. I replied to both, "Help Dave. Give him a good quote."

[303] Just to be clear, I never received this supposed email or even this supposed draft
of the email. After I revealed on February 6, 2006, to Busch my July 23, 2005,

conversation with Robb and my follow up email with my attachment about Nasso the following day, Robb wrote to me on February 7: "I thought I made it clear to you today that I resent your attempt to cover your ass by trying to imply that I somehow approved of whatever it was you were doing with Nassau [sic]. As you know, nothing could be further from the truth."

I agree with Robb on this point. In my July 24, 2005, email to Robb, I never asked for his approval and never assumed that he had given it to me. But I did leave it up to him whether or not to tell Busch—just as Busch had instructed me.

[304] On January 18, 2006, there were key exchanges among Busch, Robb, and me which proved that I was the one who told her about my association with Jules Nasso. In the first, Busch wrote: "I've knocked out a fictional account of what happened to me. Would you like to see it?"

Realizing that Robb had not told her anything about my relationship with Nasso, I decided that, in all fairness, I had no choice but to tell her—*before* she sent me her fictionalized account.

I wrote back: "Thanks for the offer, Anita. Before you send me anything, I must tell you something—in writing."

Before responding, I called Robb and told him that I was going to reveal my Nasso book project to Busch.

Robb protested my decision, saying that she would go crazy. He replied that he would tell her.

The following day, January 19, I assumed that everything was fine, based on what Robb told me:

> I'm glad that Dave, prompted by me, told you yesterday of my
> involvement with Gus Russo and Jules Nasso—which was the reason why
> I wanted to respond to your offer "in writing." In good faith, I wanted
> you to know about this before you sent me your novel. If you have any
> specific questions or concerns, please feel free to ask. As Dave told you,
> Gus and I tried but failed to make a publishing deal for Nasso's story.

As it turned out, Robb had misled me again and never told Busch anything. And, as he predicted, she went ballistic.

Referring to Ovitz in her usual code name, "Ed," she wrote:

> If [John Connolly] told Jules Nasso about Ed, then he also told
> him about the book project between us and that is probably why you
> were approached by Jules. But you probably thought about that already.

He's been trying to get to me for the past 3 1/2 years through various
people. He came to you and you engaged him.

When you were first approached to do the Jules Nasso book, given
the fact that this man was a suspect in my case, you should have told me.

In fact, I had told Busch via Robb—just as she had written in her June 12, 2005,
directive to me. Thus, as the written record showed, she first heard about it from me
on January 19, 2006. I concealed nothing. There was no betrayal on my part.

With regard to her claim that she "was terrified of Nasso," Busch wrote on
that same day:

While I BELIEVE that Jules Nasso did not have anything to do with
the threat on my life, I also have evidence that he has not told the truth on
important matters, matters of which you are unaware. (Busch's emphasis)

In other words, as of January 19, 2006, Busch did not believe that Nasso
had "anything to do with the threat on my life." But, in her sworn statement, she
insisted that my relationship with Nasso—whom she was "terrified of"—was her
latest reason why she stopped our book.

[305] Eriq Gardner, *Hollywood Reporter*, "Anita Busch, Michael Ovitz At War in
Anthony Pellicano Civil Case," January 24, 2013.

[306] Eriq Gardner, *Hollywood Reporter*, "Michael Ovitz Can't Escape Lawsuit Over
Anthony Pellicano Attack," March 4, 2013.

[307] No byline, *Los Angeles Times*, "Billionaire's ex-wife must pay $3.9 million in
Pellicano suit," October 26, 2012.

[308] Eriq Gardner, *Hollywood Reporter*, "Chris Rock Settles Hungarian Model's
Pellicano-Related Lawsuit," December 21, 2012

[309] Eriq Gardner, *Hollywood Reporter*, "Brad Grey Escapes Liability in Anthony
Pellicano Matter," January 23, 2013.

[310] James Hirsen, *examiner.com*, "Tom Cruise wins wiretapping lawsuit," March
19, 2013.

[311] Eriq Gardner and Alex Ben Block, *Hollywood Reporter*, "Tom Cruise Wins
Lawsuit Over Anthony Pellicano Wiretapping (Exclusive)," March 18, 2013.

[312] Eriq Gardner and Alex Ben Block, *Hollywood Reporter*, "*Die Hard* Director
John McTiernan Has Until April 3 to Surrender in Pellicano Case," March 18, 2013.

[313] The three asterisks (***) preceding "Mister X" was my signal to Busch to decide
whether she wanted to identify Ovitz or not. Busch made three handwritten notes

on this page of the draft book proposal: 1) she added the two words "could have," so that the sentence read, "the only person *who could have* hired Pellicano . . ." 2) Indicating that she agreed with this passage that she had earlier approved, she wrote, "already corrected this once before," next to "could have." 3) Referring to my reference to "Mister X," Busch wrote: "Why use ("Mr. X") when you just identify him to the world here?" In other words, by saying that he was the subject of Busch's series in the *New York Times*, I was saying that he was, indeed, Michael Ovitz.

[314] During her sworn deposition on July 21, 2011, Busch had the following exchange with Eric George:

> **Q:** Did you ever discuss with Dan Moldea who Mr. X was?

> **Busch:** No. He just threw that in. He would do that sometimes. He would just throw stuff in.

> **Q:** So you never discussed with Dan Moldea who Mr. X was?

> **Busch:** No. I didn't know who it was.

[315] Here is one brief exchange that illustrates this point:

> **Q:** Now, at this point in time you had already been referring to Mike Ovitz as Ed on occasions; correct?

> **A:** On occasions.

[316] On the stand, Speckin noted that one-hundred percent certainty with regard to Busch's handwritten documents was impaired by the fact that he performed his analysis for copies, not originals. Quantifying his work based on copies versus originals, Speckin told the court, "[W]e're not at the absolute pinnacle, but we're only one step below that."

[317] During her trial testimony, Busch described her sleep patterns in or about June 2003—while we were working together on the manuscript—saying: "I was having something called night terrors where I didn't know what it was, but I would wake up on the floor screaming. I didn't know what was happening to me. I thought I was losing my mind."

[318] It is a crime in State of California to intercept or eavesdrop upon any communications, including a telephone call, without the consent of all parties. (Cal. Penal Code §§ 631, 632) A first offense of eavesdropping is punishable by a fine of up to $2,500 and imprisonment for no more than one year.

[319] I also gave Ovitz's attorneys Busch's two pages of notes for January 3, 2003, in which she recounted her conversation with Mickey Freiberg. She wrote: "He

428 Hollywood Confidential

asks me if I think Bert Fields or Michael Ovitz had anything to do with the threat against me. I say no, I don't.

"We say our good-byes. I now am suspicious of Mickey."

Also, I provided the attorneys with an email I wrote to Busch on December 18, 2003, referring to this notation, asking: "How did MF know about the significance of Bert & ED last January?"

Busch responded by telephone, telling me that Freiberg had also told her in January 2003 that he knew Detective Arneson and his brother.

[320] On October 28, 2013, FBI Special Agent Corrie Lyle of Los Angeles called and asked to discuss my recent testimony at *Busch v. Ovitz*. Before speaking with her, I needed to consult with my attorney, so I asked her to give me a few minutes and call me again. I wrote a report to file which said:

> Corrie Lyle called me back at 4:37 PM. She asked if she could put me on her speakerphone, adding that another FBI special agent, Tricia Whitehill, was in the room. She basically had one question: Did I give my collaboration agreement with Anita Busch to either Anthony Pellicano or anyone on his legal team? I replied that Pellicano, his attorney and private investigator, Steven Gruel and Lynda Larsen, respectively, had tried repeatedly to get me to testify as a defense witness at Pellicano's federal RICO trial in March-April 2008.
>
> I told Lyle that I refused to testify at the trial—but that it was possible that I gave Gruel the agreement although I have no specific recollection of doing so. I did volunteer that this document was an exhibit at the recent *Busch v. Ovitz* trial.
>
> I asked her whether she was investigating Stan Ornellas, the lead FBI agent on the Pellicano case. She replied that was part of her task. She asked me if I ever heard that he had accepted money from Anita. I replied that I was as close as anyone to Anita at that time. "There is no way that Ornellas would have agreed to accept money," I said. "No way."
>
> It appears to me that Pellicano is trying to use the addendum in the collaboration agreement—in which Anita gave Ornellas seven percent of her book in the event of her death—as fodder for his current appeal before the Ninth Circuit.
>
> After our conversation, I checked my notes about my conversation with Gruel. In fact, I had sent him an FBI-302 report about Steven Seagal, which had been made public in the midst of the Peter Gotti trial in Brooklyn. I did not send him my collaboration agreement with Anita.

> Lyle asked me how Pellicano knew about the contract. I told her
> that I had written him a letter in 2006, requesting an interview. In the
> text of that letter—which was an exhibit during the recent *Busch v.*
> *Ovitz* trial—I explained to Pellicano how Anita had abandoned the book
> in favor of her civil suit in 2005.
>
> I asked her if she wanted a copy of the letter. She said she did.
> I asked her to send me an email with her request. She did so, and I
> replied with the letter attached. (My emphasis)

[321] I did not read the final transcripts of the testimonies of Busch and Robb until
November 17, 2013.

[322] Notably, Robb appeared to forget that, along with author Gus Russo, I had tried
to sell a book about Jules Nasso—which I had told Robb about before my first
conversation with Nasso.

[323] David L. Robb, *Operation Hollywood: How the Pentagon Shapes and Censors*
the Movies (New York: Prometheus Books, 2004)

[324] Robb was referring to two of my previous books, *Interference: How Organized*
Crime Influences Professional Football (1989) and *Dark Victory: Ronald Reagan,*
MCA, and the Mob (1986).

Also, on October 21, 2004, Robb wrote a review on Amazon of my 1998
book, *A Washington Tragedy: How the Death of Vincent Foster Ignited a Political*
Firestorm, saying: "Dan Moldea is one of America's best investigative reporters.
Afer [sic] you finish this book, pick up *Dark Victory: Ronald Reagan, MCA and*
the Mob, where Moldea explores the dark side of conservative America's favorite
president. It's an eye-opener."

[325] Also in her notes about Goldfine, Busch wrote: "We've had a code name for
each other for many years so his assistants (and his bosses) would never know a
reporter was calling him. We reverted to those code names."

[326] Nasso and Pellicano were hardly as close as Busch had alleged during her trial
testimony. Nasso told Gus Russo and me that he had seen Pellicano, whom he had
only met through Seagal, twice. Seagal told him to stay away from the private
detective in 1990. Later, Pellicano told me that he did not remember ever meeting
Nasso.

[327] In the latest count, Busch had falsely accused me of corruption, along with the
Los Angeles Times and the Los Angeles District Attorney's Office—not to mention
her false hunches and charges against Jules Nasso, Steven Seagal, and any number
of journalists who published anything with which she disagreed. In addition, early
during the Pellicano investigation, she had also falsely accused FBI Special Agent
Stan Ornellas of illegally leaking information about her.

[328] In an article kicking off her new website covering the entertainment industry, Finke wrote of her former publication, *Deadline Hollywood*, "I barely recognize *DH* these days. Some of those bylines I never hired and wouldn't. (Anita Busch . . . ? She's batshit crazy.)" See: Nikke Finke, *NikkeFinke.com*, "Why I Started NikkeFinke. com," June 12, 2014.

[329] The Deadline Team, *Deadline Hollywood*, "Anita Busch Joins Deadline Hollywood As Film Editor," November 14, 2013.

[330] David Robb, *Deadline Hollywood*, "WGA Urges FCC to Block Comcast-Time Warner Cable Merger," March 23, 2014. (This appears to have been Robb's first bylined story.)

[331] *The Robing Room: Where Judges Are Judged*: Hon. Elihu M. Berle. See: http://www.therobingroom.com/california/Judge.aspx?id=2507.

[332] Mike Fleming, Jr. and Dominic Patten, *Deadline Hollywood*, "LA Judge Nixes Mike Ovitz's Latest Bid in Pellicano Case; Anita Busch Suit Heading for Trial," April 3, 2014.

[333] Later, Gorry Meyer & Rudd was in a battle with Seagal for his alleged non-payment of their legal fees and hired Pellicano to help. Pellicano's file about Steven Seagal, which was discovered by federal agents during their search of his office, was about the Gorry Meyer case—and not Anita Busch.

Notably, on September 18, 2014, Judge Berle dismissed Gorry Meyer as a defendant in Busch's civil lawsuit. The firm insisted in its motion for summary judgment that Ovitz, not the firm, had hired Anthony Pellicano to investigate Busch. The firm did acknowledge that it had paid Pellicano for other work on Ovitz's behalf while he was at the Walt Disney Company.

[334] In the midst of all of the legal action swirling around *Busch v. Ovitz*, I received a phone call from a trusted friend, an investigative journalist and author, who told me that Pellicano was furious with me because of my testimony during the earlier procedural trial. Apparently, he resented the fact that I had testified as a defense witness for Ovitz in 2013, but I refused to be a defense witness for him during his criminal trial in 2008.

Also, I speculated that Pellicano, whom I always treated with respect, was upset that I revealed during my sworn testimony that he—through his associate, Lynda Larsen, verbally and in writing—had offered me the exclusive rights to his story, an offer that I turned down.

ABOUT THE AUTHOR

A specialist on investigations of organized crime since 1974, best-selling author and investigative journalist Dan E. Moldea has published eight previous nonfiction books: *The Hoffa Wars: Teamsters, Rebels, Politicians, and the Mob* (1978); *The Hunting of Cain: A True Story of Money, Greed, and Fratricide* (1983); *Dark Victory: Ronald Reagan, MCA, and the Mob* (1986); *Interference: How Organized Crime Influences Professional Football* (1989); *The Killing of Robert F. Kennedy: An Investigation of Motive, Means, and Opportunity* (1995); *Evidence Dismissed: The Inside Story of the Police Investigation of O.J. Simpson* (1997); *A Washington Tragedy: How the Death of Vincent Foster Ignited a Political Firestorm* (1998); and his memoir, *Confessions of a Guerrilla Writer: Adventures in the Jungles of Crime, Politics, and Journalism* (2013).

The first chapters of all these books are available at *www.moldea. com.*

In addition, Moldea lectures on "Investigating the Mafia" and has appeared at over a hundred colleges and universities throughout the United States, as well as on numerous national and local television and radio programs.

Made in the USA
Middletown, DE
27 February 2018